Tom —

Sincere thanks for all
you are doing for Mystic
Seaport — the Museum of America
and the Sea — and especially
the fine young men and women
& the Williams-Mystic
program in Maritime Studies.

Doug

RADM USCG (ret)

President & Director

MYSTIC SEAPORT
WATERCRAFT

MYSTIC SEAPORT
WATERCRAFT

by Maynard Bray,
Benjamin A. G. Fuller,
and Peter T. Vermilya

Mystic Seaport • Mystic, Connecticut • 2001

Mystic Seaport
75 Greenmanville Ave.
Mystic, CT 06355-0990

Manufactured in the United States of America

ISBN 0-913372-94-3 (Cloth)
ISBN 0-913372-95-1 (Paper)

*To the memory of Joseph Patrick Gribbins (1939-2001) who,
as director of publications at Mystic Seaport, added immensely
to the look and content of what you hold in your hands.*

CONTENTS

SAILING CRAFT

CHAPTER ONE
Cat-Rigged

POWER

CHAPTER ONE
Inboard-Powered

CHAPTER TWO
Outboard-Powered

PREFACE

When the National Endowment for the Arts underwrote production of the first edition of this catalog 22 years ago, it was clear evidence that, whatever the occupational or recreational use for which they were intended, the boats in Mystic Seaport's collection represent a very significant American art form. Some are true folk art, created by self-taught builders using local materials, yet having a grace and sense of rightness that transcends their simple origins. Others are art of a finer sort, representing the highest achievements in design and use of materials by the most skilled designers and builders, such as the Herreshoffs or J. Henry Rushton. All of them combine practical and aesthetic considerations in creative ways that can only be called art.

Mystic Seaport's watercraft collection did not begin to grow quite as early as its collection of marine paintings. Yet, the Museum's founders' intent to preserve watercraft as well as smaller artifacts meant that the sandbagger *Annie* became the first boat in the collection in 1931, before the Museum was two years old. The 1941 acquisition of the last American sailing whaleship, the *Charles W. Morgan*, set the stage for a greater emphasis on watercraft large and small. This trend continued through the 1960s, gaining tremendous momentum and purpose in the 1970s and 1980s during John

Gardner's tenure as the Museum's associate curator of small craft. Known as the "dean of small craft studies" and the individual most responsible for the nationwide revival of interest in traditional watercraft, John made Mystic Seaport a center for traditional American watercraft studies after he was invited to join the staff in 1969. Working with curators Edmund Lynch, Revell Carr, and Ben Fuller, shipyard directors Maynard Bray, Don Robinson, and Dana Hewson, and small craft specialists Peter Vermilya and Barry Thomas, Gardner helped identify the areas of the collection that required expansion and significant watercraft that were available for acquisition.

The first edition of *Mystic Seaport Watercraft* was written by Maynard Bray, with the assistance of his wife Anne, and published in 1979. This new edition offers dramatic evidence of the changes in the collection: From approximately 220 total watercraft in those days, the collection has grown to number just under 500 in 2001. All traditional areas of strength, such as catboats, have been selectively enhanced, but the increases among powered craft and canoes are especially great, with powered craft up from 16 to 51 and craft in the canoe category growing from 21 to 56. And, since the 1970s the Museum has made a greater effort to collect the stories that document a boat's use, as well as the boat itself. Thus, with more information about each watercraft and its context, it has been possible in many cases to provide longer and more detailed entries in this edition of *Watercraft*. The first edition included only watercraft formally accessioned into the Museum's collection. Since that time, the Museum has established its Boathouse—a boat livery that offers visitors the chance to experience a variety of traditional watercraft on the water. Some of the boats in the livery fleet are not accessioned, but they are included in this catalog, as are some of the Museum's sail-training craft and several craft used for research and recreation by the Williams College-Mystic Seaport undergraduate studies program, which was established at the Museum in 1977.

To create this new edition, Maynard Bray collaborated with Ben Fuller—Mystic Seaport curator from 1978 to 1990—and the Museum's long-time Associate Curator Peter Vermilya. Publications Director Joe Gribbins provided organizational and editorial direction and oversaw the design by Sharon Brown and Irwin Bag. After Joe's untimely death in June 2001, Andy German ably completed production of the book. Although these individuals had the greatest involvement with the project, the entire Mystic Seaport staff—from shipwrights in the Museum's duPont Preservation Shipyard to the volunteers at the Boathouse boat-livery program, special demonstration squad members, the photography department and Rosenfeld Collection staff, the staff of the Curatorial Department and Registrar's Office, and the staff of the G.W. Blunt White Library—contributed in essential ways to the successful completion of this work. In addition, we are grateful to The Chase Manhattan Foundation, Conde Nast Publications, Inc., and Mr. and Mrs. Daniel S. Gregory for contributing funding to cover the production of this important volume.

Even as this catalog of the collection is being published, Mystic Seaport is at work to create a Hall of Watercraft in which to house the major portion of its small-craft collection in an accessible manner. As the second phase of the American Maritime Education and Research Center, this almost 40,000-square-foot hall will serve as a proper gallery and permanent repository for the Museum's unparalleled collection and a fitting home for these elegant examples of American artistry afloat.

Douglas H. Teeson
President and Director
Mystic Seaport

FOREWORD TO THE 2001 EDITION

It's been almost a quarter century since the first edition of *Mystic Seaport Watercraft* was published. Coming out as it did in the late 1970s, the appearance of the book reflected the renewed and widespread interest in historical working and pleasure boats in this country. It was the first substantial example of its kind from a maritime museum, being devoted to describing what was then the largest and most extraordinary collection of historical boat types in North America. By that time Mystic Seaport had become the premier institution for craft like this. Its charming New England riverfront setting and its boats and vessels drew visitors from all over the world, then as now, and deservedly so, because the boats are such fine and unique examples of their type. Serious students of boat design, and particularly working boat design–which evolved by the rule-of-thumb methodology and the hard-won experience of men who lived or died by their ability to keep watermen safe and able–can find no single collection providing as much wisdom, industry, intelligence, and sheer beauty as the watercraft collection at Mystic Seaport.

But if the watercraft collection was noteworthy then, the boats and vessels have become even more so now. The number of watercraft there, and thus in this new edition, has more than doubled. And the vast array of types represented is breathtaking. This is especially valuable because, unfortunately for most visitors to the Museum, only a relatively limited sampling of the institution's extensive holdings can be on public display at any given time. So this book provides, as it were, a glance behind the scenes, where many of the boats reside and are patiently and lovingly cared for by individuals who know their history and their importance. It's a tool for exploring the deeper chambers of the institution in order to comprehend the enormous power of a museum to provide the historical context, insight, and understanding in the art and science of vessel, yacht, and boat design, as well as a history of maritime pursuits in this country.

Providing relevance and context for collections is a significant component of the mission of any museum, and in this age of virtual realities, synthetic experiences, and the eclipsing of education by entertainment, the unique value of true artifacts has become increasingly critical. Even now, many museums struggle to be noticed. The challenge, then, is to connect these artifacts with the lives of human beings, because it has become too easy to dismiss them as insignificant to modern times, almost no matter what–or where–they are.

Not only are the various watercraft in the collection identified here, but the contexts of their time, place, and purpose are also described, albeit briefly, offering readers a means of understanding much more than their vital statistics. As an expression of Mystic Seaport's mission to broaden awareness of the relationship of America and the sea, this book is invaluable. And it must be noted that no one authors more qualified for this project than Maynard Bray, Ben Fuller, and Peter Vermilya.

Maynard Bray, with his wife, Anne, has devoted much of his life to studying and compiling notes and resources from as many individuals, institutions, and historical publications as possible. The former shipyard supervisor and associate curator for watercraft at Mystic Seaport, Maynard Bray lives and breathes this subject matter, and his high reputation for insight, understanding, and advocacy for traditional craft is well-established worldwide. Part sailor, part historian, part designer, part boatbuilder, part curator, Maynard has made a passionate study of watercraft of all types and has brought an extraordinary combination of skills and abilities to his work over the years. He played a critical role in raising the standards by which Mystic Seaport established its prominence during the early 1970s, when interest in traditional small craft and vessels was beginning to find new shape and dimension in this country.

A devoted oarsman and sailor, and a tireless researcher and curator, Ben Fuller came to the Museum in 1978. During his 12 years as curator, he joined his expertise with that of others on the staff to refine and expand the Museum's watercraft collection. With his knowledge of the technology and traditions of the sport of boating, he made especially valuable contributions in shaping the collection to reflect developments in powerboat design and the evolution of canoes and other "personal" watercraft. As a strong advocate of the Museum's efforts to offer its visitors on-the-water experience in traditional watercraft, he established the Museum's popular Boathouse boat-livery program. Having moved to Maine as an independent researcher, educator, and exhibit specialist, he continues to advise the Museum as a member of its Yachting and Boating Committee.

Peter Vermilya arrived at Mystic Seaport as a boatbuilder, and for 30 years he has been the Museum's catboat specialist. As associate curator for the small craft collection, he has the enviable job of being daily companion to the hundreds of watercraft in storage. While managing the resource files on the collection, and communicating far and wide with watercraft experts and enthusiasts, he makes time to pursue and refine his expertise on such specialized watercraft as frostbite dinghies and gunning boats.

Embarking from Maynard Bray's groundbreaking work with the 1979 edition of this book, these three colleagues have provided a new accessibility to the public's understanding of Mystic Seaport's vessels, yachts, and boats, and their history and evolution. These impassioned professionals have turned their deep love for these craft into the kind of scholarly pursuit that will fire the curiosities of earnest students for decades and further establish Mystic Seaport's preeminence in the field. Within these pages you will find wonderful examples of ingenious interweavings of form and function in vessels and boats, some graceful and elegant, some not at all. Yet each of the examples reflects a common determination to give exquisite shape and substance to that elemental place where water, wind, and wood converge. In that respect, this work should be seen as a gathering and a celebration of individual aspirations and intentions, and of invention and sculpture, not just a collection of boats. In some cases, the boats and vessels included embody lifetimes of wisdom and experience, and represent their creators' ultimate achievements. This is the beauty of history, and of the artifacts that illustrate that history: In a way, it is a form of immortality, a reminder that the ordinary endeavors of each of us can matter, in time, if we simply acknowledge those endeavors for what they are: the unending search for perfection.

Jon Wilson
Editor-in-Chief
WoodenBoat Magazine

FOREWORD TO THE 1979 EDITION

Except for a defective and obsolete forerunner of this work, which is no longer in print, this is the first of a new kind of watercraft catalog, and as such is bound to have a profound and far-reaching influence on the current revival of classic watercraft which is now a rising tide.

It is true that a catalog of the U.S. National Watercraft Collection, prepared by Carl W. Mitman, appeared as early as 1923, and that it has since been superseded by an enlarged and completely rewritten catalog of the National Collection, compiled by Howard I. Chapelle and published in 1960. But these catalogs are lists of models, not actual vessels such as constitute the Mystic Seaport collection.

This difference is fundamental. Models, even the best of them, are only secondary sources of historic information and design detail, often defective and unreliable, while primary authority resides nowhere else but in the actual boats themselves. Moreover, this difference between a collection of models and a collection of boats relates directly to changes now taking place in maritime museums, and historical museums in general, and in the philosophy upon which museum practice is based.

Museums in the past have used models almost exclusively for displays and exhibits. The educational effect of the limited visual experience that such exhibits offer the casual museum visitor is, in most cases, both superficial and transitory. New hands-on, in-depth programs undertaken by maritime museums to interest and involve the public in activity directed to the preservation and utilization of our heritage watercraft and their adaptation to present needs and future use offer much more, and these must start with the collection and preservation of surviving examples of traditional watercraft.

Our rich heritage of classic design, which reached its peak late in the nineteenth century and for a brief interval thereafter, still survives in part in boats from that period that have survived. In great part these boats were not built from drawn designs and architects' plans, but were fabricated in accordance with an inherited trade experience and tradition which was never written down. The boats that have survived are more than repositories of unique technical information, however. They are irreplaceable historic documents, and in addition, objects of folk art as implicitly recognized by this catalog.

The models cataloged by Mitman existed as a jumbled hodgepodge packed together in the cases and on the walls of the old Watercraft Hall at the Smithsonian in Washington. Apart from such collections of models, there was not a museum in North America 50 years ago with anything that could be called a watercraft collection. The first collection of boats was started at The Mariners' Museum in Newport News, Virginia, in 1932 when a variety of small craft from all over the world, including an open, flat-bottom Portuguese fishing boat of 51 feet, were brought together for display. Beyond displaying them, nothing else was done. In 1950 these boats, numbering 85 in all, were still the largest collection of boats in this country.

From its inception, Mystic Seaport, incorporated as the Marine Historical Association in 1929, has been actively involved in numerous ways with a variety of watercraft, both large and small, but during its first 25 years the number of boats acquired was meager. Up to 1950 no more than 14 boats were accessioned. But by 1959 the number, exclusive of large vessels, had increased to 53, as listed in *Small Craft At Mystic Seaport*, published that year. Although designated as "small," boats as large as the Friendship sloop *Estella*

A. and the 45-foot Lubec carry-away boat *Regina M.* were among the boats listed.

During the 1960s, Mystic accessioned 53 more boats. From 1970 to date (1979) the collection has increased by an additional 109, nearly as many as the total number acquired over the previous 30 years. Including Mystic Seaport, there are now nine maritime museums in the eastern United States with watercraft collections of boats and/or vessels of sufficient number to be considered here. In aggregate these nine collections will probably total close to 1,000 boats, although an exact count has not yet been made. In 1950 only three of these museums were in existence, and one of them had not begun to collect boats. During the 1950s two more were founded, and the remaining four in the 1960s. Of these, three now have extensive collections, namely Bath Marine Museum (now Maine Maritime Museum), 1963; Thousand Islands Museum, 1964; Chesapeake Bay Maritime Museum, 1965.

What has happened in the East is now beginning to take place on the West Coast. A classic wooden boat museum is in the process of formation on Lake Union in Seattle, and several West Coast museums are actively seeking out and acquiring examples of local watercraft.

Activity inside museums involving boats cannot be considered apart from what is occurring outside. There is continual interaction as the one influences and affects the other. Museum involvement stimulates outside interest which in turn feeds museum involvement.

Museums are now providing instruction in seamanship and boat handling, in navigation, and in boatbuilding and boat design. They furnish building plans and information derived from their collections. They organize workshops, meets, and conferences. All such activities relate to the museum's watercraft collection, and are involved with it to a greater or lesser degree.

Meets, regattas, boat shows, and boating festivals are organized in turn outside the museums. Amateurs, apart from museums, collect and restore antique boats, and build replicas and adaptations of classic watercraft both for use and for the rewards of craftsmanship. Aesthetic appreciation also enters in. Beyond mere utility as means of transportation or of sport, the best of classic working craft over many past centuries have achieved a delicacy, grace, and purity of form which lift them into the realm of art. The beauty of boats in and of themselves is a precious part of our maritime heritage which this catalog, funded in part by the National Endowment for the Arts, proclaims and exemplifies.

Certainly one effect to be expected from this catalog of what is the largest collection of classic boats in North America will be to stimulate further collecting, serving as an example and setting standards for achievement. Other museums will use it to gauge the strengths and weaknesses of their collections. Other catalogs for other collections almost certainly will result. Museums not involved with watercraft programs will be encouraged to enter the swim.

More than anything else, what this catalog will do will be to turn the flood lights on a development within the museum field which, up to now, has been proceeding quietly and in relative obscurity. The extent of what has been achieved will come as something of a revelation to many, and can only serve to reinforce and extend impressive gains already made.

John Gardner

INTRODUCTION

Mystic Seaport's ever-growing watercraft collection compelled us to produce this revised and vastly expanded catalog. It contains about twice the number of boats and vessels as the first (1979) edition, the total count now being close to 500. The greatest growth is in small craft—boats that can be stored and exhibited indoors—with emphasis on rowboats, canoes, sailing dinghies, catboats, and the like. With these additions, the Museum and its visitors can better understand the various watercraft, how they satisfied a particular need on a particular stretch of water, and how they evolved and developed over time. Upon scrutiny, this full-size, three-dimensional "research library" of watercraft shows which of the variety of boatbuilding and shipbuilding techniques and materials proved to be most durable. An examination of details, proportions, and overall shapes yields an aesthetic and structural "feel" for a wide range of traditional watercraft that is unmatched anywhere else in these United States. Not only is Mystic Seaport's watercraft collection the largest in the country, it is the most diverse in size and type of craft.

This catalog is but a general introduction, with a photo and general information about each of the Museum's watercraft. Measured drawings represent the next level of understanding, and you'll note that, where applicable, we have mentioned their existence and availability. Seeing the actual object requires a visit to Mystic, and we realize that this isn't always possible, so we've provided further reading lists where additional key information on each of the watercraft can be found.

Magazine articles and books, many of which contain valuable new information, keep showing up in gratifying numbers, so our further reading lists often quickly become out of date. For the latest in published material on a given type of watercraft, readers might wish to contact *WoodenBoat*'s research library. That magazine maintains an ongoing bibliography for most of the types of watercraft contained in this catalog, and was the source for many of the further reading lists contained herein. Mystic Seaport's G.W. Blunt White Library and its Registrar's Office also contain both published and unpublished material on these watercraft. For most of them the Museum has additional photos—sometimes historic, sometimes alternate contemporary views—besides the ones we've included in this catalog.

Efforts are underway within the Museum to provide increased visual and textual access via the Internet, so that in the future you can learn more about these watercraft through your computer.

But nothing beats a real visit. The whaleship *Charles W. Morgan*, the training ship *Joseph Conrad*, and the fishing schooner *L.A. Dunton* can be boarded and are open year round. Although not set up for boarding because of their smaller size and limited headroom, the other floating boats on exhibit, such as the Maine sloop boat *Estella A.* and the sailing sardine carrier *Regina M.* are viewable along the waterfront throughout the year. Also included in these waterborne mid-sized craft are the sloop-rigged well-smack *Emma C. Berry* (built just down the river in Noank back in 1866), and two fishing draggers—the western-rig *Florence* (built in 1926 in Mystic) and the eastern-rig, Maine-built *Roann* of 1947. You can visit indoor exhibits featuring smaller watercraft, and can by prior arrangement view stored boats of special interest. (Within a few years you'll be able to routinely look at most of Mystic Seaport's shore-based watercraft even though most of them will be in permanent but easily viewable storage. The Museum is planning a large, accessible Hall of Watercraft with sophisticated climate controls to make this possible.)

A summer highlight not to be missed is a ride aboard the Herreshoff-built yacht club launch *Resolute* or the coal-fired passenger steamer *Sabino*, or a sail in the Cape Cod catboat reproduction *Breck Marshall*. Don't miss trying out the boats of the Museum's Boathouse—a vital livery where a range of watercraft such as pulling boats, dories, and small sailing craft can be rented, experienced, and compared with each other on the Mystic River.

Comparing, for example, several boats of the same general type can extend beyond this particular watercraft collection. By means of The Union List of Museum Watercraft, you can find where among the various museums boats of a particular type are being preserved. On behalf of the Museum Small Craft Association, Mystic Seaport maintains this Union List, and you can access it on the Museum's website, www.mysticseaport.org.

Within the Museum, there is an ongoing documentation program whereby its boats are measured and depicted on detailed drawings—both for posterity and for sale to the public. In winter, the Museum offers after-hours boatbuilding classes that focus on the same tools, skills, and materials once used to construct the boats of the watercraft collection.

Rather than risk using original watercraft, especially those that are fragile, pristine, or one-of-a-kind, the Museum often builds replicas, as with banks dories, whaleboats, and some of the small rowing or sailing boats used in the livery.

Through the efforts of the staff and others, new information about the ships and boats of the watercraft collection keeps coming to light. As a result, we have revised and amended a number of previously published descriptions. We value any relevant material, and encourage readers to come forward and share it.

Annually, in early June, Mystic Seaport holds a two-day Small Craft Workshop—an event that encourages the owners and builders of traditional boats to bring them, launch them, and use them along the Museum's wonderful waterfront. Many are available to be tried out by non-boatowners who make a point of attending that exciting weekend. Guided tours through the Museum's watercraft storage spaces take place at that time.

Other institutions hold other events relating to traditional watercraft, all of which make visiting them a worthwhile—and a generally participatory—experience.

Kindling interest and enthusiasm among its visitors—both the actual and vicarious variety—is a primary goal of Mystic Seaport. So is the conveyance of information about its collections. To that end, and until you visit in person, we hope you'll find this catalog informative and inspiring.

Maynard Bray
Benjamin A.G. Fuller
Peter T. Vermilya

September 2001

ACKNOWLEDGMENTS

To the late Joe Gribbins for his editing and layout suggestions; to Andy German who took over from Joe to finish the job and send it off to the printer; to the late Jerry Morris who got this new edition of *Watercraft* underway; to Dan Gregory for funding the lion's share of this catalog; to The Chase Manhattan Foundation and Conde Nast Publications Inc. for their financial support; to the gangs of Mystic Seaport's duPont Preservation Shipyard and Photo Lab for their help in photographing the boats; to the Museum's registrar, Rodi York, her staff, and especially Shep Johnson, who fulfilled requests for additional information promptly and completely; to Anne Bray, Research Director of *WoodenBoat*, who shared the bibliographic information upon which many of the further reading lists are based; and to our many colleagues, past and present, who have shared information and enthusiasm, contributing to the completeness of this volume.

CATALOGING CONVENTIONS

Table of Contents

The Table of Contents displays the organization of this catalog. The watercraft are divided into five section: Sailing Craft, Rowing Craft, Power Craft, Canoes, and Iceboats. Within some of the sections, there are further typological subdivisions by chapter. For example, under Sailing Craft, single-masted craft are divided into chapters on cat-rigged boats and sloop-rigged watercraft. Under rowing craft, flat-bottomed craft are differentiated from round-bottomed craft. Within these chapters there is usually a division between watercraft intended for recreation and watercraft designed for work.

Dimensions

Dimensions represent the overall length and maximum beam of hull proper, rounded off to the nearest inch. Length is measured on deck to the outer face of the stem (or extended stem of clipper-bowed craft). Beam measurements exclude guardrails and mouldings.

Accession Numbers

Accession numbers uniquely identify all objects in the Museum's collection, e.g., the whaleship *Charles W. Morgan* is 1941.761. The first four digits signify the year acquired, and those after the decimal point show in what order an object, be it boat or scrimshaw, was received by the Museum during that year. Occasionally, there is a second decimal point with numbers after it. They indicate that the boat in question is one object in a larger collection.

Further Reading Lists

Because individual entries could by no means be comprehensive in a work of this scope, further reading lists have been provided. These lists were selected from the best published material available and known to the authors at the time of writing; however, additional pertinent information is published almost daily.

Photographs

Except for a few cases in which vessel storage location made photography impossible at this time, we have attempted to provide a photograph of every relevant boat in Mystic Seaport's collection. Record shots vary in quality as they were not produced under optimum conditions and were intended primarily for record-keeping.

Historic photographs of the actual boats or similar craft were included when possible to provide the visual context for the boats' use. Many of these are from the Museum's photographic collection, which is one of the largest collections of marine photography in North America. Others were loaned by other museums or by individuals for publication in this volume, and we are grateful for their generous assistance in enhancing the visual element of this book. The photographic captions include identification numbers or credit to the lender. The Museum can provide reproductions of images that are the property of Mystic Seaport. For further information, contact

Registrar's Office
Curatorial Department
Mystic Seaport
75 Greenmanville Ave.
PO Box 6000
Mystic, CT 06355-0990

Vessel Plans

Mystic Seaport's Watercraft Plans Collection includes more-or-less complete lines plans of many vessels in the Museum's collection. Samples have been included as illustrations in a number of cases. Like the watercraft collection itself, the collection of plans is constantly expanding. If plans were available at the time of this writing, you will find a notation at the end of the boat entry, following the accession number. For further information on the availability of watercraft plans from Mystic Seaport, you may check the Museum's website at www.mysticseaport.org, or contact

    Division of Ships Plans
    G.W. Blunt White Library
    Mystic Seaport
    75 Greenmanville Ave.
    PO Box 6000
    Mystic, CT 06355-0990
    Voice: 860.572.5360

Mystic Seaport
Watercraft

Chapter One
CAT-RIGGED

Catboats come in many forms. A modern classic is the Beetle Cat, represented by Pip (1980.10), shown here sailing in the Mystic River with donor Hugh Estes at the helm. (Photo: Ken Mahler, Mystic Seaport 1979-6-137)

THE CAT RIG AND
THE CATBOAT

The word cat, where sailboats are concerned, has come to mean two distinct things: a kind of rig, the *cat rig*, and a hull form, the *catboat*.

The cat rig calls for a single fore-and-aft sail on a single mast set "well up in the eyes" or bow of the boat. Traditionally, the sail should be gaff-headed and laced to the boom, but Marconi, and leg- or shoulder-of-mutton sails can also be considered to be cat rig when the other elements are present. For the purposes of this catalog, the spritsail has also been so classified. A boat can be cat-rigged without being a catboat, but a catboat is always cat-rigged.

The catboat is an able, weatherly, shoal-draft boat with a broad-beamed hull. The classic Cape Cod catboat has a beam-length ratio of 2:1, the beam being half the waterline length.

The catboat can have either a centerboard or a keel, a counter or transom stern, an underslung or barn-door outboard rudder. It can be tiller-steered or wheel-steered, of clinker (lapstrake) or carvel construction, have a stayed or unstayed mast. Cat sloops, and two-masted cat ketches and cat yawls are recognized catboat variants if they are shoal-draft and broad of beam.

The origin and meaning of the words "cat" and "catboat" are obscure. From ancient times they have signified heavy-duty use, as in the case of a workboat.

The cat rig in its gaff-headed form derives from the square sail through intermediate transitional rigs, such as the lug sail. It antedates the catboat.

The catboat developed in the northeastern United States prior to 1850, probably from earlier hull forms. The likelihood is that the catboat developed more or less spontaneously and at the same time in various places between Cape May, New Jersey, and Cape Ann, Massachusetts. Catboats also developed independently elsewhere before the 1880s: the Biloxi catboat along the Mississippi Gulf Coast, and the plunger or "oyster sloop," as it was called, on San Francisco Bay. Catboats also exist in Europe where they are known as Unaboats. This name was derived from the American catboat *Una*, built in New Jersey in 1852 as a 16′ racing boat. She was later taken to England where she inspired the building of catboats there. Eventually, the Unaboat spread to France and Germany.

Early clinker-built catboats 12′ to 18′ in length were used in fishing and lobstering. Later, carvel construction replaced clinker construction as larger catboats were built for fishing, ferrying people, packeting goods, partying, daysailing, racing, and pleasure. Catboats now come in sizes from 12′ to 30′ with extreme examples ranging up to 40′. However, beyond 40′ the cat rig becomes inefficient and unmanageable for the catboat hull form.

Catboats come as completely open boats, as open-cockpit, half-decked boats with and without a cuddy, and as cabin boats with and without a self-bailing cockpit.

The catboat reached its highest perfection of form around 1900, at which time it was also the most familiar and common sight in any New England harbor. The decline of the catboat as a workboat occurred shortly thereafter, when the gasoline engine came into general use for boats. Power enabled new and more efficient hulls to be built for fishing. A few catboats fitted with power survived as workboats until the mid-1930s, but after the hurricane of 1938 not many were left.

After the catboat fell into disuse as a workboat, it continued to be popular for racing, pleasure sailing, and cruising for many decades because of its safety, comfort, and rig simplicity. A gradual decline in importance of the catboat after World War II has been sharply reversed by two unrelated events: the establishment of The Catboat Association in the summer of 1962, and the development of the fiberglass cruising catboat hull in the winter of 1962-63. These two events once again brought to the fore the excellent qualities of the catboat as a pleasure, racing, and cruising boat.

John M. Leavens

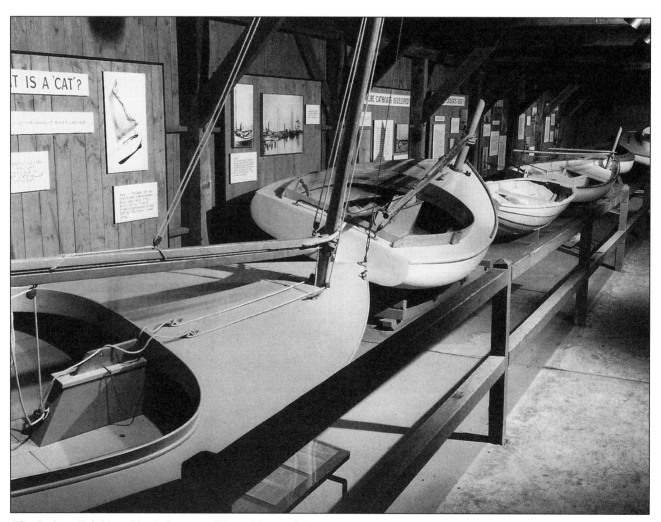

The Catboat Exhibit at Mystic Seaport. (Photo: Maynard Bray, Mystic Seaport 1975-6-15*)*

Leo Telesmanick, father of more than 3,000 Beetles, with boat presented to Mystic Seaport.
(Photo: Claire White-Peterson, Mystic Seaport 1971-9-162)

Planking a Beetle Cat at the Concordia Co.
(Photo: Maynard Bray, Mystic Seaport 1971-3-181B)

CONCORDIA BEETLE CAT
HULL #1448
12' 4" x 6' 0"   1971

Beetle Cats are one of the last traditional wooden boats still being built in quantity in the country. Virtually no changes have been made since the first one came out of John Beetle's shop in New Bedford in 1921. Since then more than 4,000 Beetle Cats have been built. These boats are now built by Beetle, Inc., 313 Smith Neck Rd., South Dartmouth, Massachusetts, 02748. They are thoroughly enjoyed by sailors of all ages, racing and daysailing.

STATUS: Unused, excellent condition.

DONOR: Concordia Co., Inc.

FURTHER READING:
Blanchard, Fessenden S. *The Sailboat Classes of North America*. Garden City, New York: Doubleday & Company, Inc., 1963.

"Building Boats." *The New Yorker*, Aug 1981. Construction commentary/Leo Telesmanick.

Coffey, Burton T. "Traditional Beetle Cat." *National Fisherman*, March, 1971.

Esterly, Diana. *Early One-Design Sailboats*. New York: Charles Scribner's Sons, 1979.

Fecteau, Loie. "A Cat With Decades of Lives." *Soundings*, Aug/Sep, 1990.

Howland, Waldo. *A Life in Boats: The Concordia Years*. Mystic, Connecticut: Mystic Seaport Publications, 1988.

——.ed. *Original Beetle Cat Boats* (several volumes). New England Beetle Cat Boat Association Booklets.

Leavens, John M. *The Catboat Book*. Camden, Maine: International Marine Publishing Co., 1973.

Lovelace, C.S. "Rainbows and Cats in the Harbor." *Nantucket Journal*, Summer/Autumn, 1991.

Mayher, Bill. "75 Years of Beetle Cats." *Maine Boats & Harbors* 42, Oct/Nov, 1996.

Pinney, William. "Fifty Years of Beetles." *Classic Boat Monthly*, Nov, 1971.

Porter, Bruce. "A Boat That's a Breeze for Kids." *Boston Globe*/Recreation Section, Oct, 1980.

Robinson, Robby. "Beetlemania." *Sail*, Dec 1996. 75th anniversary celebration.

Taylor, Roger C. *Still More Good Boats*. Camden, Maine: International Marine Publishing Co., 1981.

Vermilya, Peter T. "Building the Beetle Cats, Part I." *WoodenBoat* 51 March/April, 1983; "Part II." *WoodenBoat* 52, May/June, 1983; "Part III." *WoodenBoat* 53, July/Aug, 1983. Keel and transom construction; stem and centerboard trunk installation; fitting and bending frames, photos.

Wilson, Jon. "Concordia's Beetle Cat Shop." *WoodenBoat* 21, March/April, 1978.

Association Address:
David Akin, New England Beetle Cat Boat Association, 40 Chase Ave., West Dennis, Massachusetts 02670

ACCESSION NO. 1971.308

Wilbur Langdon
CONCORDIA BEETLE CAT
12' 4" x 6' 0"   1976-77

STATUS: Good, actively used.

DONOR: Mary Langdon

Elvira G. Tucker, Lisa, *and* Pip (left to right), *part of The Boathouse livery fleet, sailing on the Mystic River. (Photo: Sharon Brown)*

Pip
CONCORDIA BEETLE CAT
HULL #17880479
12' 4" x 6' 0"   1979

In 1980, Hugh and David Estes arranged, through the estate of their father, L. Alden Estes, to have two Beetle Cats built for the Museum in memory of their mother, Elvira Estes. While *Elvira G. Tucker* reflects their mother's maiden name, *Pip* is named for a Beetle Cat once sailed by David and Hugh Estes' late brother Ralph.

STATUS: Good, actively used.
DONOR: L. Alden Estes Estate
ACCESSION NO. 1980.10

Lisa
CONCORDIA BEETLE CAT
12' 4" x 6' 0"

STATUS: Good, actively used.
DONOR: Mark McChesney

Elvira G. Tucker
CONCORDIA BEETLE CAT
HULL # 17870479
12' 4" x 6' 0"   1979

Both *Elvira G. Tucker* and *Pip* form a major part of the Museum's very active Boathouse and are used by staff and paying customers all summer long. Luckily, these two Beetle Cats were especially ordered as an experiment in minimal maintenance, having had the paint left off ceilings, floorboards, and transoms, and no varnish used anywhere, even on traditional areas such as coamings, guardrails, and spars. These surfaces were coated in linseed oil cut with kerosene. Experience has proven that this treatment protects well, is economical of labor, and provides a handsome appearance.

   Elvira G. Tucker's hailing port is Menauhant, in honor of the Massachusetts yacht club the Estes family have belonged to for many years.

Elvira G. Tucker *participating in the summer Beetle Cat series sponsored by Mystic Seaport's Boathouse. (Photo: Sharon Brown)*

STATUS: Good, actively used.
DONOR: L. Alden Estes Estate
ACCESSION NO. 1980.11

Leo J. Telesmanick
CONCORDIA BEETLE CAT
HULL #18150180

12' 4" x 6' 0"   1980

Alma Telesmanick presented the Beetle Cat *Leo J. Telesmanick* to the Museum at the 1980 Small Craft Workshop in recognition of her husband's 50 years of building the original boats. Workshop participants shared in Leo's surprise and pleasure and listened with appreciation as he outlined the support Alma had given him and the Beetle Cat class over many years.

As is totally fitting, the *Leo J. Telesmanick* is standard-finished with sparkling varnish, buff decks, white topsides, and green bottom.

Leo J. Telesmanick, part of the Boathouse livery fleet since 1988, is enjoyed on the Mystic River by staff

Leo J. Telesmanick (second from right) *helps launch his namesake Beetle Cat in 1980. (Photo: Ken Mahler, Mystic Seaport 1980-6-24)*

and visitors from May through October each year. Since Leo's death in 2000, this boat sails on as a fitting memorial to him.

STATUS: Good, actively used.

DONOR: Alma Telesmanick

ACCESSION NO. 1980.53

The Beetle Swan at Mystic Seaport. (Photo: Judy Beisler, Mystic Seaport 2001.5P)

SWAN CATBOAT BY
BEETLE BOAT COMPANY

12' 6" x 5' 11"   ca. 1946

In the mid-1940s, Carl Beetle transferred rights to the wooden "Original Beetle Cat" to the Concordia Company and engaged in one of the earliest ventures to produce fiberglass boats. During World War II, General Electric and Owens-Corning had produced large fiberglass radar domes and other objects at GE's Pittsfield, Massachusetts, plant. In 1946, working with representatives of GE and Dick Gee, Carl Beetle designed and began to produce the Beetle Swan—also known as the BB—which is remarkably similar to the Beetle Cat (see above). Early boats required heat to cure the resins and were built in large nickel-plated copper molds at the GE plant. In 1948 Beetle switched to a resin that cured at room temperature and shifted production to his New Bedford facility.

Beetle introduced the Swan at the 1947 New York Boat Show, where it and the 16' Rebel were the first production fiberglass sailboats ever offered. The first Swans produced had fiberglass decks and coamings, but did not sell at the New York Boat Show.

Beetle cut out the decks and coamings, replacing them with wood, and sold a few at the Boston Boat Show that same year. The example now in the Museum's collection has a builder's plate stating "Molded by General Electric for Beetle Boat Company, New Bedford, Mass.," and shows evidence of this retrofit.

An ad in the January, 1948, issue of *Yachting* promoted the boat as "Tomorrow's Sailboat Today... America's Safest, Strongest, Most Beautiful Centerboard Sailboat." Americans would soon make the shift to fiberglass boats for recreation, but not before Carl Beetle ceased production of fiberglass boats in 1951.

STATUS: Fair condition with original aluminum mast and boom, fiberglassed plywood centerboard, disassembled wooden components, rudder, and nylon sail.

DONOR: Museum Purchase

FURTHER READING:

Spurr, Daniel. *Heart of Glass: Fiberglass Boats and the Men Who Made Them.* New York and Camden, Maine: International Marine/McGraw-Hill, 2000.

Vaitses, Allen. "Fiberglass Production Boats: It all Began with Carl Beetle." *National Fisherman Yearbook*, 1985.

ACCESSION NO. 2001.5

Sanshee on exhibit. (Photo: Maynard Bray, Mystic Seaport 1975-6-16)

Sanshee (ex-Kim)
CAPE COD CATBOAT
14' 4" x 6' 7"   ca. 1900-25

Sanshee is one of about 40 such boats built by Charles A. Anderson in his Wareham, Massachusetts, shop. Being small and simple they were easily handled; yet there was a good bit of room in their cockpits for a sailing party of several persons. These catboats for daysailing and racing were shrunk-down versions of the working catboats of the Cape Cod area. As one can gather from reading *The Catboat Book*, there were many different models of small catboats by many different builders, and it was rare for a builder not to be the designer as well. *Sanshee*'s builder did build boats to the designs of others on occasion. The well-known 59-foot motorsailer *Nor'Easter*, which he built in 1927,

was designed by William H. Hand, Jr.

Upon her arrival at Mystic, *Sanshee* was sailed in Mystic Seaport's Youth Training Program for a few seasons before being restored as part of the formal catboat exhibit.

STATUS: Rebuilt and refinished 1971, approximately 80% original, good condition.

DONOR: Ingersoll Cunningham

FURTHER READING:
"A Catboat for Everyman." *The Rudder*, July, 1923. Shows plans for a 22-foot raised-deck cat by Anderson with shape and construction like *Sanshee*.

The Catboat Association Bulletin 5, Oct, 1963 and 11, May, 1965. Information about Charles A. Anderson.

Barnard, William Lambert. "The Working Boats of New England: The Cape Cod Catboat." *WoodenBoat* 3, Jan/Feb, 1975.

Chapelle, Howard I. *American Sailing Craft.* Camden, Maine: International Marine Publishing Co., 1975.

Grayson, Stan. *Catboats.* Camden, Maine: International Marine Publishing Co., 1984.

Leavens, John M., ed. *The Catboat Book.* Camden, Maine: International Marine Publishing Co., 1973. The basic reference book for catboat lovers since it contains not only much information itself but has a complete and annotated bibliography.

ACCESSION NO. 1970.646
Plans for 1970.646 are available from Mystic Seaport's Watercraft Plans Collection.

Curlew

CAPE COD CATBOAT

13' 11" x 6' 9"   ca. 1900-25

Curlew is much like *Sanshee* and was used, no doubt, for pleasure as well. Little is known about her, but there is a claim that she was built by one of the Crosbys. Boats like this one were not large enough to be listed in a yacht register, and except for unusual cases they have no recorded history whatsoever. *Curlew* has not yet been examined in detail for those subtleties of construction which sometimes give a clue to a boat's origin. An old boat in need of repair when she arrived in

Catboat Curlew. *(Photo: Maynard Bray,* Mystic Seaport 1960.537*)*

Mystic, she was exhibited afloat until it was necessary to retire her to storage ashore.

STATUS: Unrestored, poor condition.

DONOR: Moses Hay Teaze

FURTHER READING:
Leavens, John M., ed. *The Catboat Book.* Camden, Maine: International Marine Publishing Co., 1973.

ACCESSION NO. 1960.537

Trio

CAPE COD CATBOAT

14' 10" x 6' 8"   ca. 1880-1912

When information from two reliable sources conflicts, as it does concerning *Trio*'s age, there are but two things to do: the issue can be confronted and resolved, if possible, and time permitting, or the conflicting information can be passed on in its raw form, as is the case here. In a letter to Mystic Seaport dated February 16, 1960, Wilton B. Crosby (nephew of the builder) says of *Trio*: "Stored here in our yard we have a 15' catboat which was built in 1880 by Wilton Crosby. We believe this boat to be the oldest Crosby catboat in existence today." Later, during a taped interview with John M. Leavens on August 3-4, 1963, Capt. Malcolm (Uncle Max) Crosby, who was also closely related to the builder, stated:

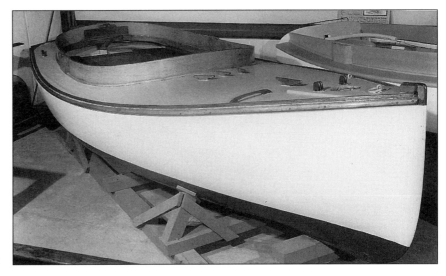

Catboat Trio. *(Photo: Maynard Bray,* Mystic Seaport 1975-6-75*)*

"*Trio* was built in 1912 by Wilton Crosby for Jack Adie."

Regardless of when *Trio* was built, she is a good boat. Huskily built, trimmed with varnished cypress and oak, she is like many of the celebrated Crosby yard's boats. With her high freeboard she should be quite dry and comfortable in a chop, in spite of her small size.

STATUS: Minor repair, substantially original, good condition.

DONOR: Wilton B. Crosby

FURTHER READING:
Crosby, Carol. "In the Crosby Tradition." *WoodenBoat* 153, Mar/Apr, 2000.
Leavens, John M., ed. *The Catboat Book,* Camden, Maine: International Marine Publishing Co., 1973.
Mason, Gregory. "The Crosbys of Cape Cod." *Motor Boating,* July, 1928.

ACCESSION NO. 1960.499
Plans for 1960.499 are available from Mystic Seaport's Watercraft Plans Collection.

Frances after restoration, 1970. (Photo: Louis S. Martel, Mystic Seaport 1970-6-140)

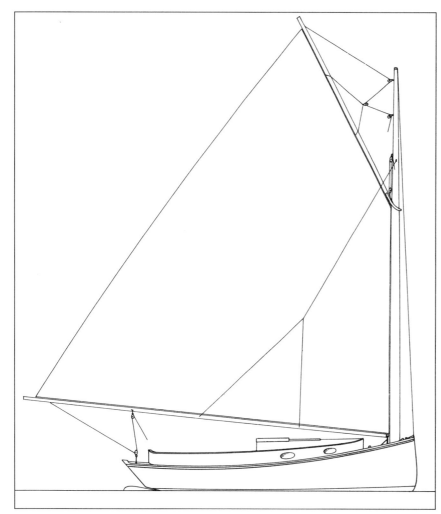

Sail Plan for Frances. *(Drawing by Edson I. Schock)*

Frances
(ex-*Buddy*, ex-*Nantucket*)
CAPE COD CATBOAT
20′ 10″ x 9′ 8″   1900

Frances was designed and built by Wilton Crosby of Osterville, Massachusetts, whose family name is almost synonymous with catboats. She is a classic example of the cruising type with her "punkin" bow, oval cabin and coaming, and natural cypress interior. Her inboard rudder was preferred at Nantucket, where *Frances* spent most of her life.

STATUS: Restored 1971, approximately 70% original, good condition.

DONOR: Stephen Peabody

FURTHER READING:

Barnard, William Lambert. "The Working Boats of New England, The Cape Cod Catboat." *Boating*, 1907. Reprinted in *WoodenBoat* 3, Jan/Feb, 1975.

Leavens, John M., ed. *The Catboat Book*. Camden, Maine: International Marine Publishing Co., 1973.

The Classic Boat. Alexandria, Virginia: Time-Life Books, 1977.

Thomas, Barry. *Building the Crosby Catboat*. Mystic, Connecticut: Mystic Seaport Publications, 1988.

ACCESSION NO. 1959.1221

Plans for 1959.1221 are available from Mystic Seaport's Watercraft Plans Collection.

Marionette

CAPE COD CATBOAT

14' 4" x 6' 4"   1888

In 1888, Edgar Jenney of Marion, Massachusetts, built *Marionette* as the only catboat to come out of his shop. She was to be a small boat for his son. She's a scaled-down Cape Cod cat, and her construction reflects her workboat heritage as well, following many standard building practices of the Crosbys of Osterville. Her shape is unusual, however. Her topsides are quite high and she has very full lines. *Marionette* is in remarkably original condition considering that she received damage in both the 1938 and 1954 hurricanes.

Marionette. *(Photo: Mary Anne Stets, Mystic Seaport 1980-2-17)*

STATUS: Complete, retains shape, structure sound.

DONOR: Robert S. Stuart
ACCESSION NO. 1980.20

Dolphin

CAPE COD CATBOAT

21' 5" x 10' 0"   1917

The cabin catboat *Dolphin* was modeled and built by Wilton Crosby of Osterville, Massachusetts, in 1917. For many years her owners used *Dolphin* as a scalloper and party boat out of Edgartown, Massachusetts. She was built to accommodate one of the many small gasoline marine engines of the time and has had a number of repowerings since, her latest being a 4-cylinder Lathrop Model LN-4. Her construction is deceptively simple. Oak structural members, cedar planking, and the typically wide sheer clamp. Over the years she's been repaired but never restored. Her iron fastenings, originally inexpensive, have not served her well over time, however.

When her working career was over, *Dolphin* was owned for many years by John Killam Murphy, one of the original principals in the Catboat Association. The annual award given by the Catboat Association to a member who has served in some exemplary way is named, most appropriately, the Dolphin Award.

STATUS: Complete, unrestored, fair condition.

DONOR: Adrian K. Lane

FURTHER READING:
Gardner, John. "Lines of Classic Cat Reveal Fine Workboat" and "Hearty Grandfather Cat Worth Some Careful Study." *National Fisherman*, July & Oct., 1971.

ACCESSION NO. 1987.138

Dolphin under sail in Fishers Island Sound. *(Photo: Mystic Seaport 1990-2-172)*

Dolphin at Mystic Seaport in 1971. *(Photo: Russell A. Fowler, Mystic Seaport 1971-8-22)*

Breck Marshall

CAPE COD CATBOAT

20′ 0″ x 10′ 0″   1986

Because the Marshall Marine Company of South Dartmouth, Massachusetts, was responsible for building so many of the fiberglass catboats sailed by Catboat Association members, they felt that a fitting tribute to company founder Breckinridge Marshall's enduring interest in small-craft history would be to fund the building of a traditional, pre-internal-combustion-engine catboat at Mystic Seaport which would then become an active exhibit.

Former Mystic Seaport Boatshop Director Barry Thomas, along with assistants Bret Laurent and Clark Poston, looked at almost all the extant pre-1920 wooden catboats in a search for suitable lines and construction examples. They settled on the lines of *Tryphenea*, said to be Crosby-built prior to 1900. They had to dig even deeper to learn about traditional Crosby family construction methods. These had never been recorded, and were all but forgotten by the 1980s. Eventually they located Horace Manley "Bunk" Crosby, Jr., who turned out to be an essential source of information. The results of this research are contained in Barry Thomas's book, *Building the Crosby Catboat.*

The boat itself is a thing of beauty, built with integrity and loaded with authenticity. *Breck Marshall* is finished in the best of the working catboat tradition: white coaming and topsides, Oregon buff cabin top and deck, dado brown trim, and French gray cockpit staving, along with galvanized hardware and manila running rigging. The inboard end of the boom is supported by the customary tripod or "crab," which eliminates stressing the mast with an attached gooseneck. Today *Breck Marshall* sails as a part of Mystic Seaport's Boathouse program of boats for rent and boats for visitors to ride, taking more than 5,000 people sailing each year, many of them for the very first time.

STATUS: Good, actively used.

ACCESSION NO. 1986.10

Plans for 1986.10 are available from Mystic Seaport's Watercraft Plans Collection.

Breck Marshall on *Fisher's Island Sound in 1987.*
(Photo: Mary Anne Stets, Mystic Seaport 1987-11-58*)*

Barry Thomas building Breck Marshall.
(Photo: Mary Anne Stets, Mystic Seaport 1986-11-277*)*

WOODS HOLE SPRITSAIL BOATS

Spritsail boats started out as working craft and are related to the well-known catboats of Cape Cod. The Woods Hole fishermen, working in an area known for its fierce current, often had to row rather than sail in order to work the eddies and slack waters in a calm. Thus the boats are proportionally narrower and generally smaller than the typical Cape Cod cat. Many spritsail boats were kept in the Eel Pond at Woods Hole and frequently had to douse their rigs to get under the bridge; the spritsail itself, along with an open cockpit with a hinged bale at the mast partners, made this easier.

The Woods Hole Yacht Club sponsored races for spritsail boats, with the fishing type in Class B and those designed especially for racing in Class A. The great yacht-design genius Nathanael G. Herreshoff, of Bristol, Rhode Island, designed *Gee* to race in Class A. To give her the largest sail that the rules allowed, he stepped the mast in a socket mounted on the stem head.

WOODS HOLE SPRITSAIL BOAT

13' 4" x 6' 0"   1913 or 1914

This boat was built by E. E. Swift, a Cape Cod cabinetmaker, for his brother, who died before Swift completed his work. The nearly finished boat lay in the family barn for 51 years before the donors obtained her. (Mrs. White is Swift's grandniece.) The boat is exquisitely built, has never yet been used, and still shows the priming coat of paint on her hull. Along with her came Swift's tools and toolbox, as well as his molds, patterns, and half models—one of which is probably of this boat. Another may be of *Susie*, built a few years earlier and now in the Museum's collection with Accession Number 1986.32. *Susie* is described below.

Woods Hole spritsail boat on display at Mystic Seaport (Photo: Maynard Bray, Mystic Seaport 1975-6-8)

STATUS: Uncompleted, original rig missing, excellent condition.

DONOR: Mr. and Mrs. John E. White

ACCESSION NO. 1968.2

Susie
WOODS HOLE SPRITSAIL BOAT

13' 4" x 6' 0"   ca. 1900

Susie was also built by Eddie Swift, but earlier than the boat described above. Eddie's father raced this boat very successfully in the Class A races for Woods Hole spritsail boats at the Woods Hole Yacht Club. In 1914, Eddie, grief-stricken over the recent death of his brother, put both *Susie* and the boat he had nearly completed for his brother into storage, where they were discovered in 1965.

The late Bob Baker, of Westport, Massachusetts, purchased *Susie* and used her as his personal boat for a number of years. He reported that she was a joy to sail: fast, responsive, and light on the helm. Recognizing her value, his widow, Anne, donated her to the Museum in 1986.

Susie at Mystic Seaport in 1986. (Photo: Deborah A. Bates, Mystic Seaport 1986.32E)

The lines and construction details of these two boats and what may be a third Eddie Swift boat, preserved at the Woods Hole Historical Society, were recorded by Dave Dillion, and they, along with the molds, make an interesting comparative study.

STATUS: Complete, excellent condition.

DONOR: Anne Baker

ACCESSION NO. 1986.32
Plans for 1968.2 and 1986.32 are available from Mystic Seaport's Watercraft Plans Collection.

Explorer (ex-T.C.)
WOODS HOLE
SPRITSAIL BOAT

13' 3" x 5' 11"   ca. 1890

The Crosbys of Osterville built this boat for Oliver Grinnell or Henry Dyer (records conflict) and she is doubtless more typical of the working spritsail boats than either of the Eddie Swift boats in the Museum's collections (1968.2 and 1986.32). Nearly destroyed by the 1938 hurricane, she was purchased in 1943 by the donor.

To economize on material, the slot for her centerboard was formed by wedging open a saw kerf in the keel timber, which is softened first by steaming. This feature, as well as the half-dovetailed frame ends, are familiar Crosby innovations.

Cockpit of Woods Hole spritsail boat Explorer *in 1970 after refinishing. (Photo: Louis S. Martel, Mystic Seaport 1970-5-96)*

STATUS: Restored 1960-70, approximately 75% original, rig missing, good condition.

DONOR: Dr. Alfred C. Redfield
ACCESSION NO. 1960.196
Plans for 1960.196 are available from Mystic Seaport's Watercraft Plans Collection.

Carrie, a Woods Hole spritsail boat much like Explorer *and* Sandy Ford, *underway off Woods Hole near turn of the century. (Photo: Source unknown, Mystic Seaport 1975.176)*

Sandy Ford launching, 1973. (Photo: Mary Anne Stets, Mystic Seaport 1973-6-20)

Sandy Ford

WOODS HOLE SPRITSAIL
BOAT REPRODUCTION

13' 3" x 5' 11"   1973

With John Gardner's supervision and assistance, Sylvester Costelloe of Mystic Seaport's Small Craft Laboratory duplicated *Explorer* and named her after his hometown in Ireland.

She is fitted with a small Marconi mizzen as described for the working spritsail boats by one source. But this additional sail proves more of a nuisance than a help and often is left ashore. *Sandy Ford* is an excellent, fun, stable boat to sail, and especially enjoyed by young families because of her ample cockpit and relatively high topsides.

STATUS: In use, good condition.

SOURCE: Museum-built reproduction of 1960.196

FURTHER READING FOR 1968.2, 1986.32, 1960.196 & 1973.40:
Costelloe, Sylvester. "The Building of the Woods Hole Spritsail Boat." Paper for Work Study Class, 1972, on file in Registrar's Office at Mystic Seaport.

Haln, Jan. "One of the Last Spritsail Boats Leaves Home as a Museum Piece." *Maine Coast Fisherman*, May, 1960.

Herreshoff, L. Francis. *The Compleat Cruiser.* New York: Sheridan House, 1963.

Littell, Browne. "Early Days of Racing in Woods Hole." *Spritsail*, Summer, 1996. Good history in this journal of The Woods Hole Historical Collection.

Palmer, H. V. R. "Those Handy Little Boats." *Skipper*, Dec, 1968.

ACCESSION NO. 1973.40

Old Pal

WOODS HOLE SPRITSAIL BOAT

13′ 4″ x 5′ 8″   ca. 1860

This boat was bought by donor Bob McGuire's father and uncle in the 1920s from Nat Grant, a man then in his eighties who, Bob says, had used it since his youth for both commercial and recreational fishing on Buzzards Bay. McGuire family tradition says the boat was built before the Civil War in Fairhaven, Massachusetts.

Bob's father and uncle rebuilt the boat, including new keel, frames, and some new planking. They refastened it with bronze. They removed the centerboard and case when they replaced the keel. Enough of the original framing still exists to indicate that the boat was built with jogged batten-seam construction similar to that used in New Bedford-Fairhaven area boatshops. The transom, stem, thwarts (with hanging knees), and planking girths appear to be as-built and verify the Woods Hole spritsail boat shape.

STATUS: Poor condition, partially rebuilt.
DONOR: Robert W. McGuire, Jr.
ACCESSION NO. 1997.96.1

Old Pal, after arrival at Mystic Seaport's shipyard. The rudder and spars are in the foreground. (Photo: Claire White-Peterson, Mystic Seaport 1997-7-138)

Kingfisher II

NEWPORT CATBOAT

17′ 0″ x 8′ 3″   ca. 1895

One of two extant Newport-type catboats, *Kingfisher II* was built on Long Wharf in Newport, Rhode Island, by either T. Stoddard or one of the Barker brothers. Edward W. Smith, Sr., her original owner, sailed her as a yacht and used her when he made his many wonderful glass-plate photographs of Newport's waterfront scenes. These plates, many of which are published in his son's book *Workaday Schooners*, are preserved at Mystic Seaport.

Traded to Lars Larson in 1905, she was later rebuilt by Larson with a cuddy cabin and vertically staved coaming to serve as a day charter boat in Newport harbor. In 1941 Henry A. Wood, Jr., nephew of E. W. Smith, Sr., purchased the boat from Larson's estate, and she remained in the family until she was donated to Mystic Seaport.

Kingfisher II *in 1975. (Photo: Ken Mahler, Mystic Seaport 1975.5)*

STATUS: Unrestored, approximately 50% original, fair condition.

DONOR: John Benson

FURTHER READING:
Smith, Edward W., Jr., compiler. *Workaday Schooners.* Camden, Maine. International Marine Publishing Co., 1975.

ACCESSION NO. 1975.5

Unidentified lady at the helm of Kingfisher II. *(Photo: Edward W. Smith Collection, Mystic Seaport 1975-2-32)*

Button Swan

NEWPORT FISH AND LOBSTER BOAT

12' 3" x 5' 4"   ca. 1880

"The *Button Swan* is an excellent example of the type of boat that originated on Long Wharf in Newport. Here, since the early 1800s, and perhaps even earlier, were congregated the simple shops of a dozen or more Newport small boat builders who specialized in pulling boats, skiffs, ship's yawl boats and similar craft.

"Historically, the *Button Swan* is unique. She is a well-preserved, well-documented example of a small working catboat with roots reaching back 125 years or more. She was made by a man who is known to have built boats of this very type at Newport over 100 years ago for commercial fishing in Narragansett Bay and the offshore waters of the open ocean around Brenton's Reef and from Sakonnet to Point Judith. She represents an evolution in small boat design from

earlier types built at Newport and the surrounding area....Certainly no existing catboat in the Mystic Seaport collection or elsewhere can equal her in importance, and she deserves to be ranked with Bob Fish's famous 1851 catboat *Una* that gave her name to the unaboat, as catboats are known in England and on the continent.

"Button Swan [who built the boat and for whom she was later named] was born at Newport in 1833. Although his real name was William Henry Munroe, being short of stature he readily acquired the nickname of 'Button.' From youth he was closely associated with his uncle John Swan, a well-known Newport fisherman, and this association led to his nickname 'Button Swan,' a name by which he was universally known in Newport all his life." -John M. Leavens, *The Catboat Association Bulletin* 46, March, 1975.

Kingfisher, shown here, was a Newport fish and lobster boat similar to Button Swan. *(Photo: Edward W. Smith Collection,* Mystic Seaport 1981.159.10*)*

STATUS: Restored, approximately 75% original, rig missing, good condition.

DONOR: Given in memory of Capt. Fernando Fowler by the children of Cyrus P. Brown

FURTHER READING:
Brewer, John Peter. "Button Swan Revisited." *The Catboat Association Bulletin* 52, March, 1977. Description of the thorough restoration by Robert H. Baker of *Button Swan* during 1974-75. This work was sponsored by The Catboat Association.

Chapelle, Howard I. *American Small Sailing Craft.* New York: W.W. Norton & Co., 1951. Appears as Providence River catboat.

——. *The National Watercraft Collection.* Washington, D.C.: U.S. Government Printing Office, 1960. Appears as Providence River catboat.

LaFarge, Christopher Grant. "Button Swan." *Scribner's Magazine*, October, 1921. Reprinted in *The Catboat Association Bulletin* 46, March, 1975.

A rigged model (1958.886) of a similar boat is in Mystic Seaport's collections.

ACCESSION NO. 1949.145
Plans for 1949.145 are available from Mystic Seaport's Watercraft Plans Collection.

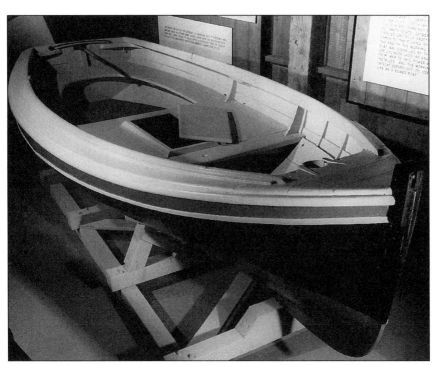

Button Swan *after restoration, 1975. (Photo: Maynard Bray,* Mystic Seaport 1975-10-163*)*

CONNECTICUT RIVER DRAG BOAT

15' 7" x 5' 9"   ca. 1890

With two men in boats like this, shad fishing was carried on in the lower Connecticut River. At night a drift net was set between the boats, and the net and the boats were allowed to drift with tide or current. When the sinking of the net buoys indicated fish caught in the gillnet, it would then be hauled back aboard, hopefully loaded with fish. The shad would then be removed and the boats rowed to the top or bottom of the reach, where a new set would be made. Sail was not used during the fishing process, but most boats were fitted with centerboards and sailing rigs. It is believed these craft did do considerable racing and daytime sailing. Drag boats were undecked aft since the net was worked over the stern.

STATUS: Restored, approximately 60% original, rig missing, good condition.

DONOR: Marshall Watrous

FURTHER READING:

Barten, Isabel. "The Search for the Shad Boat." *The Log of Mystic Seaport*, January, 1976.

Chapelle, Howard I. *American Small Sailing Craft*. New York: W. W. Norton & Co., 1951.

Morris, E. P. *The Fore and Aft Rig in America*. New Haven: Yale University Press, 1927.

Several half models of drag boats are in Mystic Seaport's collections, one of which has been drawn up by Chapelle and appears on p. 202 of his *American Small Sailing Craft*.

ACCESSION NO. 1959.808

Plans for 1959.808 are available from Mystic Seaport's Watercraft Plans Collection.

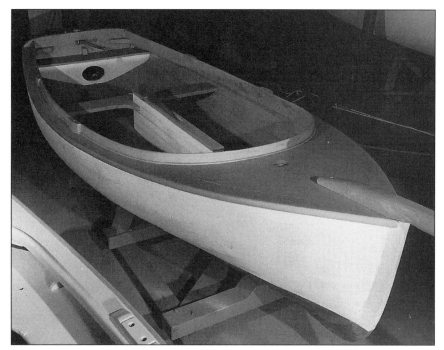

Connecticut River drag boat as she appeared in 1975.
(Photo: Maynard Bray, Mystic Seaport 1975-10-81)

Drag boats and gear at Hamburg Cove on the Connecticut River, from an old postcard. (Photo: Courtesy of Mrs. Kenneth D. Plimpton, Jr., Mystic Seaport 1972-2-34)

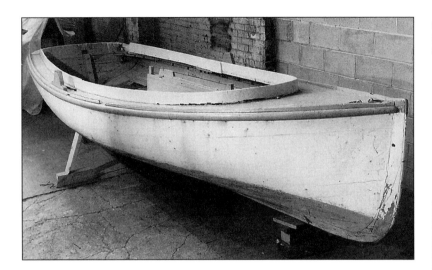

Old Indian.
(Photo: Maynard Bray,
Mystic Seaport 1976.33D)

Old Indian

CONNECTICUT RIVER
DRAG BOAT

16' 3" x 6' 1"   ca. 1882

Guilford, Connecticut, was reported to be the birthplace of this boat, built there by a man named Hall. After a short working career, fishing for bluefish as well as shad, she was purchased in 1893 by a divinity professor from Yale University. It is likely that she was used by him as a pleasure boat until World War I. Her history after that is cloudy until she was purchased by Paul Stubing in 1957, at which time she was still in the Guilford area. Somewhere along the line there was considerable repair which replaced the keel, floor timbers, and most of the frames. A new transom, centerboard trunk, and after deck have also been installed. In spite of her age and all the repair, she has retained her handsome shape and is a pleasure to look at.

STATUS: Evidence of considerable repair, including that noted above, fair condition.

DONOR: Mystic Seaport purchase from Paul Stubing

FURTHER READING:
(Same as for 1959.808)

ACCESSION NO. 1976.33

Old Indian *when acquired by Paul Stubing. Steam-bent coaming both forward and aft complemented her wine-glass stern wonderfully. (Photo: Courtesy of Paul Stubing)*

Owner Paul Stubing hauling a lobster trap aboard Old Indian *from waters off Noank. (Photo: J.E. Swedberg,* Mystic Seaport 1976.33)

Connecticut River drag boat in 1978. (Photo: Maynard Bray, Mystic Seaport 1978-2-41)

CONNECTICUT RIVER DRAG BOAT

16' 3" x 6' 5"   ca. 1947

This boat was designed by George Stadel and built by Tim MacDonald in Old Lyme, Connecticut. Although of comparatively recent construction, it is evident that she has undergone a number of repairs and alterations.

STATUS: Considerable repair, poor condition.

DONOR: Michael Murray

FURTHER READING: (Same as for 1959.808)

ACCESSION NO. 1976.56

Katinka
DUXBURY CATBOAT

17' 0" x 6' 9"   1922

Katinka is a member of the justly renowned Duxbury catboat class that once raced out of the Duxbury Yacht Club on Duxbury Bay, south of Boston. Duxbury Bay has a tidal range of nine feet, and at low tide becomes a maze of sandbanks and twisting channels. Thus, the most successful one-design classes at Duxbury are shallow-draft. The 17-foot class of catboat draws only a few inches. George Shiverick, of nearby Kingston, modeled and built the 17-foot class as well as many other classes of sloops and cats for local clubs. He wasn't always limited to shallow draft, however, as he also built the relatively deep-draft *Vireo* (1959.455), acquired by Franklin Roosevelt to use at Campobello. Shiverick was also well-known for his motor launches, two of which (1985.80 and 1991.70), are in the Museum's watercraft collection.

Robert Walker's family sailed *Katinka* for 66 years before he gave her to Mystic Seaport. *Katinka* was always professionally maintained, and her present condition reflects the good care she's always had.

STATUS: Original, good condition.

DONOR: Robert Miller Walker

Katinka *in storage at Mystic Seaport. (Photo: Maynard Bray, Mystic Seaport 1988.116A)*

FURTHER READING:
Lawson, Frank Benson and Margaret Farnsworth Lawson. *Duxbury Bay.* Duxbury, Massachusetts: The Duxbury Rural and Historical Society, 1993.

ACCESSION NO. 1988.116

George W. Shiverick (1870-1943), builder of Katinka *and three other boats in Mystic Seaport's collection. (Photo: Courtesy of Mr. & Mrs. Roger Shiverick, Mystic Seaport 1975.384.15)*

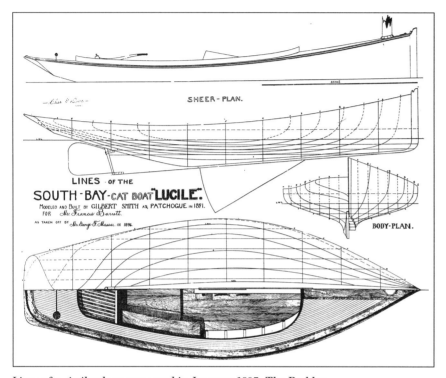

Lines of a similar boat appeared in January 1897, The Rudder.
(*Mystic Seaport 1978-1-112*)

Great South Bay catboat 1960.4 in 1975. (Photo: Maynard Bray,
Mystic Seaport 1975-6-99)

*Gilbert Smith as a young man. (Photo:
Courtesy of Long Island Maritime
Museum, Mystic Seaport 1975-5-264)*

GREAT SOUTH BAY CATBOAT

21' 5" x 7' 0"   ca. 1890

This is one of the many catboats designed and built by Gil Smith of Patchogue, Long Island, a notable builder of racing sailboats. The catboats of Great South Bay are generally narrower with less freeboard than those of Cape Cod, doubtless because of the smoother water of Great South Bay. Smith usually did away with the plumb stem in his later boats, giving them a rounded profile sometimes called a knockabout bow.

STATUS: Unrestored, some repair, fair condition.

DONOR: Thomas H. Anderson

FURTHER READING:
Bigelow, Paul. "Gil Smith, Master Boatbuilder." *Long Island Forum*, June/July, 1966.

DeFontaine, W. H., and Paul Bigelow. "Gilbert (Gil) Smith, a Great South Bay Legend." *Yachting*, March, 1966.

Massa, George Farragut. "South Bay Cats." *The Rudder*, Jan, 1897. Contains drawings of Smith-built cat *Lucile* drawn by C. G. Davis.

Morrison, Christopher. "Great South Bay Catboats, Gil Smith, and a Model of *Pauline*." *Nautical Research Journal*, Dec, 1994.

ACCESSION NO. 1960.4
Plans for 1960.4 are available from Mystic Seaport's Watercraft Plans Collection.

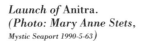

Anitra underway on the Mystic River. (Photo: Mary Anne Stets, Mystic Seaport 1990-8-188)

Launch of Anitra. (Photo: Mary Anne Stets, Mystic Seaport 1990-5-63)

Anitra
GREAT SOUTH BAY CATBOAT
21' 0" x 7' 1" 1988

The lovely *Anitra* is a Museum-built replica of the Great South Bay Class B catboat *Pauline*, modeled and built by Gil Smith of Patchogue, Long Island. *Pauline* is now in the collection of the Long Island Maritime Museum of West Sayville, Long Island, a rich repository of related Gil Smith plans, models, and photographs. The plumb stem, relatively flat sheer, low freeboard, and narrow beam are typical of Gil Smith's early work. Catboats that worked the sheltered waters behind the barrier beaches of both Long Island and New Jersey shared these characteristics and differed markedly from the robust Cape Cod cats, which faced more demanding conditions.

Anitra graces Mystic Seaport's waterfront where she provides ample evidence of the respect and affection felt toward the late Sven Hansen, whose friends created the Sven Hansen fund to enable the research and construction of this graceful reproduction.

STATUS: Good, actively used.

SOURCE: Museum-built

ACCESSION NO. 1988.10

Plans for 1988.10 are available from Mystic Seaport's Watercraft Plans Collection.

Anitra under construction in the Museum's boat shop. (Photo: Mary Anne Stets, Mystic Seaport 1989-3-54)

ADDITIONAL CATBOAT READING:

"A Catboat for Everyone." *The Rudder*, July, 1923. Cape Cod catboat.

Barnard, William Lambert. "The Working Boats of New England: The Cape Cod Catboat." *WoodenBoat* 3, Jan/Feb, 1975.

Bunting, William H. *Portrait of a Port: Boston, 1852-1914*. Cambridge, Massachusetts: The Belknap Press of Harvard University Press, 1971.

——. *Steamers, Schooners, Cutters, and Sloops: Marine Photographs of N. L. Stebbins*. Boston, Massachusetts: Society for the Preservation of New England Antiquities, 1974.

The Catboat and How to Sail Her. The Catboat Association, 1978. Sailing technique, comments, illustrations.

Chapelle, Howard I. *American Sailing Craft*. Camden, Maine: International Marine Publishing Co., 1975. Cape Cod catboats, history, design, construction, plans.

Grayson, Stan. *Catboats*. Camden, Maine: International Marine Publishing Co., 1984. History, photos, plans.

——. "Catboats." *Nautical Quarterly* 11, Summer, 1980.

——. "Vessels Such as These." *Nautical Quarterly* 42, Summer, 1988.

Heckman, Richard, ed. *Yankees Under Sail*. Dublin, New Hampshire: Yankee, Inc., 1968.

Leavens, John M. *The Catboat Book*. Camden, Maine: International Marine Publishing Co., 1973. History, photos, plans.

Mason, Gregory. "The Crosbys of Cape Cod." *Motor Boating*, July, 1928.

"More About Anderson Cats." *The Catboat Association Bulletin*, Oct, 1963. Cape Cod catboat.

Schoettle, Edwin J. *Sailing Craft*. New York: The Macmillan Company, 1945. Francis Sweisguth design *Scat II*; Charles D. Mower design *Mary Ann*; Francis Sweisguth design *Silent Maid*.

Taylor, Roger C. *Good Boats*. Camden, Maine: International Marine Publishing Co., 1977.

Thomas, Barry. *Building the Crosby Catboat*. Mystic, Connecticut: Mystic Seaport Publications, 1989. Construction details, photos, plans.

The editors of *Yachting*. *Your New Boat*. New York: Simon and Schuster, 1946.

Catboat Association Address: Walter M. Fife, The Catboat Association, P.O. Box 427, Stockton Springs, Maine 04981

Museum-built catboats Breck Marshall *and* Anitra. *(Photo: Mary Anne Stets,* Mystic Seaport 1990-8-196*)*

"Dress ship" on a Great South Bay catboat, ca. 1900. (Photo: Courtesy of Long Island Maritime Museum, Mystic Seaport 1975-5-295*)*

Brand new Great South Bay cats at Gil Smith's boat shop, ca. 1900. (Photo: Courtesy of Long Island Maritime Museum, Mystic Seaport 1975-5-291*)*

Blue Wing, *similar to the Great South Bay catboats in the Museum's collection. (Photo: Courtesy of Long Island Maritime Museum,* Mystic Seaport 1975-5-290*)*

NORTH HAVEN DINGHY
14' 3" x 4' 10"

These dinghies are considered the oldest one-design class in the country, having been first raced in 1887. They still compete each summer in their home waters, the Fox Island Thoroughfare between the islands of Vinalhaven and North Haven, Maine. The origin of this particular boat is uncertain, but she was probably built sometime after 1900. Other boats of this class are being preserved by the Maine Maritime Museum, Bath, Maine, and by the Penobscot Marine Museum, Searsport, Maine.

A North Haven dinghy sails her home waters in mid-coast Maine. (Photo: Courtesy of Maynard Bray)

STATUS: Restored 1972, approximately 90% original, excellent condition.

DONOR: George Lewis

FURTHER READING:

Blanchard, Fessenden S. *The Sailboat Classes of North America.* New York: Doubleday & Co., Inc. 1968.

Brown, C. Pennington. "The North Haven Dinghies." *Down East,* August, 1974.

Esterly, Diana. *Early One-Design Sailboats.* New York: Charles Scribner's Sons, 1979.

Richardson, Eleanor Motley. *North Haven Summers: An Oral History.* Andover, Massachusetts: Catharine Little Motley, 1992.

Slaughter, Sam C. "Age Before Beauty." *Yachting,* July, 1952.

———. "Three Score and Ten." *Yachting,* April, 1959.

White, Anne B. "Over the Years." *Down East,* August, 1974.

ACCESSION NO. 1971.383

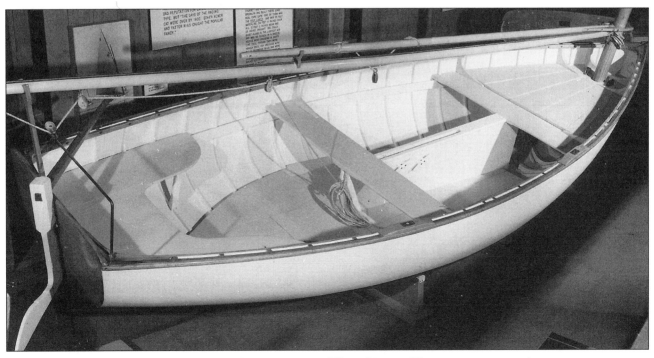

The North Haven dinghy on display at Mystic Seaport in 1975. (Photo: Maynard Bray, Mystic Seaport 1975-6-5*)*

The 11'6" Herreshoff dinghy replica built by Barry Thomas sails on the Mystic River. (Photo: Ken Mahler, Mystic Seaport 1976-6-20)

HERRESHOFF DINGHY
JOB #3403

11' 6" x 4' 1"   1905

"Job 3403 was an 11'6" boat for sailing and rowing. Model of *Columbia*'s lifeboat reduced 10/12 scale; it was ordered on 6 February 1905 for W.B. Duncan, Jr. As far as I can make out 50 boats were built to this design, the first in 1901 and the last in 1922." *From a letter–William A. Baker, Francis Russell Hart Nautical Collections,* *Massachusetts Institute of Technology, to J. Revell Carr, Mystic Seaport, September 24, 1974.*

A replica of this boat was built by Barry Thomas of Mystic Seaport's Small Craft Lab in 1975, utilizing Herreshoff Manufacturing Company construction methods. The monograph by Thomas (see Further Reading) describes this building process in detail.

STATUS: Original including sail, excellent condition.

DONOR: George Nichols, Jr., M.D.

FURTHER READING:

Herreshoff, L. Francis. *The Common Sense of Yacht Design.* New York: The Rudder Publishing Co., Inc., 1946. See Chapter entitled "Small Craft."

Thomas, Barry. *Building the Herreshoff Dinghy: The Manufacturer's Method.* Mystic: Mystic Seaport Publications, 1977.

ACCESSION NO. 1974.930

Plans for 1974.930 are available from Mystic Seaport's Watercraft Plans Collection.

The original 1905 boat, now in storage at Mystic Seaport. (Photo: Ken Mahler, Mystic Seaport 1974-11-219)

HERRESHOFF DINGHY
JOB #18152

12' 9" x 4' 7"   1928

This dinghy was modeled by N.G. Herreshoff and built by the Herreshoff Manufacturing Company. The original half model, now in possession of the donor, has pencilled on its back "12 ft sailing dinghie for *Shuttle*. NHG. Coconut Grove 1928." *Shuttle* was a 70' twin-screw commuter launched in 1928 by the Herreshoff Manufacturing Company for the donor's father, Junius S. Morgan.

STATUS: Unrestored, mostly original, fair condition.

DONOR: John P. Morgan II

FURTHER READING:

Yachts by Herreshoff. Herreshoff Manufacturing Company. Bristol, Rhode Island: Privately printed, probably 1935. Shows photograph of *Shuttle* with what appears to be this boat on deck.

ACCESSION NO. 1973.89

H.M. Co. Job #18152 in storage at Mystic Seaport.
(Photo: Maynard Bray Mystic Seaport 1975-10-83)

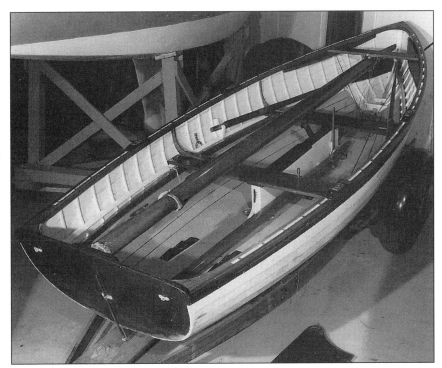

Herreshoff sailing dinghy 1318 as she appeared in 1975.
(Photo: Maynard Bray, Mystic Seaport 1975-10-84)

HERRESHOFF DINGHY
HULL #1318

14' 1" x 4' 11"   1935

Conceived by N.G. Herreshoff in 1934, this 14' sailing dinghy was one of his last designs (at age 86), and built especially for Henry S. Morgan early in 1935. This boat features a free-standing two-piece pivoting mast, rope steering, and wishbone boom with lever-operated draft control for the sail.

STATUS: Unrestored, original, excellent condition, on its original Herreshoff trailer.

DONOR: Henry S. Morgan

FURTHER READING:

Correspondence between N.G. Herreshoff and Henry S. Morgan, containing much of the rationale for the design of this boat and her fittings, is on file in the Registrar's Office at Mystic Seaport.

ACCESSION NO. 1974.1058

The Herreshoff Amphi-Craft on its trailer. (Photo: Maynard Bray, Mystic Seaport 1978-2-44)

HERRESHOFF AMPHI-CRAFT
HULL #1388

13' 1" x 4' 9"   ca. 1936

The Great Depression was truly depressing the market for yachts when, in the later years of its existence, the Herreshoff Manufacturing Company concentrated most of its effort on the building and promotion of smaller boats. This Amphi-Craft is an example; she could be sailed, rowed, or fitted with an outboard motor, and the fact that she was sold with a custom trailer made her an appealing item for middle-class sailors. Such a concept was a far cry from earlier times when wealthy yachtsmen came to the Herreshoffs for 40' daysailers and 72' one-designs. The Amphi-Crafts were designed by N.G. Herreshoff's oldest son, Sidney, who developed a number of other interesting boats for the Herreshoff Manufacturing Company during this time.

STATUS: Original, complete with its Herreshoff trailer, good condition.

DONOR: Rudolf F. Haffenreffer IV

FURTHER READING:
Bray, Maynard, and Carlton Pinheiro. *Herreshoff of Bristol.* Brooklin, Maine: WoodenBoat Publications, 1989.

Yachts by Herreshoff. Herreshoff Manufacturing Company. Bristol, Rhode Island: Privately printed, probably 1935. Contains advertising material for the Amphi-Craft.

ACCESSION NO. 1975.461

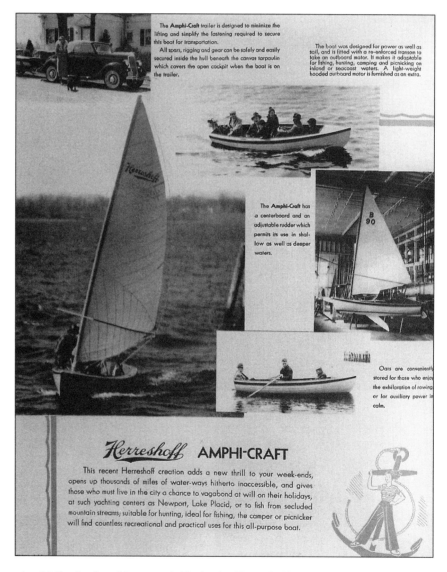

Amphi-Craft advertising page in Yachts by Herreshoff.

THE FROSTBITE DINGHY

In the early-1930s, frostbite dinghy sailors, who raced small boats during the winter months, originated most of the practices that make up today's modern dinghy racing and had a major national impact on intercollegiate and junior sailing programs.

Frostbite dinghy racing formally started on January 2, 1932, with a regatta on Manhasset Bay, New York, although owners of large boats had been informally racing their small tenders since the late 1920s. Within a year, activity had expanded to yacht clubs on both coasts, the Great Lakes, and to university sailing programs. Frostbiting was popular because it extended the season, was relatively inexpensive during depression-era times, and involved the best sailors, designers, and builders.

The North American Dinghy Association (NADA) was set up in 1932 to bring order into what had quickly developed from an informal activity to one that was highly competitive and chaotic. The NADA set up rules, sanctioned events, and over a three-year period oversaw the division of the boats into three major classes, each of which was further divided into one-design and open classes. Class A included the traditional dinghies meant to tow, row, and sail equally well, and Class B included the dinghies meant only for competitive sailing. By 1934, disparities within each class led participants to establish a one-design class for both A and B. Class D included smaller, less-expensive dinghies.

By World War II, most of the classes were self-governing and the NADA was no longer needed. Today, frostbiting takes place in general-purpose classes, such as Laser, Sunfish, and Blue Jays, as well as boats specifically designed for frostbiting.

Spectators gather for an early frostbite dinghy race at City Island, New York, on February 7, 1932. A variety of dinghies, including Lymington prams and Ratsey International dinghies, can be seen.
(*Photo:* ©Mystic Seaport, Rosenfeld Collection 50149F)

LYMINGTON PRAM

11' 3" x 4' 10"   ca. 1930

By the late 1920s, the various Transatlantic and Fastnet Races had brought many influential American yachtsmen to Cowes, England. There they experienced how much fun it was to sail one of the various pram classes, often called scows, sailed at Cowes and elsewhere. They particularly enjoyed the Lymington pram, which was built across the road from the loft of the Ratseys, the great English sailmaking family.

These same American yachtsmen were customers of George Ratsey, Sr., who had come to the United States in the 1920s to set up an American branch of the family firm at City Island, New York.

In response to their requests, George began to import Lymington prams in 1930. Some of the prams he sold, some he gave away to his best customers and friends. Arthur Knapp remembers that George imported some 25 to 30, and that he gave one apiece to Bill Taylor and Jim Robbins, both newspapermen. He kept this one for himself, which later came to the Museum. Three of these prams were in the fleet of nine boats that took part in the first formal frostbite regatta, January 2, 1932, in Manhasset Bay, New York.

STATUS: Unrestored, original, poor condition.

DONOR: John F. & Susan S. Scheffel

FURTHER READING:

Grayson, Stan. *The Dinghy Book*. Camden, Maine: International Marine Publishing Co., 1981.

Howland, Waldo. *A Life in Boats: The Years Before the War*. Mystic, Connecticut: Mystic Seaport Publications, 1984.

North American Dinghy Association. *Yearbook*. 1932-33, 1934-35, 1938, 1939-40.

Taylor, William H. "Twenty Years in a Dinghy." *Yachting*, January, 1952. Most of the history of frostbiting must be dug out of the pages of *Yachting* and *The Rudder*.

Walker, Stuart H. *Performance Advances in Small Boat Racing*. New York: W.W. Norton & Co., 1969.

Wetherill, Samuel. "Viva Dinghy Sailing!" *Yachting*, January, 1943.

ACCESSION NO. 1982.17.3

Lymington pram at Mystic Seaport. (Photo: Mary Anne Stets, Mystic Seaport 1982-2-126)

RATSEY INTERNATIONAL DINGHY

11' 4" x 4' 9"   ca. 1939

Sherman Hoyt, a member of the afterguard of the J-boat *Enterprise*, sailed a Lymington pram around Newport Harbor during the America's Cup defense in the summer of 1930, creating quite a bit of interest among the yachtsmen of the spectator fleet. The boats proved to be so popular that sailmaker George Ratsey, Sr., imported some and then arranged to have the Lymington pram built locally by the Henry B. Nevins yacht yard at City Island, New York. This is one of the Nevins-built prams, which is nearly identical to the Lymington pram, 1982.17.3 (above).

The Ratsey International dinghy in storage at Mystic Seaport. (Photo: Maynard Bray, Mystic Seaport 1975-10-82)

STATUS: Unrestored, original, good condition.

DONOR: Roberts Parsons

FURTHER READING:
(Same as 1982.17.3)

ACCESSION NO. 1965.812

DYER "HOOGAAR"
11' 2" x 4' 6"   ca. 1931

In 1931, inspired by George Ratsey's teasing, Bill Dyer had Phil Rhodes design him a proper dinghy for his Dutch-built "hoogaars" yacht *Filalou*. Fittingly, Rhodes came up with a boat with a wide beam and a tumblehome bow. Instantly popular with his friends, the "Hoogaar"dinghy was in production at Dyer's boatyard in Providence, Rhode Island, by the fall of 1931. More than 200 were built.

In December of 1931, H. Martyn Baker of Manhasset, New York, had a friendly dispute with his neighbor William Taylor, claiming his Hoogaar was faster than Taylor's Lymington pram. They decided to race their boats on January 2, 1932, at the Knickerbocker Yacht Club. Taylor, then a sports columnist with the New York *Herald Tribune* (later a great editor of *Yachting*), mentioned the race in his paper, drawing a crowd of over 100 spectators, and a few more boats, for what was to be the first frostbite regatta. Colin Ratsey won the grand prize in a Lymington pram.

Designed to be all-around utility dinghies, both the Hoogaar and the Lymington pram were rapidly outclassed for racing, and Dyer eventually replaced the Hoogaars in 1934 with the smaller, less expensive Class-D dinghy.

STATUS: Excellent condition. Rig not original.
DONOR: Roland S. Bailey
FURTHER READING:
(Same as for 1982.17.3)
Henderson, Richard. *Philip L. Rhodes and His Yacht Designs*. Camden, Maine: International Marine Publishing Company, 1981.
ACCESSION NO. 1982.12

Hoogaars compete in an early frostbite race at Port Washington, New York, on January 31, 1932. (Photo: ©Mystic Seaport, Rosenfeld Collection 50133F)

Dyer Hoogaar sailing dinghy 1982.12. (Photo: Maynard Bray, Mystic Seaport 1982.12A)

DYER DINK
#D-223
10' 0" x 4' 4"   ca. 1937

Bill Dyer built the first boat to the North American Dinghy Association's Class D Rule in early 1934 and introduced it at the New York Boat Show that year. The boat was to Philip L. Rhodes's design number 387 and was designated by the NADA as the Class D One-Design. The boat filled the need for a less-expensive, multipurpose dinghy that could be carried atop a car. Dyer's Providence boatyard, which relocated in Warren, Rhode Island, as The Anchorage after the 1938 hurricane, sold about 850 by the time production ceased in 1952. Most were sailing dinghies, but some were for oars only, and a few were equipped with a small gas engine.

STATUS: Unrestored, original, including sail, excellent condition.
DONOR: Given in memory of Alfred L. and Grace L. Fish by Edith P. Osborne, Doris T. Little, and Winifred T. Gelinas
FURTHER READING:
Davis, Arthur W. "Jeff." *Yachting in Narragansett Bay 1921-1945*. Providence, Rhode Island: Providence Journal Company, 1946.
Henderson, Richard. *Philip L. Rhodes and His Yacht Designs*. Camden, Maine: International Marine Publishing Co., 1981.
North American Dinghy Association. *Yearbook*.
ACCESSION NO. 1972.47

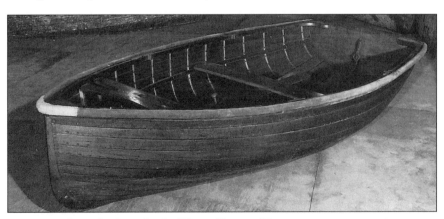

The original wooden Dyer Dink. (Photo: Maynard Bray, Mystic Seaport 1975-10-85)

Sizzle

CLASS M DINGHY
D-124

10' 0" x 4' 7"

The North American Dinghy Association declared that boats built to the D Class Rule, but not to Rhodes design 387, were to be D Open-Class boats. Dyer built a few at The Anchorage. Mystic Shipyard in West Mystic, Connecticut, built approximately 50 to a design by Charles Mower and marketed them as the M Class dinghy. Cape Cod Shipbuilding also offered a D Open-Class model.

STATUS: Original, excellent condition, unrestored.
DONOR: Mrs. Joseph G. Horne
FURTHER READING:
(Same as 1982.17.3)
ACCESSION NO. 1990.126

D-Class frostbite dinghy Sizzle. (*Photo: Maynard Bray, Mystic Seaport 1990.126A*)

Dads

ALDEN X-CLASS DINGHY
#133

11' 5" x 4' 8"

In 1932, the North American Dinghy Association (NADA) was set up to resolve an unfair situation in which highly developed sailing dinghies were competing in frostbite dinghy races against original all-around utility dinghies. Under NADA rules, Class A was for the original style of dinghy, intended to tow, row, and sail equally well. Disparities within the class led the the establishment of a one-design class.

The Class A sailors chose John Alden's Class A Design No. 561, combined it with a loose-footed Marconi sail, and called it the X Class. Promoted by sailors like Hugh Kilmer, H. Curtis Hall, and Sam Wetherill at the Larchmont, New York, Yacht Club and George Hart, Walter Rowe, and Ed Devlin at the Essex, Connecticut, Yacht Club, the class grew rapidly in size.

The Essex X-Class fleet showed its spunk when it issued a challenge to the Royal Bermuda Yacht Club to race one club's dinghies against the other's in Bermuda, to take place in April of 1934.

The challenge was accepted and six X-Class boats raced against six 12' Bermuda dinghies, with the American team coming out on top. The motivation for the challenge came partly from Walter Rowe's contacts in the diplomatic corps and partly from the fact that all the stateside harbors in the Northeast were iced in for almost the entire winter of 1934. The challenge was repeated in 1935.

STATUS: Excellent, original, unrestored.
DONOR: Lillian Hall Fisher, Marcus B. Hall, Jr., Roland Lowe Hall, Anne Lowe Hall Davis
FURTHER READING:
Carrick, Robert W., and Richard Henderson. *John G. Alden and His Yacht Designs*. Camden, Maine: International Marine Publishing Co., 1983.
ACCESSION NO. 1997.154.1

"Frostbite" dinghies were not limited to winter waters. Here, X-Class dinghies like Dads *meet on opposing tacks while racing at Miami in 1936. (Photo: ©Mystic Seaport, Rosenfeld Collection 73689F)*

Chip

CLASS-B ONE-DESIGN DINGHY

11' 6" x 4' 6"   ca. 1935

In late 1932, the governing body of frostbite racing, the North American Dinghy Association (NADA), sought to further fair competition by dividing existing dinghies into Class A for utility dinghies and Class B for racing-only dinghies. Design advances continued to produce faster, more-expensive boats, and by early 1934 some participants in Class B decided to establish a one-design class. William F. Crosby, editor of *The Rudder*, ran a design competition in the magazine, judged by a committee headed by noted yachtsman Cornelius Shields. The team of Nicholas Potter and William Strawbridge won the contest, and the first group of 21 Class-B One-Design dinghies was built by the Herreshoff Manufacturing Company of Bristol, Rhode Island, by November 1934 for $325 apiece. Later, the "BO dinghies" were built by George Lauder's Fairfield Boat Works, in Fairfield, Connecticut. Lauder's list price was $285. *Chip* is one of the latter boats and was sailed out of the Manhasset Bay Yacht Club, traditional home of frostbite dinghy racing.

STATUS: Excellent condition, original, unrestored.

DONOR: Mrs. William B. Campbell, III
FURTHER READING:
"Winner Announced in Dinghy Competition." *The Rudder*, August, 1934.
ACCESSION NO. 1988.77

Designer Nicholas Potter (forward) and dinghy-racer and yacht broker Drake Sparkman (at helm) try out Sparkman's new Class B dinghy in October, 1934. (Photo: ©Mystic Seaport, Rosenfeld Collection 70125F)

The Class B frostbite dinghy Chip *at Mystic Seaport. (Photo: Maynard Bray,* Mystic Seaport 1988.77B*)*

Outsider

PENGUIN DINGHY
#1377

11' 6" x 5' 0"   1947

Bill Dyer asked Philip L. Rhodes to design a simple frostbite dinghy in 1933. Rhodes came up with the Penguin, a hard-chine, arc-bottom boat that initially was built of 1/4" mahogany panels using batten-seam construction. The boat was too extreme and did not catch on with frostbite sailors until *Yachting* published the plans in May of 1940. By then, plywood was widely available and the boat could be built easily by amateurs. The boat became quite popular and was adopted as a youth training boat by many yacht club programs. By 1980, more than 10,000 Penguins were being sailed in the U.S. alone. The hull is built of wood or fiberglass today.

Runyon "Runie" Colie won the Penguin National Championship seven times in *Outsider*, sailing out of New Jersey's Mantoloking Yacht Club. The boat was built in 1947 by the David Beaton & Sons Boatyard, also of Mantoloking.

STATUS: Excellent condition.
DONOR: Runyon Colie
FURTHER READING:
(Same as 1982.17.3)
Henderson, Richard. *Philip L. Rhodes and His Yacht Designs.* Camden, Maine: International Marine Publishing, 1981.
International Penguin Class Dinghy Association. *Handbook.*
ACCESSION NO. 1988.56

Penguin dinghy Outsider. *(Photo: Maynard Bray,* Mystic Seaport 1988.56A*)*

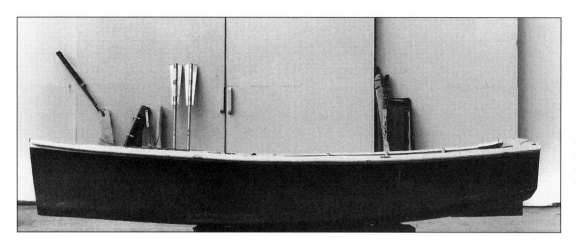

The Penguin dinghy Sawdust *in storage at Mystic Seaport. (Photo: Mary Anne Stets, Mystic Seaport 1984.154A)*

Sawdust
PENGUIN DINGHY
#7044
11′ 6″ x 5′ 0″   1962

Bruce Lockwood built *Sawdust* for himself in 1962. The boat came to the Museum unusually well equipped and reflects Bruce's penchant for experimentation.

STATUS: Good condition.
DONOR: Bruce Lockwood
FURTHER READING:
(Same as 1988.56)
ACCESSION NO. 1984.154

Fragile
INTERCLUB (IC) CLASS
DINGHY
11′ 6″ x 4′ 7″

Olin Stephens, of the design firm Sparkman & Stephens, designed the Interclub dinghy in 1939 to fit the requirements of a group of frostbite dinghy sailors from the Larchmont, New York, Yacht Club. The first group of about 100 dinghies was built of molded plywood between 1939 and 1953. In 1953, Cape Cod Shipbuilding began to build the boats in fiberglass. The class is still widely sailed as a frostbite dinghy.

STATUS: Excellent condition, upgraded over time to remain competitive.
DONOR: John Walsh
FURTHER READING:
Kinney, Francis S., and Russell Bourne. *The Best of the Best: The Yacht Designs of Sparkman & Stephens.* New York: W.W. Norton & Co., 1996.

ACCESSION NO. 1998.64.1

Interclub dinghies race on a cold and dreary January day at Larchmont, New York, in 1954. (Photo: ©Mystic Seaport, Rosenfeld Collection 139295F)

Butterfly
DEVELOPMENT CLASS DINGHY
BY L.F. HERRESHOFF

18' 2" x 5' 0"   1930

In 1927, William Atkin created a rule for a small two-person sailing boat called the Development Class. The idea was "to develop the fastest hulls (within the limits of the rule) possible with 125 square feet of sail." There weren't many restrictions–none on hull length. Beam had to fall in a range; all had to be monohulls; and "no punt, parabolic, elliptical, round, or scow snoots allowed." Scantlings controlled weight with about 200 pounds being the practical minimum. The class caught on at the Huntington Yacht Club on Long Island, with designers such as Charles Mower, Billy Atkin himself, Olin Stephens, and others joining the fun.

Some boats were given names based on "the more potent modern drinks concocted after the manner of the laws of the U.S. as sponsored by Mr. Volstead, the Anti-Saloon League... popular and deadly drinks." Huntington owners adopted the skull and crossbones for their sails and called themselves the Suicide Class.

Following the designs and descriptions of the boats published in Atkin's *Fore An' Aft* magazine, L. Francis Herreshoff and one of his steady clients, Charles A. Welch of Marblehead, got interested. L. Francis designed a 19' boat (Design No. 48) and had three built. A Marblehead challenge ensued. Three of the Huntington boats were loaded aboard the schooner *Sunbeam* and taken to Marblehead where they were trounced soundly by Skipper Herreshoff's creations. Two of the L. Francis boats sported double-luff rotating rigs, a ketch and a cat. The

third was a sloop. The double-luff boats took top honors.

In 1930, L. Francis designed another Development Class boat, Design No. 30 for Charlie Welch, and two were built at Lawley's. He kept this one and called her *Butterfly*; Welch took the other naming her *Flutterby*. Both were simpler than his earlier designs, a little smaller, lapstrake, and cat-rigged with a conventional sail, a rig considerably easier to handle than the earlier double-luffed boats. They retained the wide side decks and elegant shapes. For three years, they raced each other in Marblehead waters. *Butterfly* was saved by the donor's father from an owner who had let the boat go. Welch's *Flutterby* was sold to a Nantucket family. She later migrated to California; now restored, she's still sailing.

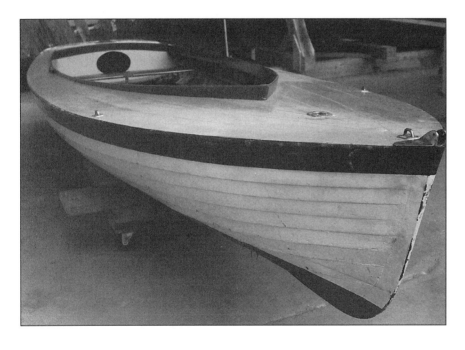

L. Francis Herreshoff's Development-Class dinghy Butterfly. *(Photo: Judy Beisler, Mystic Seaport 1988.78C)*

STATUS: Good restored condition.
DONOR: Robert Smith
FURTHER READING:
Atkin, William. "The Suicide Fleet Looks in at Marblehead." *Fore An' Aft*, November 15, 1928.

Bray, Maynard, and Carlton Pinheiro. *Herreshoff of Bristol*. Brooklin, Maine: WoodenBoat Publications, 1989.

Capt. Kid. "The Huntington Yacht Club's Development Class, Popularly Known as the Suicide Class." *Fore An' Aft*, May, 1928.

Corwin, Hiliary. "The Development Class." *Fore An' Aft*, December 15, 1927.

Herreshoff, L. Francis. *The Common Sense of Yacht Design*. Jamaica, New York: Caravan-Maritime Books, 1975.

McSwiney, Thomas. "Development in the Wishbone Rig." Stuart H. Walker, ed., *Performance Advances in Small Boat Racing*. New York: W.W. Norton & Co., 1969, 169-76.

Miller, Mark. "Flattery for *Flutterby*." *WoodenBoat* 46, May/June, 1982.

Suicide interest stayed alive in Florida, and a number of boats were built in the 1950s and 1960s. Interest is now reviving.

ACCESSION NO. 1988.78

Pig in a Bag
DEVELOPMENT CLASS DINGHY
BY N.G. HERRESHOFF
HULL #1149

20' 1" x 5' 0"   1930

Pig in a Bag under sail as a two-masted cat ketch. (Photo: Courtesy of Mr. and Mrs. Walter H. Page, Mystic Seaport 2001.104.2)

The tale in the Nichols family has this boat getting her name because she was bought sight unseen by George Nichols. The story goes on to say that the sight-unseen purchase was key to getting the Herreshoff yard to build a non-Herreshoff-designed J-Boat, Clinton Crane's *Weetamoe*. True or not, it's a good story, and Nathanael Herreshoff, then in semi-retirement, got a pair of Development Class boats built to his design. (The other went to George Nichols's brother-in-law and partner in the syndicate, Junius Morgan.) *Pig*'s contract, dated September 19, 1929, was five days before *Weetamoe*'s; she was shipped on the 26th of April. N.G. Herreshoff became interested in the Development Class through his son, L. Francis, and these boats permitted him to try out ideas involving aerodynamics and sail control at a modest scale.

This boat set the standard for later HMCo. efforts with other dinghies such as the Amphi-Craft, sharing with them wide side decks, user-friendly features like oar-storing brackets, and a wishbone or horizontal curved sprit rig. *Pig in a Bag* has five mast steps, two of them using detachable partners, giving her the potential to be sailed with rigs ranging from a sloop to a three-masted cat ketch. A removable "slip-thwart" allows a sleeping bag to be stretched on the floorboards, and a continuous tiller line attached to the rudder lets her be steered from anywhere in the boat. A watertight compartment aft provides both buoyancy and a dry place to stow gear. Whether or not Nichols and Morgan relaxed from the rigors of America's Cup trials by racing their Development Class boats isn't recorded, but *Pig* proved useful enough that she was still being sailed (and bailed) until she came to Mystic Seaport.

STATUS: Good original condition with all equipment.
DONOR: Mr. and Mrs. Walter H. Page in memory of George Nichols, Jr.
ACCESSION NO. 1990.74

Pig in a Bag in *storage at Mystic Seaport.*
(Photo: Maynard Bray, Mystic Seaport 1990.74A)

DEVELOPMENT CLASS DINGHY BY STRAWBRIDGE & FAIRFIELD

16' 0" x 4' 10"   1933

William Strawbridge, influenced by his friend L. Francis Herreshoff, designed this fast sailing dinghy, a boat similar to L. Francis Herreshoff's *Butterfly* (1988.78) and N.G. Herreshoff's *Pig in a Bag* (1990.74). Strawbridge's 16' Development Class dinghy was an evolution of two successful frostbite dinghies he had designed a few years earlier. In light airs she was fast enough to sail with the slippery, and much larger, 30-Square-Meter-Class sloops that shared her home port in Northeast Harbor, Maine. The boat has a modern dinghy hull shape, reminiscent of a Finn, and was always sailed with two sharpie-style sails. When Strawbridge sailed the boat in heavy gusty air, he kept the mizzen sheeted hard and slacked the main to ease the boat and luff into the gust, one advantage of the cat-ketch rig. Built by George Lauder's Fairfield Boat Works in 1933 of fine Virginia cedar, this boat was stored from 1946 until she came to Mystic Seaport in 1980.

STATUS: Good original condition; after mast step removed.
DONOR: William J. Strawbridge, Sr.
ACCESSION NO. 1980.14

The William Strawbridge Development Class dinghy in storage at Mystic Seaport. (Photo: Maynard Bray, Mystic Seaport 1980.14A)

Twilight

MARCO POLO SAILING DINGHY

11' 8" x 4' 7"   1961

L. Francis Herreshoff included this pram-shaped, flat-bottom dinghy when he prepared drawings of his Marco Polo design as a "how-to-build" series for *The Rudder* magazine. With a slim and seaworthy double-ended hull and a three-masted schooner rig, the 55' Marco Polo was to be a practical ocean voyager in a world made safe after World War II. Her deck had a space set aside where the dinghy could rest, bottom up, when at sea. Although few yachts were built to the Marco Polo design (a bitter disappointment for Herreshoff), far more of these Marco Polo dinghies came into being because of their singular appeal. Their carrying capacity is phenomenal for a 12' undecked craft, and because the interior isn't cluttered with the usual sailing dinghy's centerboard trunk (she has leeboards), there is plenty of space in which to move around or stow gear.

Allan Vaitses, the donor's father and a friend of L. Francis Herreshoff, built *Twilight* in his Mattapoisett, Massachusetts, boatshop–a place where several other L. Francis Herreshoff designs were constructed.

STATUS: Original, good condition.
DONOR: Gail Vaitses Elen
ACCESSION NO. 1991.91

Marco Polo dinghy Twilight.
(Photo: Maynard Bray, Mystic Seaport 1991.91A)

John G.

SAILING DINGHY

12' 10" x 4' 11"   ca. 1930-31

Sailing dinghy John G. *from Pine Island Camp. (Photo: Maynard Bray,*
Mystic Seaport 1990.142A)

This lapstrake, round-bottom, cat-rigged sailing dinghy was built by John Gardner circa 1930-31 while he was the workshop counselor at Pine Island Camp, a traditional summer camp for boys established in 1902 on Pine Island in Great Pond, Belgrade Lakes, Maine. Dr. Eugene L. Swan, the camp's director, bankrolled John's project with a hundred-dollar bill, the first that John had ever seen. There was no power on the island, and John with the help of a few young campers built the boat entirely with hand tools. Her Marconi rig called for a 21' mast, which Dr. Swan insisted be cut down to 18' in the interest of safety. C.J. Swan, youngest of the three Swan brothers, was a fine sailor, and he took over the boat when it was first launched. The boat was named in John's honor, long after he left the camp.

The design, a precursor to frostbite dinghies popular in the mid-1930s, was by Charles D. Mower, a prominent New York yacht designer. Mower's plans appeared in popular boating magazines like *The Rudder, Motor Boating,* and *Yachting,* which John eagerly read. Mower wrote with clarity, without pretense, and encouraged amateur construction of his versatile boats. Mower claimed to have built his first boat in a stable and his second under a rough shed, and this appealed to John, who learned boatbuilding as a boy with his

family on the banks of the St. Croix River in Maine.

The hull is planked in 3/8" northern white cedar, with steam-bent white oak frames 7/8" x 5/8" on 8" centers, and copper-rivet-fastened at the laps and through the frames. Brass screws are used elsewhere, and the inwale, 1-3/4" x 5/8", is fastened to the frames with copper rivets. The 3/16" steel-boilerplate centerboard is missing, but the hole for the pivot pin and the block for the pennant remain. Her two-piece stem and staunch stern knee are in excellent condition, and plank laps are still tight.

After years of summer sailing at the camp, *John G.* was modified to carry an outboard, and eventually retired from service. In 1990, 60 years after her launching, she was donated to Mystic Seaport where John Gardner again laid eyes on her. He expected her to be in rough shape, but after close inspection

on her arrival, he was inspired to write a piece for the *Pine Needle,* the Pine Island Camp newsletter, proclaiming his amazement at her condition: "True, the centerboard, rudder and rig were gone, and the paint had long since turned to shoddy grime. But what I saw, while battered, was essentially repairable. She had lost none of her original shapeliness, no planks were missing or broken, rivets were tight, bent timbers remained unbroken."

Despite the research, John was unable to confirm her exact date of construction, nor the design, although all signs point to the Snapper, published in *Motor Boating* in 1925. As far as is known, *John G.* is the oldest documented boat which John Gardner built.

STATUS: Fair Condition.
DONOR: Benjamin B. Swan
ACCESSION NO. 1990.142

The John G. *leads the Pine Island Camp fleet racing across Great Pond. (Photo: Courtesy of Pine Island Camp,* Mystic Seaport 1993.12.27)

DYER DHOW OF PLYWOOD
9' 0" x 4' 5"   ca. 1943

This is the original model of the now-ubiquitous Dyer Dhow. In 1942, Philip L. Rhodes and William Dyer collaborated on the design from which hundreds of Dhows were built for use as lifeboats during World War II; these little boats saw service aboard PT boats, submarine chasers, and aircraft rescue boats. They were originally built of 3/16" waterproof plywood panels over oak framing, but soon after the war The Anchorage, as Dyer's boatbuilding operation was known, switched to that new material, fiberglass (see Dyer Dhow 1965.392), and offered the same basic model in various lengths and freeboards.

STATUS: Good, unrestored.
DONOR: Mystic Seaport purchase
FURTHER READING FOR 1991.173 AND 1965.392:
Blanchard, Fessenden S. *The Sailboat Classes of North America*. New York: Doubleday & Co., 1968.

The Editors of *Yachting. Your New Boat.* New York: Simon and Schuster, 1946.

Henderson, Richard. *Philip L. Rhodes and His Yacht Designs*. Camden, Maine: International Marine Publishing Co., 1981.

ACCESSION NO. 1991.173

The 1940s plywood Dyer Dhow. (Photo: Maynard Bray, Mystic Seaport 1991.173A)

DYER DHOW OF FIBERGLASS
9' 0" x 4' 5"   ca. 1949

In 1942, to fulfill a navy contract for lifeboats, Bill Dyer of The Anchorage, Inc. in Warren, Rhode Island, began to build these 9' dinghies of molded plywood. Conversion was made to fiberglass in 1949. As of March 2000, nearly 6,600 boats of this type have been built. This Dyer Dhow is believed to be the first boat of the fiberglass series. Mystic Seaport's community sailing program and the *Joseph Conrad* Summer Camp Program for boys and girls ages 10 to 15, both sail-training activities, use a fleet of 40 of these boats.

STATUS: Unrestored, original, rig missing, good condition.
DONOR: Anonymous
ACCESSION NO. 1965.392

The Mystic Seaport Dyer Dhow under sail on the Mystic River. (Photo: Mary Anne Stets, Mystic Seaport 1975-8-220)

The 7' 8" Dyer Dot Little Lulu. *(Photo: Maynard Bray, Mystic Seaport 1984.157A)*

Little Lulu
DYER DOT
7' 8" x 4' 0"   ca. 1940

Bill Dyer's boatyard, The Anchorage of Warren, Rhode Island, developed the Dyer Dot just before World War II and built 68 as tenders and 18 with an additional sliding-gunter sailing rig. The first sailing model was built for noted yachtsman Hobey Ford in February of 1939. The butterfly mast partners, spars, and bronze hardware were all typical high-quality Anchorage details. Plywood sides and bottom kept the cost down.

STATUS: Good; centerboard missing, centerboard case blocked.
DONOR: John Sindall
FURTHER READING:
Grayson, Stan. *The Dinghy Book.* Camden, Maine: International Marine Publishing Co., 1981.
ACCESSION NO. 1984.157

Teal
ROOKIE CLASS SKIFF
9' 0" x 3' 6"   1930s

Henry Richardson Shepley designed the Rookie Class in part to test his theory about the best way to get young children into sailing. He felt that if youngsters were provided with a boat that was small enough and light enough to be completely controlled by the children themselves, they would learn to sail as readily and naturally as they learned to walk or swim.

About 50 of these little boats were spread between the Marion and Cohasset yacht clubs on Buzzards Bay, Massachusetts, during the 1930s and were used by children ranging in age from four to eight for within-the-breakwater sailing. Some were still sailing at Cohasset in the mid-1980s.

The boats were built by Charles Anderson and a Mr. Parry of Wareham, Massachusetts. Simply built, the boats had single-plank sides, a centerboard, a short foredeck, and set a single 36-square-foot leg-o-mutton sail using iron rings for mast hoops. The first boats built cost $25 apiece.

STATUS: Good, unrestored. Rig missing.
DONOR: Mrs. T.E. Drew
FURTHER READING:
Swan, William U. "Break 'Em in Early." *Yachting*, August, 1933.
ACCESSION NO. 1987.44

The Rookie-Class sailing dinghy Teal. *(Photo: Deborah Patterson, Mystic Seaport 1987.44B)*

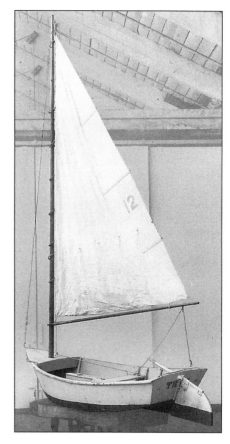

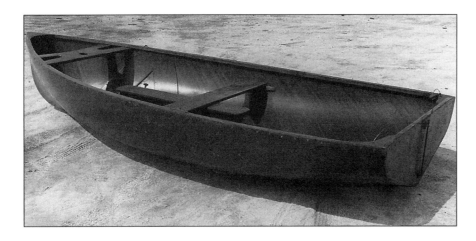

The International 12 in storage at Mystic Seaport. (Photo: Maynard Bray, Mystic Seaport 1975-5-236)

INTERNATIONAL TWELVE-FOOT CLASS
#1-12

11' 6" x 4' 9"   ca. 1940

"The International 12 was designed by an Englishman whose name, I believe, was Hall. I believe the first boats were built early in 1941 and went to the U.S. Coast Guard Academy. Much like the other boats, the 12' International was converted to fiberglass production during the 1950s, and about the only boats which have been built have been to occasionally replace the Coast Guard Academy fleet, and the most recent ones have been delivered in 1969. In all, only about 150 boats have been built." *From a letter–W.H. Dyer Jones of The Anchorage, Inc. to Maynard Bray, March 21, 1975.*

The International 12, an English-dinghy type, and a smaller sister to the International 14, was designed by H.C. Hall. This first Anchorage boat was introduced at the New York Motor Boat Show in 1941, and that spring the Coast Guard Academy ordered 30 boats. As noted, this fleet was supplemented by fiberglass boats in the 1950s and 1960s. The last six were shipped to the Academy in 1969. The Academy's fleet of International 12s raced through 1977.

STATUS: Unrestored, original, rig missing, good condition.
DONOR: Anonymous
ACCESSION NO. 1965.391

Little Haste
RIVERSIDE DINGHY
HULL #77

11' 5" x 4' 6"   ca. 1955

Fenwick Williams successfully designed this V-bottom, sprit-rigged dinghy to be easy and inexpensive to build. To achieve this he specified batten-seam construction, pine or mahogany planking, and sawn frames with plywood gussets. He also kept the chine low forward to avoid the severe twist in the planks that can make a planking job difficult. Even with a professionally built sail, an amateur could build the boat for under $75 in 1934. Although not fast in light air, the design proved to be stiff and moved well in a moderate breeze.

The boats raced as a class on the Mianus River at Riverside, Connecticut. George Lauder's Fairfield Boatworks of Greenwich, Connecticut, built the first 20 boats in the fleet in 1936. A second group of boats was built in the 1950s by Brand, working in the old Palmer Brothers factory in Cos Cob. *Little Haste* is one of the latter boats.

STATUS: Good condition.
DONOR: Peter F. Littlefield
FURTHER READING:
Anable, Anthony. *The History of the Riverside Yacht Club, 1888-1972.* Riverside, Connecticut: Riverside Yacht Club, 1974.

"A Practical Sailing Skiff." *The Rudder,* March, 1934.

ACCESSION NO. 1982.18

Riverside-Class dinghy Little Haste. *(Photo: Maynard Bray, Mystic Seaport 1982.18A)*

The 11' 7" canvas-covered dinghy in storage. (Photo: Maynard Bray, Mystic Seaport 1986.83A)

SAILING DINGHY, POSSIBLY BY OLD TOWN

11' 7" x 4' 5"

Old Town and other canoe builders like Penn Yan followed the market and moved to building small sailing, rowing, and outboard powered boats. These boats typically followed the standard flat-frame, canvas-covered construction of the canoes. This sailing dinghy was probably built by Old Town, but the maker's decal and serial number are no longer visible. Certainly their 1955 11-1/2' Standard model looks much like this boat, and had a sliding gunter rig like this one. Canvas-covered boats of all kinds, which could be speedily built on production lines, were not, superseded until the advent of fiberglass.

STATUS: Good condition, now covered in fiberglass in place of canvas, equipped with full rig and oars.

DONOR: Edward P. Boyhen
FURTHER READING:
Audette, Susan T. *The Old Town Canoe Company: Our First Hundred Years.* Gardiner, Maine: Tilbury House, 1998.

Speltz, Robert. *The Real Runabouts IV: Outboard Edition.* Lake Mills, Iowa: Robert Speltz, 1982.

ACCESSION NO. 1986.83

SAILING DINGHY BY N. BLAISDELL AND SONS

11' 2" x 4' 4"   ca. 1930

To meet the needs of the growing shipbuilding business at Bath, Maine, Nicholas Blaisdell set up as a boatbuilder with a partner in 1879. When shipbuilding declined and yachtbuilding increased in the new century, Blaisdell changed his product as well. In 1894 his partner quit and he took his sons Philip and Charles into the shop. In 1919 they moved across the river to Woolwich. His sons built increasingly for the yacht trade. This sailing dinghy is typical of the light lapstrake craft built on the New England coast to serve a flourishing recreational boat market during the first half of the twentieth century. The Maine Maritime Museum has several Blaisdell-built boats in its collection.

STATUS: Fair condition, without rig, floorboards, or centerboard trunk.
DONOR: Robert D. Scott
FURTHER READING:
Baker, James F. "'Stardust,' A Tribute to Philip Blaisdell." *Yachting*, June, 1945.

Baker, W.A. *A Maritime History of Bath, Maine, and the Kennebec Region.* Bath, Maine: Maritime Research Society of Bath, 1973.

ACCESSION NO. 1990.143

The 11' 2" Blaisdell sailing dinghy. (Photo: Maynard Bray, Mystic Seaport 1990.143A)

SAILING DINGHY FROM DION'S YACHT YARD

15' 1" x 5' 2"   ca. 1930

Primarily because of her molded sheerstrakes, one line of thinking has this as a Herreshoff-built boat. On closer inspection, however, she doesn't quite conform, and the construction list from the Herreshoff Manufacturing Company shows no boat of her dimensions. She's a fine sailing dinghy, nevertheless, which seems to have been converted from a strictly rowing boat after she was built. In the 1970s she was located at the Salem, Massachusetts, boatyard once managed by the donor, but there is no record of her history prior to that.

STATUS: Substantially original, good condition.
DONOR: Leo A. Dion
ACCESSION NO. 1980.119

The unidentified Dion dinghy in storage at Mystic Seaport. (Photo: Ken Mahler, Mystic Seaport 1981-2-81)

Alice M. Thomas

SAILING DINGHY

10' 10" x 4' 1/2"   ca. 1910

Thomas family tradition has it that this lovely sailing tender was built by George Lawley & Sons in 1910 at the same time the Lawley yard was building the family's sloop *Whisper*. John Pickering Thomas designed *Whisper* himself for racing and probably would not have been satisfied with a tender by any builder but Lawley.

The *Alice M. Thomas* is built to high standards, with cedar planking fastened with bronze to bent oak frames. The boat's scantlings are slightly heavier and it is missing some of the construction details found in most Lawley-built dinghies of the time.

STATUS: Excellent condition and shows good care.
DONOR: Mary Alice Thomas Nichols
ACCESSION NO. 1987.71

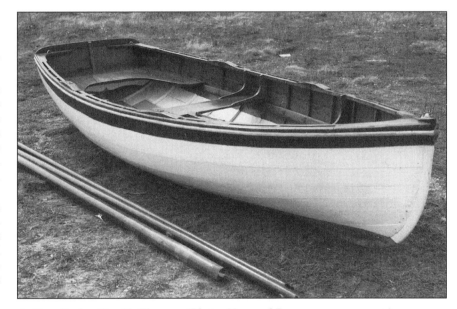

Sailing dinghy Alice M. Thomas. *(Photo: Maynard Bray,* Mystic Seaport 1987.71A)

BAHAMIAN SAILING DINGHY
10' 1" x 4' 0"

The donor reported that this dinghy was built in the Bahamas, and her wide transom, fine sheer, quick turn of the bilge, and hollow bow suggest the shapely boats of those islands. Similar boats have been built for fishing and transportation on Abaco and other islands for generations by the Alburys, Winer Malone, and other families. With the increase of yachting and tourism in the Bahamas in the 1950s, these boat-builders found a new recreational market for their boats among American sailors, who enjoyed the excitement of sailing a Bahamian-style dinghy with its tall leg-of-mutton or Marconi cat rig. Unlike most Bahamian dinghies, this one had a daggerboard for increased lateral resistance.

STATUS: Original, excellent condition, but lacking daggerboard and tiller.
DONOR: Dr. H.R. Kuhn
FURTHER READING:
Adams, Kurt. "Going the Abaco Route." *WoodenBoat* 135, Mar/Apr, 1997.
Hylan, Doug. "The Alburys of Man O' War Cay." *WoodenBoat* 135, Mar/Apr, 1997.
ACCESSION NO. 1984.183

The Bahamian sailing dinghy in storage at Mystic Seaport. (Photo: Deborah Bates, Mystic Seaport 1984.183F)

SAILBOARDS AND BOARD BOATS

Natives of the Amazon used movable masts on their sailing rafts, but the modern sailboard goes back only to the 1930s. The idea first took form when surfer Tom Blake, tired one afternoon from paddling his surfboard, added a mast, sail, and foot rudder and called it a "sailing surfboard." While a few others like Mystic's Ernie Post may have experimented with building board boats of plywood (see 1990.32), the idea finally took off in 1948, when iceboat-builders Al Bryan and Cort Heyniger added a sail and rudder to a paddle board and called it a Sailfish. Though it was a sailboard, it was intended to be sailed sitting down.

In the early 1960s, Pennsylvanian S. Newman Darby began to experiment with a rectangular board sailed standing up. With his wife and brother, Darby applied for a patent and set up a production company for their "Sailboard" in 1964, but they only built 160 before a fire ended production in 1966. A few years later, California surfer Hoyle Schweitzer, assisted by aeronautical engineer James Drake, came up with a workable sailing surfboard, which they patented in 1968. Its performance at the 1970 America's Teacup Regatta (a regatta for small, inexpensive high-performance boats held as a contrast to the America's Cup) led to a demand for the sailboard soon to be known as the Windsurfer.

Another board boat that turned heads at the America's Teacup Regatta was Bruce Kirby and Ian Bruce's Weekender, which soon entered production as the Laser, a greatly refined descendant of the Sailfish. The Windsurfer, Laser, and similar board boats appealed to many who had never owned a boat and have added a new dimension to competitive and recreational sailing ever since.

SAILFISH BY ALCORT
11' 7 1/2" x 2' 7 1/2"

The hundreds of thousands of board boats in use today can be said to be the descendants of the Sailfish of 1948. As iceboat builders, Alex Bryan and Cort Heyniger of Waterbury, Connecticut, knew "fast is fun." A Red Cross staffer asked them to build paddle boards for surf rescue, but he did not want to pay what they cost, and left Al and Cort with the plans and prototype. They redesigned the board with a canoe sail. Several tries later they had the "Sailboard." A marketing friend, inspired by a mounted sailfish on his wall, recommended a name change. Their simple Sailfish got a boost to national recognition when one of *Life Magazine*'s music editors tried the boat and sailed it better than her date. *Life* published an appealing view of Sailfish sailing in August 1948, and Alcort got its marketing start. The boat was easy to set up and sail; unlike most boats it could be righted quickly when capsized; and it planed readily in a breeze. Built with plywood deck and bottom and mahogany sides, the Sailfish was available as either a kit or a finished boat. Kit production stopped in the mid-1960s, as did Sailfish production, to be superseded by the larger Sunfish, which had a well for the sailors' feet.

This Sailfish was the display model in the Leominster, Massachusetts, marine dealership of Joe Goodhue, one of Alcort's top dealers in 1962. That year you could get a kit for $187 and a finished boat for $297. The larger Sunfish, first built about 1953, was $395 in wood, $447 in fiberglass. The company has changed hands, and now Vanguard Racing Sailboats builds the Sunfish.

Alcort's advertising for the Sailfish emphasized the ease and excitement of board sailing. (Photo: Mystic Seaport, 2001.6)

STATUS: Like new, with display names painted on deck.

DONOR: Museum purchase

FURTHER READING:

Sutphen, Duncan. "The Sailfish." *The Rudder*, February, 1949.

White, Will. *The Sunfish Bible*. Sarasota, Florida: Omega Cubed Press, 1996.

ACCESSION NO. 2001.6

WINDSURFER
COMP MODEL
#357064

12' x 2' 4"   1983

By the end of 1968, perhaps 12 sailing surfboards existed, all built by California surfer Hoyle Schweitzer, who worked with a friend, aeronautical engineer James Drake, to come up with a practical and marketable way to marry a sail to a surfboard. The sport took off after Schweitzer got national publicity with his board at the America's Teacup Regatta in 1970. The switch from fiberglass to polyethylene for the hulls in 1970-71 made it lighter, easier to manufacture, and more affordable. Bert Salisbury, the first non-Californian to order some of the early boards, suggested "Windsurfer" for the product name, and before long that became the generic term for any sailboard.

This board is one of the second generation Windsurfer designs. By the time it was built, Windsurfer had built over 350,000, and hundreds of thousands of licensed and pirated Windsurfers had been built in Europe, where the sport took off faster than in the United States. The donor used this board in Santa Barbara, California; hence its oil stains.

STATUS: Good, sailable condition.

DONOR: Joseph Knowles

FURTHER READING:

Drake, James R. "Wind Surfing: A New Concept in Sailing." *American Windsurfing* 4, #4, 1996.

Kirby, Bruce. "America's Teacup." *One-Design and Offshore Yachtsman*, Dec, 1970.

"Origins of Windsurfing." *American Windsurfing* 5, #1, 2, 1997.

Taylor, Glenn. *A Complete Guide to the Sport of Windsurfing*. Palo Alto, California: Bay Windsurfing, 1979.

ACCESSION NO. 2000.137

The Comp Model Windsurfer at Mystic Seaport.
(Photo: Judy Beisler, Mystic Seaport 2000.137A)

LASER CLASS
#0
13' 10" x 4' 7"   1970

In 1970, the Advertising Director of *One-Design and Offshore Yachtsman* suggested to the magazine's editor, Bruce Kirby, a regatta to be called the America's Teacup, with invitees to sail monohulls that cost under $1,000 and multihulls under $1,200. Kirby, also a successful International 14 designer, created a boat for the event that he called the Weekender. The boat, "built from scratch during the week before the event," and named *TGIF*, was sailed by Olympic champion Hans Fogh. It did well, tying with the Banshee for best performance. Kirby and his Canadian builder, Ian Bruce, saw a market for this lively 135-pound one-design, renamed it the Laser, and went into promotion and production. The introductory price was $695. The inaugural America's Teacup regatta also saw the national debut of two other boats that were to change the look of small-boat sailing: the Hobie Cat and the Windsurfer.

This boat is the first Laser off the production line and the third built. Kirby gave her #0, as the first two Lasers built were test prototypes. She was sailed by Kirby until he gave her to Mystic Seaport in 1988.

In the years since 1970, *One-Design and Offshore Yachtsman* became *Sailing World*, and the Weekender/Laser has been built in tens of thousands. The Laser became an Olympic-class boat in 1996.

Laser Class #0. (Photo: Maynard Bray, Mystic Seaport 1988.76A)

STATUS: Excellent unrestored condition, complete with equipment.

DONOR: Bruce Kirby

FURTHER READING:
Barrett, Peter. "Carte Blanche." *One-Design and Offshore Yachtsman*, Dec, 1970.

Kirby, Bruce. "America's Teacup." *One-Design and Offshore Yachtsman*, Dec, 1970.

Association Address:
c/o Allan Broadribb, 8466 N. Lockwood Ridge Rd., Suite 328, Sarasota, Florida 34243 (813) 751-6216

ACCESSION NO. 1988.76

The first Laser advertisement.

Barnegat Bay sneakbox shown here without rig. (Photo: Maynard Bray, Mystic Seaport 1975-5-69)

BARNEGAT BAY SNEAKBOX

12′ 1″ x 4′ 2″   ca. 1910

The sneakbox is another of the many boats designed for bird shooting. This type is unique in hull shape because of its overhanging or so-called "spoon" bow and rounded deckline. Along with a pair of bottom runners, the spoon bow supposedly makes the sneakbox amphibious so that it can sail on ice as well as water. The low freeboard can be easily concealed with grass to hide the boats from the birds.

Either Samuel Perrine of Barnegat, New Jersey, or his son Howard built this particular boat. Sneakboxes in later years have been adapted for racing by yacht clubs on Barnegat Bay.

STATUS: Unrestored, original, rig missing, good condition.

DONOR: Mr. and Mrs. Ernest H. Fontan

FURTHER READING FOR 1961.915 AND 1981.124:

"A Perrine Sneakbox, Famous Boat of Barnegat in Maritime Museum." *Beach Haven Times* (NJ), May 9, 1962.

Bishop, Nathaniel H. *Four Months in a Sneakbox*. Detroit: Gale Research Press, 1976. Reprint of 1879 edition.

Blanchard, Fessenden S. *The Sailboat Classes of North America*. New York: Doubleday & Company, 1968.

Chapelle, Howard I. *American Small Sailing Craft*. New York: W. W. Norton & Co., 1951.

Guthorn, Peter J. *The Sea Bright Skiff and Other Jersey Shore Boats*. New Brunswick, New Jersey: Rutgers University Press, 1971. Well-researched history of sneakboxes, both for gunning and racing. Also covers Nathaniel Bishop's influence on the boat's development.

Herreshoff, L. Francis. *The Compleat Cruiser*. New York: Sheridan House, 1963.

Schock, E. B. "The Barnegat Sneakbox." *The Rudder*, Feb, 1907.

Schoettle, Edwin J., ed. *Sailing Craft*. New York: The MacMillan Co., Inc., 1927. Two chapters on history of sneakboxes and their development into racing boats.

ACCESSION NO. 1961.915

Plans for 1961.915 are available from Mystic Seaport's Watercraft Plans Collection.

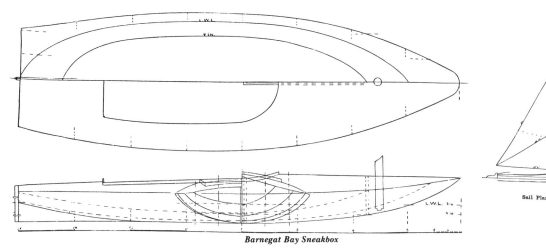

Barnegat Bay Sneakbox

Sail Plan.

Barnegat Bay sneakbox from W. P. Stephens' book Canoe and Boat Building, *1889 edition.*

BARNEGAT BAY SNEAKBOX
12' 4" x 4' 10"

Tim Eastland saved this boat from the Old Lyme, Connecticut, landfill where it had been left by the builder's grandson. Although Connecticut-built, it is typical of sneakboxes that were being built by the hundreds as late as the 1930s and 1940s for waterfowl gunning and as sail trainers for youngsters, primarily in the Barnegat Bay area of New Jersey.

This boat is equipped with a pivoted centerboard whose box is conventionally placed on the centerline. Boats meant specifically for gunning often were equipped with a daggerboard installed off center up forward, allowing more space in the cockpit for the gunner. The planking is laid off parallel to the keel and nailed to sawn frames shaped to a master pattern. The deck beams forward of the cockpit land on a unique structural member called the harpin, a shelf-like piece fastened to the frame heads.

Sneakboxes originated in the marshes behind the barrier islands of Barnegat Bay, starting in the 1830s and reaching a peak of development around 1879, the year Nathaniel Bishop's *Four Months in a Sneakbox* was published.

Sneakbox donated by Timothy Eastland. (Photo: Kenneth E. Mahler, Mystic Seaport 1981-2-91*)*

The popularity of this book caused sneakboxes to be widely built and shipped beyond New Jersey in both finished and kit form.

STATUS: Poor.

DONOR: Timothy Eastland

FURTHER READING FOR 1961.915 AND 1980.124:

Dodd, Richard. *A Heritage in Wood*. St. Michaels, Maryland: Chesapeake Bay Maritime Museum, 1992.

Drinker, Pemberton H. "Sneakbox." *WoodenBoat* 20, Jan/Feb, 1978. History, performance commentary, photos, plans.

Esterly, Diana. *Early One-Design Sailboats*. New York: Charles Scribner's Sons, 1979. Comments, photos, plans.

Gardner, John. *Building Classic Small Craft, Vol. I*. Camden, Maine:

International Marine Publishing Co., 1977. Building comments, plans.

Luck, Charles E. Jr., "The Largest One-Design Class." *The Rudder*, May, 1926. History, photos.

Spectre, Peter H. "The Boats of Autumn." *WoodenBoat* 68, Jan/Feb, 1986. Comments, list of builders.

Stark, Eric L. "The Barnegat Bay Sneakbox." *WoodenBoat* 47, July/Aug, 1982. Design and construction, history, photos.

ACCESSION NO. 1980.124

Brownie
SEAFORD SKIFF
12' 7" x 4' 2"   ca. 1883

Brownie and her once-numerous sisters were used by guides and New York sportsmen in the waters of Great South Bay, New York, and environs for hunting and fishing. In spite of a small sail area these boats are fast due to their exquisitely modeled hulls. Charles Verity is believed to have built this boat.

STATUS: Unrestored, original, good condition.

DONOR: G. Gorton Baldwin

ACCESSION NO. 1962.674
Plans for 1962.674 are available from Mystic Seaport's Watercraft Plans Collection.

Brownie as she appeared in 1975. (Photo: Maynard Bray, Mystic Seaport 1975-5-46*)*

Ro Ro
SEAFORD SKIFF
13' 6" x 4' 4"

In spite of being heavily built, this hunting skiff is a very handsome model. Although the Seaford skiff took its name from and is supposed to have originated near Seaford, Long Island, most surviving boats bear a close resemblance to the melon-seed type of boat from New Jersey waters. This boat with its skeg construction seems particularly like the melon seed. Her building date is not known, but her framing method with the frame faces being square to the boat's centerline would indicate that she is a very old boat.

Seaford skiff Ro Ro *in 1978. (Photo: Maynard Bray, Mystic Seaport 1978-2-45)*

STATUS: Hull has been stripped of paint and is dried out and weak, poor condition.

DONOR: Morgan Bowman MacDonald III

ACCESSION NO. 1976.149
Plans for 1976.149 are available from Mystic Seaport's Watercraft Plans Collection.

SEAFORD SKIFF
14' 7" x 4' 3"   ca. 1948

This is one of about 70 Seaford skiffs built by Paul A. Ketcham, Amityville, Long Island. These were modified versions of boats built in the late-nineteenth century by Samuel Gritman. Ketcham's modifications for recreational sailing included slightly more freeboard, and moving mast and centerboard aft. These boats provided Great South Bay sailors with an inexpensive and lively racing craft, and one of local historic origin.

STATUS: Excellent condition.

DONOR: John O. Zimmerman

FURTHER READING FOR 1962.674, 1972.264 AND 1976.149:

Martin, Humbert O. "The Seaford Skiff." *The Amityville Record* (NY), Oct 11, 1962.

Thomas, Barry. "The Melon Seed and the Seaford Skiff." *The Log of Mystic Seaport*, Summer 1974.

Weeks, George L., Jr. "The Seaford Skiff." *Yachting*, Feb, 1952. Good history by one who was there during some of it.

ACCESSION NO. 1972.264

Plans for 1972.264 are available from Mystic Seaport's Watercraft Plans Collection.

The Seaford skiff 1972.264 underway on the Mystic River. (Photo: Maynard Bray, Mystic Seaport 1975-10-208)

Vixen
COTUIT SKIFF
14' 6" x 5' 5"   1948

These are the class boats of the Cotuit Mosquito Yacht Club of Massachusetts that have been raced there each summer by young people since before 1910. Although *Vixen* was built by Cecil Bigelow (the famous schooner *Niña* was built by his father) to plans drawn up by J. Murray Watts, the original fleet was built without any drawings at all. Stanley Butler produced most of them and later on Watts measured one of his boats, *Scamp*, from which his drawings were made.

STATUS: Unrestored, complete, good condition.

DONOR: Dr. Benjamin V. White

FURTHER READING:
Cotuit Mosquito Yacht Club. *Summary of Yachting Activities*. Cotuit, Massachusetts: Privately printed by C. M. Y. C.

Esterly, Diana. *Early One-Design Sailboats*. New York: Charles Scribner's Sons, 1979. Comments, photos, plans.

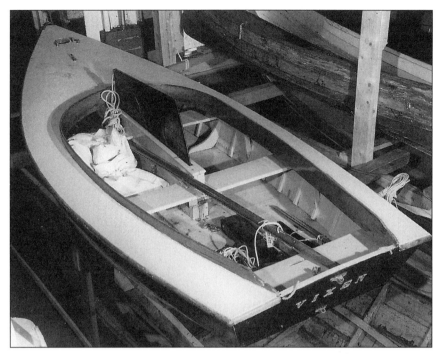

Cotuit skiff Vixen *in 1975. (Photo: Maynard Bray, Mystic Seaport 1975-10-80)*

Paine, Art. "The Artist's Eye." *WoodenBoat* 99, Mar/Apr, 1991.

ACCESSION NO. 1973.407

Cotuit skiffs racing. (Photo: Courtesy of Benjamin V. White, Mystic Seaport 1978-2-98)

W.B.
SHARPIE SKIFF
15′ 9″ x 5′ 1″   ca.1888

W.B. looks like the working sharpie skiffs once used by the oystermen of Fair Haven, Connecticut, but the donor, who owned her since new, always used her for pleasure. He states that *W.B.* was scaled down from the large (35-foot) sharpies. *W.B.* is fitted with three mast steps for either a one- or two-masted rig.

STATUS: Approximately 75% of the bottom was replaced and other repairs were made in 1967, fair condition.

DONOR: Winchester Bennett

ACCESSION NO. 1951.4206
Plans for 1951.4206 are available from Mystic Seaport's Watercraft Plans Collection.

W. B. rigged as a small oyster sharpie skiff. (Photo: Ken Mahler, Mystic Seaport 1974-10-164)

Under original ownership, W. B. was sailed either as a cat or a cat-ketch, the latter with two masts. (Photo: Courtesy of Mrs. W. E. Hoblitzelle, above, Mystic Seaport 1975-4-142; right, Mystic Seaport 1975-4-143)

W. B.
SHARPIE SKIFF
REPRODUCTION

15' 9" x 5' 1"   1979

Sailing *W. B.* proved to be such a good experience that Museum boatbuilder Willits Ansel built a reproduction so that the original could be preserved ashore. The *W. B.* reproduction is actively used on the waterfront; a favorite game is getting her underway and sailing all over the river and back to her mooring leaving the tiller lashed the entire time. Like the original, the reproduction can be rigged as a cat as well as a cat ketch.

STATUS: In use, excellent condition.

SOURCE: Mystic Seaport-built reproduction

FURTHER READING for 1951.4206 and 1979.113:

Chapelle, Howard I. *American Sailing Craft*. Camden, Maine: International Marine Publishing Co., 1975.

——. *American Small Sailing Craft*. New York: W. W. Norton & Co., 1951.

——. *The Migrations of An American Boat Type*. Washington, D.C.: Smithsonian Institution Bulletin 228, 1961.

Gardner, John. *Building Classic Small Craft, Vol. 1*. Camden, Maine: International Marine Publishing Co., 1977. 18' sailing sharpie, building comments, plans.

State of Connecticut Shell Fish Commission. *Report*, 1901. Page 47 shows photographs of commercial sharpie skiffs under sail.

ACCESSION NO. 1979.113

The W. B. sharpie skiff reproduction with Maine sloop boat Estella A. *in the left background. (Photo: Mary Anne Stets,* Mystic Seaport 1992-6-172*)*

SHARPIE SKIFF

15' 8" x 5' 3"

It takes a second glance to see the elegance and integrity of this boat through the rough finish and structural repairs. According to the donor, this boat is considered to be the last of the sailing sharpies of Norwalk, Connecticut, and may date from as early as 1808. If so, it is one of the oldest surviving American small craft.

The shape is pure New Haven square-sterned sharpie, but each chine is made up of pieces that fit between the frame feet rather than being a single length mortised to receive them. The chine pieces serve as a way to join the bottom cross planking to the sides rather than to provide any longitudinal strength. The sides are made up of three cypress boards apiece and are held in alignment by the frames put in on the flat.

Three-quarter-length side decks give the boat needed transverse stiffness, as the midships thwart has been left out to provide working room as well as a place to stand while working. An extra rubstrake in way of the side decks protects the planking from wear.

The spars that came with the boat indicate a high-aspect sprit rig with about 140 square feet of sail area, which would move this boat along quite well.

STATUS: Rough condition, repaired, paint removed.
DONOR: Captain John C. Stone
ACCESSION NO. 1987.96

The early sharpie skiff in storage in 1987. (Photo: Maynard Bray, 1987.96A)

Sea Through
WESTPORT SHARPIE

14' 0" x 4' 9"   ca. 1906

Around Westport, Massachusetts, when local flat-bottomed skiffs grew bigger than 10' and sported center-boards and sailing rigs they were called sharpies. This was the old name of these flat-bottomed skiffs as they developed around New Haven, Connecticut, where sharpies were built in sizes from 12' to 35', largely for the oyster fishery.

Westport sharpies and skiffs like this one had relatively straight sides and slightly raking stems, topsides made from one or two planks, generally no chine logs, and frames only to support seats. This one has two-plank, ship-lapped sides that look to be flush, and a chine log that was added as a repair in 1962.

This boat's builder is unknown, but she is similar to the Tripp and Briggs Westport sharpies delineated by Bob Baker. She has a gaff rig and a "modern" 1962 sail from a Beetle Cat.

STATUS: Fair, unrestored, with original repairs, complete rig.

DONOR: Weldon P. de Meurers

FURTHER READING:
Buckley, Jennifer, and A. W. Baker. "Simplicity, Skiffs and Sharpies." *WoodenBoat* 66, Sept/Oct, 1985.

Hall, Henry. *Report on the Shipbuilding Industry of the United States.* Washington, D.C.: U.S. Government Printing Office, 1884.

"The Westport Skiff." *WoodenBoat* 32, Jan/Feb, 1980.

ACCESSION NO. 1982.131

Westport sharpie Sea Through. *(Photo: Judy Beisler,* Mystic Seaport *1982-131B)*

Westport sharpie Sea Through *under sail. (Photo: Courtesy of John Gidley,*

WESTPORT SAILING SKIFF ATTRIBUTED TO "KIT" BRIGGS

11' 0" x 3' 11"

Anne Baker found this lovely Westport skiff when she was consulting on a house restoration project in Westport, Massachusetts. She instantly recognized it's construction characteristics as probably having been built by Christopher "Kit" Briggs of Westport, Massachusetts, and brought the boat to the attention of the Museum.

The two rowing seats are supported by dissimilar risers. The aft seat sets into horizontal slots cut into a shaped vertical board, while the forward seat sets into slots cut down into cleats fastened to the side planks.

The single, roughly square spritsail attaches to the mast with leather "hoops." There is no centerboard, leeboards, or rudder.

STATUS: Good but worn condition.
DONOR: Robert and Donna Brayton
ACCESSION NO. 2000.121

The Westport sailing skiff at Mystic Seaport. (Photo: Judy Beisler, Mystic Seaport 2000.121A)

A GOOD
LITTLE
SKIFF

CONCORDIA CO
So Wharf
So Dartmouth

In his 1970 pamphlet, A Good Little Skiff, R.D. "Pete" Culler sketched the design and the pleasures of a simple, versatile water-craft. (G.W. Blunt White Library, Mystic Seaport)

Pete Culler, Waldo Howland, George Kelley

GOOD LITTLE SKIFFS

13' 6" x 4' 0"

When John Gardner planned the initial Small Craft Workshop weekend to be held at Mystic Seaport in June of 1970, he accompanied the invitations with the request that participants submit a small boat design that met a lengthy list of requirements. Captain R.D. "Pete" Culler responded by compiling some sketches of what he called a "Good Little Skiff" into a booklet, to which Waldo Howland contributed cogent text, and a few copies were handed out that weekend. The concept was an immediate success.

John Gardner said it best: "This rugged little 13-1/2' flat bottomed, cross-planked skiff with her more than 4 feet of beam is distinctive in several respects: for her able, seakindly performance, her jaunty good looks, and not the least, for her simple inexpensive construction that makes her especially attractive to the amateur builder. Here is a flat-bottomed boat with character in the real sense of that much-abused word. Her flaring clinker sides, raking stern, well-rockered bottom, and ample sheer unite to

produce a striking craft, one that rows and sails equally well. The boat can navigate both in deep and shoal water and can run aground and sit upright on the beach without damage"

The design has inspired many to build it in various lengths. At Mystic Seaport, Barry Thomas and his John Gardner Boatshop crew built three 13-1/2' Good Little Skiffs for use by Museum

A Good Little Skiff at Mystic Seaport's 1972 Small Craft Workshop. (Photo: Lester Olin, Mystic Seaport 1972-6-143)

visitors at the Museum's Boathouse boat livery. The boats are named, with great respect, for "Pete" Culler, Waldo Howland, and George Kelley.

STATUS: Excellent condition, original and unrestored, seasonally in the water.

DONOR: Mystic Seaport-built

FURTHER READING:

Culler, Robert D., and Howland, Waldo. *A Good Little Skiff*. Privately printed, 1970. This little pamphlet, produced in limited numbers, can be seen at Mystic Seaport's G.W. Blunt White Library.

Culler, Robert D. *Skiffs and Schooners*. Camden, Maine: International Marine Publishing Co., 1974.

——. *Boats, Oars, and Rowing*. Camden, Maine: International Marine Publishing Co., 1978.

——. "What Makes Classics Real." *The Mariners Catalog*, 3, 1975.

A Good Little Skiff in an idyllic setting at Mystic Seaport's 1972 Small Craft Workshop. (Photo: Lester Olin, Mystic Seaport 1972-6-131)

Dixie Belle

SAILING SKIFF BY CULLER

18' 6" x 4' 8"   1971

When Waldo Howland needed a boat for use on the thin water near his winter home at Captiva Island, "Pete" Culler built him a Good Little Skiff lengthened out to 18' 6", but he kept the beam to a narrow 4' 8". The added length made the boat more stable and able to handle better under both sail and oar. Pete equipped the boat with a special rudder, with a blade that can be drawn part way

up into its cheeks, similar to a centerboard within its case. He didn't advise the use of this rudder unless needed for shallow water.

Waldo Howland used *Dixie Belle* for many years in the shallow bays and rivers around his winter home at Captiva Island, Florida, before giving the boat to the Museum in 1993. Waldo maintained the boat with house paint and linseed oil and sailed with sprit-rigged tanbarked sails. The boat is a wealth of small refinements that reflect Howland's many years of experience sailing with a traditional rig.

STATUS: Good condition.

DONOR: Waldo Howland

FURTHER READING:

Burke, John. *Pete Culler's Boats*. Camden, Maine: International Marine Publishing Co., 1984.

Culler, R.D. *Skiffs and Schooners*. Camden, Maine: International Marine Publishing Co., 1974.

Stambaugh, Karl. *Good Skiffs*. Marblehead, Massachusetts: Devereux Books, 1988.

ACCESSION NO. 1993.69.1

Pete Culler's enlarged Good Little Skiff variation, built as Dixie Belle *for Waldo Howland. (Photo: Judy Beisler, Mystic Seaport 1993.69.1D)*

Pete Culler's long, slim sailing skiff Owl. *(Photo: Mary Anne Stets, Mystic Seaport 1982-2-71)*

Owl

SAILING SKIFF BY CULLER

18' 8" x 4' 1"   1976

"Pete" Culler was well known for his skiff designs, all of which have more than the usual amount of flare to their topsides, and transoms that rake enough to discourage the use of outboard motors. Pete originally developed this larger-than-usual skiff design for Waldo Howland, then head of the Concordia Company. *Dixie Belle* (1993.69.1, left) was the first, followed by *Owl*. Both boats have three rowing positions; a centerboard, rudder, and sternsheets for sitting make them convenient to sail. With simple boats like this, Pete demonstrated that skiffs can be both handsome and versatile, especially when a sailing rig is part of the design.

STATUS: Original, good condition.
DONOR: Roger Wing
FURTHER READING:
(Same as for 1993.69.1)
ACCESSION NO. 1981.81
Plans for 1981.81 are available from Mystic Seaport's Watercraft Plans Collection.

Pete Culler's clipper bateau Otter. *(Photo: Deborah Bates, Mystic Seaport 1984.147.2D)*

Otter

CLIPPER BATEAU BY CULLER

17' 6" x 3' 1"   1971

According to John Burke in his wonderful book, *Pete Culler's Boats*, the design of *Otter* followed that of a larger bateau that Pete designed for a client but never got the chance to build. Pete built *Otter* for himself and spent many a calm morning using her in the sheltered waters near his Hyannis, Massachusetts, home. Although tiddlish in the extreme because she's so narrow, *Otter* is as slippery under oars as her namesake. Pete contrived a tiny spritsail rig for her,

Otter display's Culler's fine detailing. In the foreground are the leeboard and the block that secured it to the gunwale. (Photo: Maynard Bray, Mystic Seaport 1984.147.2A)

complete with a single leeboard that shifted from side to side so as always to be to leeward. When they first showed up at Mystic Seaport's annual Small Craft Workshop, Pete and *Otter* caused a sensation: big man in a boat that seemed way too small.

STATUS: Original, excellent condition.
DONOR: Dr. Nicholas Freydberg
FURTHER READING:
Burke, John. *Pete Culler's Boats*. Camden, Maine: International Marine Publishing Co., 1984.

Culler, R.D. *Skiffs and Schooners*. Camden, Maine: International Marine Publishing Co., 1974.

ACCESSION NO. 1984.147.2
Plans for 1984.147.2 are available from Mystic Seaport's Watercraft Plans Collection.

Pete Culler sails Otter *at Mystic Seaport's 1974 Small Craft Workshop. (Photo: Mary Anne Stets, Mystic Seaport 1974-6-84F7)*

CAT-RIGGED SAILING BOAT
13' 3" x 4' 2"

This boat was dropped off at Mystic Seaport for "research," and was so nicely built and shaped that she was added to the collection. She is a carvel-planked, full-sectioned ship's boat type, with a small deck and coaming added after she was built. She has riveted construction, with floor timbers between each bent frame and natural crook knees to hold things together. Her vague history is that she was left in Maine by an English vessel, although she does not appear to be of English construction.

STATUS: Unrestored condition with serious structural problems, no spars or sails.

DONOR: Unknown

ACCESSION NO. 1979.210

Cat-rigged sailing boat in 1980. (Photo: Mary Anne Stets, Mystic Seaport 1980-2-48)

Cat-rigged Whitehall type in 1975. (Photo: Maynard Bray, Mystic Seaport 1975-4-145)

WHITEHALL-TYPE SAILBOAT
11' 0" x 4' 1"

Unfortunately, nothing is known about the origin or the original appearance of this beautifully shaped craft, but it is interesting to speculate, and her sail plan has been developed on just that basis.

STATUS: Relic, hull only.

DONOR: Russell Clark

FURTHER READING:
Gardner, John. "Comments Here & There." *National Fisherman*, Feb 1973. Describes acquisition by Mystic Seaport.

ACCESSION NO. 1973.22
Plans for 1973.22 are available from Mystic Seaport's Watercraft Plans Collection.

Nixie *in 1975, among other boats in storage at Mystic Seaport.*
(Photo: Maynard Bray, Mystic Seaport 1975-10-110)

Captain Charlton Smith sailing
Nixie. *(Photo: Courtesy of Gerald Smith,*
Mystic Seaport 1980.132.2)

Nixie
KEEL CAT BY BURGESS
23′ 4″ x 7′ 7″   1885

Launched in 1885 with a cat rig, *Nixie* is one of the last survivors of Edward Burgess's work. This famous designer developed three successful defenders of the America's Cup, *Puritan*, *Mayflower*, and *Volunteer*, and a great many other yachts during his short but brilliant career. Built by William B. Smith in South Boston, *Nixie* later was rigged as a cutter and was rebuilt for cruising in 1939 by Captain Charlton Smith.

STATUS: Hull only—cabin, deck, cockpit, and rig are missing, fair condition.

DONOR: Given in memory of Edward Burgess by his grandson, Dr. Frederic Tudor

FURTHER READING:
Atkin, William and John. *The Book of Boats*. Camden, Maine: International Marine Publishing Co., 1976.

Gardner, John. "*Nixie*." *The Log of Mystic Seaport*, Spring, 1981.

Smith, Charlton. "The Re-birth of *Nixie*." *New England Yachtsman*, 1939.

Storrow, Charles. "Rediscovering the *Nixie*." *The Log of Mystic Seaport*, Winter, 1996.

Yachting, March 1951. Contains a biography of Edward Burgess.

ACCESSION NO. 1973.714

Nixie *as she looked after her original cat rig was altered, from H. A. Mott's* Yachts and Yachtsmen of America, *published in 1894.* (Mystic Seaport 1963-11-14)

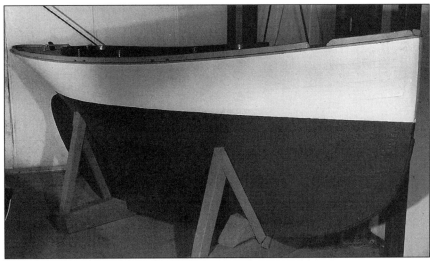

Snarleyow in 1975 at Mystic Seaport. (Photo: Maynard Bray, Mystic Seaport 1975-10-87)

Snarleyow
KEEL CAT BY HARVEY
14′ 11″ x 3′ 8″   1882

This toy-like cutter was designed by John Harvey, one of the leading English designers of the fashionable and larger "plank-on-edge" cutter yachts, and was owned for a number of years by the author, boatbuilder, and yachting historian W. P. Stephens. *Snarleyow* was built in New York by John C. Smith in 1882. It is believed that she first appeared looking much like the catboat *Dodge* illustrated in C. P. Kunhardt's book, *Small Yachts*; and that sometime later Stephens changed her rig to that of a cutter. In hull form, *Snarleyow* represents the typical English cutter-yacht of the 1870s and 1880s, only very much reduced in size.

STATUS: Unrestored, rig missing, fair condition.

DONOR: Eleanor Stephens

FURTHER READING:
Kunhardt, C. P. *Small Yachts.* New York: Forest and Stream Publishing Co., 1887, and Brooklin, Maine: WoodenBoat Publications, 1985.

Stephens, W. P. *Traditions and Memories of American Yachting.* New York: Hearst Magazines, 1945, and Brooklin, Maine: WoodenBoat Publications, 1989. Contains good description of sloop and cutter controversy.

ACCESSION NO. 1952.498
Plans for 1952.498 are available from Mystic Seaport's Watercraft Plans Collection.

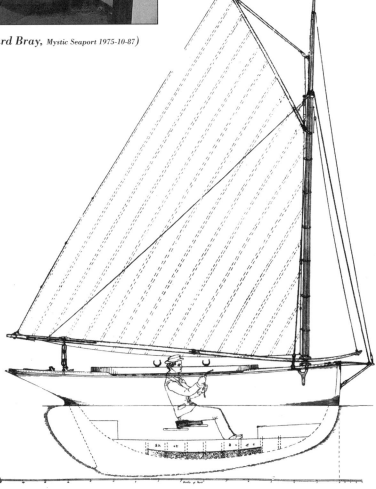

Shown above is the sail plan of the catboat Dodge *(a boat almost identical to* Snarleyow*) from C. P. Kunhardt's book* Small Yachts, *published in 1887. Kunhardt had this to say: "The horns of the boom extend some distance forward of the mast. If a tripping line is taken from the fore end of these horns, passed through a block slung at the hounds of the rigging and from thence through a leading block or bullseye at the deck on one side of the boom, the tripping line acts as a purchase to keep the boom down at the outer end when the main sheet is slacked for the purpose of running before the wind. For steering, tiller ropes lead from a yoke forward to a footboard, canoe fashion, leaving the crew with both hands free. An oscillating seat low down accommodates the skipper and this can be slid fore and aft to trim with a passenger on board."*

Chapter Two
SLOOP-RIGGED

Annie *in the water at Mystic Seaport. (Photo: Claire White-Peterson,* Mystic Seaport 1975-8-141*)*

Annie
CLASS A RACING
SANDBAGGER

28' 9" x 12' 4"   1880

One of *Annie*'s distinctions is that she was the first boat in Mystic Seaport's collection, acquired in 1931. D. O. Richmond modeled her and she was built in his Mystic River shop for Henry Tift of Mystic, Connecticut, and Tifton, Georgia. Racing sandbaggers was a popular sport before 1885, when the overall length alone determined their racing handicaps and one could crowd on as much sail as a boat seemed able to carry. With so great a spread of canvas, just to keep from capsizing was

a challenge, let alone winning the race. The idea was for the large crew to position themselves along with several 50-pound sandbags far enough to windward to balance the press of wind on the sails. Squally weather or frequent tacking called for quick and expert movement; it was exciting sport. Sandbaggers were raced in several classes according to their size; *Annie* raced in Class A with the other large boats, while on the other end of the scale were the smaller boats of about 20 feet. Much of the racing and building took place near New York City where the sport originated, but *Annie*'s

successful career was in eastern Long Island Sound near where she was built, and in Florida waters where she was shipped during the winter. Like the many other aging and outclassed sandbaggers, *Annie* became a working craft and was in this state when acquired by the Museum.

Today she has the spectacular appearance of a sandbagger but can hardly be considered original. A number of changes were made during her early years to make her faster, and in 1902 she was totally rebuilt after a fire. At least twice since then, in 1950 and again in 1968, she was given an

Annie is shown here under full sail and with full crew of men and sandbags. (Photo: From the collection of Mystic Seaport, Mystic Seaport 1949.843*)*

almost completely new hull, and her rig was, of course, restored to that of a typical sandbagger. A restoration begun in 2001 used newly discovered information to restore *Annie* more accurately, illustrating in full scale an important era in yachting history— when the base of the sail plan was more than twice the length of the hull itself!

STATUS: Restored 1950, 1968, and 2001 after earlier modifications and rebuildings, little original, floating exhibit, good condition.

DONOR: Dr. C. K. Stillman

FURTHER READING:

Chapelle, Howard I. *History of American Sailing Ships.* New York: W. W. Norton & Co., Inc., 1935.

Davis, Charles G. "Captain Tom Webber." *Yachting,* June, 1947.

Fuller, Benjamin A.G. "Blue-Collar Boat Sailing." *The Log of Mystic Seaport,* Autumn, 1996.

——. "Sandbaggers." *WoodenBoat* 118, May/June, 1994.

Kemp, Dixon. *A Manual of Yacht and Boat Sailing,* London: Horace Cox, 1886.

Kunhardt, C. P. *Small Yachts, Their Design and Construction.* New York: Forest and Stream Publishing Co., 1891 and WoodenBoat Publications, 1985.

Lee, Lance. "Sailing Puffin." *The Apprentice,* Autumn, 1990.

Lizee, Maurice, and John Burton. Interview by Nancy d'Estang, Dec. 1991, Mystic Seaport Shipyard Oral History Archives, G.W. Blunt White Library.

Lynch, Edmund E. "Wood, and Weather." *The Log of Mystic Seaport,* Winter, 1969.

Napier, Rob "Sandbaggers in General, *Cruiser* in Particular." *Nautical Research Journal,* March, 1989.

Peterson, Wm. N. *Mystic Built: Ships and Shipyards of the Mystic River, Connecticut, 1784-1919.* Mystic, Connecticut: Mystic Seaport Publications, 1989.

Shannon, Liam. "Sandbaggers." *Nautical Quarterly,* Spring, 1979.

Simmons, William E. "The Sandbagger." *The Rudder,* March, 1906.

Smith, A. Cary. "Small Yacht Racing in 1861." *The Rudder,* October, 1906.

Stephens, W. P. *Traditions and Memories of American Yachting.* New York: Hearst Magazines, 1945 and Brooklin, Maine: WoodenBoat Publications, 1989.

Teuscher, Philip Thornycroft. "A Sandbagger for all Seasons." *Sea History,* Summer, 1985.

"The New Haven Boat Race." *The Log of Mystic Seaport,* September, 1968. Article re-printed from the Mystic Press of October 6, 1881.

"The *Rival.*" *The Rudder,* April, 1892, Sep. and Oct, 1893.

A half model, reputedly duplicating *Annie*'s original builder's model, two rigged models, and several half models of sandbaggers are in Mystic Seaport's collection. The Museum also has W. P. Stephens's collection of manuscripts and drawings, many of which relate to sandbaggers, and Charles G. Davis's manuscripts, which include the lines he took off *Annie* in 1931. South Street Seaport, the Long Island Maritime Museum, the Museum of the State of New York in Albany, and the Musée du Bateau in Douarnenez, France, each has a sandbagger in its collection.

ACCESSION NO. 1931.4

Galena under sail in Long Island Sound. (Photo: Courtesy of Dr. Frederic Tudor, Mystic Seaport 1972-5-111)

Galena (ex-Fox, ex-Cockle)
CUTTER TYPE
18' 9" x 6' 5"   1913

James E. Graves of Marblehead, Massachusetts, built this boat to the design of James Purdon. *Cockle*, as she was first named, was to be used as a pleasure boat by a couple of boys. Later she belonged to W. Starling Burgess whose young son, Frederic, sailed her extensively around Provincetown, where the family lived at the time. Purdon based his design on the English "plank-on-edge" cutters of the 1880s.

STATUS: Restored 1969-72, approximately 60% original, good condition.

DONOR: James Geier

FURTHER READING:
Darvin, Tom. *The Rudder Treasury*. New York: The Rudder Publishing Co., 1953. A reprint of *The Rudder*, March, 1915.

Tudor, Dr. Frederic. Letter published in *The Log of Mystic Seaport*, Spring, 1972.

ACCESSION NO. 1957.537
Plans for 1957.537 are available from Mystic Seaport's Watercraft Plans Collection.

Galena, then called Fox, *at Mystic Seaport in 1958.*
(Photo: Louis Martel, Mystiuc Seaport 1958-6-69)

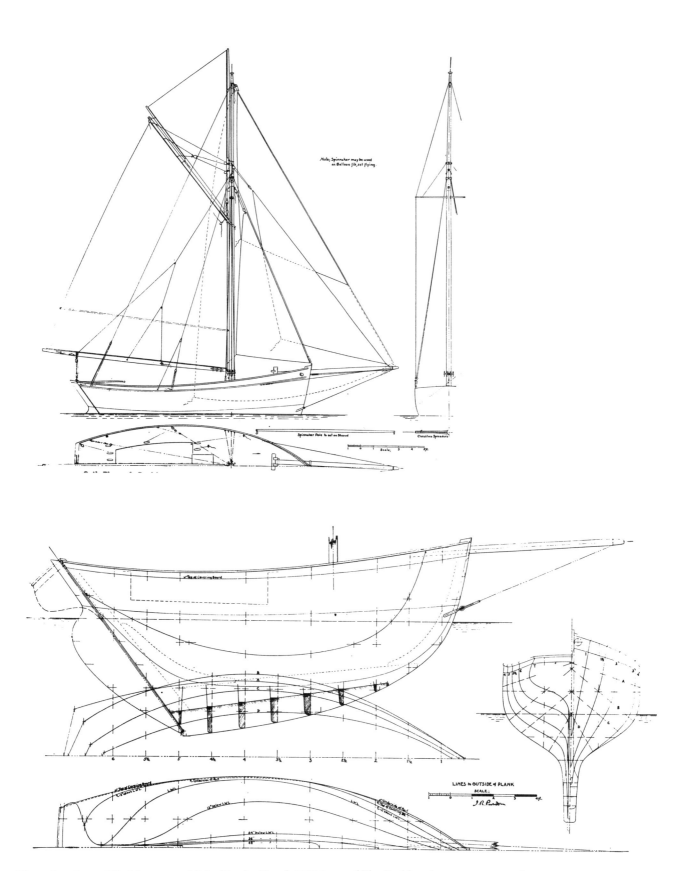

These drawings of Cockle *were published in the March 1915 issue of* The Rudder. *(Mystic Seaport 1978-1-110)*

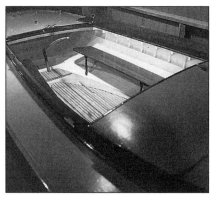

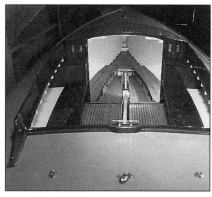

Views of Alerion's cockpit and deck layout taken in 1973. (Photos: Lester D. Olin, Mystic Seaport 1973-2-128)

Alerion *as drawn for publication by S. H. Lincoln, 1978.*

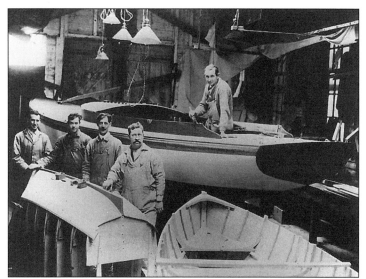

Alerion *in the small-boat shop of the Herreshoff Mfg. Co. before launching. The partly planked dinghy was designed to fit upside down over Alerion's centerboard trunk for shipment to Bermuda. Charlie Sylvester, second from the left, has identified the other workmen, left to right, as Ernest Adler, Sylvester, Henry Vincent, James Clarkson, and Willard Kenney. (Photo: Courtesy of Clarence Herreshoff, Mystic Seaport 1969-5-14A)*

Alerion *being weighed on a steelyard before being put overboard at Bristol, Rhode Island. (Photo: L. Francis Herreshoff Collection, Mystic Seaport, Mystic Seaport 1976-3-28)*

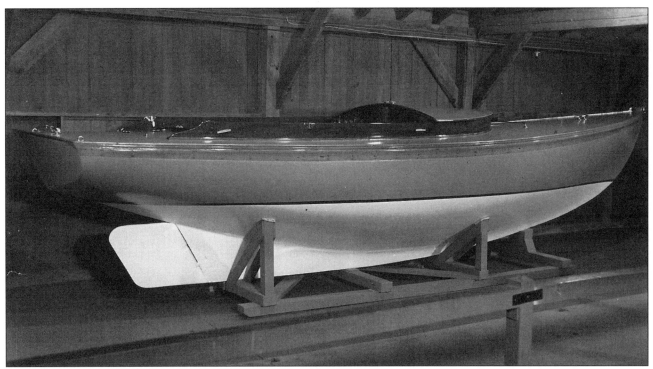

Alerion as she looked in 1973 at Mystic Seaport. (Photo: Lester D. Olin, Mystic Seaport 1973-2-128)

Alerion III
HERRESHOFF
CABIN DAYSAILER
HULL #718

26' 0" x 7' 7"   1913

The beautiful *Alerion*! She is the favorite of many, and a number of people return to the Museum just to see her again. Indeed, she is one of Herreshoff's most exquisite creations. "Mr. Nat" or "Capt. Nat" as N. G. Herreshoff was called, was 64 years old when he designed this boat (the third of that name) for himself. His career was perhaps at its zenith, and *Alerion*'s beauty and simplicity reflect his genius every bit as much as one of his America's Cup defenders did. After being built by the Herreshoff Mfg. Co. in Bristol, Rhode Island, she was shipped to Bermuda where "Capt. Nat" spent part of each winter. Just what inspired her shape is not known for certain, but she was a rather distinct departure from his previous designs, most of which had the longer overhangs and full keels typical of the Universal Rule racers. *Alerion* became an inspiration for her designer, and within

the next year or two he came out with the 12½-footers, Newport 29-footers, Fish class, and Buzzards Bay 25s–all with somewhat similar hull shapes. One other boat, *Sadie*, was built in 1914 using *Alerion*'s offsets but with some minor changes. She is now in the collection of The Herreshoff Marine Museum, in Bristol, Rhode Island.

Captain Nat discarded *Alerion*'s original gaff rig after a few years and put a sliding gunter mainsail on her, which had a sprit equal in length to the boom and which, when raised, became almost an extension of the mast itself. It is with this rig that she is exhibited.

STATUS: Refastened and refinished in 1972, otherwise mostly original, excellent condition.

DONOR: Isaac B. Merriman, Jr.

FURTHER READING:
Barker, Warren. "*Curlew.*" *WoodenBoat*, 138, Sept/Oct, 1997.

Bray, Maynard, and Carlton Pinheiro. *Herreshoff of Bristol.* Brooklin, Maine: WoodenBoat Publications, Inc., 1989.

Bray, Maynard. "Reversing Curves." *WoodenBoat*, 138, Sept/Oct, 1997.

Davis, Arthur W. *Jeff Davis's Log.* Providence: Providence Journal Publishing Co., 1937. Chapter 14 contains a sketch and anecdote about "Capt. Nat." and *Alerion.*

Herreshoff, L. Francis. *The Writings of L. Francis Herreshoff.* New York: The Rudder Publishing Co., 1943. Contains an account of an exciting sail from New York to Bristol in *Alerion.* (Republished in *The L. Francis Herreshoff Reader.* Camden, Maine: International Marine Publishing Co., 1978.)

Pesare, Michael J. "*Sadie* and *Alerion III.*" *Herreshoff Marine Museum Chronicle*, 1992.

Skerry, Amory S. "*Alerion.*" *The Log of Mystic Seaport*, September, 1969. A good write-up by one of her former owners.

Taylor, Roger C. *Still More Good Boats.* Camden, Maine: International Marine Publishing Co., 1981.

See also applicable portions of list for 1963.595, *Nettle.*

ACCESSION NO. 1964.631

Nettle on display at Mystic Seaport in 1978.
(Photo: Mary Anne Stets, Mystic Seaport 1963.595A)

Nettle
BUZZARDS BAY
12-1/2-FOOT CLASS
HULL #762

15' 10" x 5' 10"   1914

In concept, these popular daysailers are not unlike the earlier Newport fishing boat (1949.145) in that they do not have centerboards or after decks; the tiller penetrates the wineglass transom; the mast is held by a bail at the partners, and the side decks are unusually narrow.

Whether or not her designer, N. G. Herreshoff, was influenced by these local fishing boats with which he was intimately familiar is problematical, but there can be no doubt that his own *Alerion*, modeled two years earlier, inspired the shape of this boat's forebody. The combination of a hollow waterline and full foredeck almost always creates a lovely shape. It was a common one for many nineteenth-century small craft, but one which was abandoned when racing rules started to penalize long waterline lengths.

The 12½s, as the class was usually called, were built in greater number (about 360) and over a longer time span (1914-43) than any other Herreshoff boat. After the first batch of boats, which included *Nettle*, a number of changes were made. For example, some later 12½s had Marconi rigs, mahogany trim, plywood decks, and alternate cockpit arrangements. The 12½s are also called Buzzards Bay Boys Boats, Doughdishes, and Bullseyes.

After World War II, when the Herreshoff yard was closing down, it first licensed the Quincy Adams yard to build 12½-footers. After 51 boats, that contract was canceled and Cape Cod Shipbuilding took over the building rights, patterns, molds, etc., and went on to build about 30 more wooden 12½s before switching to fiberglass in the early 1950s. Since then nearly 900 fiberglass Bullseyes have been sold by Cape Cod. That builder also produces a

Herreshoff 12½-footer under sail about 1950. (Photo: Courtesy of Norman Fortier)

more traditional version, also in fiberglass but with wood trim, called the H-12. Edey & Duff's Doughdish is similar.

Nettle herself was purchased by Charles Francis Adams as a Christmas gift for his daughter, Catherine. Nearly 50 years later, after three generations learned to sail in her, Nettle was given to Mystic Seaport by her original owner.

STATUS: Restored 1975-77, approximately 85% original, excellent condition.

DONOR: Mrs. Henry S. Morgan

FURTHER READING:

Blanchard, Fessenden S. *The Sailboat Classes of North America.* New York: Doubleday & Co., Inc., 1968.

Bray, Maynard. "Herreshoff Legacies." *Nautical Quarterly* 37, Spring, 1987.

——. "Restoration of 12½-footers." *WoodenBoat* 56 & 57, Jan/Feb, Mar/Apr, 1984. Rebuilding by Steve Ballentine.

Bray, Maynard, and Carlton Pinheiro. *Herreshoff of Bristol.* Brooklin, Maine: WoodenBoat Publications, Inc., 1989.

Esterly, Diana. *Early One-Design Sailboats.* New York: Charles Scribner's Sons, 1979. Comments, photos, plans.

Fulmer, Scott. "Restoration in Paradise." *Shavings,* Nov, 1991. The Center For Wooden Boats, Seattle.

Mendlowitz, Benjamin, and Joel White. *Wood, Water and Light.* New York: W. W. Norton & Co., 1988.

Yachts by Herreshoff. Herreshoff Manufacturing Co., Bristol, Rhode Island: Privately printed, ca. 1935. Contains advertising material on the 12½s.

ACCESSION NO. 1963.595
Study plans for 1963.595 are available from Mystic Seaport's Watercraft Plans Collection.

12½-footers under construction in the Herreshoff shops sometime in the 1930s. (Photos: Courtesy of Charles Sylvester, Mystic Seaport 1974-4-79 and 1974-4-75)

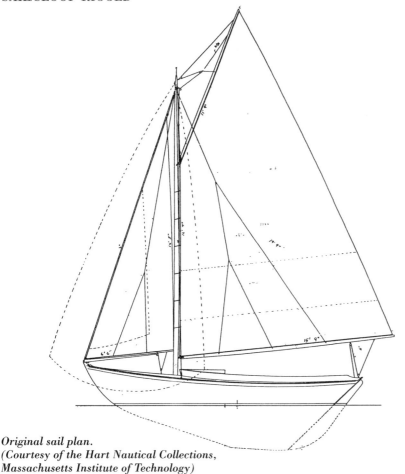

Original sail plan.
(Courtesy of the Hart Nautical Collections,
Massachusetts Institute of Technology)

Merry Hell

FISH-CLASS SLOOP BY
HERRESHOFF
HULL #1379

20' 9" x 7' 2"   1936

As with *Blazing Star* (1985.23), N. G. Herreshoff created the Fish Class from a half model he'd made earlier for another purpose–in this case for the well-known 12½-footers of which *Nettle* (1963.595) is one. The Wizard of Bristol simply remeasured the model with a change in scale to produce this 5' longer and proportionally larger boat. The original Fish-Class fleet numbered 22 boats, all delivered to their owners in the spring of 1916. They were boats that attracted attention beyond the confines of Long Island's Seawanhaka Corinthian Yacht Club, which sponsored the first fleet, and as the years passed more were built, later versions like *Merry Hell* carrying

Merry Hell *at Mystic Seaport. (Photo: Maynard Bray, Mystic Seaport 1980.116B)*

Marconi rigs rather than gaff. Some were fitted with the lovely molded sheerstrakes that became a kind of trademark of the Herreshoff yard. Ultimately the Herreshoff Mfg. Co. turned out more than 40 of these boats. At least half are still sailing—and with justification, for they are truly a great design.

A Fish-Class derivative called the Marlin Class was developed for cruising, having a longer cabin, a pair of berths, and an inboard engine. Later, after the Herreshoff yard closed,

Cape Cod Shipbuilding obtained the rights to the design and continued producing the Marlin in fiberglass, stretching the hull out with a counter stern and giving it a streamlined cabin trunk of molded fiberglass and a taller, masthead rig.

Merry Hell is one of the very last Fish-Class sloops built, and is about as pure an example as one is apt to find. She's had good care and very little use, and was for many years in covered storage in Charlevoix, Michigan, prior to her arrival at Mystic Seaport.

STATUS: Original, good condition.

DONOR: Pat Spitzmiller, in memory of Henry L. Stein

FURTHER READING:
Archives of Seawanhaka-Corinthian Yacht Club at Mystic Seaport.

Parkinson, John Jr. *The Seawanhaka-Corinthian Yacht Club: The Early Twentieth Century.* New York: 1965.

See also applicable portions of list for *Nettle* (1963.595).

ACCESSION NO. 1983.116

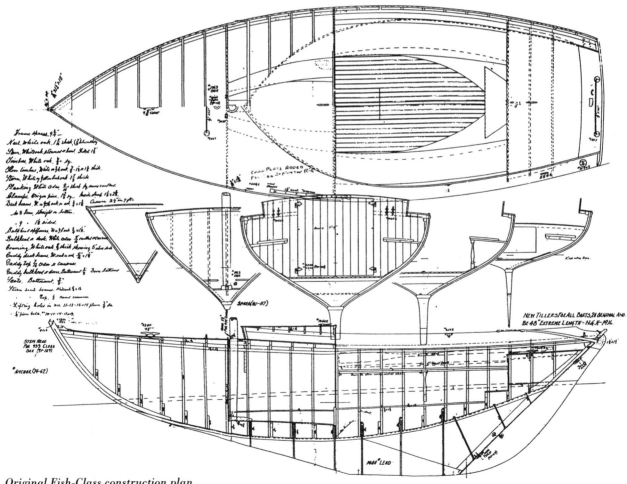

*Original Fish-Class construction plan.
(Courtesy of the Hart Nautical Collections,
Massachusetts Institute of Technology)*

Fiddler *being moved into her exhibit, 1972. (Photo: Lester D. Olin,* Mystic Seaport 1972-6-233*)*

Fiddler
HERRESHOFF BUZZARDS BAY 15' CLASS

24' 9" x 6' 9"   ca. 1902

N. G. Herreshoff designed this class in 1898, and the first boats sold for $666.66 according to the Herreshoff Manufacturing Co. records. *Fiddler* was built a few years later for Miss Caroline M. Dabney, who was also her first skipper, and apparently a good one, for in 1904 she won the championship sponsored by the Beverly Yacht Club of Marion, Massachusetts. As years passed, Miss Dabney became Mrs. Parker and in 1933 her son, Augustin, outdid his mother, and *Fiddler* won the Van Rensselaer Cup, presented to the champion "15" of all Buzzards Bay.

In all, about 90 boats were built to this model, some having ballast keels six inches lower and known as Newport 15-footers, and others with Marconi rigs and pointed coamings which came out in 1922 as the Watch Hill 15-footers.

STATUS: Restored 1971, approximately 65% original, good condition.

DONOR: Augustin H. Parker, Jr.

FURTHER READING:
Bennett, Jenny. "Project Profile: The Return of the E-Class." *WoodenBoat* 124, May/June, 1995.

——. "The Herreshoff 15." *The Boatman* 30, Nov/Dec, 1995.

Bray, Maynard. "Replacing a Keel and Centerboard Trunk." *WoodenBoat* 124, May/June, 1995.

Cheever, David. "The Herreshoff Fifteens." *The Log of Mystic Seaport*, Summer, 1972.

See also applicable portions of list for 1963.595, *Nettle*.

ACCESSION NO. 1959.1286

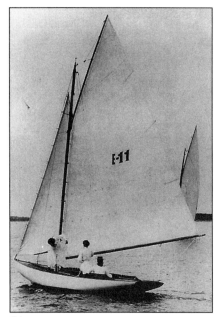

Fiddler is shown here being sailed by her original owner, Miss Caroline Dabney, and a crew of two other women. (Photo: Gift of Augustin H. Parker, Jr., Mystic Seaport 1960.348*)*

Fiddler *and others of her class racing in light weather. (Photo: Gift of Augustin H. Parker, Jr.,* Mystic Seaport 1960.349*)*

Blazing Star as she arrived at Mystic Seaport in 1985. (Photo: Nancy d'Estang, Mystic Seaport 1985-3-67)

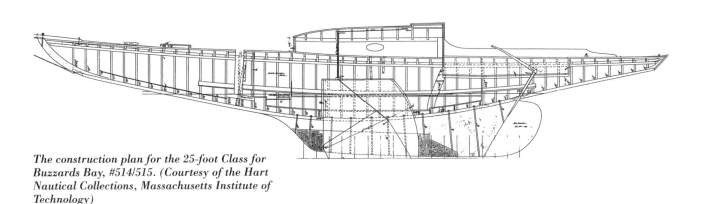

The construction plan for the 25-foot Class for Buzzards Bay, #514/515. (Courtesy of the Hart Nautical Collections, Massachusetts Institute of Technology)

Blazing Star (ex-Barracouta)

HERRESHOFF
BUZZARDS BAY 25′CLASS
HULL #515

41′ 6″ x 10′ 6″   1899

By the time C. M. Baker ordered this boat, N. G. Herreshoff had spent a decade producing custom sailboat designs. He arrived at his hull shapes by modeling rather than by drawing lines on paper, and many times he would modify one of his existing models into what may have appeared to be a new design. He did this for *Blazing Star* and her sister *May Queen* by remeasuring an existing half model to an altered scale (about $^{14}/_{12}$ of that used originally for Mr. Baker's earlier sloop *Edith*, HMCo. Hull #486). These two new boats, according to the drawings, were called Buzzards Bay 25s, although there is a later Herreshoff design also known by that class name.

The records indicate that *Blazing Star* spent most of her days in New Brunswick and Nova Scotia (as *Barracouta*). She may have been the very first yacht in Canadian registry, having shown up at St. Andrews in 1911. She remained in Canada for 70 years, and was sailing out of Chester, Nova Scotia, when Mystic Seaport acquired her in 1985.

STATUS: Original, fair condition.

DONOR: John B. McCurdy

FURTHER READING:
See applicable portions of list for 1963.595, *Nettle*.

ACCESSION NO. 1985.23

Kittiwake sailing in Gardiner's Bay at the eastern end of Long Island, her home waters for many years. (Photo: Courtesy of Norman Fortier)

Kittiwake (ex-Louise)
HERRESHOFF
CABIN DAYSAILER
HULL #678

30' 9" x 8' 2"   1907

No other boats were built to this model: she was a special boat, designed by N. G. Herreshoff for Louise Tiffany, and cost $1,875 when new. She was purchased in 1944 by W. B. Lockwood who, a few years later, outfitted her with a new Sparkman & Stephens-designed Marconi rig and put on a new deck and cabin. Then, as *Kittiwake*, raced mostly by Mr. Lockwood's daughter Mary, this boat became a consistent winner in eastern Long Island Sound. Her hull is double-planked above the waterline; an unusual feature for so small a boat, but one which has proven itself, since her topsides after all this time are still flawless.

STATUS: Rig converted to Marconi, good condition.

DONOR: W. B. Lockwood

FURTHER READING:
See applicable portions of list for 1963.595, *Nettle*.

ACCESSION NO. 1974.929

Kittiwake on her mooring in the Mystic River, 1975. (Photo: Maynard Bray, Mystic Seaport 1975-6-148)

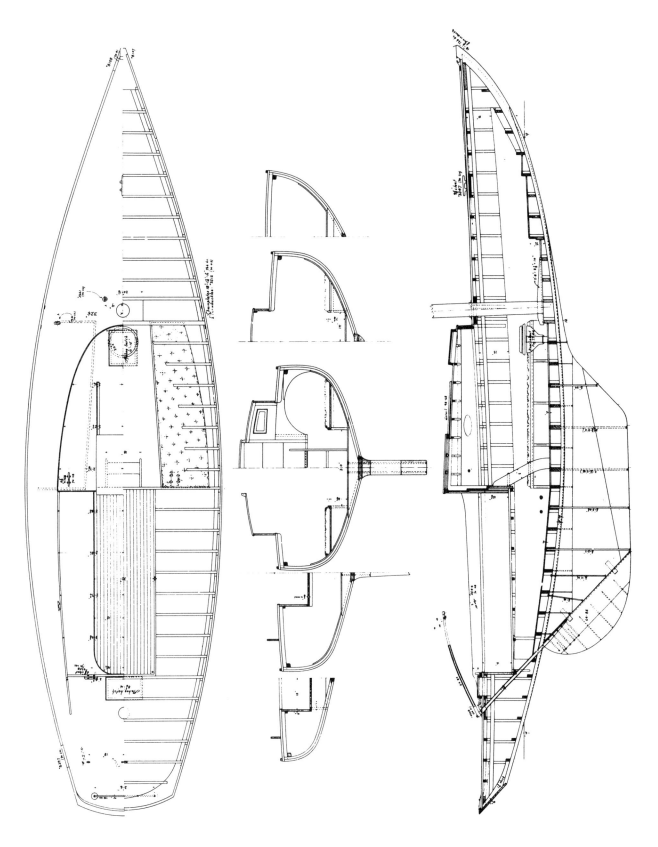

Original Herreshoff Manufacturing Co. construction plan for Hull #678. (Courtesy of the Hart Nautical Collections, Massachusetts Institute of Technology)

*Fantasy returning from the Crosby yard in Osterville, Massachusetts, where she was restored in the same shop where she was built 56 years before.
(Photo: Louis S. Martel, Mystic Seaport 1970-4-184)*

*Fantasy, in the foreground, seems to be doing well in this race with other Wiannos.
(Photo: Courtesy of Wilton Crosby, Mystic Seaport 1972-6-335)*

Fantasy
WIANNO SENIOR CLASS #11
25' 4" x 8' 5"   **1914**

Not only are the "Senior boats," as the Crosbys call them, still racing in large numbers each summer, most of the fleet consists of the old wood boats, with a few newer fiberglass sisters. H. Manley Crosby designed them, and the first batch of 13 boats, which included the Museum's *Fantasy*, came out in 1914. Since then more than 150 wooden Seniors have been launched from the Crosby Yacht Building and Storage Co. of Osterville, Massachusetts. It was here that *Fantasy* was taken for a restoration in 1970. She had been owned by the donor since new.

Perhaps the most famous Wianno Senior is *Victura*, #94 which was owned by the Kennedys of Hyannisport and was raced by JFK for many years. *Victura* is now on display at the John F. Kennedy Library in Boston.

STATUS: Restored 1970, approximately 60% original, good condition.

DONOR: James G. Hinkle

FURTHER READING:
Blanchard, Fessenden S. *The Sailboat Classes of North America.* New York: Doubleday & Co., 1968.

Esterly, Diana. *Early One-Design Sailboats.* New York: Charles Scribner's Sons, 1979.

Farrell, Jane. *The History of Cape Cod's Own...The Wianno Senior.* Privately printed, August 1969.

Gray, F. C., Jr. "The Wianno Senior, 1914-1964." *Yachting,* March, 1965.

Howes, Malcolm. "The Wianno Senior." *WoodenBoat* 91, Nov/Dec, 1989.

"The Wianno Y. C. One-Design." *The Rudder,* April, 1915.

Trimble, Nancy. "Celebrating the Senior." *Nautical Quarterly* 48, Winter, 1989.

Wianno Senior Class Association. *The Senior: 75 Years of the Wianno Senior Class,* 1989.

Association Address:
Wianno Yacht Club, Bridge St., Osterville, Massachusetts 02655 (508)428-2232

ACCESSION NO. 1965.820

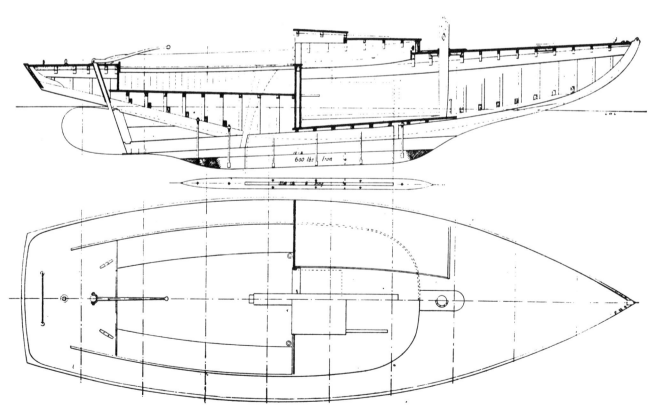

Plans of the new Wianno class as they appeared in the April 1915 issue of The Rudder *magazine.*
(*Mystic Seaport 1973-2-191, 192*)

NORTHEAST HARBOR
A CLASS #7

27' 9" x 7' 3"   1911

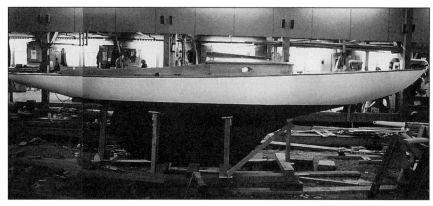

Northeast Harbor A Class #7 in 1976 being repainted at Mystic Seaport.
(Photo: Jack Deupree, Mystic Seaport 1976-3-155)

Remarkable is the fact that this boat, which has never had a name, was owned and well used by five generations of the Morris family from 1914 until she was given to Mystic Seaport in 1975. Each summer they raced her with the others of her class; but the season was short, lasting usually from July 4th until Labor Day. She was under cover the rest of the year and was cared for by professionals, which is why she's in such wonderful condition today. This boat and 23 others like her were built for the Eastern Yacht Club of Marblehead, Massachusetts, by the George F. Lawley & Son yard to the design of Edwin A. Boardman. Their racing days in Marblehead were brief, however, a result of too much competition from other classes racing there at the time. After only a few years they were sold as a class to members of the Northeast Harbor Fleet and other nearby clubs to become the Northeast Harbor A Class. As time

went on, more boats were built, this time by the Rice Bros. yard in East Boothbay, Maine. With the new boats, the class numbered 45 and racing was keen up until World War II. Since then the fleet has dwindled, although the class did sail its fiftieth anniversary race with six boats. This boat is perhaps the best remaining example of the entire class.

STATUS: Original except for a deck overlay of plywood. Excellent condition.

DONOR: William B. Morris, Thomas D. C. Morris

FURTHER READING:

Esterly, Diana. *Early One-Design Sailboats.* New York: Charles Scribner's Sons, 1979. Comments, photos, plans.

Haskins, Sturgis. "Old Designs, One Designs Live in Maine." *National Fisherman,* Jan, 1975.

Robinson, W. E. "From Knockabout to Raceabout." *The Rudder,* May, 1900.

Welles, Edward R. III. "Grand Old One-Design Class Still Races off Northeast Harbor." *Down East,* Sept, 1964.

——. "A Grand Old One-Design." *Yachting,* July, 1961.

——., ed. *Mariner Notes and Antiques, Vol. 1, No. 4.* Maine Antique Boat Society, Inc., 1977.

ACCESSION NO. 1975.452

A boat #7 in Mount Desert waters.
(Photo: Courtesy of William B. Morris, Mystic Seaport 1977-5-95)

A boat #7 strapped down in a stiff breeze.
(Photo: Courtesy of William B. Morris, Mystic Seaport 1977-5-89)

Vireo
KNOCKABOUT SLOOP BY SHIVERICK

25′ 5″ x 7′ 0″   1912

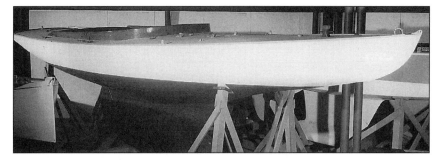

Vireo in 1975. (Photo: Maynard Bray, Mystic Seaport 1975-6-10)

Herbert Yerxa of Boston ordered *Vireo* from well-known boatbuilder George W. Shiverick of Kingston, Massachusetts, in 1912, planning to teach his 12-year-old daughter to sail. Yerxa, his wife, and their two children were avid sailors at the Corinthian Yacht Club in Marblehead, Massachusetts. Their new boat came out the same year as the Corinthian club's new 15-foot class—a similar but less-refined design by Alden—and the Eastern Yacht Club's 17-foot class, which would become the Northeast Harbor A Class (1975.452, on the opposite page). The knockabout sloop, without bowsprit, had been developed at Marblehead 20 years earlier, and *Vireo* was a good example of the type, which was thought ideal for families and children. With a lead keel, she could not capsize, and two air-filled compartments kept her from sinking. At 15 feet on the waterline, she was a popular size for day racing or teaching a teenager to sail. Her long bow and stern overhangs provided buoyancy and allowed her to sail faster by increasing her waterline length when she heeled over, and a whole family could fit in her cockpit. In Marblehead during the 'teens, *Vireo* had a reputation for speed. She was the "fastest knockabout of her overall length around Marblehead. . . . Very stiff and able," an "ideal single hander," according to John Alden.

When Yerxa offered *Vireo* for sale in 1920, Assistant Secretary of the Navy Franklin D. Roosevelt was looking for a boat to teach his five children his favorite pastime of sailing. Roosevelt bought *Vireo* for $700 and took her to the family's summer compound at Campobello Island on a U.S. Navy destroyer. Although he had only about 20 days of vacation at Campobello in 1920 and 1921 before he was paralyzed by polio, FDR happily used this boat to rediscover the waters of his childhood and spend time with his older children, showing them how to sail.

The Roosevelts used *Vireo* very little after FDR's illness. After the Hammer family purchased the Campobello property in the 1950s, they donated the boat to Mystic Seaport.

STATUS: Unrestored, original, fair condition, cosmetic treatment for exhibition in 2001.

DONOR: Victor Hammer

FURTHER READING:
Alden, John. Correspondence with Franklin D. Roosevelt, Papers of Franklin D. Roosevelt, Group 10—June-July 1920. Franklin D. Roosevelt Library, Hyde Park, New York. Copies in Correspondence file, 1959.455, Registrar's Office, Mystic Seaport.

Corinthian Yacht Club, Marblehead. *Yearbooks.* 1912-20.

German, Andrew W. "*Vireo*: A Boat for Franklin D. Roosevelt." *The Log of Mystic Seaport,* Summer, 2001.

Hudson, George S. "The Corinthians of Marblehead." *Yachting,* January, 1913.

Klein, Jonas. *Beloved Island: Franklin & Eleanor and the Legacy of Campobello.* Forest Dale, Vermont: Paul S. Eriksson, 2000.

Robinson, W.E., "From Knockabout to Raceabout," *The Rudder,* May, 1900.

John Alden sent FDR this photo of Vireo *speeding along under reefed sails at Marblehead. (Photo: Courtesy of FDR Library, Hyde Park)*

Roosevelt, James. *My Parents: A Differing View.* Chicago: Playboy Press, 1976.

Ward, Geoffrey C. *A First-Class Temperament: The Emergence of Franklin Roosevelt.* New York: Harper & Row, 1989.

ACCESSION NO. 1959.455
Lines taken off 1959.455 in the year 2001 are available from Mystic Seaport's Watercraft Plans Collection.

FDR, some of his children, and friends, aboard Vireo *off Campobello, in the summer of 1920. (Photo: Courtesy of FDR Library, Hyde Park, Mystic Seaport 1959-10-8)*

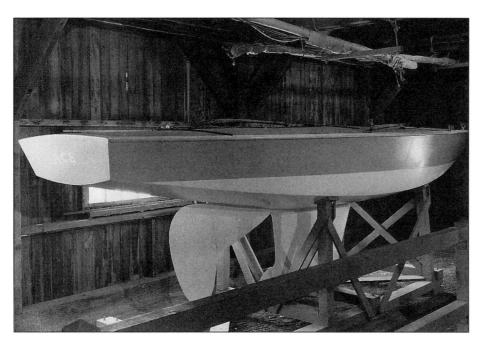

The Star-Class sloop Ace *as she appeared on exhibit in 1970. (Photo: Lester D. Olin,* Mystic Seaport 1970-6-173)

Ace
INTERNATIONAL STAR
CLASS #202

22' 8" x 5' 10"   1925

When the International Star Class Yacht Racing Association was formed in 1922, there were 110 registered boats. Fifty years later there were 5,763, and today the Stars are still going strong. Good going for a 1911 design!

Francis Sweisguth of William Gardner's office drew the plans, expanding the Bug class of 1906. Until 1921, Stars carried a sliding gunter mainsail, and for the next eight years a Marconi sail was used of about the same proportions. The present sail plan was adopted in 1929. Over 500 different builders have produced registered boats all over the world.

Ace was built by the Purdy Boat Company of Port Washington, New York, for Adrian Iselin II who sailed her to victory in the world's championship her first year and again eleven years later in 1936.

STATUS: Unrestored, has been extensively rebuilt and rerigged by owner, good condition.

DONOR: C. Oliver Iselin, Jr.

FURTHER READING FOR 1961.912 AND 1983.102:
"Altair Wins Elder Trophy." *The Rudder,*

Sept, 1918. History, early racing, photos.

Blanchard, Fessenden S. *The Sailboat Classes of North America.* New York: Doubleday & Co., 1968.

"Details of the New Star Rig." *The Rudder,* June, 1930. Rig modification, plan.

Elder, George W. *Forty Years Among the Stars.* Port Washington, Wisconsin: Schanen and Jacque, 1955. Elder is considered the "father" of the Star Class Association.

Esterly, Diana. *Early One-Design Sailboats.* New York: Charles Scribner's Sons, 1979. Comments, photos, plans.

Hubbard, Walton Jr. "The New Star Rig." *Sea,* Feb, 1938. Rig modification, photos.

Korper, George W. "The Organization of a Successful Racing Class." *The Rudder,* Jan, 1933. History, class association.

Log of the Star Class. ISCYRA annual publication.

Lucke, Charles E. Jr. "The Star Class Goes Modern." *Yachting,* April, 1930. Rig modification, comments, plans.

——. "Peggy Wee of Long Island Sound, Victor in 1930 Star Internationals." *The Rudder,* Nov, 1930.

——. "The Stars Come of Age." *Yachting,* January, 1932.

——. "A Quarter Century for the Stars." *Motor Boating,* Nov, 1936. Contains photo of *Ace.*

Ogilvy, C. Stanley. "50 Years of Stars." *Motor Boating,* May, 1961.

"One Design Classes." *The Rudder,* Dec, 1911. Contains construction and sail plans for original boats.

Persson, Seth. "Twenty Years of Star Boats." *The Rudder,* Aug, 1931.

A Pictorial History of the Star Class, 1911-2001. n.p.: International Star Class, 2001. Contains photos of *Ace.*

Reinke, Tom. "The Rising Star: A Classic Keelboat Turns 75." *Small Boat Journal,* Dec/Jan, 1987. History, photos.

Schoettle, Edwin J., ed. *Sailing Craft.* New York: The MacMillan Co., 1927.

"Star Class Internationals." *The Rudder,* Oct, 1925. Racing, international trophy competition, photos.

"Star Class in 1932 Games." *The Rudder,* May, 1931. Olympic contender, brief comments.

"Star Class Most Successful." *The Rudder,* November, 1922. History, growth of class, photos, plan.

The Editors of *Yachting. Your New Boat.* New York: Simon and Schuster, 1946.

Trimble, Nancy. "Starboats." *Nautical Quarterly* 41, Spring, 1988. History, photos, racing.

Association Address:
International Star Class, 1545 Waukegan Rd., Glenview, Illinois 60025. (847) 729-0630 (Inquire for plans information.)

ACCESSION NO. 1961.912

Ace, early in her racing career before the new rig was put in. (Photo: Morris Rosenfeld, Gift of Mrs. C. O. Iselin,
Mystic Seaport 1962.242.1*)*

When the boat was new, plans of the Star One-Design Class appeared in the December, 1911, issue of The Rudder.
(Mystic Seaport 1978-1-108)

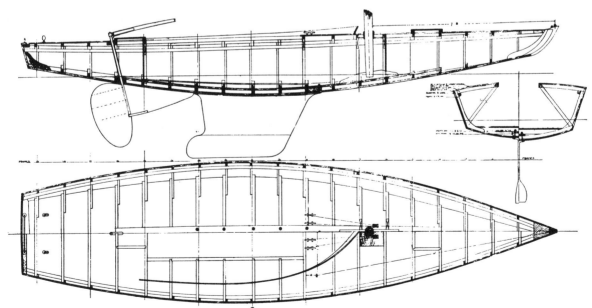

Construction Plan of Star One-Design Class. Dimensions: 22.7 Ft. O. A., 15.4 Ft. W. L., 5.8 Ft. Breadth, 3.4 Ft. Draught, Sail Area 280 Sq. Ft., Ballast 830 Lb. on Keel

Ceti on her arrival at Mystic Seaport. (Photo: Claire White-Peterson, Mystic Seaport 1983-9-101A)

Ceti

INTERNATIONAL STAR CLASS #7

22' 8" x 5' 10"   1911

Star class sloops were originally very simple boats, as these photos of *Ceti* indicate. One of the first Stars, built in 1911 by Isaac Smith of Port Washington, New York, *Ceti* spent her life on Lake Massawippi, North Hatley, Quebec, and was never changed from her original sliding gunter rig, sailing until 1980. During her very first years she was raced out of Rye, New York, by George D. Barrow, then given to the donor's father, Warren A. Ransom, and his brother Frank, and shipped to Quebec. There, according to the donor, the "chief form of pleasure with the *Ceti* is to load my family and several boxes of food in it, tow a canoe behind, and anchor somewhere up the lake and go ashore, cook lunch or supper as the case may be, and hope for enough wind to get home. It is a cruising boat on a minute scale as far as I am concerned." Now, of course, Stars are highly refined racing machines, but older boats could serve a family just as *Ceti* did once their competitive days were done.

STATUS: Good condition, rudder replaced, otherwise original.

DONOR: Miss Louise Ransom

FURTHER READING:
(Same as for *Ace*, 1961.912)

ACCESSION NO. 1983.102

Star boat Ceti—probably on Lake Massawippi, North Hatley, Quebec. (Photo: Mystic Seaport 1984.57.2)

Triple Threat
ATLANTIC CLASS
HULL #2513

30' 6" x 6' 6"   1929

Abeking & Rasmussen of Lemwerder, Germany, built a hundred of these 'round-the-buoys racers in 1928, '29, and '30, mostly for Long Island Sound yachtsmen. Within a few years, several of the fleet, however, including *Triple Threat* (originally raced as *Skipper* from Warwick, Rhode Island), got as far as Blue Hill, Maine. W. Starling Burgess designed the Atlantics and certainly influenced the choice of their builder–a natural one for him since A. & R. was already building other Burgess-designed sailing craft. The Atlantics served as trainers for youngsters and skill-honers for older sailors. Responsive and able because of their sleek underwater lines, but wet because of their low freeboard, the ever-popular Atlantics remain active today—still under the auspices of the Atlantic Class Association. The current fleet represents diminished numbers and, for the most part, fiberglass replacement hulls instead of the original wood.

The Atlantics were among the first designs to shed overhanging booms and running backstays, and their handsome sail plans still look reasonably modern. The mainsail can be easily hoisted and furled from the cockpit and is sufficiently large and powerful so that a small and easily handled jib is all that's ever needed for good on-the-wind performance.

Triple Threat, like the other boats of this mahogany-planked class, suffered broken frames early and required sister framing. Finally, in the 1960s, after several idle years in her boathouse, she underwent an extensive rebuild by Frank L. Day, Jr., in his Brooklin, Maine, shop. His work matched the original–which, in spite of some structural problems, was of unusually high quality–and infused much-needed new life into *Triple Threat*'s worn-out hull. His was a museum-quality restoration, although at the time no one anticipated a museum would be her final resting place.

STATUS: Restored, excellent condition.

DONOR: Mrs. Richard Niehoff

FURTHER READING:
Blanchard, Fessenden S. *The Sailboat Classes of North America.* Garden City, New York: Doubleday & Co., 1963.

Herreshoff, L. Francis. "W. Starling Burgess." *The Rudder*, May, 1947. Brief obituary by Starling Burgess's old friend.

Howland, Llewellyn. "The Burgess Legacy." *WoodenBoat* 71, 72, 73, 74, July/ Aug, Sept/Oct, Nov/Dec, 1986, and Jan/Feb, 1987. Four-part series on Edward Burgess and his son Starling; the Atlantic is discussed in issue 74.

"The Atlantic Coast One-Design Class." *Yachting*, November, 1928.

Association Address:
c/o Ward Campbell, P. O. Box 121, Cold Spring Harbor, New York 11724 (516)692-6227

ACCESSION NO. 1993.155

Triple Threat *under sail in Maine waters. (Courtesy of Benjamin Mendlowitz)*

Duchess
COMET CLASS #444
16' 0" x 5' 0"   1937

Duchess on her original trailer. (Photo: Maynard Bray, Mystic Seaport 1988.48A)

Working to a commission from Mrs. Elliot Wheeler of Oxford, Maryland, who wanted an inexpensive, fast centerboard boat for her sons, designer C. Lowndes Johnson created the Comet in 1932. He borrowed the hard chines, low freeboard, and relatively large sail area from the Star, a boat in which he was a world champion. The first Comet, *Zoea*, now in the collection of the Chesapeake Bay Maritime Museum, was built by Ralph Wiley of Oxford for $120, a price that netted Ralph just ten dollars. This new one-design, first called a Crab, then a Star Jr., received a lot of press in 1933, being featured in *Yachting*'s design section and in their boat show booth. Motivation for *Yachting*'s support probably lay in needing a boat that would interest readers in the same way that *The Rudder*'s Snipe, designed a

few years before, was doing in those Depression years. The Comet is still a rival of the Snipe: Comet partisans say that their larger sail plans and lighter hulls make them better and faster boats. But Snipes were first into the market, and there are more of them.

Duchess was built by the donor's father in 1936-37 as one of three boats built from kits that winter by members of the Bayside Yacht Club. The kits

were furnished for $165 by the venerable Skaneateles Boat and Canoe Co., founded in 1893, a company that was changing its product to suit the times. *Duchess* won fleet championships in 1937, 1940, 1941, and 1942, then was taken over by the donor who continued racing until 1953. Donor "Duke" Dayton restored *Duchess* to pristine condition before giving her to the Museum.

CONDITION: Excellent, on original trailer with all equipment.

DONOR: Walter S. Dayton, Jr.

FURTHER READING:
"A Young Brother of the Stars for Chesapeake Bay." *Yachting*, March, 1932.

Blanchard, Fessenden. *The Sailboat Classes of North America*. Garden City, New York: Doubleday & Co., 1968.

Dodds, Richard J. S., and Pete Lesher, eds. *A Heritage in Wood: The Chesapeake Bay Maritime Museum's Small Craft Collection*. St. Michaels, Maryland: The Chesapeake Bay Maritime Museum, 1992.

Hanson, John K. "Built to Win: The Comet Class." *WoodenBoat* 13, Nov/Dec, 1979.

Jett, Starke. "The Comet's Tale." *Classic Boat* 98, August, 1996.

Lucke, Jr., Charles E. "A 20th Birthday." *Yachting*, February, 1952.

Slane, James F. "Johnson's 'Comet.'" *Yachting*, March, 1934.

"The Comet, a Rapidly Growing Class." *Yachting*, November, 1935.

The Editors of *Yachting*. *Your New Boat*. New York: Simon and Schuster, 1946.

Association Address:
Anne Filbert
4658 North Shore Drive
Westerville, Ohio 43082
(614) 965-1628

ACCESSION NO. 1988.48

Duchess under sail. (Courtesy of Walter S. Dayton, Jr., Mystic Seaport 1988-5-40)

Good News III

INTERNATIONAL SNIPE
CLASS #6025

15' 8" x 5' 1"   1947

In 1931 the Florida West Coast Yachting Association conceived a "trailer class" boat, whose length was not to exceed 16 feet or its sail area 100 square feet, and asked William F. Crosby to draw the plans. Crosby went one better; he not only produced the drawings but published them as a "How to Build" article in *The Rudder* for which he was editor. It was the Depression and people were turning to smaller boats, particularly types they could build themselves. Within a year 150 Snipes had been built (The name "trailer class" was abandoned in favor of a sea bird, the magazine's usual custom for its "How to Build Series.") When the Snipe Class International Racing Association was formed in November of 1932, 250 boats were registered. Five years after Crosby's article, the Snipes were the largest one-design racing class in the world with 1,950 boats. In 1966 there were 16,000.

Good News III was a fast boat. Skippered by Ted Wells, one-time SCIRA Commodore, she was a three-time winner and a five-time runner-up in the national championships. She was built in California by Louis Varalyay.

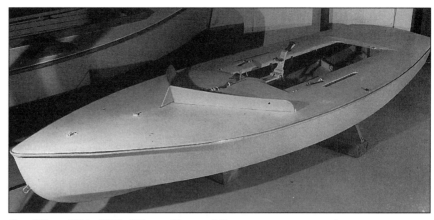

Good News III in 1975. (Photo: Maynard Bray, Mystic Seaport 1975-6-82)

STATUS: Fiberglass-covered, modern racing gear added, good condition.

DONOR: August F. Hook

FURTHER READING:
Adams, Ed. "Snipes: A Pretty Short Trip." *Sail*, April, 1989. Photos, racing.

Blanchard, Fessenden S. *The Sailboat Classes of North America*. Garden City, New York: Doubleday & Co., 1968.

Crosby, William F. *Boat Sailing*. New York: Rudder Publishing Co., 1935.

——. "How to Build the Snipe." *The Rudder*, July, 1931.

——. *Racing Small Boats*. New York: The MacMillan Company, 1940.

——. "The Snipe Story." *Yachting*, June, 1953.

How to Build 20 Boats, No. 10. Greenwich, Connecticut: Fawcett

Publications, Inc., 1950. 15' 6" William F. Crosby Snipe-class one-design.

Gilreath, Harold L. *Building the Plywood Snipe*. Wilton, Connecticut: Snipe Class International Racing Association, 1962.

Lazarus, Paul. "William Crosby's Snipe." *WoodenBoat* 89, July/Aug, 1989.

Pickering, Jeff. "…But Not Forgotten." *Australian Sailing*, Feb, 1983.

Reynolds, Mark. "From the Experts— Snipe." *Yacht Racing/Cruising*, Oct, 1982.

"800 Boats in Three Years." *The Rudder*, June, 1934.

Association Address:
Thomas Payne, Snipe Class International, 4096 Chestnut Drive, Flower Branch, Georgia 30542. (Write for plans information.)

ACCESSION NO. 1966.304

Half-Hitch

SEA SCOUT SLOOP

13' 2" x 5' 8"   1940

Half-Hitch was built by Mystic Seaport Trustee James Harvie and his father, John Barr Harvie, at Barrington, Rhode Island, in 1940 from a design by Edson I. Schock. The natural crook knees used in her construction are from a family apple tree blown down in the hurricane of 1938.

Professor Schock of the University of Rhode Island designed these sturdy 13' sloops in 1938 as a gift to the Narragansett Sea Scout Council, naming the design the Narragansett Bay Sea Scout. The vessel was intended to be a do-it-yourself project, built and sailed by Sea Scouts. Before World War

II, 20 Sea Scouts were built on Narragansett Bay and 117 plans were sold to other Sea Scout units.

The Harvies made some modification to the original design, using mahogany planking rather than plywood, and slightly lengthening the deck. Mr. Harvie donated the *Half-Hitch* to the Williams College-Mystic Seaport Program in 1986.

STATUS: Very good condition; garboards and centerboard trunk replaced at Mystic Seaport.

DONOR: James Harvie

FURTHER READING:
Williams, J. Harold. *Scout Trail 1910-1962, History of the Boy Scout Movement in Rhode Island. An Eyewitness Report*. Providence, Rhode Island: Rhode Island Boy Scouts and Narragansett Council, Boy Scouts of America, 1964.

Plans for "Sea Scout," Edson I. Schock Design No. 43, are available from Mystic Seaport's Watercraft Plans Collection.

Half Hitch under sail. (Photo: Courtesy of Williams College-Mystic Seaport Maritime Studies Program)

Pantooset on exhibit at Mystic Seaport in 1959. (Photo: Louis S. Martel, Mystic Seaport 1955.1201)

Pantooset

HALF-RATER CLASS

26' 5" x 7' 0"   1907

Built in South Boston by W. J. Edwards for use with the steam yacht *Pantooset*, this daysailer is equipped with lifting eyes at each end and was normally carried, along with a variety of other boats, on the larger yacht's davits. The big *Pantooset*, owned by the donor's uncle, came out in 1902. She was designed by W. J. J. Young and built by Bath Iron Works, Bath, Maine.

STATUS: Unrestored, mostly original, poor condition.
DONOR: Cleveland Bigelow
ACCESSION NO. 1955.1201

When not in use, the Half Rater Pantooset *was carried on the davits of the steam yacht whose name she bore. She is shown here with her rig still standing. (Photo: Gift of Charles F. and Walter S. Almy, Mystic Seaport 1951.4261.2)*

Tineke. *(Photo: Maynard Bray,* Mystic Seaport 1975-6-34*)*

Tineke

12-SQUARE-METER
SHARPIE US 1
HULL #2826

19' 8" x 4' 10"   1933

For the 1956 Melbourne Olympics, the 12-Square-Meter Sharpie Class was selected as a boat for a crew of two. The type was virtually unknown in the United States. A U. S. Air Force Colonel in the Netherlands bought this one, which had been built by Abeking & Rasmussen, and offered it to the North American Yacht Racing Union for the competition. NAYRU recruited Eric Olsen and Stan Renehan to sail her, and they went to Holland in July of 1956 to try the boat out on the Loosdrecht Plats. Then the boat and the two U. S. sailors went to Melbourne. In the 1956 Olympics, Olsen and his crew finished 9th out of 13 competitors, swamping once and fouling out once, a creditable job considering their brief practice time. In the 1960 Olympics, the Flying Dutchman replaced the 12-Square-Meter Sharpie.

These boats were designed by Hans Kroger in 1931 for a design competition as an inexpensive sporting sailboat for German lakes. A decade later the boats had spread all over Europe. They were relatively inexpensive and simple to build because of their batten-seam construction and hard-chine hull shape. They are still popular on the lakes, bays, rivers, and canals of Holland and Germany, and may be found in England and other European countries as well. Sail area has grown to 16 square meters, still in a high-aspect-ratio spinnakerless sliding gunter rig, and cockpits have become self-bailing.

STATUS: Excellent original condition.

DONOR: Merrill Stubbs

FURTHER READING:
Roosevelt, Julian K. "The Olympics." *Yachting*, February, 1957.

Valent, Ron. "The Sharpie: Still an Affordable One-Design." *The Boatman*, Feb/March, 1993.

ACCESSION NO. 1957.850

Tineke. *(Photo: From the collection of Mystic Seaport,* Mystic Seaport 1957.850*)*

Eddystone Light in 1975. (Photo: Maynard Bray, Mystic Seaport 1975-10-79)

Eddystone Light under sail in home waters near Rochester, New York, about 1935. (Photo: Courtesy of H.V.R. Palmer, Jr.)

Eddystone Light
INTERNATIONAL 14-FOOT CLASS

14′ 0″ x 4′ 6″   1935

The International 14s were probably the first high-performance planing sailboats, a distinction they held from 1933, when they were first recognized as a class, until the early 1950s when other classes were introduced. The modern 14-footers originated in England when Uffa Fox became interested in the National 14s, as they were called in 1927, and came out with a radical new design the following season. That year his new *Avenger* won the Prince of Wales Cup and went on to win many other races, at one time having a record of 52 wins out of 57 starts. About this time the class became an international one and boats began appearing in other countries. In the United States one of the first four boats built to race in this class was *Eddystone Light*. She and the three others were modeled after one of the Uffa Fox boats and built by the Rochester Boat Works. The International 14 Class is still very active and has about 5,000 boats on its register.

STATUS: Unrestored, substantially original, excellent condition.

DONOR: Howard V. R. Palmer, Jr., and Richard V. Palmer

FURTHER READING:
"A New 14-Foot International Dinghy. *Yachting*, January, 1944.

Blanchard, Fessenden S. *The Sailboat Classes of North America.* Garden City, New York: Doubleday & Co., 1968.

Douglass, Gordon K. "The Inimitable International 14-Footer." *The Rudder*, September, 1940.

——. "The Why of the International 14." *Yachting*, April, 1943.

Bunnell, Steve. "The I-14s." *Northwest Yachting*, June, 1993.

Fox, Uffa. *Sailing, Seamanship, and Small Yacht Construction.* New York: Charles Scribner's Sons, 1934.

——. *Sail and Power.* New York: Charles Scribner's Sons, 1937.

——. *Uffa Fox's Second Book.* Camden, Maine: International Marine Publishing Co., 1980. *Alarm*, 14′ 0″ Uffa Fox International 14 Class.

Hanson, John. "Built to Win: The International 14." *WoodenBoat* 20, Jan/Feb, 1978.

"International 14." *International Dinghy*, July/Aug, 1977.

"International 14—Fast, Fun, Forever!" *Sailing World*, April, 1988. Design commentary, racing rules, photos.

Palmer, H. V. R. "It Was a Matter of Love at First Sight." *Skipper*, Feb, 1955.

Schoettle, Edwin J., ed. *Sailing Craft.* New York: The MacMillan Co., 1927.

The Editors of *Sailing World*. "The International 14." *Sailing World*, April, 1988.

The Editors of *Yachting. Your New Boat.* New York: Simon and Schuster, 1946.

"The 14-Foot International One-Design Dinghy." *Yachting*, March, 1938.

Vaughan, T. J. *International Fourteen Foot Dinghy 1928-1964.* London: International Fourteen Foot Dinghy Class Association of Great Britain, 1964. Handbook and history.

Walker, Stuart H. *The Techniques of Small Boat Racing.* New York: W. W. Norton & Co., 1960.

Association Address:
c/o Julio Magri, 16952 Kennedy Rd., Los Gatos, California 95119 (408) 358-7090.

ACCESSION NO. 1974.1030

*George Lauder sails the
Fairfield Knockabout in
the summer of 1983.
(Photo: Courtesy of
James M. Brown III)*

FAIRFIELD
KNOCKABOUT CLASS SLOOP
17′ 5″ x 5′ 5″   1938

George Lauder's Depression-era Fairfield Boat Works in Greenwich, Connecticut, offered skilled boatbuilders a chance to work at their trade during those lean years when they might otherwise have ended up pushing a broom or standing in a breadline. Had Lauder been less philanthropic, or had he less taste in boats, the Fairfield knockabout wouldn't have happened. Small and beautiful and made like fine furniture, she is clearly a craft for the carriage trade—very different from the then-prevailing, built-for-a-price daysailing boats that the austere 1930s encouraged. The Herreshoff influence shows in her molded teak sheerstrakes, steam-bent coaming, and specially cast, bronze bow chocks as well as in the overall quality of construction. Under sail, two persons are about the limit for the small oval cockpit which, because of its distance from the rudder, requires a remote steering system. Confined amidships, neither skipper nor crew can adversely affect the boat's trim, and the extensive deck adds a measure of safety.

STATUS: Original, good condition.

DONOR: The estate of George Lauder

FURTHER READING:
Gribbins, Joseph. "George Lauder's Nautical Garden." *Nautical Quarterly* 23, Autumn, 1983.

ACCESSION NO. 1987.75.6

*Fairfield Knockbout sloop shortly after arrival at Mystic Seaport.
(Photo: Nancy d'Estang, Mystic Seaport 1987-8-71)*

ALDEN O BOAT
18' 3" x 7' 2"

In all, some 600 of John Alden's O boats may have been built, according to Richard Henderson, author of *John G. Alden and his Yacht Designs*. The Alden office drew several variations of the O boat. The wider one, represented by this boat, was designed with a smaller rig for windier sailing. The O boat was to be a trainer for youngsters–sloop-rigged so as to have all the sails and most of the rigging of the larger racing boats into which they would "graduate." The first of these boats went to Marblehead in 1921, but before long fleets appeared up and down the coast as these practical and affordable little daysailers caught on. O boat orders went to a variety of mostly New England builders and, as might be expected, workmanship standards varied considerably. Their iron fastenings limited the lives of most O boats, and they required extensive rebuilding as they aged. If they were lucky like this one, they got it; if not, they were abandoned. Mystic Seaport's O boat was especially lucky. She was the last restoration Bob Baker carried out before he died–and Baker was known for his fine and careful work.

STATUS: Restored, good condition.

DONOR: Kathie R. Florsheim

FURTHER READING:
"Alden-Designed Knockabout." *The Rudder*, Mar, 1923.

Carrick, Robert W., and Richard Henderson. *John G. Alden and His Yacht Designs*. Camden, Maine: International Marine Publishing Co., 1983.

"Designs: 18' O Boat." *WoodenBoat* 32, Jan/Feb, 1980 and 42, Sept/Oct, 1981.

Esterly, Diana. *Early One-Design Sailboats*. New York: Charles Scribner's Sons, 1979.

Schoettle, Edwin J. *Sailing Craft*. New York: The Macmillan Co., 1945.

ACCESSION NO. 1989.51

Alden O boat. (Photo: Maynard Bray, Mystic Seaport 1989.51A)

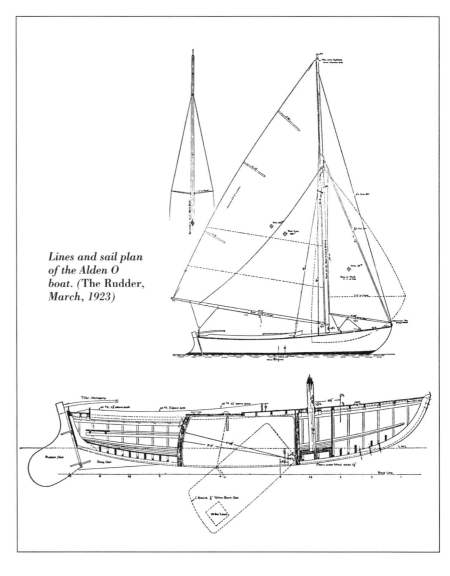

Lines and sail plan of the Alden O boat. (The Rudder, March, 1923)

Tautog
SAKONNET ONE-DESIGN CLASS SLOOP

18' 5" x 6' 3"   1938

John G. Alden designed these keel sloops for his fellow summer residents of Sakonnet, Rhode Island. As he said to *Tautog*'s donor, he stretched out the popular Herreshoff 12½, giving this design a proportionally heavier keel, higher freeboard, and a taller Marconi rig, and producing a boat more able to handle the open water off Sakonnet Point. *Tautog* was Alden's own boat for a season and the only one of the original ten that survived the hurricanes of '38, '44, and '54 (although she sank and was recovered each time). Alden sold *Tautog* to the donor's father in 1938, but kept sailing her. She and the original other nine were built by the Casey Boatbuilding Co. of Fairhaven, Massachusetts. Palmer Scott built more in 1947, and Harry Towne also added to the class that year and again in 1954 after he had established his shop in Bristol, Rhode Island, on the site of the old Herreshoff yard.

STATUS: Fair condition, 60% sister-framed, cosmetically rough.

DONOR: Elizabeth Brayton Dawson in memory of David A. Brayton and John G. Alden

FURTHER READING FOR 1985.7 AND 1990.136:

Carrick, Robert W. and Richard Henderson. *John G. Alden and his Yacht Designs*. Camden, Maine: International Marine Publishing Co., 1983.

The Editors of *Yachting*. *Your New Boat*. New York: Simon and Schuster, 1946.

"The Sakonnet One-Design." *Yachting*, May, 1939.

ACCESSION NO. 1985.7

Sakonnet Class Tautog. *(Photo: Deborah A. Bates, Mystic Seaport 1985.7A)*

Blossom. *(Photo: Mary Anne Stets, Mystic Seaport 1990.136)*

Blossom
SAKONNET ONE-DESIGN CLASS SLOOP

18' 5" x 6' 3"   1954

Blossom is one of the 1954 boats, and it is interesting to see the differences. *Tautog* has a stern stowage compartment not present on *Blossom* and the later boats, and has higher seats and slightly heavier frames. The aft deck is one frame longer on *Tautog* than on *Blossom*. And by 1954 chrome-plated bronze hardware had become the style instead of the older plain bronze. These boats, prewar and postwar, represent almost the last of the old tradition of one-designs created for specific waters and conditions.

STATUS: Good condition, 40% sister-framed, complete equipment included.

DONOR: Howard R. Merriman, Sr.

ACCESSION NO. 1990.136

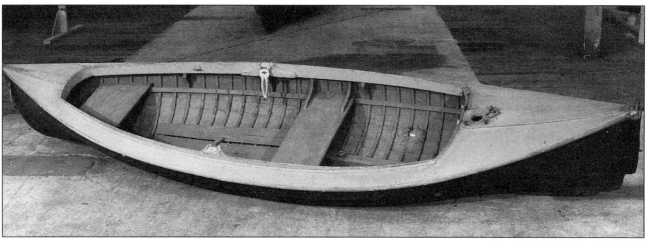

Double-ended sailboat 1975.22 in 1978. The trunk for her "radix" centerboard can be seen just ahead of the middle seat. She is fitted with outrigger oarlocks. (Photo: Maynard Bray, Mystic Seaport 1978-2-43)

HALF-DECKED
DOUBLE-ENDED SAILBOAT

13′ 11″ x 3′ 9″   ca. 1900

With her two quite different rigs, a boat like this must have been a fun one to own. In addition to the lug rig shown, she has a big gaff sloop rig that requires a bowsprit for the tack of its jib. Whether she is one of a kind or part of a class or type is not known, although perhaps further research will turn up more someday. In his *Canoe and Boat Building*, W. P. Stephens shows a similar, but larger, boat in Plate XLVIII called *Clio*. She was the 1887 champion of her class, unnamed in the book, at Toronto Bay on Lake Ontario.

STATUS: Some repair has been made, poor condition.

DONOR: Thomas C. Sutton

FURTHER READING:
Stephens, W. P. *Canoe and Boat Building*. New York: Forest and Stream Publishing Co., 1889.

ACCESSION NO. 1975.22
Plans for 1975.22 are available from Mystic Seaport's Watercraft Plans Collection.

In addition to the small lugsail rig shown here, this boat came with a much larger sloop rig carrying a big gaff mainsail and a jib set from a removable bowsprit. (Photo: Courtesy of Thomas C. Sutton)

Hampton-boat type, The Seagull. *(Photo: Courtesy of Mrs. Charles A. Grobe, Jr.*, Mystic Seaport 1982-3-111*)*

The Seagull

HAMPTON-STYLE DAYSAILER BY CHARLES EATON

14' 4" x 4' 0"   1933

This boat looks a lot like the larger Hampton-style workboats—no wonder since she was built at Blastow's Cove on Little Deer Isle, Maine. She was ordered by the donor's aunt, Marian Lawrence, who summered with her aunt, Lina Lawrence, at nearby Swain's Cove. After a few other builders were found to be too busy, Charles Eaton got the job. He figured he could do a 14-15' boat in about three weeks, and he was off by only a few days. He and the owner sailed the boat around to Swain's Cove only 25 days after the order was placed. There she was based for the next 40 years, often sailing to nearby islands for picnics. The boat lost her original gaff rig as a result of capsizing in a squall ten years after she was built, a mishap from which the owner and her aunt were lucky to be rescued. The replacement rig was Marconi, and that was the only change during all her years of use.

As the donor remembers: "She was a good sturdy boat which didn't ghost very well and was not particularly easy to row due to certain conflicts with the centerboard housing and the boom. She sailed nicely when there was enough wind, even when loaded down with four or five people, an old-fashioned picnic basket and Lina's bags of ferns and tins of berries. She gave a number of people a lot of fun."

The Seagull has lapstrake planking on flat bent frames, and is fitted with two rowing positions. Her sweeping sheer is handsome and clearly relates her to local working watercraft. Charles Eaton built what he knew.

STATUS: Fair condition, unrestored, with sail and spars.
DONOR: Mrs. Charles A. Grobe, Jr.
ACCESSION NO. 1981.112

The Seagull. *(Photo: Maynard Bray*, Mystic Seaport 1981.112A*)*

Patience
CONCORDIA SLOOP BOAT
17' 10" x 5' 3"   1964

Developed by Waldo Howland and Pete Culler of The Concordia Company, the sloop boat was to fill the gap between the company's wooden-hulled Beetle Cats (page 7) and its larger cruising boats. The design is loosely based on New England working craft–the Kingston sailing lobsterboats and the Connecticut River sailing shad boats–as well as being influenced by the sailing dinghies of the Bahamas. Concordia printed a brochure and built several boats, although production never came close to that of

Patience *on her arrival at Mystic Seaport in 1978. (Photo: Mary Anne Stets,* Mystic Seaport 1977-4-211)

the smaller and less-costly Beetle Cats that the shop put together with such elaborate construction efficiency. The following, excerpted from the

brochure, tells more: "Like her older sisters, our sloop is handy and maneuverable. She holds her course and does not rely on constant use of the rudder. At anchor she lays quietly head to wind with mainsail set. She is sufficiently heavy and of such design that she carries her way well. Shooting a mooring or coming alongside another vessel or a float can be accomplished without haste or confusion. There are no shrouds, and as both boom and gaff have jaws it is possible to sail by the lee or lay alongside with wind abaft the beam."

Many years have passed since Concordia built its last sloop boat, although similar boats have been built more recently in Kennebunkport, Maine, to Pete Culler's slightly beamier design as part of The Landing School's boatbuilding curriculum.

STATUS: Original, good condition.

DONOR: Joseph W. Outerbridge

FURTHER READING:
Burke, John. *Pete Culler's Boats.* Camden, Maine: International Marine Publishing Co, 1984.

O'Brien, Mike. "The Buzzards Bay Sloop." *WoodenBoat* 122, Jan/Feb, 1995.

ACCESSION NO. 1978.223

Patience *under sail in the Mystic River in 1978. (Photo: Ken Mahler,* Mystic Seaport 1978-6-83A)

Breeze (ex-Maria)

NOANK LOBSTER SLOOP
BY WAYLAND MORGAN
OFFICIAL NO. 516837

26' 1" x 12' 1"   1898

With increasing commercialization of the oyster fisheries, small shoal-draft sloops spread down Long Island Sound from the waterways around New York City, starting in the days before the Civil War. In the small fishing village of Noank, Connecticut, and in nearby towns, a distinctive type developed, better suited to deeper waters and lobstering than the shallower New York oyster sloops. These came to be called Noank sloops, no matter where they were built. In hull shape they most closely resemble Cape Cod catboats, and indeed many eastern Long Island Sound boats could be rigged either as cats or sloops.

Breeze is the last remaining example of these small Noank sloops. She was built as *Maria* by Francis Wayland Morgan, a third-generation Noank boatbuilder, at the yard shared by his father and brother. By then both Wayland and his brother Augustus made most of their living fishing, building boats only occasionally. Louis Peterson was Wayland's client, and named the new boat for his wife, Maria. According to local history, when built she had a 6-hp Lathrop engine as an auxiliary. It was a daring expense, as James W. Lathrop had only begun to build engines the year before. Like her larger smack cousin, *Emma C. Berry*, she had a wet well to hold her catch of lobsters. The original engine was aft of the wet well.

In 1915, Frederick C. Sweet of Groton bought her and changed her name to *Breeze*. Shortly thereafter, he had Charles Butson of Groton remove the centerboard trunk that extended forward of the wet well into the cabin, and shorten the well, leaving enough space to put an engine in the cabin with its shaft running in a tube through the well. Depth was added to the keel, and the cockpit sole was raised to make it self-draining. Under this configuration she sailed and worked out of Groton. Other repairs were made as *Breeze* aged, including a general shortening of

Frederick C. Sweet sails Breeze *in the Thames River, circa 1946-47. (Photo: Courtesy of William H. Babcock, Jr., Mystic Seaport 1978.255)*

the rig, once occasioned by hitting the railroad bridge that crosses the Thames at New London, and repairs made after she went ashore at Gales Ferry in the hurricane of 1938. The donor, also of Groton, bought *Breeze* in 1967, the year before Sweet died, and sailed her for pleasure for a number of years.

STATUS: Fair, unrestored.

DONOR: William H. Babcock, Jr.

FURTHER READING:
Chapelle, Howard I. *American Small Sailing Craft.* New York: W.W. Norton & Co., 1951.

Peterson, William N. *Mystic Built: Ships and Shipyards of the Mystic River, Connecticut, 1784-1919.* Mystic: Mystic Seaport Publications, 1989.

"Power in Oyster and Fishing Boats." *Motor Boat*, January 10, 1905, 13-15. Has an excellent diagram that shows engine profile and placement, typical in these sloops.

ACCESSION NO. 1979.15
Plans for 1979.15 are available from Mystic Seaport's Watercraft Plans Collection.

Mystic Seaport's modelmaker, William S. Quincy, built a model of *Breeze*, Accession Number 1990.25.

Frederick C. Sweet sculls a skiff out to Breeze, *moored in the Thames River, ca. 1940, below the old road bridge and the railroad bridge that shortened her rig. (Photo: Mystic Seaport, 1979-4-80)*

Emma C. Berry

NOANK SMACK
OFFICIAL NO. 7971

45' 9" x 14' 8"   1866

Mystic Seaport's interest in acquiring this vessel began in 1966 when, owned by F. Slade Dale of Bay Head, New Jersey, she returned to Noank, the coastal Connecticut village where she was built, to celebrate her centennial anniversary. After Slade Dale donated her to the Museum, the *Berry* underwent an extensive rebuilding and restoration, which returned her to her original configuration as a smack, with a sloop rig and a wet well for carrying live fish and lobsters to market. During further rebuilding in 1988, shipwrights restored her deck, deck arrangement, and tiller steering to that of the early fishing smacks of southeastern Connecticut. Sailing tests in 1992 proved her to be an agile design.

After her 1866 launching for fisherman John Berry, at the R.&J. Palmer yard in Noank, the *Emma C. Berry* fished local waters for nearly 30 years–some of the time as a fish carrier rather than a fisherman–and was registered first in Stonington, then in New London. In 1886, she was rerigged as a schooner to divide the rig for easier handling. In 1894 she was sold to an owner in Maine where she was to remain for many years, working as a wet-well lobster smack, as a bait carrier, and in the cargo trade. She'd been abandoned by 1931 when a young wooden boat enthusiast, Slade Dale, was attracted by her lines. Dale sailed her to Bay Head, had her extensively rebuilt, used her as a yacht, and occasionally hauled pilings and materials for building his business, the Dale Yacht Basin.

The *Berry* is the only remaining example of the famed yacht-like smacks of Noank, vessels that also were involved in fishing, wrecking, and salvaging as far south as Key West.

STATUS: Restored at Mystic Seaport 1969 to 1971 and 1987 to 1988. Little original. Excellent condition.

DONOR: F. Slade Dale

FURTHER READING:

Ansel, Willits D. "Reframing the *Emma C. Berry*." *The Log of Mystic Seaport*, Winter, 1970.

——. *Restoration of the Smack Emma C. Berry at Mystic Seaport, 1969-1971.* Mystic: The Marine Historical Association, Inc. 1973.

Baird, Spencer Fullerton. *Conditions of the Sea Fisheries of the South Coast of New England in 1871 and 1872.* Washington, D.C.: U.S. Government Printing Office, 1873.

Baumer, David. "Fishing Vessels of the Northern Gulf Coast Red Snapper Fishery." Thesis, East Carolina University, 1991.

Chapelle, Howard I. *The National Watercraft Collection.* Washington, D.C.: U.S. Government Printing Office, 1960.

Dale, F. Slade. "Old Emma Comes to Barnegat." *Yachting*, June & July, 1933.

Dempster, Henry. *The Deck-Welled Fishing Boat and the Fisheries and Fish Reform: Being Dialogues on Those Important Subjects with Full Information on the Oyster Question.* Glasgow: Aird and Coghill, 1868.

d'Estang, Nancy, and Kevin Dwyer. *Handbook for the Shipyard of the*

Restoration of the Emma C. Berry. Mystic Seaport Manuscripts Department, 1992.

——. "Reconsidering the *Emma C. Berry*." *The Log of Mystic Seaport*, Summer, 1990.

d'Estang, Nancy, Gary Adair, Karl Robinson, Dean Seder, Quentin Snediker. "The *Emma C. Berry* Under Sail." *The Log of Mystic Seaport*, Winter, 1993.

"1880 Noank Smack Model Arrives From Norway." Mystic Seaport. *The Wind Rose*, August, 1987.

Goode, George Brown. *The Fisheries and Fishery Industries of the United States.* Washington, D.C.: U.S. Government Printing Office, 1887.

Hall, Henry. *Report on the Shipbuilding Industry in the United States.* Washington, D.C.: U.S. Government Printing Office, 1884.

Knapp, Edward. "The Smacks of Noank." Mystic Seaport Manuscripts Department.

Mystic Press. 1881, 1883.

New London Day. 1882.

New London Democrat. 1866.

Under sail again in Fishers Island Sound is the Noank Smack Emma C. Berry *after her most recent restoration. (Photo: Mary Anne Stets, Mystic Seaport 1992-9-193)*

The Shipyard's Howard Davis works on a new deck beam during the Berry's *1987-88 restoration. (Photo: Nancy d'Estang,* Mystic Seaport 1987-9-394*)*

Billethead from the Emma C. Berry *during refinishing in 1970. (Photo: Louis Martel,* Mystic Seaport 1970-4-199*)*

London County Historical Society.

These newspapers, in these years, contained frequent reports of the activities of Noank's fishing fleet.

Martin, Kenneth R., and Nathan R. Lipfert. *Lobstering and the Maine Coast.* Bath, Maine: Maine Maritime Museum, 1985. Has quite a bit on lobster smacks-the *Berry*'s later career.

Peterson, William N. *Mystic Built: Ships and Shipyards of the Mystic River, Connecticut, 1784-1919.* Mystic: Mystic Seaport Publications, 1989.

Stevenson, Charles H. *The Preservation of Fishery Products for Food.* Washington, D.C.: U.S. Government Printing Office, 1899. Good discussion of well-smacks, 341-43.

"The Schooner *Smack Grampus.*" *Field and Stream*, January 20, 1887.

Wall, Richard B. "The Wall Scrapbook." New London, Connecticut: *The New London Day* microfilm, 1907 to 1929, New

ACCESSION NO. 1969.231
Plans for 1969.231 are available from Mystic Seaport's Watercraft Plans Collection.

Smacks rafted up at New York's Fulton Fish Market in the 1880s. (Photo: Courtesy of Albert Barnes Collection, The Mariners' Museum)

Two smacks similar to the Emma C. Berry *lie in the Mystic River, ca. 1874, in this photo by E.A. Scholfield. (Photo:* Mystic Seaport 1965.828*)*

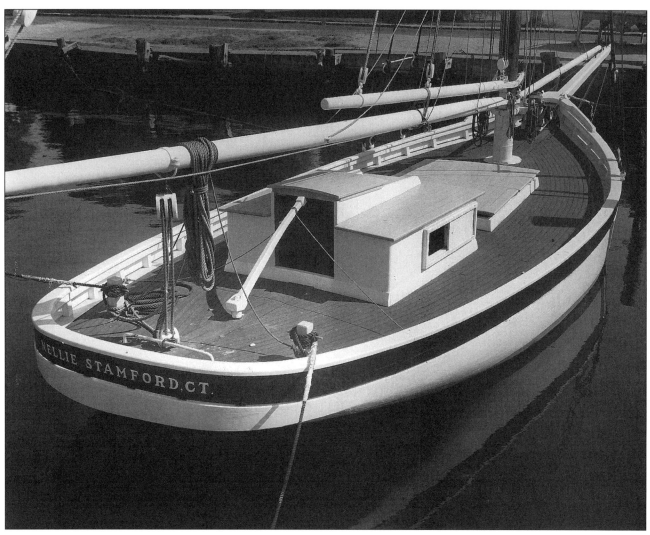

Oyster sloop Nellie *in 1975.*
(Photo: Maynard Bray,
Mystic Seaport 1975-6-27)

Nellie

OYSTER DREDGING SLOOP
OFFICIAL NO. 130578
32' 7" x 12' 9"   1891

Working in deeper water than the tonging boats and manned with a crew of two or three, boats such as *Nellie* towed their four or five dredges over the natural oyster beds off the shores of Long Island Sound. With slackened sheets they more or less drifted slowly over the beds with the tide. The boat's heading was controlled with the jib sheet and centerboard; the dredges were hauled back as they became full. During a drift from one end of the bed to the other there might be time for anywhere from two to six hauls, whereupon the boat would be sailed back against the tide to begin another

drift. The oysters, dumped on deck from the dredges, were culled from the rocks and other debris between hauls. The oystering season opened in the fall and lasted until spring. Power was not permitted in the boats until 1921, and even then its use was restricted to running between the harbor and the oyster beds. The last sailing dredger had long gone in 1969 when the law was changed to permit dredging under power on natural beds.

Most of the oyster sloops were like *Nellie* with gaff mainsails, cabins aft, and low-sided shallow hulls with centerboards. Most were unlike her, however, in that they had square rather than round sterns. *Nellie* was built in Smithtown, Long Island, and fished at Long Island until coming to Connecticut in 1900. Then, she was one of 350 sailing craft licensed to dredge on Connecticut's natural beds. After she received an engine about 1914, she probably worked the Ryle family oyster grounds near Stamford, Connecticut. Her sailing rig was long gone when Mystic Seaport acquired her, but the Museum has restored her to represent a sailing oyster dredge.

STATUS: Rig restored 1965, hull restored 1972 and 2001, approximately 40% original, good condition.

DONOR: Purchased for Mystic Seaport by Society for the Preservation of the *Nellie A. Ryle*

FURTHER READING:

Agassiz, G. "The Romance of the Oyster." *National Magazine*, January, 1909.

Chapelle, Howard I. *American Small Sailing Craft*. New York: W.W. Norton & Co., 1951.

Connecticut Shell Fish Commission. *Annual Report of the Connecticut Shell Fish Commission*, 1895, 1900.

Ingersoll, Ernest. *The Oyster Industry: Tenth Census of the United States*. Washington, D.C.: U.S. Government Printing Office, 1881.

Jones, Stephen. *Working Thin Waters*. Hanover, New Hampshire: University Press of New England, 2001. Documents the uses of a vessel similar to *Nellie* through the 1900s.

Kochiss, John M. *Oystering from New York to Boston*. Middletown, Connecticut: Wesleyan University Press for Mystic Seaport, 1974.

Teuscher, Philip. "The Oral History Project." Sound Archives, G.W. Blunt White Library, Mystic Seaport.

ACCESSION NO. 1964.1551

Plans for 1964.1551 are available from Mystic Seaport's Watercraft Plans Collection.

Oyster dredging at Port Chester, New York. (Photo: Courtesy of Fred Lovejoy, Mystic Seaport 1969-1-385)

Nellie was operating as a powerboat when Mystic Seaport acquired her. (Photo: J.M. Kochiss, Mystic Seaport 1968-2-99)

Estella A. *sailing in Fishers Island Sound in 1974 after her restoration.* (*Photo: Ken Mahler,* Mystic Seaport 1974-10-195)

Estella A.

MAINE SLOOP BOAT
OFFICIAL NO. 201627

34′ 5″ x 11′ 9″   1904

Friendship sloops are what these boats are called now, but to the Maine fishermen who used them they were known simply as "sloop boats." Although the Muscongus Bay area was where most were built, other towns besides Friendship produced them. *Estella A.* came from Bremen Long Island, Maine. Her builder was R.E.

(Rob) McLain whose son, Newell McLain, of Thomaston, was an indispensible source of information during the boat's restoration. Needless to say, the term "Friendship sloop" is not used by him.

These boats were built as lobsterboats and often were sailed by one man. Once there were hundreds of them, and they swung from moorings in most every Maine harbor just as the

engine-driven lobsterboats do today. Engines were their undoing; as soon as powerplants became dependable there was no need for a sailing hull. During the transition to power around the turn of the century, some of these boats carried small auxiliary engines, which were rigged for hauling traps as well as for propulsion. *Estella A.* was so equipped when new, having a two-cylinder, 9-hp Knox engine.

102

Used sloop boats became somewhat of a glut on the market in the 'twenties and 'thirties as fishermen changed to the powerboats that evolved into today's lobsterboats. The better ones–those not left on the beach to die–made economical yachts and were purchased and sailed "up to the west'ard" by their new owners. *Estella A.* herself was sold by her original owner, H.J. (Jack) Ames of Matinicus, in 1930 to the donor's late husband, who sailed her from his Jamestown, Rhode Island, summer home for the next 27 years. During this time her rig was converted to Marconi, outside lead ballast was added, and the cabin was enlarged.

The Gloucester sloop boats possibly were the forebears of these smaller but similar craft. In any event the charm of these boats keeps them popular and was the basis for forming the Friendship Sloop Society in 1961, an organization whose annual Sloop Days have become a well-attended and much-publicized affair. Several stock models are now built of fiberglass, and occasionally an amateur or professional will build a new Friendship in wood.

STATUS: Restored 1970-72 by Newbert & Wallace, Thomaston, Maine, little original, floating exhibit, good condition.

DONOR: Mrs. Duncan I. Selfridge

FURTHER READING:

Barnard, William Lambert. "The Working Boats of New England, the Maine Sloop." *Boating*, 1907. Reprinted in *WoodenBoat* 2, Nov/Dec, 1974.

Bray, Maynard E. "Good and Simple." Friendship Sloop Days Program, 1971.

Burnham, H.A. "Lobstering Under Sail." *WoodenBoat* 161, July/Aug, 2001.

Chapelle, Howard I. *American Sailing Craft.* Camden, Maine: International Marine Publishing Co., 1975. 2nd edition.

——. *American Small Sailing Craft.* New York: W.W. Norton & Co., 1951.

——. "The Friendship Sloop." *Yachting*, July, 1932.

Duncan, Roger F. *Friendship Sloops.* Camden, Maine: International Marine Publishing Co., 1985.

——. "Sloops of Friendship." *Yachting*, February, 1965.

Goode, George Brown. *The Fisheries and Fishery Industries of the United States.* Washington, D.C.: U.S. Government Printing Office, 1887.

Jones, Herald A., ed. *It's a Friendship.* Rockland, Maine: The Friendship Sloop Society, 1965.

——., ed. *Ships That Came Back.*

Rockland, Maine: The Friendship Sloop Society, 1962.

Kelly, Alice. "Friendships Never Die." *The Rudder*, July & August, 1946.

McKean, Robert B. "We Build a Friendship Sloop." *Yachting*, December, 1939.

"Old Time Yard and Builder's Son Help Restore '04 Fishing Sloop." *National Fisherman*, January, 1971.

Richards, Joe. *Princess, New York.* Indianapolis, Indiana: Bobbs-Merrill, 1956.

Roberts, Al, ed. *Enduring Friendships.* Camden, Maine: International Marine Publishing Co., 1970.

Taylor, William H. "The Friendship Sloop is Back." *Yachting*, December, 1946.

Wasson, George S. *Sailing Days on the Penobscot.* New York: W.W. Norton & Co., 1949. *Chapter VI*, "Lobster Sloops and Tidal Bores," describes the sloops used at Isle au Haut, Maine.

Winslow, Sidney L. *Fish Scales and Stone Chips.* Portland, Maine: Machigonne Press, 1952.

One rigged model of a small Friendship sloop is in Mystic Seaport's collection. Mystic Seaport has considerable unpublished material on sloop boats. A comprehensive report on *Estella A.*'s restoration is on file in the Registrar's office.

ACCESSION NO. 1957.498
Plans for 1957.498 are available from Mystic Seaport's Watercraft Plans Collection.

Most Maine sloop boats were used by lobstermen for hauling traps, as illustrated in George B. Goode's Fisheries and Fishery Industries of the U.S. *(1887). (Photo:* Mystic Seaport 1972-8-6*)*

Regina M. *sailing in Fishers Island Sound in 1994 after restoration. (Photo: Mary Anne Stets, Mystic Seaport 1994-7-178A)*

Regina M.

SARDINE CARRIER
OFFICIAL NO. 206136

45' 2" x 13' 6"   1900

Carrying herring or mackerel from Maine coastal weirs to the canning factories was her early trade. Originally a sloop, *Regina M.*'s first conversion was to power–a 7-hp Fairbanks Victor engine. Just before coming to Mystic Seaport in 1940, she was converted to pinky schooner appearance, with bulwarks that swept aft past the rudder post. Her origin remains uncertain. Her admeasurement and original U.S. license of 1909 were granted for *Regina M.*, a gas-engine vessel built in Perry, Maine, in 1900. However, the oral tradition of the Passamaquoddy Bay area theorizes that she was built on Indian Island, New Brunswick.

During 1993 and 1994, *Regina M.* was rebuilt by Mystic Seaport and restored to her original sloop configuration, the pinky stern eliminated. She now represents the only hull form known to remain of the sloop-rigged sardine carriers from Passamaquoddy Bay–the region where the U.S. sardine canning industry began in 1875.

STATUS: Rebuilt 1955-64 and restored 1993-94 with all new material; excellent condition.

DONOR: C.D. Mallory, Sr.

FURTHER READING:

Bennett, Paul E. *Sardine Carriers and Seiners.* Freeport, Maine: Paul E. Bennett, 1992.

Burns, L.C. "Maine Herring Carriers." Parts I to VII. *The Quoddy Times.* Eastport, Maine, 1982, 1983.

Chapelle, Howard I. "The Lubec Carryaway Boats." *Yachting*, July, 1940.

——. *American Small Sailing Craft*: New York: W.W. Norton & Co., 1951.

Crowley, Michael. "Sardine Carriers." Parts I and II. *WoodenBoat* 58 and 59, May/June and July/Aug, 1984.

——."Utilitarian Beauty: Sardine Carriers Have Graced the Maine Coast for More Than 100 Years." *Maine Boats and Harbors*, August-September, 1993.

"Fish Curing." *Scientific American*, January 4, 1902.

Fix, Peter. *Handbook for the Shipyard of the Restoration of* Regina M. Mystic Seaport Manuscripts Department, 1994.

Gifford, Leslie. "*Regina*, an Echo from the Past, A Treasure for the Future." *The Log of Mystic Seaport*, Summer, 1994.

Goode, George Brown. *The Fisheries and Fishery Industries of the United States.* Washington, D.C.: U.S. Government Printing Office, 1887.

Hall, Ansley. "The Herring Industry of the Passamaquoddy Region, Me." *Report of the U.S. Commission of Fish and Fisheries for the Year Ending 30 June 1896.* Washington, D.C.: U.S. Government Printing Office, 1898.

"International Passamaquoddy Fisheries Commission." *Science*, April 14, 1931.

Lawrence, E.M. "A History of Sardine Canning." *Canning Trade*, January, 1914.

MacKean, Ray, and Robert Percival. "Sailing Sardine Carrier c. 1910." *The Little Boats: Inshore Fishing Craft of Atlantic Canada.* Fredericton, New Brunswick, Canada: Brunswick Press, 1979.

Maine Sardine Council. *Maine Sardine History: History and Anthology.* New York: D. Appleton & Co., 1911.

Stevenson, Charles H. *The Preservation of Fishery Products for Food.* Washington, D.C.: U.S. Government Printing Office, 1899.

Webber, F.C. "The Maine Sardine Industry." *Bulletin No. 908.* U. S. Dept. of Agriculture. Washington, D.C.: U.S. Government Printing Office, 1921.

Wilbur, Richard, and Ernest Wentworth. *Silver Harvest.* Fredericton, New Brunswick, Canada: Fiddlehead Poetry Books and Goose Lane Publishers, Ltd., 1986.

ACCESSION NO. 1940.338
Plans for 1940.338 are available from Mystic Seaport's Watercraft Plans Collection.

Regina M. under auxiliary power in Rockland Harbor, 1928. (Photo: John F. Leavitt Collection, Mystic Seaport 1967-11-26)

At left is an engraving of a sardine boat being unloaded. From Goode's Fisheries and Fishery Industries, 1887. (Photo: Mary Anne Stets, Mystic Seaport 1978-2-5)

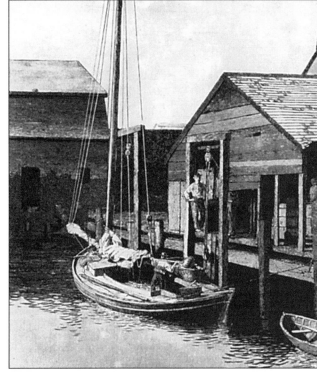

Regina M. lies on the beach at low tide, showing the shape of her hull, her long sternpost, and the aperture cut for a propeller. The caption for this photo in The Motor Boat, *April 10, 1910, noted that she could motor at 7 mph as she made her deliveries of herring to Eastport from as far away as Machias, Maine, and Grand Manan, New Brunswick.* (Photo: Mystic Seaport, 1993-7-20)

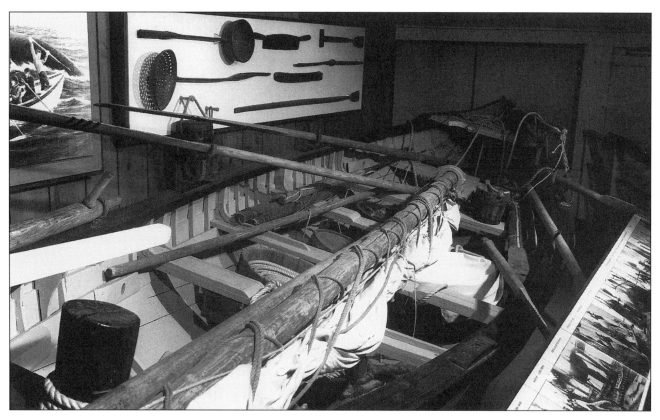

Whaleboat 1968.60 on exhibit in 1975. (Photo: Maynard Bray, Mystic Seaport 1975-5-428)

WHALEBOAT

28' 11" x 6' 6"   ca. 1920

This boat arrived aboard the *Charles W. Morgan* in 1941. Before that her history is unknown, but it is likely that she was off the *John R. Manta,* the *Wanderer,* or the *Charles W. Morgan* herself, as these were the last vessels to sail from New Bedford in search of the whale. Every whaleship carried a few of these boats hung from davits and ready for lowering away whenever a whale was sighted. Whaleboats were developed and refined over many years and at the end became quite standardized. Each was manned by a boatsteerer (whose job it was to harpoon the whale) four other oarsmen, and one of the whaleship's mates who was in command. If the whale was to leeward and there was some wind, sail was hoisted and the whaleboats were sailed—oftentimes right up to the whale—to make their kill. The hinged mast partner made quick work of striking the rig, and oars could be quickly shipped for

maneuvering, at which time a steering oar was run out to replace the rudder.

At first whaleboats were lapstrake, but it was later found best to have a boat with a smooth skin at the waterplane in order to sneak up on the whale without the chortling noise common to lapstrake craft. Battens fastened behind each of the flush-planked seams kept the hulls from drying out and leaking after long periods out of the water.

While the whaleboat itself is strong and flexible, it is also light in weight. But with six men, oars, paddles, a sailing rig, two tubs of line, harpoons, lances, and other gear it becomes much heavier.

Mystic Seaport has four other original whaleboats in its collection, all in only fair condition and in most instances much-repaired. They are similar in size and appearance to 1968.60 above and are therefore not illustrated. Accession numbers of these whaleboats are 1955.679, 1958.690, 1972.327, and 1986.94.1.

STATUS: Restored 1968, approximately 50% original, good condition.

DONOR: Anonymous

FURTHER READING:
Ansel, Willits D. *The Whaleboat, 1850-1970: A Study of Design, Construction, and Use.* Mystic: Mystic Seaport Publications, 1978.

Hall, Elton W. *Sperm Whaling from New Bedford.* New Bedford, Massachusetts: Old Dartmouth Historical Society, 1982.

Murphy, Robert C. *A Dead Whale or a Stove Boat.* New York: Houghton Mifflin, 1967.

Ronnberg, Erik A.R., Jr. *How to Build a Whaleboat.* New Bedford, Massachusetts: The Old Dartmouth Historical Society, 1985.

ACCESSION NO. 1968.60
Plans for 1968.60 are available from Mystic Seaport's Watercraft Plans Collection.

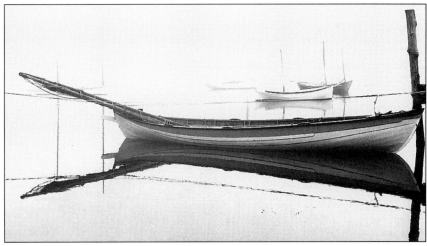

LEONARD MODEL WHALEBOAT REPRODUCTIONS

29' 11" x 6' 6"   1972-73

This boat and two others like her were built by the staff of the Museum's shipyard with several purposes in mind. The *Charles W. Morgan* needed to be outfitted with serviceable boats, having at least one for waterfront demonstration purposes. Willits Ansel (who subsequently built the first boat) was researching a book on whaleboats and felt the experience of building and testing one would add considerable validity to his project; and there was a need for some staff experience in boatbuilding skills. Since the early 1970s, when these boats were built, the *Morgan*'s normal complement of seven boats (five on davits and two spares on the boatskids) has been satisfied with the construction of three Leonard and five Beetle-model whaleboats.

When not in use, mast, boom, and sprit were bundled up, along with the sail, and shoved under an after thwart, leaving most of the rig overhanging the stern. (Photo: Maynard Bray, Mystic Seaport 1975-6-117)

The Leonard shop is believed to have produced the boat from which R.O. Davis of William Hand's office drew up a set of plans sometime before 1930. These plans, now part of the Davis-Hand Collection at MIT, were used to build these boats. The other two boats built to this design are similar in size and appearance and are not illustrated here. Their accession numbers are 1973.449 and 1973.488.

STATUS: Fair condition.

DONOR: Mystic Seaport-built reproduction

FURTHER READING:
Ansel, Willits D. *The Whaleboat, 1850-1970: A Study of Design, Construction, and Use.* Mystic: Mystic Seaport Publications, Inc., 1978.

ACCESSION NO. 1972.883
Plans for 1972.883 are available from Mystic Seaport's Watercraft Plans Collection.

A whaleboat race attracts onlookers among Mystic Seaport's summer visitors. (Photo: Claire White-Peterson, Mystic Seaport 1974-6-127)

(Photo: Maynard Bray, Mystic Seaport 1972-11-85)

The first Museum-built Beetle whaleboat was rigged with a sprit mainsail instead of the sliding gunter rig. (Photo: Ken Mahler, Mystic Seaport 1975-6-110)

BEETLE MODEL WHALEBOAT REPRODUCTION

28' 6" x 6' 4"   1974

Peter Vermilya of the Mystic Seaport staff built this whaleboat, helped out from time to time by a number of persons, among them the English boatbuilder Harold Kimber. She duplicates, as closely as possible, the Beetle whaleboat at The Mariners' Museum, Newport News, Virginia. That boat was one of the last built by the most prolific of all whaleboat builders, Beetle of New Bedford, specifically for The Mariners' Museum about 1930. She has never been used and is a really remarkable craft–so remarkable that Mystic Seaport naval architect Robert C. Allyn, along with Willits Ansel, traveled from Mystic to Newport News to measure the boat and take pictures of her. Upon their return, detailed plans were drawn and this boat was built from them. It's easy to see why Beetle was so successful; this boat is unquestionably better-looking than the Leonard model and, like the original, is superbly put together. She divides her time between the davits of the *Charles W. Morgan* and the waters of the Mystic River. She was rigged with a spritsail instead of the sliding gunter mainsail of the other boats.

Four more of these Beetle-model whaleboats have been built at Mystic Seaport since this one was launched, and one of them has been donated to an Australian maritime museum. Their accession numbers are 1980.148, 1987.80, 1989.36.1, and 1989.36.2.

STATUS: In use, excellent condition.

DONOR: Mystic Seaport-built reproduction

FURTHER READING:

Ansel, Willits D. *The Whaleboat, 1850-1970: A Study of Design, Construction, and Use*. Mystic: Mystic Seaport Publications 1978.

Howland, Llewellyn. *Sou'west and by West of Cape Cod*. Cambridge, Massachusetts: Harvard University Press, 1948.

Ronnberg, Erik A.R., Jr. *How to Build a Whaleboat*. New Bedford, Massachusetts: The Old Dartmouth Historical Society, 1985.

ACCESSION NO. 1974.1027
Plans for 1974.1027 are available from Mystic Seaport's Watercraft Plans Collection.

Sail plan of the Beetle-model whaleboat drawn by R.C. Allyn in 1974.

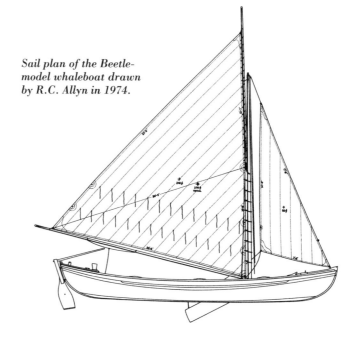

Chapter Three
KETCH-RIGGED

Quiet Tune

AUXILIARY KEEL
DAYSAILER

29' 6" x 7' 10"   1945

L. Francis Herreshoff designed *Quiet Tune* for Edwin Hill, who wanted a beautiful little boat for daysailing along the Maine coast. Hill's Pemaquid harbor mooring allowed him convenient access to both coastal and deepwater sailing grounds, so *Quiet Tune* had to be versatile, able to perform in a variety of conditions. A small gasoline engine (now diesel) got her dependably home after the wind died. Hodgdon Bros. of nearby East Boothbay built this boat along with a couple of Francis Herreshoff's H-28 ketches, and a study of the drawings for the two designs reveal similarities, although *Quiet Tune*'s more elegant hull shape–intended for professional rather than amateur construction–sets her apart from the H-28. Edwin Hill and Herreshoff shared a passion for beautiful boats, and after a decade with *Quiet Tune* Hill commissioned the slightly larger and equally lovely *Araminta*, built by Norman Hodgdon in 1954.

A single person, if reasonably experienced, finds *Quiet Tune* easy to sail, but there's room for as many as five or six, comfortably sprawled in the tub-like cushioned cockpit. From that vantage point, eye level is high enough to see over the low cabin and yet low enough for looking out under the sails and really enjoying the view, as well as the sensation of speed as the water rushes by close at hand. *Quiet Tune* is every bit as sensitive to sail as she is lovely to look at, and if ever there were a representative boat to prove that a thing of beauty is a joy forever, this little ketch would be a leading candidate.

Quiet Tune came to Mystic Seaport in perfect condition, a rare occurrence for donations, having been thoroughly refurbished and refinished by her donor. Shortly before her trip east, she won for him the coveted Opening Day Yacht Inspection Sweepstakes award from the Newport Harbor (California) Yacht Club.

Former owners Barry and Dorothy Thomas sail Quiet Tune *in 1976.*
(**Photo:** Mystic Seaport 1990.37.1043)

STATUS: Restored, in use, excellent condition.

DONOR: Daniel E. and Joan G. Carter, trustees of the Carter Living Trust

FURTHER READING:
Bolger, Philip C. "L. F. Herreshoff, Part II." *WoodenBoat* 56, Jan/Feb, 1984.

Herreshoff, L. Francis. *The Common Sense of Yacht Design.* Jamaica, New York: Caravan-Maritime Books, 1974.

——. *Sensible Cruising Designs.* Camden, Maine: International Marine Publishing Co., 1973.

ACCESSION NO. 1994.31

Canoe yawl *Half Moon* in 1975. *(Photo: Maynard Bray, Mystic Seaport 1975-6-35)*

Half Moon
CANOE YAWL

18' 3" x 5' 5"   ca. 1930

Half Moon was built by A. W. Barlow and Herbert Salisbury of Providence and Pawtucket, Rhode Island, to old drawings of the *Iris* by J. A. Akester which appear in W. P. Stephens's *Canoe and Boat Building* (see Further Reading). She is neither a canoe nor a yawl; however, the name canoe yawl was frequently used to describe this type of one-person cruising boat.

STATUS: Unrestored, some parts missing, fair condition.

DONOR: Captain Elwell B. Thomas
FURTHER READING:
Garden, William. *Yacht Designs*. Camden, Maine: International Marine Publishing Co., 1977. 18'6" William Garden canoe yawl; George F. Holmes canoe yawl.

Herreshoff, L. Francis. *The Compleat Cruiser*. New York: Sheridan House, 1963.

——. *Sensible Cruising Designs*. Camden, Maine: International Marine Publishing Co., 1991. 28' L. F. Herreshoff-designed canoe yawl *Rozinante*.

"Iris, Eighteen-Foot Canoe Yawl." *Yachting*, December, 1933.

Leather, John. *Albert Strange: Yacht Designer and Artist, 1855-1917*. Edinburgh: Pentland Press, 1990.

MacGregor, John. *The Voyage Alone in the Yawl Rob Roy*. London: Rupert Hart-Davis, 1954.

O'Brien, Mike. "*Otter*: An Albert Strange Canoe Yawl." *Small Boat Journal*, Aug/Sept, 1984. Design, comments, plans.

Stephens, W. P. *Canoe and Boat Building: A Complete Manual for Amateurs*. New York: Forest and Stream Publishing Co., 1889.

——. *Traditions and Memories of American Yachting*. New York: Hearst Magazines, 1945, and Brooklin, Maine: WoodenBoat Books, 1989.

Taylor, Roger C. *Good Boats*. Camden, Maine: International Marine Publishing Co., 1977. Contains chapter on the canoe yawl *Iris* with some material published in *Yachting* in December, 1933.

ACCESSION NO. 1959.1209
Plans for 1959.1209 are available from Mystic Seaport's Watercraft Plans Collection.

Plans of the canoe yawl Iris *taken from W. P. Stephens'* Canoe and Boat Building, *1889 edition.* Half Moon *was built from these lines, although her rig was altered somewhat.*

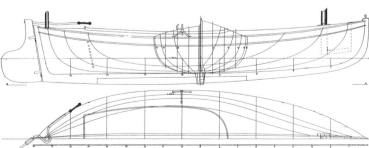

Noman's Land boat in 1973. (Photo: Mary Anne Stets, Mystic Seaport 1973-2-74*)*

Josiah Cleveland, builder and original owner of the Noman's Land boat, in his shop around 1875. (Photo: Courtesy of Charlie Sayle, Mystic Seaport 1972-5-35*)*

Rodney Cleveland aboard his Noman's Land boat. (Photo: Courtesy of Mrs. Rodney Cleveland, Mystic Seaport 1972-2-147*)*

NOMAN'S LAND BOAT

19′9″ x 6′2″   ca. 1882

The name came from a small island off the Massachusetts coast south of Martha's Vineyard, which in the summer (because of its nearness to the fishing grounds) became home to many fishermen and their families. Their colony has long since disappeared, and landing on the island is now prohibited since unexploded bombs, remainders of military target practice, cover the island.

Noman's Land never had much of a harbor, and in bad weather the boats were hauled up on the beach over greased skids by oxen. The Noman's Land boat with its double-ended hull could be launched stern first into the surf and rowed into deep water where sail was set.

Josiah Cleveland built this boat, and it remained in the Cleveland family until acquired by Mystic Seaport. In later years an engine was installed, and the rig was changed to that of a catboat with a gaff sail, but her wet well was not disturbed and remains intact today.

STATUS: Stripped to its original structure, rig missing, fair condition.

DONOR: Purchased from Rodney V. Cleveland with money from the Storrs fund

ACCESSION NO. 1952.1115
Plans for 1952.115 are available from Mystic Seaport's Watercraft Plans Collection.

Orca

NOMAN'S LAND BOAT

19' 9" x 6' 5"   ca. 1882

Of batten-seam rather than lapstrake construction, her hull was built in Fairhaven, Massachusetts, by Delano for Onslow Stuart who took her to his Chilmark shop for finishing. She was never actually used at Noman's Land but fished until about 1920 from the Gay Head area of Martha's Vineyard. *Orca*, too, had an engine and single mast when the donor acquired her in the 1950s. *Orca* is now back to her original rig with two masts, both of which, being short, are easily unstepped. The foremast has a bail at its partners to make the task even easier.

STATUS: Restored by donor in the 1950s, hull rebuilt at Mystic Seaport in 1970, approximately 75% original, good condition.

DONOR: Robert H. Baker

FURTHER READING
for 1952.115 and 1963.592:

Orca *under sail on the Mystic River in 1974. (Photo: Ken Mahler,* Mystic Seaport 1974-10-139)

Allen, Joseph C. *Martha's Vineyard Boats.* New Bedford, Massachusetts: Reynolds Printing, n.d.

Brewington, Dorothy E. R., and M. V. "Some Notes on the Boats of Noman's Land." *The Mariner,* July, 1932.

Cabot, David. "The New England Double Enders." *The American Neptune* 12, April, 1952.

Chapelle, Howard I. *American Small Sailing Craft.* New York: W. W. Norton & Co., 1951.

——. *The National Watercraft Collection.* Washington, D.C.: U. S. Government Printing Office, 1960.

Gardner, John "Comments Here & There: Sailing is made simple in Boston; a Noman's Land boat in your future?" *National Fisherman,* Sept, 1975.

Goode, George B. *The Fisheries and Fishery Industries of the United States.* Sect. V, Vol. II. Washington, D.C.: U. S. Government Printing Office, 1887.

Herreshoff, L. Francis. *The Compleat Cruiser.* New York: Sheridan House, 1963.

Howland, Llewellyn. *Sou'west and by West of Cape Cod.* Cambridge, Massachusetts: Harvard University Press, 1948. Vivid description of life at Noman's Land including use of a boat.

Huntington, Frederick R. "A Noman's Land Double Ender." *Yachting,* April, 1932.

Huntington, Gale. "Nomansland, Salt Codfish and the Nomansland Boat." *The Dukes County Intelligencer,* Nov, 1975.

Leavens, John M. "The Cat-rigged Island Double Ender." *National Fisherman,* Aug, 1976.

——. "The Noman's Land Boat." *The Log of Mystic Seaport,* October, 1976.

Morris, E. P. *The Fore and Aft Rig in America.* New Haven, Connecticut: Yale University Press, 1927.

Taylor, Roger C. *Good Boats.* Camden, Maine: International Marine Publishing Co., 1977.

Taylor, William H. "The Nomansland Sailboat." *Yachting,* March, 1932.

Wood, Annie M. *Noman's Land, Isle of Romance.* New Bedford, Massachusetts: Reynolds Printing, 1931.

ACCESSION NO. 1963.592
Plans for 1963.592 are available from Mystic Seaport's Watercraft Plans Collection.

Glory Anna II sailing in the Mystic River after her restoration at Mystic Seaport. (Photo: Russell A. Fowler, Mystic Seaport 1971-11-144)

Glory Anna II

BLOCK ISLAND COWHORN REPRODUCTION

23' 0" x 9' 0"   1948

Proving that an open cockpit can be seaworthy, cowhorns were used both winter and summer in the rough waters of Block Island Sound. Among small working vessels only the pinky seems to enjoy such a reputation for seaworthiness.

Before the Old Harbor breakwater was built in 1873, cowhorns (which they resembled because of their high ends) were numerous, as they could be hauled up on the beach during bad weather. Larger craft having the same appearance and known simply as Block Island boats gradually displaced the cowhorns after that date, however.

The originals had all vanished by the time artist Paule Loring became interested in them. But working from models and photographs and with the help of H. I. Chapelle and others, he conceived this reproduction, built in Wickford, Rhode Island, by L. Howard. From the start her deck layout was different–altered to suit Loring's needs–and by 1970 she sported a high pilot house and a cut-down ketch rig. Saving only the hull, the Museum modified her appearance to that of the original *Glory Anna.*

Paule Loring was best known and loved for his "Dud Sinker" cartoons which were published in each issue of *National Fisherman.*

STATUS: Rebuilt and restored to original configuration, in use, good condition.

DONOR: Purchased for Mystic Seaport by Thomas R. Wilcox

FURTHER READING:
Ansel, Willits D. "Loring's Cowhorn Sails Again." *National Fisherman,* April, 1972.

——. "The Repair and Replacement of Stems." *WoodenBoat* 39, Mar/Apr, 1981.

Cabot, David. "The New England Double Enders." *The American Neptune* 12, April, 1952.

Chapelle, Howard I. *American Small Sailing Craft.* New York: W. W. Norton & Co., 1951.

"Pole Harbor," Block Island, where Cowhorns were kept. Cowhorns were replaced by larger Block Island boats after the breakwater (background) was built. (Photo: Courtesy of Mrs. Paule Loring, Mystic Seaport 1970-10-226)

The original Block Island Cowhorn Glory Anna *as she lay rotting on the beach near Cormorant Cove on Block Island about 1930. (Photo: Courtesy of Mrs. Paule Loring, Mystic Seaport 1970-10-238)*

—. *The National Watercraft Collection.* Washington, D.C.: U. S. Government Printing Office, 1960.

Davis, Charles G. *Ships of the Past.* Salem, Massachusetts: The Maritime Research Society, 1929. Has chapter dealing with the larger Block Island boats; includes plans.

Hall, Henry. *Report on Shipbuilding Industry of the United States.* Washington, D.C.: U. S. Government Printing Office, 1884.

Herreshoff, L. Francis. *The Compleat Cruiser.* New York: Sheridan House, 1963.

Holle, Beverley. "The Block Island Cowhorn." *WoodenBoat* 22, May/June, 1978.

Hyslop, John. *Forest and Stream,* Jan 3, 1884.

Morris, E. P. *The Fore and Aft Rig in America.* New Haven, Connecticut: Yale University Press, 1927.

Nicholson, Paul C. *The Block Island Double Ender.* Rhode Island Historical Society Collections (Oct 1923).

Ritchie, Ethel Colt. *Block Island Lore and Legends.* Block Island: Norman Associates, 1955.

Taylor, Roger C. *Good Boats.* Camden, Maine: International Marine Publishing Co., 1977.

Thompson, Winfield M. "Adriaen Block, His Yacht and His Island." *The Rudder,* March, 1912.

—. "Roaring Bessie." *The Rudder,* April, 1912.

ACCESSION NO. 1970.763

Cadet as she arrived at Mystic Seaport in 1955. (Photo: From the collection of Mystic Seaport, Mystic Seaport 1955.318G)

Cadet

DOUBLE-ENDED HAMPTON BOAT

23' 4" x 6' 6"   ca. 1846

Cadet afloat on the Mystic River after restoration. (Photo: Louis S. Martel, Mystic Seaport 1955.318A)

Rev. Elijah Kellogg (1813-1901) had this boat built, probably by Ebenezer Durgin of Birch Island, and owned her throughout his life. She was found stored in the old Kellogg barn in the mid-1950s, and damaged such that total rebuilding was thought necessary. For Kellogg, best known for his 30-odd adventure books for boys, this boat furnished transportation from his home in Harpswell, Maine, to the many islands in Casco Bay. Many others like her were used for fishing. In 1977 a working reproduction of this boat was built by The Restoration Shop of the Maine Maritime Museum.

STATUS: Restored, little original, good condition.

DONOR: Olive French Kellogg

ACCESSION NO. 1955.318

Plans for 1955.318 are available from Mystic Seaport's Watercraft Plans Collection.

Cuspidor under sail at Bailey Island.
(Photo: Courtesy of Mrs. F. P. Luckey, Mystic Seaport 1967-2-8A)

Cuspidor
SQUARE-STERNED HAMPTON BOAT

17' 4" x 6' 0"   1902

Built by Capt. D. Perry Sinnett on Bailey Island, Maine, *Cuspidor* is typical of hundreds of such boats used for fishing and hauling lobster traps along the coast. Later Hampton boats, such as *Ocean Queen* (1988.106), show transition to power as forerunners of the modern lobster boat. *Cuspidor* was built as a pleasure boat for the late Dr. Franklin P. Luckey of Paterson, New Jersey, and Bailey Island.

STATUS: Restored 1967, approximately 90% original, good condition.

DONOR: Mrs. F. P. Luckey

ACCESSION NO. 1961.916

Plans for 1961.916 are available from Mystic Seaport's Watercraft Plans Collection.

Hampton boat Cuspidor *in 1975. (Photo: Maynard Bray, Mystic Seaport 1975-6-33)*

David Perry Sinnett's boat shop at Bailey Island, Maine. (Photo: Courtesy of Mrs. F. P. Luckey, Mystic Seaport 1967-2-80)

FURTHER READING FOR 1955.318, 1961.916, 1979.211, AND 1988.106 (as applicable):

The Apprenticeshop of the Bath Marine Museum. *The Crotch Island Pinky.* Bath, Maine: 1975. Useful as background because of the close resemblance between Crotch Island pinkys and the double-ended Hampton boats.

Audubon, John James. *Delineations of American Scenery and Character,* New York:. G.A. Baker and Co., 1926.

Bishop, W. H. *Fish and Men in the Maine Islands.* New York: Harper, 1885. Reprint from *Harper's Magazine,* Aug/Sept, 1880.

Bodge, J. "Old Times at Harpswell." *Maine Coast Fisherman,* Feb, 1954.

Cabot, David. "The New England Double Enders." *The American Neptune* 12, April, 1952.

Chapelle, Howard I. *American Small Sailing Craft.* New York: W. W. Norton & Co., 1951.

——. "The Hampden Boat." *Yachting,* July, 1938.

——. *The National Watercraft Collection.* Washington, D.C.: U. S. Government Printing Office, 1960.

Doughty, Jean. "Muffin Goes From Fish to Boats." *National Fisherman,* July, 1968. A good write-up on Sinnett family history.

Elden, A. O. "Power Boating in Casco Bay, Maine." *Yachting,* April, 1907.

Emerson, Charles. *The American Neptune,* April, 1941. Page 173 has a letter containing evidence that the square-stern Hampton boat descends from the double-ender.

"A Fundy Fishing Boat." *The Rudder,* Jan, 1900.

Gardner, John. "The Elusive Hampton Boat." *Small Boat Journal,* Nov, 1979. Written after spending 10 days with Bob Cooper of Nova Scotia studying shad boats.

——. "Comments Here and There." *National Fisherman,* June, 1989.

——. *Wooden Boats To Build And Use.* Mystic, Connecticut: Mystic Seaport Publications, 1996.

Hall, Carl F. "Looking Back One Hundred Years." *The Sea Breeze,* April, 1962.

Kellogg, Elijah. *The Young Shipbuilders of Elm Island.* Boston: Lee & Shepard, 1898. Page 259 makes reference to a boat of this type.

Lazarus, Paul. "Capable West Point Skiff has Made an Indelible Mark on Maine Fisheries." *National Fisherman,* May, 1988. The Hampton boat compared to the West Point skiff.

Lipke, Paul. "Traditional Survivors." *Small Boat Journal,* Oct/Nov, 1988.

Malloy, Anne. "Elijah Kellogg of Elm Island." *Down East,* June, 1948.

Millet, W. H. "Original Hampton Boats." *Maine Coast Fisherman,* June, 1984.

Morris, E. P. *The Fore and Aft Rig in America.* New Haven: Yale University Press, 1927.

Post, Robert C. *The Tancook Whalers, Origins, Rediscovery, and Revival.* Bath, Maine: Maine Maritime Museum, 1985. This monograph discusses the migration of the New England double-enders.

Soule, Phelps. "The Hampton Boat." *The American Neptune* 3, April, 1943.

Watson, Warren. "The Hampton Boat of Casco Bay." *Motor Boat,* January 25, 1909.

Mystic Seaport's Casco Bay Hampton. (Photo: Mary Anne Stets, Mystic Seaport 1980-2-40)

HAMPTON BOAT

20' 4" x 6' 1"   ca. 1910

Casco Bay's fishing fleet of Hampton boats was one of the first to be successfully powered, and this square-sterned, strip-planked boat was once one of them. Conversion happened quickly after 1903. Captain David Perry Sinnett of Bailey Island, the builder of *Cuspidor* (1961.916), in a letter to *Motor Boat* in June of 1908 sketched the history: "Previous to the year 1877 the boats used by the fishermen of Casco Bay were of the whaleboat type, built in Hampton, N. H., all of lap-streak construction. I had built a few of the square sterned type. During that year a fisherman came to me and asked if I could build him a smooth hull boat, very strong. I replied that I thought I could so I made a model, got the stock together, and built a boat of strips, 1 ½ x 1 inch, nailed one on to the other and put in ten pairs of timbers, steam bent. This was the first smooth-seam boat built of narrow strips that was ever constructed in Casco Bay.... Since that time I have built one hundred and

seventy five of these strip-work boats .... Other builders soon began to build them, so that today there are very few other kinds built in the bay.

"All of these are built for motors of from 3 to 6 hp. I think there are more than three hundred of this type in use in Casco Bay....Five years ago there was only one motorboat in the bay, and now there is only one sailboat.

"As an illustration of the speed and the weathering qualities of the Casco Bay Hampton, I can speak of the following incident. On the fourth of last April a 24-foot boat, equipped with a 5 ½ hp. motor, went out to the fishing grounds from the island fifteen miles to the leeward. Shortly after the boat reached the grounds it began to blow hard, developing into a forty-mile-an-hour northwesterly gale. This boat made the run home, against the wind, in two hours and forty minutes.

"Casco Bay Hamptons are built in sizes from 16 to 32 feet long, and the price ranges from five to twelve dollars per foot."

Other builders were Alpheus Griffin on Cliff Island, Frank Johnson of Bailey Island, Walter Brewer of Peaks Island, and John Pettengill of Cliff. Any one of them could have built this boat, whose history is unknown before she was acquired by the Penobscot Marine Museum. The presence of engine mounts seems proof of original construction for, or conversion to, power; she was also fitted to carry a spritsail on a mast near the bow as well as oars. As gas engines grew in size, Casco Bay Hampton boats had their sterns filled out and became one of the ancestors of today's Maine lobster boat.

STATUS: Original, poor condition, interior missing.

SOURCE: Penobscot Marine Museum

ACCESSION NO. 1979.211

Early power Hampton boat similar to 1979.211. (Photo: Mystic Seaport 1993.17.492)

Ocean Queen
BAY OF FUNDY BOAT
24' 1" x 7' 9"   pre-1900

In the nineteenth century, double-ended, ketch-rigged fishing boats were found from New York to Newfoundland. All shared common ancestry in the colonial shallops, but they took on regional styles and names. The immediate ancestry of this Bay of Fundy boat may involve boats of the Maine shad fishery which, according to local legend, seem to have been brought east. Thus these boats, locally called "pinkies," may be closely related to Hampton boats like *Cadet* (1955.318). Whatever the evolution, the type and the fishery were speedily taken over by local fishermen and builders, who had a thriving business by 1900.

Ocean Queen is a carvel-planked double-ender with a lapped sheer strake. A feature peculiar to the Bay of Fundy is a wide plank keel, which let these boats sit upright when the Bay emptied out its 40' of tide. William G. (Greg) Hall and his son built *Ocean Queen* in their shop in Portapique Village, Colchester County, Nova Scotia. They were the chief builders of the type, both smooth and lapstrake. Their later boats went to square sterns in an evolution similar to the Casco Bay Hampton boats. In 1900 alone the Halls added seven boats to the local fleet of 20. On *Ocean Queen*, an engine box amidships for a make-and-break engine (for instance the Lunenburg-built *Acadia*), and a cuddy under the foredeck, were later additions, but she kept her centerboard and trunk. Originally these boats carried two loose-footed spritsails permanently lashed to the masts and a jib set flying. Only one set of spars, consisting of a mast and sprit, came with this boat.

STATUS: Unrestored, fair condition.

DONOR: Robert Cooper

ACCESSION NO. 1988.106

Ocean Queen. *(Photo: Maynard Bray, Mystic Seaport 1988.106)*

Owner and builder William G. Hall and his wife Jerusha are shown in a square-stern Bay of Fundy boat, circa 1893-95. (Photo: John Gardner Collection)

KINGSTON LOBSTER BOAT

19' 0" x 6' 3"   ca. 1890

The nearby yacht-building yards of the Boston area influenced the lobstermen along the Massachusetts South Shore to take up racing with their workboats. After 1885, when this fever took hold, the local builders started to adopt some of the speed-giving features of the larger yachts. They refined their products to become the speediest and most responsive of all commercial sailing watercraft, known commonly as the Kingston lobster boat. The boats of Edward Ransom were particularly fast and beautiful, as Chapelle's drawings show. Other builders, however, didn't succeed as well in producing superior boats, as was the case with William Bates, who built this one. While her sailing qualities can only be guessed at, it is doubtful if, without the usual firmness to her quarters, she could lug enough sail to be very fast. Most of these boats were half-decked, necessary to keep them dry no doubt. But the deck eliminated one of the

The Kingston lobster boat in 1958. (Photo: Louis Martel, Mystic Seaport 1958-4-47)

great conveniences of most other two-masted spritsail boats for it made it impossible to strike the foremast while underway and required a man to climb up out of the cockpit to shorten or furl the sail.

Like the *Annie A. Fuller*, this boat is strip-planked. She has a wet well on either side of the centerboard trunk in which her catch of fish was carried.

STATUS: Restored 1969, approximately 80% original, rig missing, good condition.

DONOR: Robert Hanckel

ACCESSION NO. 1956.1544

Plans for 1956.1544 are available from Mystic Seaport's Watercraft Plans Collection.

The Kingston lobster boat 1956.1544 as found in 1956 near Scituate, Massachusetts. (Photo: From the collection of Mystic Seaport, Mystic Seaport 1956-6-33)

Annie A. Fuller in 1975. (Photo: Maynard Bray, Mystic Seaport 1975-6-14)

Annie A. Fuller

KINGSTON LOBSTER BOAT

15′ 8″ x 5′ 5″   1872

This was Capt. Parker Hall's first boat; the coasting schooner *Alice S. Wentworth* was his last. During his long career in the coasting trade he owned many others, which he usually sailed single-handed all up and down the New England coast. He was quite a character, as John Leavitt describes him, and was well-known among coastermen. *Annie A. Fuller* was named for an early ladyfriend, and it is reported that he gave the boat to another friend, Capt. Freeman Closson, in later years. The boat was built on the South Shore of Massachusetts by Arthur Rogers and is an early version of what Chapelle calls the Kingston lobster boat. The more recent boats were longer and racier, with counter sterns and hollow garboards.

STATUS: Restored 1970, approximately 80% original, rig missing, good condition.

DONOR: William Bell Watkins

FURTHER READING FOR 1963.818 AND 1956.1544:

Barnard, Wm. L. "The Lobster Boats of Plymouth." *Boating*, 1907. Reprinted in *WoodenBoat* 1, Sept, 1974.

Chapelle, Howard I. *American Small Sailing Craft*. New York: W. W. Norton & Co., 1951.

Gardner, John. "Kingston Lobster Boats." *National Fisherman*, July, 1969.

Jones, Henry M. *Ships of Kingston*. Plymouth, Massachusetts: The Memorial Press of Plymouth, Massachusetts, 1926.

Leavitt, John F. *Wake of the Coasters*. Middletown, Connecticut: Wesleyan University Press for The Marine Historical Association, Inc., 1970; Mystic Seaport Publications, 1984.

ACCESSION NO. 1963.818

Plans for 1963.818 are available from Mystic Seaport's Watercraft Plans Collection.

Parker Hall at the helm of his first boat, Annie A. Fuller.
(Photo: From the collection of Mystic Seaport, Mystic Seaport 1964-4-43)

NEW HAVEN OYSTER TONGING SHARPIE

35' 4" x 6' 11"   ca. 1890

Like the dugouts (1946.643 and 1946.644) the sharpies were used for oyster tonging; however, they were a refinement responsive to changing needs and advancing technology. The tonger had to travel farther away for oysters as the beds near home became exhausted, so he needed a better sailing boat. Scarcity of large trees and an abundance of sawmills made a built-up boat more practical than one fashioned from a single log. Inexpensive, shallow, and easy to handle, the larger sharpies rigged as cat ketches proved popular not only with the tongers of Connecticut, primarily of Fair Haven, but with the oystermen in the Chesapeake and southern Atlantic coast as well.

New Haven oyster sharpie under sail in the Mystic River in 1974. (Photo: Ken Mahler, Mystic Seaport 1974-10-173)

STATUS: Rebuilt as a condition of gift in the 1950s; little original, in use, good condition.

DONOR: Ernest E. Ball

ACCESSION NO. 1947.597
Plans for 1947.597 are available from Mystic Seaport's Watercraft Plans Collection.

NEW HAVEN OYSTER TONGING SHARPIE

34' 11" x 7' 4"   ca. 1880

This boat is much like 1947.597, both representing the largest size of tonging sharpie, carrying 150-175 bushels of oysters and rigged with two masts. For winter work or in heavy weather, however, a single mast could be used, stepped just ahead of the cockpit. When the wind was too light for sailing, these sharpies could be either rowed or sculled.

STATUS: Unrestored, original, structurally weak.

DONOR: Exchange with The Mariners' Museum

New Haven oyster sharpie on exhibit in 1975. (Photo: Claire White-Peterson, Mystic Seaport 1975-9-154)

FURTHER READING FOR 1947.597 AND 1974.1031:

Chapelle, Howard I. *American Small Sailing Craft.* New York: W. W. Norton & Co., 1951.

———. *Migrations of an American Boat Type.* USNM Bulletin 22, Washington, D.C.: U. S. Government Printing Office, 1961.

———. *The National Watercraft Collection.* Washington, D.C.: U. S. Government Printing Office, 1960.

———. "The New Haven Sharpie." *Yachting,* Jan, 1927.

Hall, Henry. *Report on The Shipbuilding Industry of the United States.* Washington, D.C.: U. S. Government Printing Office, 1881.

Ingersoll, Ernest. *The Oyster Industry: Tenth Census of the United States.* Washington, D.C.: U. S. Government Printing Office, 1881.

Kochiss, John. *Oystering from New York to Boston.* Middletown, Connecticut: Wesleyan University Press for Mystic Seaport, 1974.

———. "Some Aspects of the Sharpie and Its Work." *The Log of Mystic Seaport,* January, 1976.

Morris, E. P. *The Fore and Aft Rig in America.* New Haven, Connecticut: Yale University Press, 1927.

Stephens, W. P. "The Sharpie." *Yachting,* January, 1927.

Four rigged models of oyster sharpies are in Mystic Seaport's collections, 1947.475, 1954.1511, 1959.1196, and 1979.194.

ACCESSION NO. 1974.1031

An engraving from Scribner's Monthly in 1878 shows sharpies working an oyster bed in western Long Island Sound. (Photo: Judy Beisler, Mystic Seaport 1997-2-15)

Chapter Four
SCHOONER-
AND
SQUARE-RIGGED

Brilliant *sails in a brisk breeze in 1988. (Photo: Mary Anne Stets,* Mystic Seaport 1988-6-337*)*

Brilliant

SCHOONER-YACHT
OFFICIAL NO. 231472

61' 6" x 14' 8"   1932

"The schooner *Brilliant* is the seagoing emissary of Mystic Seaport. Although she has several fine records for speed, acquired in her early days, *Brilliant*'s great claim to fame lies in the program she has served..."–Captain F.E. "Biff" Bowker in the *Log of Mystic Seaport,* Summer, 1971, describing *Brilliant*'s sail-training program for teenagers,

which began in 1953, and is the oldest sail-training program of its type in the U.S. This program served Mariner Girl Scouts from the mid-1950s to the mid-1980s; it is now open to all teenage sailors, male and female. With a professional captain, mate, and cook, *Brilliant* continues to take nine teenagers to sea in the summer months. In the spring and fall, adults 20 years and older have their chance to take the

helm and set sail.

Luck has been with *Brilliant* all her life, and shows up particularly in the good care she has been given. No trace of a seam shows in her flawless topsides, her teak deck and varnished teak trim look like new, and below decks one would find things every bit as good. Now in her eighth decade, *Brilliant* symbolizes, perhaps better than any other craft at Mystic Seaport,

Brilliant *under sail during her Girl Scout Mariner Program years. (Photo: Pam Lott,* Mystic Seaport 1985-12-34*)*

the benefits of timely, intelligent, and unfailing maintenance. But her good luck reaches beyond; the bottomed-out stock market of 1932 didn't stop Walter Barnum from ordering a first-class yacht; or from having the young and talented Olin Stephens prepare a custom design; or from encouraging the marvelously skilled workers at Henry B. Nevins's City Island yard to take whatever time was needed to do the best work they knew how. Even in her day, *Brilliant* stood out as superior. Now with the senses dulled by look-alike boats of fiberglass and aluminum, *Brilliant* turns heads wherever she goes, rekindling one's appreciation for beauty, good taste, and craftsmanship.

Staysail schooners with Marconi mainsails were the rage when *Brilliant* came out, but in spite of her old-fashioned gaff-headed rig, she made an extraordinarily fast passage to England in 1933, logging an average of 200 miles a day for nine consecutive days. But the wholesome *Brilliant* was more of a cruiser than a racer, even though Briggs Cunningham had her masts lengthened and her sail area increased when he bought her after World War II –following her stint as a Coast Guard picket patrol vessel during the war.

Since she has joined Mystic Seaport's fleet in 1953, *Brilliant* has carried more than 8,000 crew members in her several sail-training programs, and has sailed the equivalent in miles of five times around the Earth. In 1997 *she* was named Sail Training Ship of the Year by the American Sail Training Association.

A photo taken during construction in the Nevins yard gives an idea of the careful workmanship and fine materials that went into Brilliant. *(Photo: Rosenfeld Collection,* Mystic Seaport 1965-8-23F*)*

The finished main cabin with its mahogany cabinet work. (Photo: Rosenfeld Collection, Mystic Seaport 1973-6-49*)*

She has been a consistent winner in classic yacht races during the past 25 years. In 1997, for example, *Brilliant* finished first in class and first in fleet in Nantucket's Opera House Cup contest, with more than 50 yachts participating. In the summer of 2000 *Brilliant* finished first in fleet and first in class, on corrected time, in the Cutty Sark Tall Ships Race 2000 from Halifax to the Solent in England.

Brilliant's good life at Mystic Seaport is due in great measure to the interest of her former owner, Briggs Cunningham, who subsidized her expenses for many years, to Captain "Biff" Bowker, who conscientiously skippered her and superintended her care from 1962 to 1983, and to Captain George Moffett, who continues the tradition.

STATUS: In use, mostly original, excellent condition.

DONOR: Briggs S. Cunningham

FURTHER READING:

Bowker, Francis E. "To Know the Sea." *The Log of Mystic Seaport*, Summer, 1971.

——. "A Special Sort of Boat: The Schooner *Brilliant*." *The Log of Mystic Seaport*, Summer, 1982.

Fox, Uffa. *Sailing, Seamanship and Yacht Construction.* New York: Charles Scribner's Sons, 1934. Contains some worthwhile comments about *Brilliant* in an entire chapter devoted to her. Her major plans, although redrawn by the author, are included as well.

Gerard, Philip. *Brilliant Passage.* Mystic, Connecticut: Mystic Seaport Publications, 1989. A novelist's account of a cruise from Halifax to Mystic Seaport.

Loomis, Alfred F. "Two Hundred a Day." *Yachting*, October, 1933. A first-hand account of *Brilliant*'s transatlantic passage.

Nevins, Henry B. "Economy Versus Cheapness." *Yachting*, September, 1933. Contemporary comments by *Brilliant*'s builder on the fine points of a yacht built to the highest standards.

Taylor, Roger. *Still More Good Boats.* Camden, Maine: International Marine Publishing Co., 1981. Chapter 15 is an appreciation of *Brilliant*.

Van Mesdag, Martin. "*Brilliant*—Olin's Shining Example." *Classic Boat*, July, 1998. An especially good history, with emphasis on her design and construction.

Wilson, Jon. "Sailing the Schooner *Brilliant*." *WoodenBoat* 122, Jan/Feb, 1995. Jon Wilson's appreciative account of *Brilliant* and her crew on a cruise from Rockland, Maine, to Nova Scotia and back.

ACCESSION NO. 1987.77

In a photo taken at the Nevins yard on October 18, 1931, Brilliant's *hull is planked and about half caulked. (Photo: Rosenfeld Collection, Mystic Seaport 1965-8-23D)*

Australia under sail in the Chester River, Maryland, in 1935. (Photo: Frank Moorshead, Jr., Mystic Seaport 1997.14)

Australia (ex-*Alma, Ella Alida*)

COASTING SCHOONER
OFFICIAL NO. 25

72' 5" x 19' 4"   1862

When *Australia* came to Mystic in 1951 one story told was that she took part in the War of 1812 as the *Alma*. No such thing happened; this vessel is not that old. She was built in Patchogue, Long Island, in 1862 as a humble merchant vessel that her New York owners named *Ella Alida*. She was sold within a year to British owners who renamed her *Alma*. She is not the *Alma* of 1812. During the Civil War she was captured by the USS *Seneca* off the Georgia coast trying to run the Union blockade. She was sold to a Chesapeake Bay shipping firm, renamed *Australia*, and spent the next 78 years carrying cargo. She was lengthened 10' in 1879. In 1942, after an almost total rebuilding, she went into service as a yacht for the donor and her husband on Chesapeake Bay.

After arriving in Mystic the schooner was a floating barracks for Mystic Seaport's Mariner Program for ten years. *Australia*, a hundred years old by then, was not in good shape. In the early 1960s she had to be hauled out because she leaked so badly. An attempt was made at restoration but then abandoned once the degree of prior rebuilding and change was realized. Today she is a relic through which visitors may walk and see how wooden vessels are constructed.

STATUS: Relic, less than 50% original, poor condition.
DONOR: Mrs. E. Paul duPont
FURTHER READING:
Jackson, Melvin H., editor, *Historic American Merchant Marine Survey.* Salem, New Hampshire: Ayer Company, 1983.

Leavitt, John F. *Wake of the Coasters.* Middletown, Connecticut: Wesleyan University Press for Mystic Seaport, 1970, Mystic Seaport Publications, 1984.

Lyman, John. *Log Chips.* Vol. 2, No. 7, 76-80.

Maloney, John. "Sailing Into Her Third Century." *This Week*, March 19, 1939.

——. "America's Oldest Vessel." *Yachting*, June, 1939.

Smith, Edward W., compiler. *Workaday Schooners.* Camden, Maine: International Marine Publishing Co., 1975.

Snediker, Quentin, and Ann Jensen. *Chesapeake Bay Schooners.* Centerville, Maryland: Tidewater Publishers, 1992.

Documentation of *Australia*'s history and her confusion as the *Alma* is available in the G.W. Blunt White Library at Mystic Seaport as an information bulletin.

ACCESSION NO. 1951.4509

The hull of Australia, on exhibit at Mystic Seaport, is used to illustrate wooden-vessel construction. (Photo: Mary Anne Stets, Mystic Seaport 1974-1-192*)*

This model of Australia was completed in 1975 by staff modelmaker Ray Pendleton. (Photo: Mary Anne Stets, Mystic Seaport 1975.451*)*

129

L.A. Dunton at her Mystic Seaport berth in 1969. (Photo: R.A. Fowler, Mystic Seaport 1969-6-33)

L.A. Dunton

GLOUCESTER FISHING SCHOONER
OFFICIAL NO. 221150

123' 0" x 24' 11"   1921

The American fishing schooner, of which this vessel is almost the last surviving example, enjoyed a worldwide reputation for speed and beauty. These vessels combined a strong graceful hull with large carrying capacity, and a tall but simple rig that could carry a great spread of canvas. Yet once on the fishing grounds a schooner like the *Dunton* could be snugged down to carry only three fairly small sails, making it possible for the captain and cook alone to jog her back and forth while her "brood" of dories was off fishing.

There were ten of these dories,

each manned by a crew of two. They were launched from the *Dunton*'s deck early in the morning to set their baited trawls, often making several sets before returning in late afternoon to clean a deckload of fish. Fog and sudden snow squalls made for anxious times, and lost dories were not uncommon.

The *Dunton* was built by the Arthur D. Story shipyard in Essex, Massachusetts–both the builder and the town synonymous with the Gloucester fishing fleet–and designed by Thomas McManus. Felix Hogan had her built and was her first master, usually fishing for halibut in summer and haddock and cod in winter. Hogan installed an auxiliary engine in 1922, but by then

the legendary fishing schooners were on their way out. The *Dunton* was laid up in 1932. In 1934 she was sold to Newfoundland interests and fished until 1955, twice carrying salt cod across the Atlantic to Portugal. She was ultimately repowered and became a freighter carrying just enough sail to steady her. Such was her state in 1963 when she was acquired by Mystic Seaport.

Within a year her appearance had been altered to what it was originally and she was placed on exhibit. In the early 1970s the long task of "retopping" her began. It was completed in 1977 and resulted in nearly all new wood above the waterline.

The Dunton *is launched from the A.D. Story yard in Essex, Massachusetts, in 1921.*
(Photo: Courtesy of Dana Story, Mystic Seaport 1964-2-26*)*

L.A. Dunton *on the fishing grounds with crew aft baiting up trawls. The shortened rig, used when jogging, could be handled by only a few men. (Photo:* Mystic Seaport 1964-2-28*)*

Showing off her high stern and fine sheer, the L.A. Dunton lies at the Boston Fish Pier, ca. 1929. Equipped with power by this time, she has a riding sail in place of her big mainsail with its 75-foot boom. (Photo: Courtesy of Dana Story, Mystic Seaport 1991-12-55)

STATUS: Restored 1963-77. Original below waterline. Good condition.

DONOR: Mystic Seaport purchase

FURTHER READING:

Chapelle, Howard I. *The American Fishing Schooner, 1825-1935*. New York: W. W. Norton & Co., 1973.

Church, Albert Cook. *American Fishermen*. New York: W.W. Norton & Co., 1940.

Dunne, W.M.P. *Thomas F. McManus and the American Fishing Schooners*. Mystic, Connecticut: Mystic Seaport Publications, 1994. An award-winning biography of the *L.A. Dunton*'s designer.

Garland, Joseph E. *Down to the Sea: The Fishing Schooners of Gloucester*. Boston: David R. Godine, 1983.

German, Andrew W. *Down on T Wharf*. Mystic, Connecticut: Mystic Seaport Publications, 1982.

——. "Life on Board the *L.A. Dunton*." *The Log of Mystic Seaport*, Summer, 1996.

Goldie, George S. "A Winter's Fishing Trip to Georges." *Yachting*, November and December, 1910. A marvelous firsthand account of a trip in the schooner *Lizzie M. Stanley*.

Kleinschmidt, James. "Last Voyage of the *L.A. Dunton*." *The Log of Mystic Seaport*, January, 1964. See also the April 1964 issue for a description of the first phase of her restoration.

McFarland, Raymond. *The Masts of Gloucester*. New York: W.W. Norton & Co., 1947.

Pidgeon, Roy W. "A Fishing Trip to the Western Banks on the Schooner Mayflower." *Yachting*, April, 1922.

Pierce, Wesley George. *Goin' Fishing'*. Salem, Massachusetts: Marine Research Society, 1934.

Story, Dana. *Frame Up: The Story of Essex, Its Shipyards and Its People*. Barre, Massachusetts: Barre Publishing Company, 1964.

——. *The Shipbuilders of Essex*. Gloucester, Massachusetts: Ten Pound Island, 1995.

Thomas, Gordon W. *Fast and Able*. Gloucester, Massachusetts: 350th Anniversary Celebration, Inc., 1973.

ACCESSION NO. 1963.1705
Plans for 1963.1705 are available from Mystic Seaport's Watercraft Plans Collection.

Captain Felix J. Hogan (ca. 1872-1951) at the wheel of the L.A. Dunton *during a trip for halibut, ca. 1924. A Newfoundlander, Hogan came to Massachusetts as a young man and made a name for himself in command of several schooners before he and a group of investors built the* Dunton *in 1921. During the Great Depression he laid her up and retired ashore. His son Felix took this photo. (Photo: Courtesy of Hogan family, Mystic Seaport 1984-10-147)*

The Dunton *is shown at Gloucester about 1932. (Photo: Courtesy of Charlie Sayle, Mystic Seaport 1964-1-9E)*

Part of the long, laborious task of retopping the old schooner is shown here, in a photo taken in Mystic Seaport's Henry B. duPont Preservation Shipyard during the winter of 1972-73. (Photo: L.D. Olin, Mystic Seaport 1973-4-195)

The Charles W. Morgan *at sea in her whaling days. (Photo: A.E. Packard. Mystic Seaport 1978.207)*

Charles W. Morgan

WHALESHIP
OFFICIAL NO. 5380

113' 11" x 27' 8"   1841

In 80 years, from her launching in 1841 until the end of her last voyage in 1921, the *Morgan* made a record 37 voyages which earned a total of $1,400,000. Outlasting all others of her type, she is now the treasured symbol of Mystic Seaport.

The events of her long life have been well-recorded, and the more significant of these are listed here:

1841 (July)—Launched from the New Bedford shipyard owned by Jethro and Zachariah Hillman and named for her principal owner, Charles Waln Morgan. She was ship-rigged when new.

1841 (September)—Sailed on first voyage under the command of Captain Thomas A. Norton.

1849 (March)—Sold by Charles W. Morgan to Edward Robinson. Morgan regretted the sale but could not buy her back.

1859 (October)—Sailed on her 6th and most profitable voyage, from which she returned three and a half

years later with a cargo worth more than $165,000.

1863—Sold to J. & W.R. Wing who were to be her principal owners for the next 53 years.

1864—A gimballed bed was built for Captain Landers's wife who was aboard for the seventh voyage. A "gamming chair" was also fitted on the vessel for her.

1867—Vessel remeasured under the new tonnage rule; registered tonnage was changed from 351 to 313.75. Her rig was altered to that of a bark with removal of yards from the mizzenmast.

The Charles W. Morgan *in a sand berth at Mystic Seaport in 1961. (Photo: Louis Martel, Mystic Seaport 1961-8-118)*

1874-75—The *Morgan* was extensively refitted and repaired.

1881—She underwent more refitting, which included moving the anchor windlass forward, some new spars and rigging, and the fitting of double topsails on the mainmast.

1883—Double topsails were fitted on the foremast during the 12th voyage.

1886 (June)—Returned from her longest voyage of nearly five years.

1886 (October)—Left New Bedford for her new home port of San Francisco Before leaving she was refitted, repaired, and altered somewhat for Arctic whaling with reinforcement of her bow and the addition of a steam-powered hoisting engine.

1906 (June)—The *Morgan* returned to New Bedford after an absence of nearly 20 years.

1913—Back from her 33rd voyage, she was stripped and laid up at Union Wharf in Fairhaven.

1916—She was purchased by Captain Benjamin Cleveland who outfitted her to hunt sea elephants at Desolation Island. Before leaving, the *Morgan* took part in a movie titled *Miss Petticoats*.

1918—The vessel was sold to Captain John A. Cook who changed her port of hail to Provincetown. She left New Bedford in July on her 35th voyage.

1920 (September)—Set out on her 37th and last voyage.

1921 (May)—Returned, ending an active whaling career of 80 years.

The Morgan *drying sails at a New Bedford wharf around 1906.*
(*Photo:* Mystic Seaport 1982-1-134A)

1922—Took part in the Elmer Clifton movie *Down to the Sea in Ships*, for which the vessel's rig was changed to that of a ship. Afterwards she sailed to Salem to take part in another movie, *Java Head*, in which she was thinly disguised as a merchant ship.

1924-25—Purchased by artist Harry Neyland and others of a group called Whaling Enshrined. With money given by Colonel E.H.R. Green, she was repaired, repainted, outfitted and ultimately moved to Green's estate at South Dartmouth, Massachusetts, where she was placed in a bed of sand and opened to the public.

1935—Colonel Green died, leaving no provision for her future.

1938—Already falling into disrepair, the *Morgan* was jostled and damaged further by the great hurricane.

1941—At the age of 100, she was acquired by Mystic Seaport, removed from the sand at South Dartmouth to be placed in a similar berth at Mystic after being towed there less than a month before World War II was declared.

1942—She was opened as an exhibit after being rigged and painted.

1947—Many new spars and much rigging were renewed with all of the masts, including the three lowers, being removed for the purpose.

1952-62—The hull was retopped above the 'tween deck by being given new topsides, bulwarks, and weather deck.

1967—The *Charles W. Morgan* was declared a National Historic Landmark.

1968-72—The entire 'tween deck was rebuilt. New steam-bent boat davits were made up and fitted.

The Morgan *hauled at Fairhaven in 1906.*
(*Photo:* Mystic Seaport 1980-8-6)

Laid up in Fairhaven from 1913 to 1916. (Photo: Courtesy of the Kendall Whaling Museum)

1973-76—The ceiling and standing knees were renewed in the area between the two decks.

1973 (December)—The *Morgan* was refloated after nearly 50 continuous years in the sand.

1974 (January to June)—She was hauled on the new lift dock at Mystic Seaport's Henry B. duPont Preservation Shipyard for an inspection and other work. While at the shipyard she was refastened, recaulked, and resheathed. A new false keel and worm shoe were fitted and her rig was overhauled and converted to that of a double topsail bark. The captain's day cabin was refinished. She was returned to a new berth in the center of the Museum, afloat, and open to visitors.

1977-84—An extensive rebuilding over a period of seven years replaced virtually every part of the vessel visible above the waterline, and restored her to her appearance and structure during the 1895-1905 era. The rebuilding process also enabled Shipyard Documentation staff to record structural and other details.

1986-91—Further rebuilding and restoration work included the living spaces aft of amidships and on deck.

1991—Mystic Seaport celebrated the 150th anniversary of the *Morgan's* launching. She was now displayed with as complete an outfit of whaling gear, stores, and personal gear as she had ever had in her time at the Museum.

With all flags flying, the Morgan *is opened for public visits at Colonel Green's estate in South Dartmouth in 1925.* (**Photo:** Mystic Seaport 1960.453)

STATUS: Under continuing restoration and maintenance, lower hull original, good condition.

DONOR: Mystic Seaport purchase

FURTHER READING:

Ashley, Clifford. *The Yankee Whaler*. Garden City: Halcyon House, 1942.

Bray, Maynard. "The Magnificent *Morgan*." *The Log of Mystic Seaport*, Spring, 1974.

Church, Albert Cook. *Whaleships and Whaling*. New York: W.W. Norton & Co., 1938.

Dow, George F. *Whale Ships and Whaling*. Salem, Massachusetts: Marine Research Society, 1925.

Goode, George Brown. *The Fisheries and Fishery Industries of the United States*. Washington, D.C.: U.S. Government Printing Office, 1887.

Leavitt, John F. *The Charles W. Morgan*. Mystic, Connecticut: The Marine Historical Association, Inc., 1973, Mystic Seaport Publications, 1998.

Starbuck, Alexander. *History of the American Whale Fishery* (Part IV of the Report of the U.S. Commission on Fish and Fisheries). Washington, D.C.: U.S. Government Printing Office, 1878.

ACCESSION NO. 1941.761

Plans for 1941.761 are available from Mystic Seaport's Watercraft Plans Collection.

The Morgan *about to be refloated in 1973. (Photo: Lester Olin, Mystic Seaport 1973-11-49)*

The refloated Morgan *is hauled for the first time in nearly 60 years in 1974 on Mystic Seaport's lift dock. (Photo: Thomas Lamb, Mystic Seaport 1974-1-41)*

The Morgan *returns to her wet berth and her station as an exhibit in 1974. (Photo: Mary Anne Stets, Mystic Seaport 1974-7-388)*

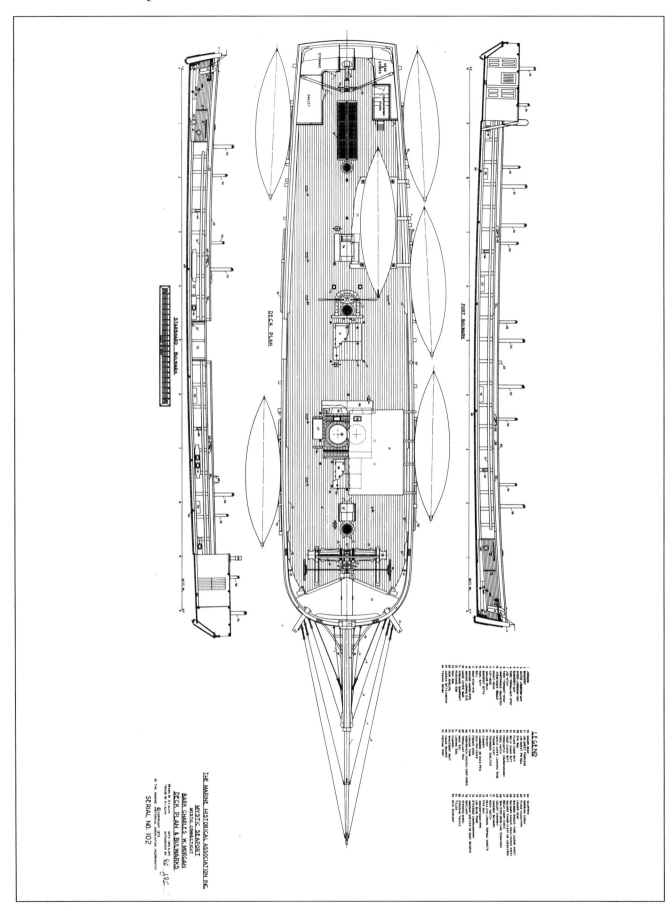

Charles W. Morgan, *plan of deck and bulwarks, drawn by Robert C. Allyn at Mystic Seaport in 1972.* (**Photo:** *Mystic Seaport 1976-9-192*)

Rendering of the Morgan's lower hold forward, with foremast step on top of the keelson and "pointers" for reinforcing the bow against North Pacific ice, drawn by Kathy Bray. (Photo: Mystic Seaport 1985-3-105)

Charles W. Morgan, *profile and rigging plan, drawn at Mystic Seaport in 1972 by Robert C. Allyn.* (**Photo:** Mystic Seaport 1972-12-203A)

Kathy Bray sketch of the Morgan's bow reinforced for North Pacific whaling. (**Photo:** Mystic Seaport 1985-3-104)

Joseph Conrad, *ex-Georg Stage, in her berth at Mystic Seaport in 1990. (Photo: Claire White-Peterson,* Mystic Seaport 1990-8-106*)*

Joseph Conrad (ex-Georg Stage)

SCHOOLSHIP

OFFICIAL NO. 235832

111' 0" x 25' 2"   1882

"A single topsail full-rigged ship crossing three royals, she was 100 feet on the waterline, 25 feet beam, drew 12 feet, grossed 212 tons. She had been, when I found her, for 52 years a schoolship for the Danes. She was built by Burmeister and Wain in Copenhagen in 1882, of Swedish iron; her name was the *Georg Stage*, after the shipowner who financed her building, and she had been training 80 young Danes annually. Built for safety, she was exceptionally strong and as able and seaworthy as a good ship could be made." Thus Alan Villiers described the little ship he would rename *Joseph Conrad*, giving a sketch of her history in his book *Cruise of the Conrad*. (One correction to Villiers: The little ship was built for Carl Frederick Stage, but named for his son Georg Stage, who had died young of tuberculosis.)

Training her cadets in piloting, sail-handling, and general seamanship, the *Georg Stage* cruised the Baltic and North Sea annually. Although she was equipped with a steam engine and retractable propeller, she rarely operated under power. In 1905 her routine was interrupted tragically when a steamship plowed into the *Stage* at night, sending her to the bottom with the loss of 22 boys. Raised and repaired, with the addition of watertight bulkheads, the ship returned to service until a new *Georg Stage* was launched in 1934.

Villiers bought the old ship and sailed her around the world during 1934-36. Afterwards, the *Conrad* became millionaire G. Huntington Hartford's yacht for two years. She then served as a training vessel for the U.S. Maritime Commission during World War II. She came to Mystic Seaport as a donation from the Maritime Commission in 1947 and has been on exhibit ever since.

The schoolship Georg Stage *in Copenhagen Harbor at the turn of the century with 80 Danish boys aboard. (Photo: Holger Knoidsen, The Danish Maritime Museum, SR-42:47;* Mystic Seaport 1962.1252*)*

STATUS: 1969, lower hull lined with ferro-cement; 1977, partially replated; 1984-85, maindeck frame repaired, new teak decking laid, arrangement of maindeck structures returned to 1934 configuration; 1987 fo'c'slehead ironwork repaired and new teak planking laid; 1995, poop deck ironwork repaired and new teak planking laid.

DONOR: U.S. Maritime Commission

FURTHER READING:

The Joseph Conrad, *1882-1982.* Mystic: Mystic Seaport, 1982.

Underhill, Harold A. *Sail Training and Cadet Ships.* Glasgow: Brown, Son & Ferguson, Ltd., 1956. Contains photographs and plans of this vessel as both *Georg Stage* and *Joseph Conrad.*

Villiers, Alan. *Cruise of the Conrad.* New York: Charles Scribner's Sons, 1950.

——. *The Making of a Sailor.* New York: William Morrow & Company, 1938.

——. *Stormalong.* New York: Charles Scribner's Sons, 1937.

Mystic Seaport's *Joseph Conrad* archive includes three rigged models, four ships logs, three crew diaries, three movies, 16 oral-history interviews, and an extensive collection of photographs and drawings.

ACCESSION NO. 1947.1948

Plans for 1947.1948 are available from Mystic Seaport's Watercraft Plans Collection.

Under Alan Villiers's ownership and command, the Joseph Conrad *is shown leaving Sydney, Australia, on December 18, 1935 bound for Melbourne. (Photo: Andrew Lindsay Collection,* Mystic Seaport 1990.97.2.1)

After a wintry transatlantic passage, the Joseph Conrad *reached New York in January 1935 during Alan Villiers's two-year 'round-the-world cruise. Morris Rosenfeld and Sons photographed the little ship in New York Bay.* (**Photo:** Mystic Seaport 1978-3-18)

With a flying bridge atop her chart house and a motor launch in her davits, the Joseph Conrad *sails as the private yacht of G. Huntington Hartford in the late-1930s.* (**Photo:** Mystic Seaport 1973-11-99)

At Mystic Seaport, the Demonstration Squad furls the Conrad's *foretopsail. (Photo: Mary Anne Stets, Mystic Seaport 1972-8-128)*

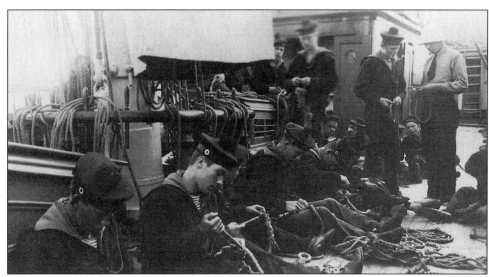

Seagoing schoolboys practice rope splicing aboard the Georg Stage in 1933. (Photo: Captain Junker Collection, Mystic Seaport 1985-5-252)

ROWING CRAFT
Chapter One
FLAT-BOTTOMED

Kathy

BUTTHEAD SKIFF (PUNT), BY CULLER

10' 8" x 4' 2"   1970

Designed, built, and given the "butthead skiff" classification by Captain R.D. "Pete" Culler of the Concordia Company, this skiff rows easily in spite of her blunt appearance. She is stable, rugged, and because of her high freeboard can be used as a work platform without shipping water over her sides. For work around the waterfront she is ideal. As Captain Pete says, "she is a good beach boat with her long snout, as one can step ashore dry."

STATUS: In use, excellent condition.
DONOR: Purchased for Mystic Seaport by John R. Deupree
FURTHER READING:
Burke, John. *Pete Culler's Boats.* Camden, Maine: International Marine Publishing Co., 1984.

Culler, R.D. *Skiffs and Schooners.* Camden, Maine: International Marine Publishing Co., 1974. Contains information on building similar boats by the designer and builder of this one.

Gardner, John. *Building Classic Small Craft.* Camden, Maine: International Marine Publishing Co., 1977. Has chapter on building punts.

ACCESSION NO. 1970.647
Plans for 1970.647 are available from Mystic Seaport's Watercraft Plans Collection.

The butthead skiff Kathy *is lowered into the hold of the* Charles W. Morgan *to do some unusual work.*

With the Morgan's *hold flooded with water, work beneath her 'tween deck was done from the butthead skiff. (Photos: Russell Fowler,*
Mystic Seaport 1972-1-90 and 1972-1-94*)*

SAMPAN BY CULLER
10' 2" x 4' 0"   1975

As a finishing touch on his new Concordia-built schooner *Welcome*, a traditionally rigged vessel designed by Nelson Zimmer, Arthur Snyder ordered this distinctive tender designed by Pete Culler. Culler called this boat a sampan because of her resemblance, in miniature, to her Asian counterpart. Although Pete built most of the small craft he designed, many of them were commissioned through Concordia, which handled the material ordering, billing, and other paperwork. This left Pete free to do what he did best–design and build boats. Sleek is hardly a word suitable for a square-ended boat of any description, but compared to Pete's "butthead skiff" design (see *Kathy*, on the previous page), this sampan is noticeably more graceful.

STATUS: Original, good condition.
DONOR: Arthur F.F. Snyder
FURTHER READING:
Burke, John. *Pete Culler's Boats.* Camden, Maine: International Marine Publishing Co., 1984.
Culler, R.D. *Skiffs and Schooners.* Camden, Maine: International Marine Publishing Co., 1974.
ACCESSION NO. 1980.8
Plans for 1980.8 are available from Mystic Seaport's Watercraft Plans Collection.

Pete Culler's 10' 2" "sampan." (Photo: Judy Beisler, Mystic Seaport)

SKIFF BY PALMER
10' 0" x 4' 1"

In the early days of the Palmer Bros. marine engine company, boats to accommodate the engines were among the Palmer products. These were contracted to builders in the neighborhood of the Cos Cob engine plant. This skiff is not one of these, however, being totally unsuited to the inboard marine engines that Palmer built. This boat is a classic three-plank-per-side, cross-planked skiff with a Palmer Bros. builder's plate. Such a small skiff would have served well as a rowing tender for a larger boat, and that may have been how it was marketed.

The 10' Palmer Bros. skiff. (Photo: Judy Beisler, Mystic Seaport 1996.82L)

STATUS: Good structural condition, paint stripped.
DONOR: Maritime Center at Norwalk

ACCESSION NO. 1996.82
Plans for 1996.82 are available from Mystic Seaport's Watercraft Plans Collection.

FLATIRON SKIFF

10' 3" x 3' 11"

Flatiron skiff was the common name given to these boats because of their resemblance to the housewife's old-fashioned iron. Boats like this, with their two-plank sides and cross-planked bottoms, were not only easy to set up and build, but didn't require hard-to-get material; in fact, scraps from many boat shops oftentimes would do nicely.

Thousands of flatiron skiffs have been built–some well-constructed and nicely modeled, others crudely hammered together. This particular boat, whose origins are not known, was duplicated in 1977 in small numbers by students enrolled in various education programs at Mystic Seaport.

STATUS: Original, fair condition.
DONOR: Edward A. Ackerman

FURTHER READING:
Chapelle, Howard I. *American Small Sailing Craft.* New York: W.W. Norton & Co., 1951.
Culler, R.D. *Skiffs and Schooners.* Camden, Maine: International Marine Publishing Co., 1974.
Gardner, John. "The Flatiron Skiff." *National Fisherman,* January and April, 1961.
Stambaugh, Karl. *Good Skiffs.* Marblehead, Massachusetts: Devereux Books, 1998.

ACCESSION NO. 1976.72

The classic small flatiron skiff, builder unknown. (Photo: Ken Mahler, Mystic Seaport 1976-8-3)

SKIFF FROM SOUTHPORT, MAINE, BY BREWER

10' 11" x 3' 9"

Osborne (Ob) Brewer built this skiff and many like her for lobstermen and summer people. Most were kept and used within sight of Brewer's shop on Cozy Harbor in the village of West

Southport. The harbor is small and sheltered, so great seaworthiness and speed were not of much concern. Brewer died about 1960, and most of his skiffs were constructed long before then. Nevertheless, quite a few of them are still active.

STATUS: Original, good condition.
DONOR: Timothy S. Brewer

FURTHER READING:
Chapelle, Howard I. *American Small Sailing Craft.* New York: W.W. Norton & Co., 1951.
Gardner, John. "The Flatiron Skiff." *National Fisherman,* January and April, 1961.
Stambaugh, Karl. *Good Skiffs.* Marblehead, Massachusetts: Devereux Books, 1998.

ACCESSION NO. 1970.392

The 10' 11" Osborne Brewer flatiron skiff. (Photo: Maynard Bray, Mystic Seaport 1975-5-244)

WESTPORT SKIFF REPLICA
11' 0" x 3' 11"   ca. 1985

This skiff is a replica of a Westport, Massachusetts, skiff built by Fred Tripp around 1942 for Thomas Earle. At one point it was owned and documented by Bob Baker, an expert on the type, who drew up a set of plans in his own artistic but accurate style. Bob wrote about building the type in an article in *WoodenBoat Magazine* in which he said the type rowed well, was good through the surf, and often was towed, sometimes two at a time, behind commercial swordfishermen on Buzzards Bay. Like Tripp's other skiffs, the boat has hanging knees and frames set perpendicular to the sheer.

This replica was built by students in the Williams College-Mystic Seaport undergraduate program under the guidance of shipwright Kevin Dwyer. In season, it is used daily.

STATUS: Seasonally in the water, excellent condition.
DONOR: Mystic Seaport-built reproduction
FURTHER READING:
"The Westport Skiff," *WoodenBoat* 32, Jan/Feb, 1980.
Baker, Bob. Letter. *WoodenBoat* 33, Mar/Apr, 1980.

The 12' 2" Noank skiff Clara. *(Photo: Mary Anne Stets,* Mystic Seaport 1973-3-580*)*

Clara

SKIFF FROM NOANK, CONNECTICUT
12' 2" x 4' 2"   ca. 1930

Noank fishermen used boats like this to row to their larger vessels from the shore. When not in use these "sharpies," as they were called, were hauled out on wooden ramps or runways at the water's edge, or tied to haulout lines set up between the land and stakes driven into the bottom a short distance offshore.

STATUS: Paint stripped to bare wood, some repair, approximately 90% original, poor condition.
DONOR: Maynard E. Bray
FURTHER READING:
(Same as for Brewer skiff 1970.392)

ACCESSION NO. 1973.87

Three women use a similar skiff to go bathing along the shore near Noank or Groton, Connecticut, ca. 1910. (Photo: Courtesy of Larry Jacobsen, Mystic Seaport 1994-6-37)

NOANK SHARPIE SKIFF

12' 8" x 4' 7"   1980

Students in the Williams College-Mystic Seaport program, under the direction of Willets Ansel, built this reproduction of a Noank sharpie skiff to be used with a lobstering exhibit intended to re-create a representative section of the shoreline of Noank, Connecticut, ca. 1890-1900. The exhibit includes a lobster shack, pier, ramp, lobster car, and this sharpie skiff lying next to the lobster shack. The boat was based on the lines of *Clara* (1973.87), another skiff from Noank, described above.

STATUS: Used seasonally, excellent condition.

DONOR: Mystic Seaport-built reproduction

ACCESSION NO. 1980.46

The replica Noank skiff built by Williams-Mystic students. (Photo: Gene Meyers, Mystic Seaport 1980-7-73)

SHARPIE SKIFF FROM NOANK, CONNECTICUT

14' 9" x 3' 9"   ca. 1900

This skiff was locally built for use in Mr. Babcock's small boat livery at Groton Long Point, Connecticut. Two of Mr. Babcock's customers could row this boat at the same time from the two rowing positions.

Although a sharpie in shape, this skiff is not typical sharpie construction. There is no chine log to take the bottom fastenings. The builder avoided splitting the bottom edge of the lower side planks by tapering the plank thickness from 1/2" at the top to 3/4" at the bottom. The frame feet stop some two inches shy of the bottom; all fastenings are iron, with the two side planks clench-nailed at the lap.

CONDITION: Good.
DONOR: Adrian Pearsall
ACCESSION NO. 1986.92

The 14' 9" skiff from Noank.
(Photo: Deborah Patterson,
Mystic Seaport 1986.92D)

SKIFF FROM UNCASVILLE, CONNECTICUT

13' 11" x 3' 5"   ca. 1912

Fourteen dollars reputedly was paid for this skiff when she was brand new. Fred Perkins built her part way up the Thames River at Uncasville for use in that area. Although without a centerboard or rudder, she has provision for a mast and probably set a small sail when the wind was fair. Her seats are removable, held in by turnbuttons. Her unusually narrow bottom and the fact that she could be rowed triple-banked contributed to her speed–up to a point. But her run is probably too steep and she is too short on the waterline to do much but drag a lot of water when rowed hard.

STATUS: Original, transom damaged, good condition.
DONOR: H. Downer Johnson, Jr.
FURTHER READING:
Dolbeare, Harward B. *A History of Point Breeze on the Thames.* Privately printed. Illustration on page 11 shows a similar boat.
ACCESSION NO. 1974.471

The 13' 11" x 3' 5" skiff from Uncasville.
(Photo: Maynard Bray,
Mystic Seaport 1975-5-4)

The Housatonic River oyster skiff. (Photo: Ken Mahler, Mystic Seaport 1981-2-50)

HOUSATONIC RIVER TONGING SKIFF

20' 7" x 5' 0"   1938

This sharpie-type skiff was built by George Irving Culver & Son, of Stratford, Connecticut, for oyster tonging on the Housatonic River. J. Fletcher Lewis bought the boat for use in his duties as Harbormaster of Stratford. He had the boat extensively repaired by Louis Chagnon of Stratford Marina, who replaced the original cross-planked bottom with two layers of plywood and removed two inches from the lower side planks when he replaced the chines. The keel and stem were also replaced and a stern seat installed. The donor, George Edwards, bought the boat from Fletcher Lewis in 1975 and used the boat in Stratford for oyster tonging under outboard power. He would tow a 38"-wide dredge from a cleat mounted on the side deck, and this large skiff could carry about 25 bushels of oysters.

Edwards feels that the Culvers built the boat to an early model, one suited more for oars than power. As such, the boat's sides are brought in narrower aft, limiting ability to use power and reducing carrying capacity. When limited to oars, the tonger had to use his knowledge of the tides, as these boats were heavily built to withstand hard usage and were not easily rowed.

STATUS: Poor.
DONOR: George Edwards
ACCESSION NO. 1980.87

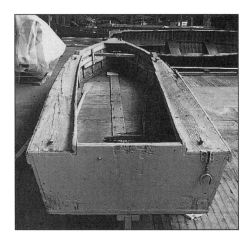

At left, the Housatonic River oyster skiff in Mystic Seaport's collection. (Photo: Ken Mahler, Mystic Seaport 1981-2-48). Below, similar skiffs at Stratford, Connecticut, in the early 1940s. (Photo: Courtesy of George Edwards, Mystic Seaport 1980.87)

SKIFF FROM COS COB BY SPENCER

11' 2" x 4' 3"

This handsome flat-bottom skiff was built by George P. Spencer of Cos Cob, Connecticut. The donor, Edward Payne, told the Museum in 1986 that he had owned the boat for over 50 years. He also said that the fore-and-aft bottom shape made the boat easy to row or scull. The three lapstrake side planks are dory lapped forward at the stem, but not aft where the hood ends fit into notches in the transom. The transom is notched for sculling and reinforced for use with an outboard motor. Altogether, this is a pleasant yacht tender.

STATUS: Excellent condition. Donor replaced bottom planking.
DONOR: Edward Payne
ACCESSION NO. 1986.51

The 11' 2" skiff from Cos Cob. (Photo: Deborah Patterson, Mystic Seaport 1986.51D)

SKIFF FROM CLIFF ISLAND, MAINE, BY PETTENGILL

13' 11" x 4' 3"   1932

John H. Pettengill built this skiff three years before he died. Although better known locally as a policeman, he had previously been well-known for his Casco Bay-style lobsterboats, having built more than a hundred of them. Pettengill's skiffs all had an extreme amount of rocker in the stern, useful in landing and getting off beaches, and were typically built with two planks to a side with a very wide garboard and a sheer strake whose top edge was kept straight. At the time he built this skiff, Cliff Island had four active boatshops, all of which imported wood to the island. Skiffs like this took about a week to build. This one sold for $35 when the donor bought her in 1934 to use as a tender on nearby Chebeague Island.

STATUS: Excellent condition; donor cut transom notch for unsuccessful outboard experiment.
DONOR: Henry Hubbell
ACCESSION NO. 1986.44

The 13' 11" skiff built by John H. Pettengill. (Photo: Maynard Bray, Mystic Seaport 1986.44A)

SKIFF FROM OSTERVILLE
11' 6" x 3' 11"

Townie Horner wrote Mystic Seaport that he had picked this boat up when friends were cleaning out their garage in Osterville, Massachusetts. The boat is typical of the flat-bottom skiffs that were widely used prior to World War II by both summer and local people to get to their moored boats. Summer people rowed and local people sculled, Townie said. The boats were most often painted white or gray, but a bright one like this boat was not unusual. Heavy after a season in the water, the boats were stable. These boats began to be

The 11' 6" skiff from Osterville. (Photo: Maynard Bray, Mystic Seaport 1988.24A)

replaced by the lighter, smaller plywood after World War II and all but disappeared when fiberglass became the preferred "no-maintenance" material.

STATUS: Excellent condition.
DONOR: Townsend Horner
ACCESSION NO. 1988.24

SKIFF BY STANNARD
11' 1/2" x 4' 7 1/2"   1942

Elliot Spencer received this flat-bottom skiff for his birthday in 1942. He used it on Long Island Sound near Westbrook, Connecticut, for fishing and as a general workboat for many years before giving it to Mystic Seaport.

Horace Stannard came from a family of Westbrook boatbuilders. Born in 1878, he started building boats in the early-1930s and continued until his death in the mid-1950s. He was known primarily for his fishing and commercial craft up to 45 feet in length. He worked from half models.

The boat is "all of a piece." All the

scantlings are in scale, the workmanship is uniformly good but not precious, and the shape is lovely. A lively sheer at the rail and chine indicate the boat would tow and row well.

STATUS: Excellent.
DONOR: Elliot Spencer
ACCESSION NO. 1988.117

The 11' 1" skiff built by Horace Stannard. (Photo: Maynard Bray, Mystic Seaport 1988.117A)

"PEE WEE" SKIFF BY PALMER SCOTT

6' 1" x 3'   ca. 1950

Some traditional boat types like flat-bottom skiffs lend themselves to being built in plywood, available in quantity after World War II. New Bedford's Palmer Scott Company meant this "Pee Wee" as a child's skiff; it is a bit small for adults. Using a fore-and aft seat meant that the boat could be easily trimmed for carrying a passenger or to compensate for different crew sizes.

The boat was used by young people on the Kenyon Estate in South Kingston, Rhode Island.

Palmer Scott's "Pee Wee" skiff for children. (Photo: Maynard Bray, Mystic Seaport 1991.165.1A)

STATUS: Excellent original condition.
DONOR: Estate of Ann Kenyon Morse
ACCESSION NO. 1991.165.1

Asa Thomson takes time out for a smoke while the varnish dries. (Photo: Courtesy of Mrs. L. Francis Thomson)

SKIFF FROM NEW BEDFORD, MASSACHUSETTS BY THOMSON

11' 2" x 4' 3"   ca. 1925

This unusual model of the skiff, with its high freeboard and kicked-up bottom aft, would probably remove her from the flatiron category. For such a basic shape, however, she is rather elegantly constructed with a double-planked bottom, delicate side framing, special brass oarlocks and sockets, and a beautifully worked out stemband and cap having an integral towing eye. She is varnished inside and out and has a built-in bait well under the hinged middle seat. Her large skeg is reinforced by a "sternpost" that runs up the outside of the transom and has done its intended job well. Strangely enough,

she has no seat knees whatsoever; yet she doesn't seem to have suffered because of it.

Her builder, Asa Thomson, was born in 1859 and set up his boatbuilding shop in New Bedford in 1885. By the time this skiff was built, Thomson had nearly a lifetime of experience behind him. Some of those years were spent building delicate and exquisitely finished canoes; thus, it is no wonder that his latter-day skiffs were highly regarded. They were apparently his own design and were particularly valued as tenders. High sides allowed several persons to be carried in safety; a flat bottom permitted easy landing on a beach; the absence of bottom framing made her quick and simple to clean out; and the turned-up run aft kept her bow high when being towed. This last feature

also prevented her stern from dragging water with a load of passengers aboard. After being hauled out of the water for a few days, even in the hot summer sun, she could be put overboard without fear of leaking thanks to her double-planked bottom. Like all Thomson boats, she is fastened with copper and brass throughout.

STATUS: Original, good condition.
DONOR: Richard F. Hunt
FURTHER READING:
Phalen, Dan. "Asa Thomson's Elegant Skiffs." *WoodenBoat* 29, July/Aug, 1979.
Stambaugh, Karl. *Good Skiffs.* Marblehead, Massachusetts: Devereux Books, 1998.
ACCESSION NO. 1976.148
Plans for 1976.148 are available from Mystic Seaport's Watercraft Plans Collection.

The Asa Thomson skiff in storage at Mystic Seaport. (Photo: Maynard Bray, Mystic Seaport 1978-2-47)

Monhegan Island shore scene with dories and fish houses.
(Photo: Courtesy of The Hudson Collection, Mystic Seaport 1968-11-72E)

Monhegan shore fishermen tending a stop seine from a
banks dory. (Photo: Courtesy of The Hudson Collection,
Mystic Seaport 1968-11-72D)

This Milton J. Burns watercolor depicts shore fishermen with their
dories, ca. 1880. (Mystic Seaport Collections, Mystic Seaport 1975.32)

Nested dories. (Photo: Maynard Bray, Mystic Seaport 1975-6-112)

This Milton J. Burns
illustration of cod
fishermen hauling a trawl
line from their dory was
published in Harper's
Weekly, *October, 1885.*
(Mystic Seaport 1976.181)

DORIES

Derived from earlier French and colonial flat-bottomed watercraft, the dory with its characteristic flaring sides, raking ends, and fore-and-aft bottom planks had emerged along the North Shore of Massachusetts Bay by the 1790s. Originally a beach fishing boat, easy to launch and land in the surf, the dory was adopted for fishing on the offshore banks in the 1850s. There, its stability, capacity, and ability to stack on the deck of a fishing schooner with thwarts removed made it the boat of choice for more than 60 years.

Few other small craft measure up to the dory when it comes to simplicity and seaworthiness. Inexpensive and easy to build, the dory became the first mass-produced American small craft as the fishing fleet consumed thousands per year. Shops in Amesbury, Massachusetts, and Lunenburg, Nova Scotia, specialized in turning out the heavy banks dories for fishing.

Dory variations include ones with convex or "round" sides known as Swampscott dories (after the town where they were developed). Because of their increased stability, Swampscott dories were sometimes fitted with centerboards and rigged for sailing. Bateaux, dory-skiffs with wide transoms, and certain wherries share the dory's characteristic construction form.

BANKS DORY FROM SCHOONER *BLACK HAWK*

18′ 3″ x 5′ 1″   ca. 1940

Of unknown origin, this dory last saw service aboard the 63-foot auxiliary schooner *Black Hawk*, which, after conversion from a yacht, fished commercially from New London and Noank during the 1940s and '50s. *Black Hawk* was perhaps the last dory fisherman to sail out of southeastern Connecticut. *Black Hawk*'s plans are shown in the June 1922 issue of *The Rudder*.

STATUS: Restored, mostly original, equipped, good condition.

DONOR: H.H. Kynett

FURTHER READING:
Bunting, W.H. *An Eye for the Coast.* Gardiner, Maine: Tilbury House, 1998. With reference to Eric Hudson photographs, discusses dory fishing from Monhegan Island, Maine.

Chapelle, Howard I. *American Small Sailing Craft.* New York: W.W. Norton & Co., 1951.

——. *National Watercraft Collection.* Washington, D.C.: U.S. Government Printing Office, 1960.

Gardner, John. *The Dory Book.* Mystic: Mystic Seaport Publications, 1987.

——. *Wooden Boats to Build and Use.* Mystic: Mystic Seaport Publications, 1996.

Garland, Joseph E. *Adventure: Queen of the Windjammers.* Camden, Maine: Down East Books, 1985. Includes excellent photos of dories in use.

Gribbins, Joseph. "Dories." *Nautical Quarterly* 9, Winter, 1980.

ACCESSION NO. 1955.320
Plans for 1955.320 are available from Mystic Seaport's Watercraft Plans Collection.

Dory from the fishing schooner Black Hawk *as she looked in 1975. (Photo: Maynard Bray, Mystic Seaport 75-6-29)*

The schooner Black Hawk, *with her dories nested on deck, heads out of Noank. (Photo: Mystic Seaport 1989-7-41)*

Allen's Dory Shop, Lunenburg, Nova Scotia. Planing final bevel.
(Photo: Louis Martel, Mystic Seaport 1970-7-338)

Clamping garboard planks to "tombstone" sternboard.
(Photo: Louis Martel,
Mystic Seaport 1970-7-358)

BANKS DORY FROM LUNENBURG, NOVA SCOTIA

19' 8" x 5' 8"   1970

Thousands of simple, seaworthy, inexpensive, and expendable dories have been built over the years. Their first widespread use was in the cod fishery around 1860 when fishing from the decks of vessels declined in favor of small fleets of two-man dories. Banks fisherman was the name given to the schooner that carried the dories out to the fishing grounds, or banks, as they were called. The man himself was also called a banks fisherman and his boat a banks dory. Similar dories, usually larger, carried the seine twine (net) of the shore fisherman who fished for herring and mackerel with a seine, while smaller banks dories are the favored lifeboat of more modern fishing draggers. One of the advantages of the dory to the banks fisherman, other than low cost and seaworthiness, was that these boats could be stored one inside the other once the seats and other gear had been removed. Customarily, banks dories would be nested on deck in two stacks of five or six boats each while not in use.

This dory is really a by-product of a Mystic Seaport movie-making project which filmed each step in her construction while she was being built in Capt. Lawrence Allen's shop in Lunenburg, Nova Scotia. The boat and her prefabricated sister are available

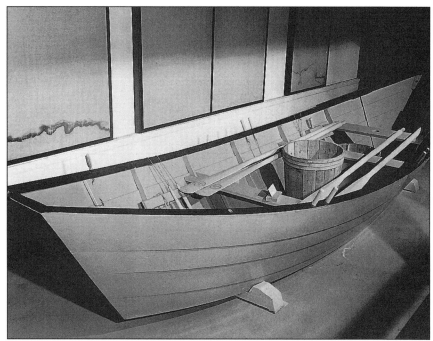

The Lunenburg dory in 1975. (Photo: Maynard Bray, Mystic Seaport 1975-5-429)

First two strakes of planking in place, and finishing and smoothing before painting. (Photo: L. S. Martel, Mystic Seaport 1970-7-319 and 1970-7-59)

for study, and the movie serves to visually preserve the way men of long experience go about building the banks dory.

STATUS: Unused, excellent condition.

DONOR: Mystic Seaport purchase

FURTHER READING:

Atkinson, Bob. "As Old as a Dory." *WoodenBoat* 18, Sept/Oct, 1977.

Gardner, John. *The Dory Book*. Mystic: Mystic Seaport Publications, 1987.

——. "Navy Dory Was Drawn at Height of Type's Use." *National Fisherman*, December, 1977.

Goode, George Brown. *The Fisheries and Fishery Industries of the United States*. Washington, D.C.: U.S. Government Printing Office, 1887.

O'Leary, Wayne M. *The Maine Sea Fisheries: The Rise and Fall of a Native Industry, 1830-1890*. Boston: Northeastern University Press, 1996.

Zimmerman, Jan. "Building the Banks Dory." *WoodenBoat* 19, Nov/Dec, 1977.

ACCESSION NO. 1970.686

Plans for 1970.686 are available from Mystic Seaport's Watercraft Plans Collection.

BANKS DORY (PREFABRICATED) FROM LUNENBURG, NOVA SCOTIA

19' 8" x 5' 8"   1970
(These are the approximate dimensions of the completed boat.)

Purchased as separated pieces, this dory has at times been partially assembled to illustrate the parts that go to make up a dory and the name of each one.

STATUS: Partly assembled, excellent condition.

DONOR: Mystic Seaport purchase

ACCESSION NO. 1970.687

The prefabricated dory on exhibit in 1975. (Photo: Maynard Bray, Mystic Seaport 1975-5-427)

The L. A. Dunton at Chubb's Wharf with dories.
(Photo: Claire White-Peterson, Mystic Seaport 1978-8-76)

TEN BANKS DORIES, MYSTIC SEAPORT REPRODUCTIONS

18' 2" x 4' 11"   1976-78

These boats were built as replacements for the worn-out banks dories exhibited aboard the Museum's fishing schooner, *L. A. Dunton*; the first one was completed in 1976. They are planked with cedar rather than pine and have hackmatack knees for frames instead of iron-reinforced oak frames; thus they are expected to far outlast the Nova Scotian dories which preceded them. Will Ansel of the Mystic Seaport staff was in charge of the dory-building program and also served as an instructor to students who helped with their building at the Museum.

Howard Chapelle's plans for Higgins and Gifford's standard model of the 1880s were used as the representative epitome of banks dory development.

Dory demonstrations are given in the summertime by Mystic Seaport staff members so visitors can see just how a dory is hoisted overboard by the schooner's dory tackles, how dories are rigged for fishing, and how they are rowed.

These dynamic drawings by I.W. Taber were illustrations for the first edition of Kipling's wonderful novel Captains Courageous *in 1897.*

162

A ten-dory-power auxiliary moves this fishing schooner clear of the harbor at St. John's, Newfoundland, in the late 'teens or early 1920s. (Photo: Courtesy of Stuart Wilson, Mystic Seaport 1973-9-5))

STATUS: In use, excellent condition.

DONOR: Mystic Seaport-built reproductions

FURTHER READING:
See also this section under *L. A. Dunton.*

Boutilier, E.L. "Recollections of Four Dorymen." *National Fisherman Yearbook,* 1996.

Chapelle, Howard I. *American Small Sailing Craft.* New York: W. W. Norton & Co., 1951.

Gardner, John. *The Dory Book.* Mystic: Mystic Seaport Publications, 1987.

——. *Wooden Boats to Build and Use.* Mystic: Mystic Seaport Publications, 1996.

Garland, Joseph E. *Lone Voyager.* Boston: Little Brown, 1963.

Goode, George Brown. *The Fisheries and Fishery Industries of the United States.* Washington, D.C.: U.S. Government Printing Office, 1887.

Grayson, Stan. "The Oldest Boatshop in the Country." *Nautical Quarterly* 31, Autumn, 1985.

"Rowing Against the Tide." *WoodenBoat* 106, May/June, 1992.

ACCESSION NOS. 1978.51, 1978.52, 1978.53, 1978.54, 1978.55, 1978.56, 1978.57, 1978.58, 1978.59, 1978.60

The Massachusetts Humane Society dory in 1975. (Photo: Maynard Bray, Mystic Seaport 1975-6-74)

BANKS DORY, MASSACHUSETTS HUMANE SOCIETY

17' 4" x 4' 8"   ca. 1900

The crew of the Siasconset, Nantucket, Life-Saving Station used this dory along with the usual double-ended surfboat. Later it was bought by Jim Coffin and used to gather seaweed for his famous clambakes. This is a slight departure from the usual banks dory in that its bottom is not rockered, and steambent, rather than sawn, frames are used.

STATUS: Paint stripped to bare wood, original, good condition.

DONOR: Charles F. Sayle

FURTHER READING:
Gardner, John. *The Dory Book.* Mystic: Mystic Seaport Publications, 1987.

Howe, M.A. DeWolfe. *The Humane Society of the Commonwealth of Massachusetts—An Historical Review 1785-1916.* Boston: The Riverside Press, 1918.

ACCESSION NO. 1963.1517
Plans for 1963.1517 are available from Mystic Seaport's Watercraft Plans Collection.

BANKS DORY FROM *ROANN*
15' 8" x 4' 8"

This five-plank dory of unknown age and origin was being used as a lifeboat on the eastern-rig dragger *Roann* when she was acquired by Mystic Seaport in 1997. The lapped frames with clips at the joints identify this as a production dory. The rot and damage indicate that this dory spent most of its time on the rack atop *Roann*'s pilothouse, not in the water.

STATUS: Fair, with damaged rails and planks to starboard, repairs to the transom, and rot in frames and planks.

DONOR: Mystic Seaport purchase

FURTHER READING:
(Same as 1955.320)

ACCESSION NO. 1997.137.1720

Carried as a lifeboat, Roann's dory rarely left the rack on the port side of her pilothouse. (Photo: Nancy d'Estang Mystic Seaport 1997-7-135*)*

The lumberman's bateau in 1973 with stern modified for an outboard motor. (Photo: Maynard Bray, Mystic Seaport 1973-7-5*)*

MAINE LUMBERMAN'S BATEAU #2556
24' 8" x 6' 0"

Until recently bateaux were used for spring log drives on the great rivers of Canada and Maine, as well as on rivers and streams in New York State's Adirondacks. They are crudely built but of rugged construction to withstand the chafe and pressure from moving logs. Neither select materials nor exacting fits were necessary to produce them.

STATUS: Stern cut off and transom added for outboard power, otherwise mostly original, fair condition.

DONOR: Great Northern Paper Co.

FURTHER READING:
Bunting, William H. *A Day's Work: A Sampler of Historical Maine Photographs, 1860-1920.* Gardiner, Maine: Tilbury House, 1997.

Chapelle, Howard I. *American Small Sailing Craft.* New York: W. W. Norton & Co., 1951.

Gardner, John. *The Dory Book.* Mystic: Mystic Seaport Publications, 1987.

Thoreau, Henry D. *The Maine Woods.* New York: Thomas Y. Crowell & Co., 1909.

"Tin Boats Take Over for Classic Bateaus On River Drive." *National Fisherman,* May, 1971.

ACCESSION NO. 1973.408

A lumberman's bateau in action during the spring pulp drive for the Great Northern Paper Company. (Courtesy of Great Northern Paper Company, Mystic Seaport 1975-3-175*)*

PISCATAQUA RIVER WHERRY

16' 5" x 4' 1"   ca. 1850

Simple in structure, as are most dory types, the long lines of this so-called wherry and her low freeboard make for easy rowing. She needed to row well for the river current is strong near Eliot, Maine, where she was built as a means of basic transportation. A flat bottom protected by a sacrificial "false bottom" of hardwood enables boarding her from the beach without damage. The reproduction of this boat was remarkably easy to build. Only 8-inch boards were needed in her topside planking, and these were easily hung without the use of steam or fancy clamping.

The Piscataqua River Wherry in 1975. (Photo: Maynard Bray, Mystic Seaport 1975-5-249)

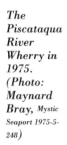

The Piscataqua River Wherry in 1975. (Photo: Maynard Bray, Mystic Seaport 1975-5-248)

Designed to stem the tidal rush of the Piscataqua River, these wherries also ventured into quiet backwaters, where they could make an easy landing on the beach. (Photo: Courtesy of Ed McClave, Mystic Seaport 1982-5-59)

She is a handsome boat and would make an ideal craft for an amateur builder, and when complete would row about as well as the more complex Whitehall, peapod, or St. Lawrence River skiff. Indeed, several reproductions of these boats have more than held their own in races for traditional small craft.

STATUS: Original, very good condition.

DONOR: David C. Wherren

FURTHER READING:
Gardner, John. *Building Classic Small Craft.* Camden, Maine: International Marine Publishing Co., 1977.

——. *The Dory Book.* Mystic: Mystic Seaport Publications, 1987.

ACCESSION NO. 1973.236

Plans for 1973.236 are available from Mystic Seaport's Watercraft Plans Collection.

In exchange for the original, Mystic Seaport built this reproduction of the Piscataqua River wherry. (Photo: Mary Anne Stets, Mystic Seaport 1973-8-13)

DOUBLE-ENDED GUNNING DORY FROM MARBLEHEAD

16' 1" x 4' 6"   ca. 1940

These boats were favored around Marblehead, Massachusetts, harbor for bird shooting. This one was built over the dory molds of William Chamberlain either by Capt. Gerald Smith or by Albert Cloutman, foreman at Graves Yacht Yard at the time, but who earlier had worked for Chamberlain. Of these boats John Gardner has written in *Building Classic Small Craft*: "The gunning dory as perfected in Marblehead by William Chamberlain is the queen of all dories, and one of the handsomest double-enders ever built anywhere, not to mention its easy speed under oars and its unexcelled rough-water ability with capable hands at the oars."

Although this boat's sheer is flatter and less handsome than the larger boat that Gardner discusses, she is nevertheless a good-looking boat.

The Chamberlain gunning dory, 1975. (Photo: Maynard Bray, Mystic Seaport 1975-5-260)

STATUS: Fiberglass-covered outside, otherwise original, good condition.

DONOR: Richard Parker

FURTHER READING:
Gardner, John. *Building Classic Small Craft*. Camden, Maine: International Marine Publishing Co., 1977.

——. *The Dory Book*. Mystic: Mystic Seaport Publications, 1987.

——. *Wooden Boats to Build and Use*. Mystic: Mystic Seaport Publications, 1996.

ACCESSION NO. 1969.99

The George Chaisson double-ended dory in 1975. (Photo: Ken Mahler, Mystic Seaport 1975-9-119)

Point Sardine Lifeboat No. 1

DOUBLE-ENDED DORY BY CHAISSON

14' 4" x 4' 6"   ca. 1920

George Chaisson, whose shop in Swampscott, Massachusetts, produced a great many boats large and small, built this handsome variation of the traditional Swampscott round-sided dory. Reportedly she was designed by John G. Alden for use as a tender on one of his well-known Malabar schooners.

STATUS: Original, although modified somewhat with the addition of a steering oar brace, very good condition.

DONOR: R. Livingston Ireland

FURTHER READING:
Gardner, John. *Building Classic Small Craft*. Camden, Maine: International Marine Publishing Co., 1977.

——. *The Dory Book*. Mystic: Mystic Seaport Publications, 1987.

ACCESSION NO. 1975.397

Nova Scotian double-ended dory in 1993. (Photo: Maynard Bray, Mystic Seaport 1990.125)

DOUBLE-ENDED ROWING DORY FROM NOVA SCOTIA

18' 6" x 4' 6"   ca. 1929

One generally thinks of Canadian-built dories as being of the straight-sided banks type carried to and from the fishing banks on the decks of schooners. This round-sided double-ender indicates that there were exceptions. Lunenburg and Shelburne were Nova Scotia's primary dory-building towns, and the evidence points to Shelburne as the place where this one was built. The donor's grandfather bought the boat sometime before 1929 to go with the family summer house in Argyle, near Yarmouth. Upon his death in 1942, his family laid up the dory and it has seen no subsequent use.

STATUS: Original, fair condition.

DONOR: Roger L. Gregg

FURTHER READING:
Gardner, John. *The Dory Book*. Mystic: Mystic Seaport Publications, 1987.

ACCESSION NO. 1990.125

DORY-SKIFF BY CHAMBERLAIN

13' 4" x 4' 2"   ca. 1930

Bought new by the donor's late husband and initially used as the tender for the family's Alden-designed, Salem, Massachusetts-based yawl *Shag*, this craft switched roles to that of a 'longshore lobsterboat when the Robinsons retired to Maine in 1945.

Recreational fishing and family outings in Johns Bay were also part of its activity. John Robinson, long associated with the Alden design office, died in 1969 and the boat has been unused since that time. A chapter of John Gardner's *The Dory Book* is devoted to this boat, and includes plans. He says of this model that "for a rowing sea boat, you can't do much better within the 14' limit."

STATUS: Some repair, fair condition.

DONOR: Mrs. John Robinson via Penobscot Marine Museum

FURTHER READING:
Gardner, John. *The Dory Book*. Mystic: Mystic Seaport Publications, 1987.

ACCESSION NO. 1986.3

Chamberlain dory-skiff 1986.3. (Photo: Deborah Bates, Mystic Seaport 1986.3A)

The Amesbury dory-skiff in 1975. (Photo: Maynard Bray, Mystic Seaport 1975-6-93)

AMESBURY DORY-SKIFF

14' 0" x 4' 0"   ca. 1930

Models such as this were favorites of fishermen and yachtsmen alike as tenders for larger craft. Most were built on the North Shore of Massachusetts Bay. This one probably came from the Lowell shop at Amesbury.

STATUS: Hull stripped of paint and fiberglass 1973, mostly original, fair condition.

DONOR: Ann W. Kenyon

FURTHER READING:
Gardner, John. *The Dory Book*. Mystic: Mystic Seaport Publications, 1987.

ACCESSION NO. 1957.290
Plans for 1957.290 are available from Mystic Seaport's Watercraft Plans Collection.

Amesbury dory-skiff as she appeared in her early days at Mystic Seaport with her hull covered with fiberglass. (Photo: L. S. Martel, Mystic Seaport 1957.290B)

Sailing dory-skiff in 1993. (Photo: Maynard Bray, Mystic Seaport 1986.97.2A)

SAILING DORY-SKIFF BY WHITTIER & LOW

14' 4" x 4' 4"   ca. 1935

Whittier & Low of Ipswich, Massachusetts, built this boat and others under the name of "Cape Ann Boats," and the builder's plate is still on the transom. She never strayed far. Her active days were before the Second World War, when the donor's father used her at the family's summer place in nearby Rockport. Luckily, she came to the Museum with her sailing rig still intact.

STATUS: Original, good condition.

DONOR: Joseph R. Worcester, in memory of Thomas Worcester

FURTHER READING:
Gardner, John. *The Dory Book*. Mystic: Mystic Seaport Publications, 1987.

ACCESSION NO. 1986.97.2

The Lancaster dory-skiff in 1993.
(Photo: Maynard Bray,
Mystic Seaport 1989.94.1A*)*

DORY-SKIFF BY LANCASTER
13' 6" x 4' 0"   1924

The donor believes that this was a "store-bought" boat, one that he and his father found on the floor of Varney's Department Store in Manchester, New Hampshire, in 1924. The nameplate indicates that C. H. Lancaster of Amesbury, Massachusetts, was the builder. The family fished from her on nearby Bow Lake each summer until 1950 when they laid her to rest next to the Steward boathouse. There, the weather took its toll and, although the boat has all her original parts and details, her condition is poor.

STATUS: Original, poor condition.

DONOR: Merrill F. Steward and Donald T. Steward

FURTHER READING:
Gardner, John. *The Dory Book*. Mystic: Mystic Seaport Publications, 1987.

ACCESSION NO. 1989.94.1
Plans for 1989.94.1 are available from Mystic Seaport's Watercraft Plans Collection.

The Mystic Seaport-built Chamberlain dory-skiff in 1971 with John Gardner at the oars.
(Photo: R. A. Fowler, Mystic Seaport 1971-11-113*)*

Harry Williams

CHAMBERLAIN DORY-SKIFF REPRODUCTION
13' 5" x 4' 0"   1971

In the early decades of the 1900s, boats of this model were built in quantity by William Chamberlain in his shop at Marblehead. Lately, in addition to this boat, there have been others built to this same model using plans published in the *National Fisherman* and in *The Dory Book* by John Gardner. Among them is the Parimar dory-skiff built in fiberglass. This reproduction is very close to the Chamberlain dory-skiff (1986.3) that was discussed on a previous page.

STATUS: In use, excellent condition.

DONOR: Mystic Seaport-built reproduction

FURTHER READING:
Gardner, John. *The Dory Book*. Mystic: Mystic Seaport Publications, 1987.

ACCESSION NO. 1971.238
Plans for 1971.238 are available from Mystic Seaport's Watercraft Plans Collection.

SWAMPSCOTT DORY BY NEWELL McLAIN

16' 10" x 4' 7"   1938

In 1938, Newell McLain built this dory at his boatshop in Thomaston, Maine. Called a Swampscott dory because of round sides, this style could be found wherever dories were built, not just where they originated on the North Shore of Massachusetts Bay. Her frames overlap at the center just like dories built with natural-crook frames. These have diamond-shaped plates that join the floor futtocks and the side futtocks. The McLain dory has three rowing positions and four thwarts. A very fancy Swampscott, all of her planks have beaded edges. It's not surprising that Newell McLain took pains to produce an extra-special boat, as he was building this one for his sons.

STATUS: Good original condition.

DONOR: Newell McLain

FURTHER READING:
Gardner, John. *The Dory Book*. Mystic: Mystic Seaport Publications, 1987.

ACCESSION NO. 1992.117

The McLain dory in 1993. The sacrificial pieces of her "false bottom" are shown at the left. (Photo: Maynard Bray, Mystic Seaport 1992.117A)

SWAMPSCOTT DORY BY CHAISSON

15' 2" x 4' 6"   ca. 1920

This production model, called a "clipper dory" by the well-known Swampscott boatbuilder George L. Chaisson, was used as a tender for a larger boat and for pleasure rowing. She's a classic Swampscott with round sides and a beautiful curve of sheerline.

STATUS: Restored 1972, approximately 85% original.

DONOR: Mystic Seaport purchase

FURTHER READING:
Gardner, John. *The Dory Book*. Mystic: Mystic Seaport Publications, 1987.

The Chaisson Swampscott dory in 1975. (Photo: Maynard Bray, Mystic Seaport 1975-5-216)

Promotional catalog describing and illustrating the standard boats built by Chaisson. Privately printed and undated. A copy of this catalog is in the library at Mystic Seaport.

ACCESSION NO. 1971.205

SWAMPSCOTT
SAILING DORY
BUILT AT MYSTIC SEAPORT

17' 3" x 4' 6"   1974

"These Swampscott boats are the aristocrats of the dory clan, and are not to be confused with their clumsier, more crudely built cousins, the heavy slab-sided working dories of the Grand Banks fishermen," wrote John Gardner in his *Building Classic Small Craft.* Gardner noted, "The true Swampscott dory....is essentially a round-bottom boat, yet with enough flat in its relatively narrow board bottom to sit upright on the beach when it grounds out. For a boat that is to be beached frequently, this is an especially desirable feature, particularly as it permits a double bottom, the outer layer of which is easily renewed when it wears thin from dragging over rocks."

Barry Thomas of Mystic Seaport's Small Boat Shop built this boat, and her plans are much like those contained in Chapter 11 of *Building Classic Small Craft.* Both boats were modeled by John Gardner after the dories of the North Shore of Massachusetts Bay.

STATUS: In use, excellent condition.

DONOR: Mystic Seaport-built

FURTHER READING:

Carter, John. "Swampscott Dories: Work or Pleasure; On the North Shore." *WoodenBoat* 36, Sept/Oct, 1980.

Gardner, John. *Building Classic Small Craft.* Camden, Maine: International Marine Publishing Co., 1977.

——. *The Dory Book.* Mystic: Mystic Seaport Publications, 1987.

——. *Wooden Boats to Build and Use.* Mystic: Mystic Seaport Publications, 1996.

ACCESSION NO. 1974.1025

Plans for 1974.1025 are available from Mystic Seaport's Watercraft Plans Collection.

December trial of the Swampscott sailing dory. Later a conventional rudder replaced the oar shown here. (Photo: Ken Mahler, Mystic Seaport 1974-12-8)

The replica Swampscott sailing dory on launching day, November, 1974. (Photo: Ken Mahler, Mystic Seaport 1974-11-166)

SAILING DORY
BY CHAISSON

16' 5" x 5' 3"   ca. 1930

"This is the only boat of its type to survive, so far as I know. Once in common use on Fisherman's Beach (Swampscott, Massachusetts) but for a rowing work boat, not fitted for sail. This boat is in practically new condition and was stored in a barn unused for something like 40 years until found and sailed for two summers by John M. Chaisson, the designer's grandson, and Paul Sherry, husband of Joan C. Sherry, Joe Chaisson's granddaughter . . ." John Gardner.

STATUS: Original, excellent condition.

DONOR: John M. Chaisson, William J. Chaisson, Joan C. Sherry

FURTHER READING for 1977.262 and 1982.85:
Gardner, John. *The Dory Book*. Mystic: Mystic Seaport Publications, 1987.

Chaisson sailing dory 1977.262 in 1978. (Photo: Maynard Bray, Mystic Seaport 1978-2-16)

——. *Building Classic Small Craft*. Camden, Maine: International Marine Publishing Co., 1977.
——. *Classic Small Craft You Can Build*. Mystic: Mystic Seaport Publications, 1993.

Promotional catalog describing and illustrating the standard boats built by Chaisson. Privately printed and undated. A copy is in the library at Mystic Seaport.

ACCESSION NO. 1977.262

SAILING DORY
BY CHAISSON

15' 1" x 4' 8"   1936

It isn't often that a boat this old comes to the Museum from its original owner completely equipped, but this one arrived with her original spars, rudder and tiller, rigging and sails. Although this sailing dory was not built with the outboard motor well, the boat was only three years old when a well was installed. Her builder charged only $90.00 for the basic boat, and another $30.00 for the sailing rig–a bargain even in those days, made possible because Chaisson specialized in building dories and became efficient at turning them out. (This is the same model as the Chaisson-built rowing dory 1971.205.) The Castle family used this boat each summer on Cape Cod's Waquoit Bay until 1963, when they laid her up for the last time.

STATUS: Original, minor repairs, good condition.

DONOR: Dr. & Mrs. William B. Castle

ACCESSION NO. 1982.85

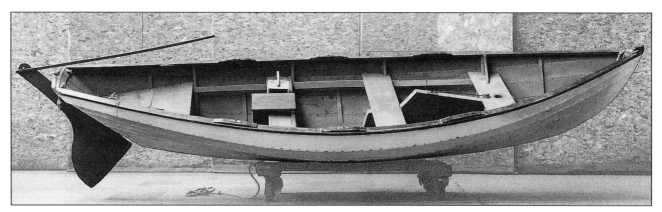

Chaisson sailing dory 1982.85. Note pads for a forward rowing station, put in even though this is a sailing version–an indication of immutable production-line boatbuilding. (Photo: Deborah Bates, Mystic Seaport 1982.85B)

Jope
SWAMPSCOTT SAILING DORY
17' 5" x 4' 6"   ca. 1900

An exceptionally pretty dory, *Jope* came complete with sailing rig. Her mainsail has the high-cut foot common to most sailing dories that kept the sail area as low as possible, yet kept the boom reasonably clear of the helmsman's head. Dories are none too stable to begin with, and keeping the rig low keeps heeling moment low. What keeps a dory like this on her feet is skipper and crew using their weight as ballast and moving to windward as the wind breezes up. For this kind of crew activity, tiller steering never worked as well as a rudder-mounted yoke with continuous steering line, reachable from either rail. This dory is so equipped. Her builder is unknown, although it's a fairly safe bet

Sailing dory Jope *in 1993 with her rudder shipped and her bundled-up sailing rig in the foreground. (Photo: Maynard Bray,* Mystic Seaport 1986.97.1A*)*

that he was from the North Shore of Massachusetts Bay, and not far from Rockport where this dory was always used.

STATUS: Original, fair condition.

DONOR: Joseph R. Worcester, in memory of Thomas Worcester

ACCESSION NO. 1986.97.1

SAILING DORY BY CHAMBERLAIN
18' 5" x 4' 9"   ca. 1930

This is similar to, but smaller than, Chamberlain's standard "Beachcomber" model. Like the "Beachcomber" she steers with a yoke and continuous steering line, led about halfway forward, allowing the helmsman to get well up to windward and still steer.

STATUS: Some repair, split in garboard planks has been reinforced with blocking, mostly original, good condition.

DONOR: Estate of Welles V. Moot

FURTHER READING FOR 1977.256 AND 1986.97.1:
(Same as for dory 1973.386)

ACCESSION NO. 1977.256

CATALOGUE
OF
POWER BOATS
Sailing and Clipper Dories
Rowboats and Skiffs
BUILT BY
WILLIAM H. CHAMBERLAIN
14 Orne Street   .   .   .   .   Marblehead, Mass.

These boats are all built under my personal supervision, by skilled workmen. They are noted for their stability and seaworthiness and their lines are the result of years of study and practical experience, and are guaranteed second to none.

The Chamberlain sailing dory in 1978. (Photo: Maynard Bray, Mystic Seaport 1978-2-56*)*

The Dion-built sailing dory in 1993. (Photo: Maynard Bray, Mystic Seaport 1990.137A)

SWAMPSCOTT SAILING DORY BY DION

17' 0" x 4' 8"   1910

With the youthful objective of voyaging to Provincetown from his Salem, Massachusetts, home, Fred Dion borrowed the molds and built this dory. Other events postponed the trip, however, and it was Fred's new wife Thias who made use of this boat, often taking their young family out rowing and sailing. Only four days before giving birth to their first child in 1914, Thias Dion rowed this dory away from her waterfront as she watched it and much of Salem go up in flames during that year's great fire. Rumor has it that Fred may have used the dory for occasional night trips during Prohibition. He always thought of the boat as his wife's, however, and put it away after she died in the 1930s. Neither he nor anyone else has used the boat since.

John Gardner discovered this sweet little boat in 1952 resting on the spar-shed rafters of Dion's Yacht Yard where he worked. He measured, drew plans, published an article in *National Fisherman*, and finally, in 1966, arranged for Fred to donate it to the Adirondack Museum in upstate New York. There it remained on exhibit until it was given to Mystic Seaport some 25 years later. Amateur builders have produced copies of this dory from Gardner's drawings and instruction in *The Dory Book*.

STATUS: Original, good condition.

DONOR: The Adirondack Museum

FURTHER READING:
Gardner, John. *The Dory Book*. Mystic: Mystic Seaport Publications, 1987.

ACCESSION NO. 1990.137

SWAMPSCOTT DORY TENDER BY DION

12' 4" x 4' 3"   ca. 1918

Dory tenders make seaworthy, easy-rowing boats, but have less initial stability than do round-bottom tenders, a potential disadvantage when boarding in a seaway. This dory tender is similar to those turned out by George Chaisson in three sizes, starting at 10'. Chaisson made frequent use of bent frames, and this tender's frames are all bent. Fred Dion befriended the Chaissons when they arrived in Swampscott from Nova Scotia, and he acquired a drawing of Chaisson's 12' tender, which he gave to John Gardner. The drawing became the subject of a chapter in John Gardner's *Classic Small Craft You Can Build*. This boat has two rowing stations, and a mast partner and step forward. Inset metal straps support the seat knees.

The Dion-built dory tender. (Photo: Judy Beisler, Mystic Seaport 1990.156A)

STATUS: Fair condition.

DONOR: L. Thomas Dion

FURTHER READING:
Gardner, John. *Classic Small Craft You Can Build*. Mystic: Mystic Seaport Publications. 1993.

——. *The Dory Book*. Mystic: Mystic Seaport Publications, 1987.

ACCESSION NO. 1990.156

BEACHCOMBER-ALPHA
SAILING DORY
BY CHAMBERLAIN

20' 10" x 4' 11"   ca. 1900

William Chamberlain modeled this boat and built many like her for the Beachcomber and Alpha Dory Clubs of Marblehead and Salem, respectively. These two clubs came into being about 1890, and interest in racing these big dories continued into the 1930s. During that time there were several changes in the rig, the most apparent being the adoption of the cross-cut battened mainsail with its rather extreme roach in place of the original sail that had an up-and-down cut.

While few boats survive today from the original fleet, a number of reproductions have been built from the very detailed drawings prepared by John Gardner for *National Fisherman* in 1964. Anyone making a study of these boats would also do well to inspect the rigged model at the Peabody Essex Museum in Salem, Massachusetts, which was carefully researched, then built in 1959 under the direction of a special committee of surviving members of the Beachcomber and Alpha clubs.

STATUS: Original, fair condition.

DONOR: Sylvester B. Kelley

FURTHER READING:
Gardner, John. *Building Classic Small Craft*. Camden, Maine: International Marine Publishing Co., 1977.

——. *The Dory Book*. Mystic: Mystic Seaport Publications, 1987.

Promotional catalog describing and illustrating the standard boats built by William Chamberlain. Privately printed and undated. A copy of this catalog is in the library at Mystic Seaport.

ACCESSION NO. 1973.386

The Beachcomber dory in 1975. (Photo: Maynard Bray, Mystic Seaport 1975-10-171)

BEACHCOMBER DORY

These dories have gained a much envied name for themselves, being adopted by the Beachcomber Club of Marblehead and the Alpha Club of Salem. They are well known for their speed, stability and sea-worthiness. They are the fastest dories of their size on the market.

15 feet bottom, 21 feet over all, $57.00

Rigged with mast, sails and oars, complete, $90.00.

7

Chamberlain's catalog description of the Beachcomber Dory.(Photo: Mystic Seaport 1978-1-122)

SAILING DORY

12' 0" x 3' 9"   ca. 1880

Although this boat's dory classification is unmistakable, her extreme topside flare and her raking ends make her an unusual version of the type. No one remembers who built her or where, only that the donor's grandfather, Willard Kent, used her for hunting and fishing on the Pettaquamsett River that empties into Narragansett Bay on its western shoreline.

This boat has metal sheathing on stem and stern, most likely as protection from ice. The absence of oarlocks indicate that it was sailed or sculled, not rowed.

STATUS: Original, good condition.

DONOR: Mr. & Mrs. G. Herbert Repass

ACCESSION NO. 1981.162.1

Sailing dory 1981.162.1 in 1993. (Photo: Maynard Bray, Mystic Seaport 1981.162.1*)*

Svarmisk

SWAMPSCOTT DORY BY CULLER

18' 8" x 5' 0"   1977

Svarmisk was built by Capt. R.D. "Pete" Culler in 1977 from a design he created in 1972 for Charlie Sayle of Nantucket. Capt. Culler considered *Svarmisk* to be a "clipper" version of the Swampscott dory, designed for recreational rowing and sailing. The boat carries a large sail plan featuring sprit-rigged main and mizzen and is fitted with two rowing stations. Constructed of pine, cedar, and oak, *Svarmisk* is believed to be the last boat Pete Culler built. Her original owner, Chris Wentz of Larchmont, New York, donated the boat to the Williams College-Mystic Seaport undergraduate studies program in 1986 for use by students. In 2001 the vessel was retired from sailing to become part of the Mystic Seaport Watercraft Collection.

STATUS: Good Condition.

DONOR: Chris Wentz

Williams College-Mystic Seaport Program students sail Svarmisk *in the Mystic River. (Photo: Courtesy of Williams College-Mystic Seaport Maritime Studies Program)*

FURTHER READING:
Burke, John. *Pete Culler's Boats: The Complete Design Catalog.* Camden, Maine: International Marine Publishing Co., 1984.

Culler, R.D. Boats, *Oars and Rowing.* Camden, Maine: International Marine Publishing Co., 1978.

ACCESSION NO. 2001.85
Plans for 2001.85 are available from Mystic Seaport's Watercraft Plans Collection.

Chapter Two
ROUND-BOTTOMED

The Bailey Whitehall on exhibit, 1978. (Photo: Maynard Bray, Mystic Seaport 1978-2-104)

BAILEY WHITEHALL

16′ 9″ x 3′ 7″   1879

Whitehalls, most experts agree, originated about 1820 as runners' boats on the New York waterfront, taking their name from Whitehall Street, near the Battery. As a deepwater sailing vessel made her way up the bay after months at sea, her crew was accosted by runners who came aboard huckstering for local brothels, ship chandlers, and the like, hot on the trail of whatever money the poor sailors had managed to earn during their passage. Runners from the ships' owners or agents might be rowed out as well in a working Whitehall boat with a couple of "Battery boatmen" at the oars.

As the years went by the boatmen of other seaports, notably Boston, adopted Whitehalls, perhaps modified, which were described by Capt. Charlton Smith as being "not under seventeen nor over twenty feet in length. The breadth not less than four feet. The depth not less than nineteen inches. They were rowed on the gunwales and had to weigh at least 265 pounds. So read the rules of the boat clubs."

Within the past 35 years there has been a renewed interest in Whitehall boats, their history, and their characteristics—understandable attention inspired by their grace and beauty. W.P. Stephens, Capt. Charlton Smith, and Howard Chapelle have been leaders in Whitehall research, but it

was the late John Gardner who fit all the pieces together in his boatbuilding and research and must be recognized as Dean of the Whitehall scholars.

Of this boat, John Gardner says in his book, *Building Classic Small Craft,* that she is "a fancy pleasure Whitehall apparently built at Boston, Massachusetts, in 1879. A sliding seat for the oarsman on runners extending over the top of the daggerboard case is a refinement not to be found in the runner's workboat. Yet in essentials the boat conforms to standard Boston Whitehall construction, although its scantlings are reduced to an absolute minimum, and its hull lines are drawn extra lean and fine. The peerless workmanship found in this boat, its exquisite lines, and delicate yet sturdy construction which has lasted so well after so many years, bespeak the hand of a master craftsman. Although we do not know the name of the builder, there is good reason to conclude that this boat came out of one of the leading Boston boatshops of the era, when the boatbuilding craft was practiced on a level which we do not begin to approach in this country today."

As far as is known, this boat is the only surviving Whitehall from the heyday of these boats from either New York or Boston. The Baileys, father and son, owned her from 1881 until she was given to Mystic Seaport 72 years later.

STATUS: Some repair but mostly original, fair condition.

DONOR: Edwin M. and David C. Bailey

FURTHER READING FOR 1954.211, 1969.584, 1974.94, 1980.5, 1978.102, AND 1998.34:

Chapelle, Howard I. *American Small Sailiaft.* New York: W.W. Norton & Co., 1951.

Gardner, John. *Building Classic Small Craft.* Camden, Maine: International Marine Publishing Co., 1977.

Smith, Charlton L. "The Whitehall Boat." *The Rudder,* August, 1943.

Stephens, Robert W. "Survival of the Fastest." *WoodenBoat* 126, Sept/Oct, 1995.

ACCESSION NO. 1954.211

Plans for 1954.211 are available from Mystic Seaport's Watercraft Plans Collection.

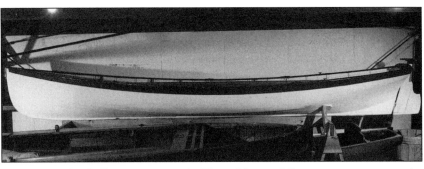

The Bailey Whitehall in storage, 1975. (Photo: Maynard Bray, Mystic Seaport 1975-10-103)

BOSTON WHITEHALL

13' 2" x 4' 0"   ca. 1900-20

Although this boat is smaller than the old working Whitehalls and was built later, probably in Maine rather than Boston, Charles Lawton called her a good representative of the nineteenth-century Boston Whitehalls. Lawton, as a young man, had built boats for the H.V. Partelow Co., a firm noted for its superior Whitehalls and its improved ways of building them. This particular boat was first pointed out to John Gardner in the early 1940s when he and Lawton, who was then an old man, worked together at Graves Yacht Yard in Marblehead. After studying the boat and learning all he could about Whitehall construction from Lawton, Gardner lost track of her until the late 1960s when she turned up again, dried out and paint sick, and was given to Mystic Seaport.

To be classed as a Whitehall type, a boat must have not only the right shape but certain other features as well. Her frames must lay square to the keel and be bevelled to fit the planking which is hung later; her frames also must be tapered so they are deeper at their heels than at their heads. Whitehalls always had an oak sheer strake, bevelled on its lower edge to fit against, and stand out slightly beyond, a matching bevel on the top edge of the binding strake as the second plank down was called. The rest of the planking was smooth-seamed, although Howard Chapelle pointed out that some early Whitehalls were lapstrake. An inwale always covered the heads of the frames and a horseshoe-shaped stern seat with a backrest was standard on Whitehall boats.

STATUS: Restored 1970, mostly original, good condition.

DONOR: William F. Peach

FURTHER READING:
(Same as for 1954.211)

ACCESSION NO. 1969.584
Plans for 1969.584 are available from Mystic Seaport's Watercraft Plans Collection.

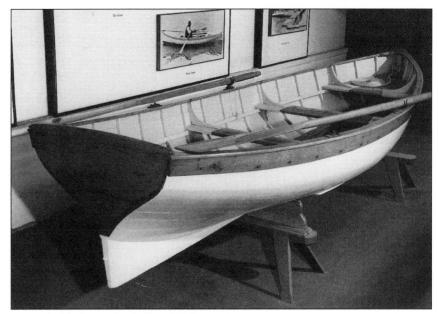

The 13' 2" Boston Whitehall on exhibit, 1978. (Photo: Maynard Bray, Mystic Seaport 1978-2-102)

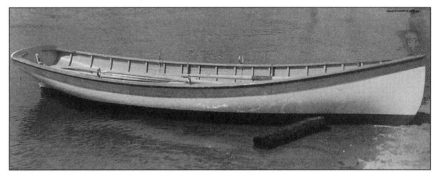

The Mystic Seaport-built Whitehall tender in 1974. (Photo: T.J. Baker, Mystic Seaport 1974-6-87)

WHITEHALL TENDER, MYSTIC SEAPORT-BUILT REPRODUCTION

14' 10" x 4' 2"   1974

Barry Thomas, Mystic Seaport's now-retired boatbuilder, built this lovely boat to lines taken from an old (ca. 1910) tender by Rice Bros., East Boothbay, Maine, now in the Maine Maritime Museum. But the new boat's construction was altered to that of a classic working Whitehall and building her this way yielded the first-hand experience and photos needed to produce an authoritative book on the subject. The Whitehall has always been a favorite of amateur builders, and many plans of this boat have been sold.

STATUS: In use, excellent condition.

SOURCE: Museum-built reproduction

FURTHER READING:
(Same as for 1954.211)

ACCESSION NO. 1974.94
Plans for 1974.94 are available from Mystic Seaport's Watercraft Plans Collection.

Sheldon Whitehall in storage in 1980. (Photo: Mary Anne Stets, Mystic Seaport 1980-2-37)

WHITEHALL BY SHELDON

15' 0" x 4' 1"   ca. 1900

On the Massachusetts-Rhode Island border sits the town of Sheldonville, Massachusetts, in the midst of what was once a large cedar swamp and stands of hardwood. There, in 1825, Col. Rose Sheldon started a boatbuilding business furnishing ship's boats in various styles to the shipbuilders of Massachusetts, Cape Cod, Buzzards and Narragansett Bays. The business turned out packet boats, yawl boats, reach, long, and surf boats as well as a few gigs, lifeboats, and

launches. In 1866, Col. Sheldon died and his son Orin took over, moving aggressively into the burgeoning recreational market of the 1880s. Among the company's offerings were plain but nicely finished Whitehalls like this one, which once had a seatback for passengers and a rudder to give them something useful to do. The Sheldon company also built St. Lawrence River skiffs that were similar to 1975.177, and established a "wareroom" in

Boston. Sheldon even became a dealer for Globe Marine Engines and a builder of gasoline-powered launches.

STATUS: Original, good condition.

DONOR: Townsend Hornor

FURTHER READING:
(Same as for 1954.211)

ACCESSION NO. 1980.5
Plans for 1980.5 are available from Mystic Seaport's Watercraft Plans Collection.

Elysea

BOSTON SHIP CHANDLER'S WHITEHALL BY SAMUEL I. McQUAY

16' 3" x 4' 5"   1976

Following the plans of the Boston Ship Chandler's Whitehall published by Howard I. Chapelle in his *American Small Sailing Craft*, "Doc" Fisher commissioned the Eastern Shore boatbuilder, Sam McQuay of Whitman, Maryland, to build *Elysea*. Since light round-bottom construction was unusual for a Maryland builder, McQuay's neighbor, Josef Liener, retired superintendent of the Philadelphia Naval Shipyard's Small Boat Shop, supervised. The result is an elegant product, given to the Museum for use on its waterfront. *Elysea* is equipped with an awning, a sail, a stern sheets backrest, a rudder, and custom oars. In use, she tracks so well it seems like she is on rails, making her less

Sailing Whitehall Elysea *in use in 1976. (Photo: Mystic Seaport 1976-3-136)*

maneuverable than many boats under oars, and a real challenge to sail in and out of tight quarters. The original design, which dates to sometime before 1876, of course, was meant for open harbor use, carrying passengers and gear, where holding course in a cross wind at varying loadings was important.

STATUS: In use, excellent condition.

DONOR: Dr. Donald E. Fisher

FURTHER READING:
(Same as for 1954.211)

ACCESSION NO. 1978.102

WESTCOTT WHITEHALL

14' 9" x 4' 4"   ca. 1977

This boat has been temporarily retired from the Museum's Boathouse livery fleet, where it provided patrons with the experience of rowing a Whitehall. The shape is quite attractive, and the boat was constructed using straight-forward plank-on-frame methods. Heavily built, the boat has 5/8" planking screw-fastened to 1" x 3/4" oak frames bent in on the flat. Some broken frames and a number of repairs point to a history of heavy use and periods of neglect. Finish details vary on similar structural members, indicating that the boat may have been originally built by a team, not a single individual.

STATUS: Good to fair condition.
DONOR: Jack & Suzanne Westcott
ACCESSION NO. 1998.79.1

Whitehall 1998.79.1. (Photo: Dennis Murphy, Mystic Seaport 1998.79.1H*)*

Donoghue

WHERRY/WHITEHALL ATTRIBUTED TO GEORGE KNEISS

17' 11" x 3' 9"   ca. 1870

It's hard to fine a nicer pulling boat than *Donoghue*, resurrected from a basket case by Bob Baker's skill, study, and thought. The Bakers got the wreck of a beautiful pulling boat from Jack Kochiss about 1968, with the story that she was built and used around Clinton, Connecticut. "Beautiful....*Donoghue* What a labor of love that was.....She was just dead grey wood but it was wonderful and...when we brought her back to Newport and took her up to Warren, everyone teased us about this hulk," Bob Baker remembered.

Baker brought her back into shape with patience, poking, and prodding, then taking off her lines. From those he built outside molds, then stripped out the boat's interior. After a soaking to

limber her up, gently into the mold she went, and she fit exactly. With the shape locked in, the keel, stem, sternpost, and frames could be replaced. All the planks, which defined the shape, were saved except for her sheer strakes. In replacing them, Baker precisely duplicated the mid-plank beading. Floorboards, stretchers, gratings, and a backboard were newly built. Her folding outriggers are based on ones that Baker saw in a period catalog, whose base precisely matched the indentation and fastening patterns in the boat.

The bead in the center of the sheer strakes is exactly like one on *Azulykit* (1987.25), and that, plus a few other details, is why Baker felt both had been built by the same hand. The question is open and would take some inquiries into Connecticut census data to see if George Kneiss worked in Connecticut and removed to San Francisco.

Donoghue is Whitehall-built, with cedar planks riveted to bent oak frames

that overlap at the keel. She has "T. Donoghue" branded twice on the inner transom and starboard and port on the inside of the planks below the sheer strakes, as well as on a second plank to port. Evidently, Mr. Donoghue wanted to make the boat easy to identify. The interior was a nice Band-Aid pink, Bob thought from combining red and blue lead paint, something not uncommon. The Bakers intended to use her, so a modern aesthetic prevailed and they painted the interior with French gray.

Donoghue was built fancy, and Baker's new work followed the theme. Besides the bead in outboard center of the sheer strakes (which lap the next plank down), both risers are beaded, as are the seats and the inboard top edge of the plank below the sheer strakes. Her seat knees pass under the seats and are fastened together, providing a light, strong beam across the boat in the manner of Norwegian small boats.

Baker called her a wherry in the English sense of a lightly built pleasure boat, feeling that the term Whitehall should be best reserved for the more heavily built working types. Judging from period writings about rowing, she could have been referred to as a wherry, a Whitehall, a New York work boat, or just a club boat.

Several reproductions of *Donoghue* have been built, one of which is rowed hard in Maine and on the New England open-water race circuit. She is fast and hard to beat, pulling 9' 6" oars on her 5' span between outriggers. However, her

light construction suffered from trailer transportation, as was found out during a Boston Harbor race, when bailing became necessary. To combat this, she has been given a half frame between each original frame. She balances beautifully with a light coxswain; a few stones in the stern can substitute, reducing her tendency to turn upwind when rowing across wind in a real breeze. It is surprising that more *Donoghue*s are not on the water.

STATUS: Good, worn condition. Rebuilt by Bob Baker, with parts added as above.

DONOR: Anne (Mrs. Robert H.) Baker

FURTHER READING: (Same as for 1954.211)

ACCESSION NO. 1998.34

Plans for both *Donoghue* and *Azulykit* are available from Anne Baker, 29 Drift Rd., Westport, Massachusetts 02790.

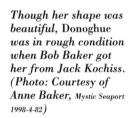

Though her shape was beautiful, Donoghue *was in rough condition when Bob Baker got her from Jack Kochiss. (Photo: Courtesy of Anne Baker,* Mystic Seaport 1998-4-82*)*

Bob and Anne "Pete" Baker take their children Nat and Sarah for a spin in Donoghue *at an early Mystic Seaport Small Craft Workshop. (Photo: Courtesy of Anne Baker,* Mystic Seaport 1998-4-88*)*

Sailing Whitehall Azulykit. *(Photo: Deborah Patterson, Mystic Seaport 1987.25D)*

Azulykit
SAILING WHITEHALL BY GEORGE KNEISS

15' 0" x 4' 3"   ca. 1890

In 1963, Bob Baker and his wife Anne moved to Tomales Bay, California, to research small boats and their connections to the East. A block from their house in Inverness, they spotted and stopped at a shop. Peering through the windows they saw "thousands of little boats. The place had been a livery back in the 'forties...and there were all kinds of neat things in there, at least there seemed to be." Once they found the owner, Brock Schreiber, they got in. Over the next months they measured and drew several of the boats they found, and Brock gave them one. They found *Azulykit* under another house, a

discovery Anne made while walking home from the post office. Twenty-five dollars later, Bob had an early birthday present. Local lore is that she had been built by a George Kneiss about 1890.

Azulykit has the shape and floor timber-frame construction typical of working Whitehalls, in addition to a centerboard trunk and mast step. She has unusual details, such as the construction of her stern seat, extra light and long thwart knees, and a double bead cut into the center of the sheer strakes. Her name was carved into the backrest at the stern.

Later the Bakers obtained and restored *Donoghue* (previous page), a light, narrow Whitehall-type that Bob called a wherry (using the old English sense of the term for a lightly-built pleasure boat). She was said to have been built about 1870 in the vicinity of

Clinton, Connecticut. His examination of telling details found on both boats convinced him that the same builder had built them both, perhaps moving from Connecticut to California. Unfortunately, census work has not yet confirmed this; the only thing certain is that both boats have similar details and were built 3,000 miles apart.

STATUS: Well-worn, no longer usable.
DONOR: Anne (Mrs. Robert H.) Baker
FURTHER READING:
(Same as for 1954.211)
ACCESSION NO. 1987.25
Plans for both *Azulykit* and *Donoghue*, the similar Connecticut boat, are available from Anne Baker, 29 Drift Rd., Westport, Massachusetts 02790.

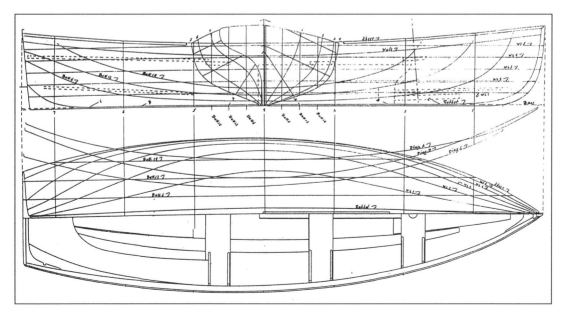

Lines for Azulykit *as drawn by Bob Baker.*

General Lafayette
on exhibit in 1978.
(Photo: Maynard
Bray, Mystic Seaport
1978-2-101)

American Star was taken to Lafayette's estate outside Paris in the 1820s
and has been preserved there ever since. This photo was taken about 1971.
(Photo: H. Grey, Mystic Seaport 1976-2-50)

General Lafayette *underway on the Mystic River.*
(Photo: Ken Mahler, Mystic Seaport 1975-7-87)

General Lafayette

EARLY NINETEENTH-CENTURY PULLING BOAT, MYSTIC SEAPORT-BUILT REPRODUCTION

27' 4" x 3' 10"   1975

John Gardner built this near-replica of the New York Harbor racing gig *American Star* (ca. 1820). The original, which defeated the British boat *Dart* in a now-famous race during the winter of 1824, was presented to General Lafayette when he visited the United States a short time later. Lafayette prized the gift; he took her to his chateau just outside Paris and placed her inside out of the weather, where she has since remained. Realizing her importance as the oldest American small boat known to exist, Gardner seized the first opportunity to view, study, and record her lines and structural details with the idea of duplicating her at the Museum.

Compared with the small-boat construction that most of us know today, these boats were very differently put together, being planked with thin 1/4-inch cedar over an alternating

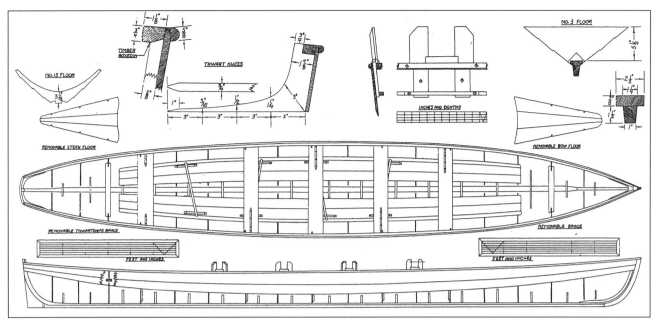

General Lafayette as drawn by John Gardner in 1993.

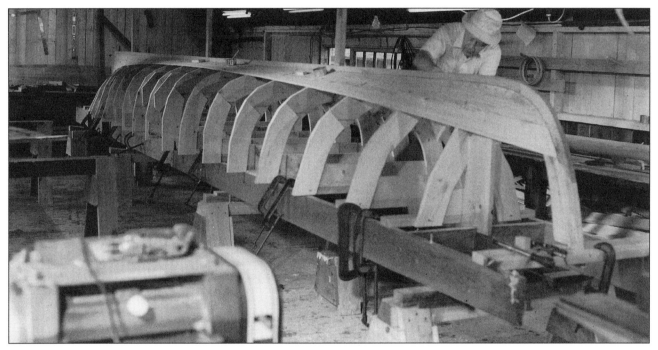

John Gardner planking up the pulling boat General Lafayette *in 1974. (Photo: Ken Mahler, Mystic Seaport 1974-9-127)*

structure of substantial floor timbers and very light steam-bent frames. For her great length she is quite light; yet, due largely to her gunwales and seats, she is stiff and strong. *General Lafayette* is fun to row, fast and responsive, but not the boat to use if the course isn't straight, or nearly so.

STATUS: Excellent condition.

SOURCE: Museum-built reproduction sponsored by John R. Deupree

FURTHER READING:
Gardner, John. *Building Classic Small Craft*. Camden, Maine: International Marine Publishing Co., 1977.

——. "Early Days of Rowing Sport." *The Log of Mystic Seaport*, Winter, 1971.

——. "The *American Star*." *The Log of Mystic Seaport*, Fall, 1972.

——. *Wooden Boats to Build and Use*. Mystic, Connecticut: Mystic Seaport Publications, 1996. Chapter 11 is about this boat.

ACCESSION NO. 1974.1026

DOUBLE GIG

24' 8" x 3' 9"   ca. 1870

This boat was probably built just after the Civil War, when rowing took the country by storm. Rowing clubs increased from a dozen before the war to almost 300 in 1873. In the clubs of that time, this boat would have been called an in-rigged gig, with rowlocks—in this case flat thole pins on top of the gunwale, like those of the *General Lafayette* (1974.1026). She is set up to be rowed by two, with a passenger or two, or a coxswain. Her structure features a longitudinal hogging timber or keelson that runs over the frames and runs upwards to support the seats. She has six lapped planks per side, riveted to bent oak frames set a foot apart. She was found hanging in a barn in Salisbury, Connecticut. Although her history is not known, she is a fine

The double gig at Mystic Seaport. (Photo: Judy Beisler, Mystic Seaport 1996.80.1G)

example of the type of boat commonly found in the rowing clubs of the 1880s.

STATUS: Excellent original condition, cosmetically worn. Missing centerline floorboards and stretcher, but with rudder, yoke, and oars. Two broken tholes.

DONOR: Pat Patterson

FURTHER READING:

Mendenhall, Thomas C. *A Short History of American Rowing.* Boston: Charles River Books, ca. 1980.

Waters, Balch & Co. *The Annual Illustrated Catalogue and Oarsman's Manual for 1871.* Troy, New York: Waters, Balch & Co., 1871.

Woodgate, W.B. *Boating.* Boston: Little, Brown, and Co.; London: Longmans, Green & Co., 1888.

ACCESSION NO. 1996.80.1

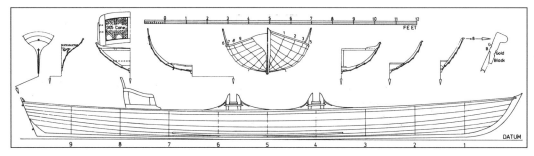

Drawings of a similar Thames River skiff from Working Boats of Britain.

Gytha

THAMES RIVER SKIFF BY E. MESSUM & SONS

23' 8" x 4' 2"   ca. 1880

Great Britain's Thames River skiff, a popular recreational boat of the Victorian era, evolved out of the working Thames waterman's passenger wherries in the 1870s. The sharply flaring sides of these boats allow oars to get a maximum spread on a minimum waterline beam. They were lightly built to a high standard and equipped with spoon oars and efficient stretchers (foot braces). Light gratings in bow and stern allow gear to be stored there, while the passengers' seat is placed well forward of the stern, allowing a very long fine run. The passenger backrest is often caned for comfort and light weight, or made of ornamental cast iron. Picnic supplies or camping gear go in a box under the passenger seat, and there is a

canvas canopy for camping. In addition to all the usual skiff features, *Gytha* has elaborate painted and gold-leafed decorations under the rowlocks and in the stern sheets. Her oars are monogrammed and her tiller ropes embellished with decorative rope work. She was one of thousands that were built on the Thames by some 300 builders at the height of Thames rowing popularity. In 1889, 12,000 pleasure boats were registered there.

James Lawrence bought this Thames River skiff for use on the Nashua River near Groton, Massachusetts, sometime around 1880 from E. Messum & Sons of Richmond (near Hampton Court Palace on the Thames), one of the better-known builders. She lived in a boathouse on the river until she came to the Museum, a fine example of sophisticated light oar-on-gunwale boatbuilding, donated by James Lawrence's grandson.

STATUS: Excellent unrestored original condition, except for one damaged plank.

DONOR: John Lawrence

FURTHER READING:

Jerome, Jerome K. *Three Men in A Boat.* London: Arrowsmith, 1889.

McKee, Eric. *Working Boats of Britain, Their Shape and Purpose.* London: Conway Maritime Press in Association with the National Maritime Museum, 1983.

Spectre, Peter H. "A Week Along the Thames: Rowing a Camping Skiff Through the Heart of England." *WoodenBoat* 74, Jan/Feb, 1987.

Vine, P.A.L. *Pleasure Boating in the Victorian Era.* Chichester, Sussex, U.K.: Phillimore & Co. Ltd., 1983.

Woodgate, W.B. *Boating.* Boston: Little, Brown, and Co.; London: Longmans, Green and Co., 1888.

ACCESSION NO. 1989.52

Mary A.

PULLING BOAT FROM SOUTHPORT, MAINE

12' 6" x 3' 10" ca. 1910

Rowing for pleasure was what "rusticators" who came to country cottages each summer from the cities did in boats like this. Most were owned by the summer people themselves and were kept at their floats or at the yacht club. Others were sometimes rented by summer hotels to their guests. This particular boat is believed to have been built by one of the McFarlands and was last used at Southport, Maine.

Mary A. *at Mystic Seaport in 1975. (Photo: Maynard Bray,* Mystic Seaport 1975-5-6)

STATUS: Some repair, approximately 85% original, fair condition.
DONOR: Maynard E. Bray
FURTHER READING:
Clifford, Harold B. *The Boothbay Region,* 1906 to 1960. Freeport, Maine: Bond Wheelwright Co., 1961.
Gardner, John. *Building Classic Small Craft.* Camden, Maine: International Marine Publishing Co., 1977.
ACCESSION NO. 1973.88

Livery boats at Dennett's Wharf, Castine, Maine. (Photo: Courtesy of Joel White)

Pulling boat Limpet *with rudder and backrest in place.*
(Photo: Judy Beisler, Mystic Seaport 1982.35B)

Limpet

PULLING BOAT FROM CASTINE, MAINE

12' 1" x 4' 1" ca. 1920

For years a common sight on a Castine summer day was this boat being rowed by Miss Dorothy Blake (her dog as passenger) and any nieces, nephews, and other friends that might be handy, heading to nearby islands or up the Bagaduce River. *Limpet* was kept at Dennett's Wharf, having been built by J.M. Dennett, the father of Jake Dennett who ran the wharf. The Dennett family also ran a boat livery and took summer parties to the islands for picnics. Miss Blake rowed *Limpet* until she was late in her seventies, then gave her to Philip Booth. Booth in turn passed her to Joel White of Brooklin, Maine. After Joel's restoration, the donor persuaded Joel to part with *Limpet* and rowed the boat with family and friends for about eight years.

Limpet may be similar to the boats the Dennetts built for their livery fleet, as she is heavier than similar-sized yacht tenders. She has square-sectioned bent oak frames, oak trim, a spruce sheer strake, and is carvel-planked. She would have been easy to row from her forward rowing position, as that position has provision for a foot brace.

STATUS: Good condition. Complete with oars, oarlocks, backrest, rudder and yoke.
DONOR: Edward Leonard
ACCESSION NO. 1982.35

PULLING BOAT
BY WARDWELL

14' 0" x 4' 6"   ca. 1930-40

For an amateur, Dr. I.F. Wardwell did a commendable job building this boat to modified Whitehall lines. Both frames and floors are joggled to fay tight against the planking between laps, a good idea to back up and help strengthen the unusually thin planking. However, her garboards are too wide, even for thicker planking, and in spite of the little use this boat has seen they have already started to buckle.

STATUS: Refinished 1973, original, good condition.

DONOR: Charles A. Betts, Jr.

FURTHER READING:
Gardner, John. *Building Classic Small Craft.* Camden, Maine: International Marine Publishing Co., 1977.

ACCESSION NO. 1949.323
Plans for 1949.323 are available from Mystic Seaport's Watercraft Plans Collection.

Wardwell pulling boat in 1975.
(Photo: Maynard Bray, Mystic Seaport 1975-10-104)

Capt. Hook
PULLING BOAT FROM SOUTHPORT, MAINE

11' 11" x 3' 10"   ca. 1920

This boat was also found in Southport, Maine, and is quite similar to *Mary A.* (1973.88) on the preceding page. Known simply as round-bottom rowboats along the Maine coast, they descend directly from the Whitehall boats of New York and Boston.

STATUS: Restored by donor in 1973, approximately 80% original, fair condition, retired from livery service in Mystic Seaport's Boathouse, and replaced by a Museum-built replica.

DONOR: Richard W. Conant
FURTHER READING:
(Same as for pulling boat 1973.88)

ACCESSION NO. 1974.472
Plans for 1974.472 are available from Mystic Seaport's Watercraft Plans Collection.

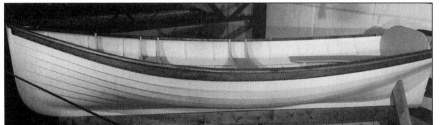

The pulling boat from Southport in use in 1975.
(Photo: Maynard Bray, Mystic Seaport 1975-5-251)

Helen N. in storage in the early 1970s.
(Photo: Mary Anne Stets, Mystic Seaport 1972.930)

Helen N.
PULLING BOAT

16' 9" x 3' 10"

Similar in shape to a Whitehall but of different and lighter construction, *Helen N.* was found by the donor in a Gloucester, Massachusetts, boatyard in 1961. He bought her on the spot and afterwords tried unsuccessfully to track down her history.

STATUS: Original, fair condition.

DONOR: Michael D. Sturges

ACCESSION NO. 1972.930

Winona *in 1993.*
(Photo: Maynard Bray,
Mystic Seaport 1979.70A)

Winona
PULLING BOAT
BY BARTLETT

16' 0" x 4' 2"   ca. 1911

Jared Bartlett of Sabbath Day Point on
New York's Lake George built this boat
for the donor's grandfather, William
Hathaway Van Cott, Jr., a Hell's
Kitchen teacher undoubtedly in need of
a summer break. Van Cott's summer
neighbors at the Divinity Bay summer

colony were all ministers. The boat's
name is supposed to mean "flashing ray
of light," but the donor recalls that, "It
might as well have been called the Love
Boat as it was the silent witness to many
young couples who went off for their
'funny moons' and often had the
pleasure of drifting around in the
moonlight." Mrs. Flint also comments
that "Getting in the boat to go to church
was better than horse and buggy on the
hot dusty road. As for other purposes,
this would have been forbidden on the

Sabbath. This gave church-going a
plus." In lines *Winona* resembles a
Whitehall, and her builder, "Uncle
Jed," may have sent away for the design.
She has closely spaced, steam-bent
frames and light lapstrake planking.

STATUS: Good, mostly original, some
reframing, repainted from original
varnish finish.
DONOR: Mrs. Janet B. Flint
ACCESSION NO. 1979.70
Plans for 1979.70 are available from Mystic
Seaport's Watercraft Plans Collection.

GIG FROM
STEAM YACHT *NOMA*

24' 10" x 5' 1"   ca. 1890

The 263-foot *Noma* came out in 1892
from the Staten Island yard of Burlee
Shipbuilding & Dry Dock Co. Clinton
Crane designed her for railroad mogul
W.B. Leeds who used her a few years,
after which she belonged to the Astors,
then the Wanamakers, finally going to
foreign registry as *Vega* in the early
1930s. Her gig was an insignificant part
of *Noma*'s small-boat complement, for
also on davits were a couple of naphtha
launches, a racing sailboat of about 25
feet, and another gig. Each of this gig's
four-man crew pulled one oar. A
splendid model of *Noma* is in Mystic
Seaport's collection.

STATUS: Mostly original, good
condition.
DONOR: Bard College

FURTHER READING:
Crane, Clinton H. *Clinton Crane's
Yachting Memories*. New York: D. Van
Nostrand Co., 1952.

Hofman, Erik. *The Steam Yachts*.
Tuckahoe: John De Graff, Inc., 1970.

ACCESSION NO. 1959.967
Plans for 1959.967 are available from
Mystic Seaport's Watercraft Plans
Collection.

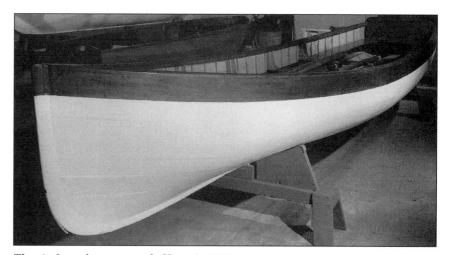

The gig from the steam yacht Noma *in 1975.*
(Photo: Maynard Bray, Mystic Seaport 1975-6-76)

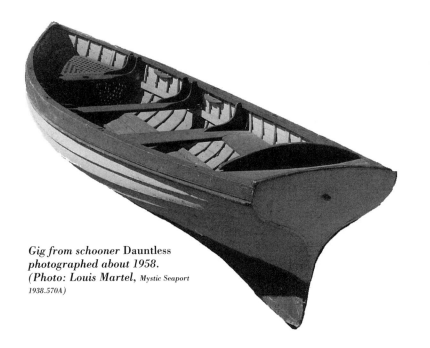

Gig from schooner Dauntless
photographed about 1958.
(Photo: Louis Martel, Mystic Seaport
1938.570A)

GIG, PROBABLY FROM SCHOONER *DAUNTLESS*

16' 2" x 4' 3"   ca. 1870

The famous schooner-yacht *Dauntless* was built as *L'Hirondelle* at Mystic, Connecticut, in 1866. Three years later, under the ownership of James Gordon Bennett and with the name *Dauntless*, she raced across the Atlantic against the America's Cup challenger *Cambria*, losing by only one hour. Unfortunately there is some doubt as to whether this gig belonged to *Dauntless*, although photos show a similar craft on her davits. In any event, *Dauntless* ended her days on the Connecticut River at Essex as the first headquarters of the Dauntless Club, and was an inspiration for the name of the Dauntless Shipyard there.

Mystic Seaport has in its collection two rigged models and a very fine series of photographs of the schooner *Dauntless*.

STATUS: Some repair, mostly original, fair condition.

DONOR: Dr. C.K. Stillman

FURTHER READING:
Bunting, W.H. *Steamers, Schooners, Cutters and Sloops*. Boston: Houghton Mifflin Co., for the Society for the Preservation of New England Antiquities, 1974. A photograph and good writeup of *Dauntless* appear on p. 29.

Perry, Lawrence. "*Dauntless*—A Boat With a Great Heart." *Yachting*, December, 1911. A good biography of the schooner *Dauntless* which covers her racing career.

ACCESSION NO. 1938.570
Plans for 1938.570 are available from Mystic Seaport's Watercraft Plans Collection.

Dauntless *under sail, with a gig hoisted on her port davits.*
(Photo: *Mystic Seaport 1969.196A.12*)

*The ship's boat
Ethel in 1979.
(Photo: Mary
Anne Stets,*
Mystic Seaport 1979-10-73*)*

Ethel
SHIP'S BOAT
14' 0" x 4' 11"

Not all boats are fancy-built, and *Ethel*
is a good example of plain construction.
Her planks are not well lined off, and
unmatched side to side. She was clench-
nailed with round galvanized nails,
longer than they needed to be. Yet she is
still serviceable and well-suited to
carrying a heavy load: a boat relatively
beamy, and yet with a fine high stern
that can stand serious immersion
without dragging. She still has her stern
hoisting ring, but the ring in the bow
seems to have fallen victim to
rebuilding. She has her original short
tiller, rudder, and spars for a leg-of-
mutton rig. Bronze quarter knees, seat
knees, and mast partner indicate that
her builder was producing enough boats
to warrant the investment in patterns
and castings to save construction time.
Her keel has been replaced, and other
repairs have been made by a succession
of owners who thought well enough of
how she rowed and sailed to keep her
intact. She was found abandoned on a

A ship's boat like Ethel *is stowed across the deckhouse of the bark* Alice *in this
photo taken on a passage from New York to New Zealand, ca. 1900.
(Photo:* Mystic Seaport 1996.113.1.6*)*

beach in Wellfleet on the east side of
Cape Cod in the early years of this
century. "W.F. Graham" is incised
under the paint inside the transom and
on the backrest, which has been
overpainted with "Ethel." The identity
of these vessels is unclear–if indeed they
are vessel names. A likely candidate is
an 1875 British bark named *Ethel*,

whose master was F. Graham. Another
is a bark named *Ethel* built in 1881 in
Portland, Maine.

STATUS: Fair condition, mostly
original.
DONOR: Thomas D. Leary
ACCESSION NO. 1979.117

Favorite *in 1975. (Photo: Maynard Bray, Mystic Seaport 1975-4-268)*

Favorite
PULLING BOAT

11' 9" x 4' 0"   ca. 1900

Favorite is smooth inside as well as out because she has no frames. Her hull is strip-planked and held in shape with extra-large seat knees which extend below as well as above the seats. Her lines are much like those of a Whitehall even though her construction is far removed from normal Whitehall practice.

STATUS: Refinished 1969, original, good condition.

DONOR: Elwell B. Thomas

FURTHER READING:
Gardner, John. *Building Classic Small Craft.* Camden, Maine: International Marine Publishing Co., 1977.

ACCESSION NO. 1940.504
Plans for 1940.504 are available from Mystic Seaport's Watercraft Plans Collection.

Punch
PULLING BOAT BY CULLER

17' 8" x 4' 1"   1970

This is a modified Whitehall model designed and built by Captain R.D. Culler of Concordia Co., Inc. As "Pete" Culler said of *Punch*, "...it is not a boat suited to beach work as a steady thing. It is quite slow in turning, and on account of this sculls very well. The charm of these boats seems never to die out, even in a modern age–if one wants the best, along with the cost of it and the few drawbacks, the Whitehall is it."

STATUS: In use, excellent condition.

DONOR: B. Glenn MacNary

FURTHER READING:
Burke, John. *Pete Culler's Boats.* Camden, Maine: International Marine Publishing Co., 1984.

Culler, R.D. *Skiffs and Schooners.* Camden, Maine: International Marine Publishing Co., 1974.

——. *Boats, Oars & Rowing.* Camden, Maine: International Marine Publishing Co., 1978.

ACCESSION NO. 1974.1011
Plans for 1974.1011 are available from Mystic Seaport's Watercraft Plans

Punch *in 1975. (Photo: Maynard Bray, Mystic Seaport 1975-10-209)*

PULLING BOAT, PROBABLY
FOR LIVERY USE

13' 7" x 3' 8"

Quite probably this is a livery boat which, along with others like her, might have been kept by a lakeside summer hotel for use by its guests. Or it might have belonged to a boat livery to be rented out for public use. It is apparent that shortcuts were taken by whoever built her, for she was not produced with a discriminating buyer in mind. For example, her garboards, when fitted to the keel batten, were allowed to run out past it to be cut off flush later after fastening, so that what appears to be the keel is in reality only a chafing strip to protect the garboards from damage. Thus built, the garboard seam is hidden and cannot be caulked later. Yet, in spite of the quick and dirty way she is built, there is nothing at all second-rate about her shape; she is one of the most graceful pulling boats in the entire collection.

STATUS: Original, fair condition.

DONOR: John S. Van Etten

ACCESSION NO. 1973.728
Plans for 1973.728 are available from Mystic Seaport's Watercraft Plans Collection.

The 13' 7" livery boat in 1975. (Photo: Maynard Bray, Mystic Seaport 1975-4-263*)*

Whitehalls in front of The Lake View House, a Lake George summer hotel. (Photo: Seneca Ray Stoddard, Mystic Seaport 1985.60.1*)*

Quitsa Pilot *with designer/builder Pete Culler in the stern. (Photo: Ben Fuller,* Mystic Seaport 1985-6-151*)*

Quitsa Pilot
PULLING BOAT BY CULLER
18' 4" x 3' 5"

Although Pete Culler usually went for heavy construction ("a little weight doesn't hurt," he was fond of saying), there were a few exceptions. This fast gig, at 151 pounds, is one of them. Compared to Culler's other boats, the pieces that he used in this one are tiny! But the result is just what the donor, Dr. Freydberg, who commissioned Pete to design and build her, was looking for–a long, slim, easily driven vehicle with a sliding seat for extra oar-power. Elegant would be a proper description. Details in wood were one of Pete Culler's trademarks, and although his detailing was recognizable from boat to boat, it was hardly ever the same. Pete Culler's drawings rarely give a sense of such detail–there's only enough there to build a basic boat–and only a portion of his shaping and sculpting has been committed to record through photographs and sketches. It is fortunate indeed that, through donors such as Dr. Freydberg, many of Pete Culler's creations are in Mystic Seaport's watercraft collection where people can study them.

STATUS: Original, excellent condition.

DONOR: Dr. Nicholas Freydberg

FURTHER READING:
(Same as for 1974.1011)

ACCESSION NO. 1984.147.1

Plans for 1984.147.1 are available from Mystic Seaport's Watercraft Plans Collection.

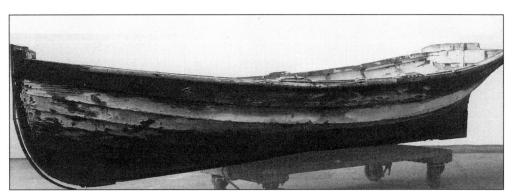

Yawl boat 1986.43.
(Photo: Deborah Patterson,
Mystic Seaport 1986.43B)

YAWLBOAT POSSIBLY FROM THE U.S. NAVY
12' 1" x 4' 7"

This stoutly built yawlboat looks very like the rugged boats built to United States Navy standard designs and specifications, yet she is smaller than the smallest listed in the 1900 standard navy design book. Her high-grade riveted lapstrake construction, the generous use of bronze knees and braces, together with a shape that would row easily, is probably what influenced the late Bob Baker to add her to his collection as a fine (albeit modest) example of a ship's boat.

STATUS: Fair, some planks broken or missing.

DONOR: Mrs. Robert H. Baker

FURTHER READING:
Hichborn, Philip. *Standard Designs for Boats of the United States Navy.* Washington, D.C., U.S. Government Printing Office, 1900.

ACCESSION NO. 1986.43

Mullins pressed-steel pulling boat. (Photo: Deborah Patterson, Mystic Seaport 1984.175B)

PULLING BOAT BY MULLINS

13' 10" x 3' 8"   ca. 1900

In 1895, W.H. Mullins of Salem, Ohio, brought the machine age into boatbuilding by producing his first pressed-steel rowboat, a boat similar to this Mullins "Prince" model. Instead of making a hull of many bits of wood as was then the custom, Mullins made it from a few sheets of steel pressed to shape. While wooden boatbuilders like the Lowell dory shop in Amesbury, Massachusetts, had simplified wooden boatbuilding by using patterns and assembly jigs, and accomplishing repetitive tasks by means of piecework, with the Mullins process boatbuilding truly became boat manufacturing. Of the thousands built, not many of these steel boats have survived as they rusted quickly once their coating was worn through. As a shape, Mullins used the omnipresent Whitehall style for its pulling boats, equipping them with air tanks to keep them afloat in case of a capsize. By 1905, the company moved into commercial production of motor launches, which were a newly popular pleasure craft. In that year a Mullins Prince sold for $30, which was less than the price of a wood/canvas canoe.

STATUS: Good condition, missing thwarts and platforms over bow and stern tanks.

DONORS: Bill Howard and Richard G. Crevier

FURTHER READING:
W.H. Mullins Co. *Pressed Steel Boats, Catalog No. 13.* Salem, Ohio: The W.H. Mullins Co., ca. 1915-20.

Speltz, Robert. *The Real Runabouts, Volume III.* Albert Lea, Minnesota: Robert Speltz, 1980.

ACCESSION NO. 1984.175

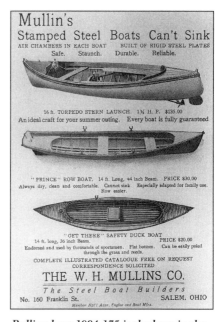

Pulling boat 1984.175 is the boat in the center of this flyer–price $30.

Lawton in 1975. (Photo: Maynard Bray, Mystic Seaport 1975-6-94)

Lawton
PULLING BOAT BY GARDNER

14' 8" x 3' 11"   1970

John Gardner modeled this boat with the entrance of a St. Lawrence River skiff and an especially buoyant afterbody inspired by lifesaving requirements of the Red Cross. She was beautifully built by Gardner, who used Whitehall construction features such as bevelled frames and a closed gunwale. He named her after Marblehead's one-time sage of small craft, Charles A. Lawton, one of his mentors—"Somehow in talking with Charlie, I became enamored of the Whitehall."

STATUS: In use, excellent condition.

DONOR: Built at Mystic Seaport

FURTHER READING:
Gardner, John. *Building Classic Small Craft.* Camden, Maine: International Marine Publishing Co., 1977. Source of above quote by John Gardner.

——. "Toward a Better Rowboat." *National Fisherman,* January, 1971.

ACCESSION NO. 1971.236

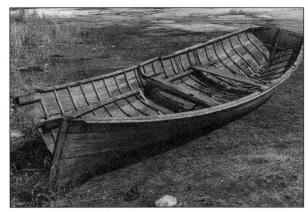

Partelow-built pulling boat 1973.39 in 1975.
(Mystic Seaport 1975-5-185)

(All photos by Maynard Bray)

Lenox model pulling boat 1973.235 in 1975. (Mystic Seaport 1975-5-195)

Lake boat 1973.25 in 1975. (Mystic Seaport 1975-5-192)

Lapstrake pulling boat 1974.1065 in 1975. (Mystic Seaport 1975-1-1)

PULLING BOAT RELICS

These boats were brought to Mystic Seaport for study. Measured drawings have already been made of some of them. It is doubtful if any restoration work will be done; however, such relics are often more valuable if simply preserved for future reference.

FURTHER READING, RELICS:

Gardner, John. "Whitehall and Canoe–An Era Ends." *The Log of Mystic Seaport,* Summer, 1973.

——. *Building Classic Small Craft.* Camden, Maine: International Marine Publishing Co., 1977.

Illustrated catalog of Partelow Co. Privately printed and undated. A copy is in the library at Mystic Seaport.

Plans for 1973.39, 1973.25, and 1973.235 are available from Mystic Seaport's Watercraft Plans Collection.

Accession No.	Dimensions	Donor	Remarks
1973.39	14' 0" x 3' 10"	Dwight P. Quigley	Partelow-built, ca. 1890
1973.235	15' 6" x 3' 10"	Matthew Griswold, Jr.	Lenox model
1973.25	15' 8" x 3' 6"	Thomas R. Wilcox	Lake boat
1974.1065	15' 0" x 4' 0"	Robert Worsley	Rabbeted bottom board, planked down like wherry

RANGELEY LAKE BOAT

14' 7" x 3' 3"   ca. 1915

Less delicate than the Adirondack guide
boat or the St. Lawrence skiff, Rangeley
boats were mostly used for the same
purpose: taking city sportsmen out
fishing. It is probable that a St.
Lawrence River skiff inspired the
Rangeley. Regardless of origin, these
slippery and beautiful boats became
popular in the 1870s and remained so
for the next 50-odd years. This boat was
probably built by C.W. Barrett. Since
she was laid out for single-person use,
she is smaller than the usual two- or
three-person 17-footer.

STATUS: Original, good condition.

DONOR: Godfrey W. Kauffmann

FURTHER READING:
Gardner, John. *Building Classic Small
Craft*. Camden, Maine: International
Marine Publishing Co., 1977.

Rangeley Lake boat in 1975. (Photo: Maynard Bray, Mystic Seaport 1975-4-252)

——. "Rangeley Boat." *National
Fisherman*, January-April, 1968,
September-October, 1969.
——. "The Rangeley Boat." *The Log of
Mystic Seaport*, Winter, 1973.
ACCESSION NO. 1974.1007

RANGELEY LAKE BOAT FOR OUTBOARD MOTOR

15' 11" x 4' 0"   ca. 1920

The small outboard motor was a terrific
boon for the guides who took their
sportsmen clients onto the big waters of
Maine's Rangeley Lake region. There,
most fishing was guided and most boats
ran to 17' for a party of two and a
guide. Before the outboard, the guide
had to row to where the fish were in the
still of the morning before the wind
came up. Once the outboard was
introduced, builders modified their
boats by installing a transom and
widening them aft above the waterline,
while retaining the double-ended shape
below so the boats could still be rowed
with ease. The round seats mounted
atop the thwarts are a common feature
of the Rangeley Lakes boat, to make
sitting at an angle and casting easier.

*Transom-
sterned
Rangeley
Lake Boat
in 1993.
(Photo:
Maynard
Bray,
Mystic Seaport
1979.46A)*

STATUS: Original, fair condition.

DONOR: George H. Stadel, Jr.

FURTHER READING:
(Same as for 1974.1007 and 1978.165)

ACCESSION NO. 1979.46

Museum trustee Clifford Mallory and builder's wife Dorothy Thomas try one of the Museum-built Rangeley Lake boats. (Photo: Claire White-Peterson, Mystic Seaport 1978-8-18B)

Nelson B.

RANGELEY LAKE BOAT REPRODUCTION

14' 7" x 3' 4"   1978

This reproduction of Rangeley Lake boat 1974.1007 in Mystic Seaport's collection and shown on the facing page was the first of a production run of about 20 boats, a project that inaugurated the Small Boat Shop's research into the production methods of original builders. This ten-year project also produced a run of Rushton pulling boat reproductions, a series of melonseeds and Delaware River tuckups, and culminated in the study and reproduction of the Crosby catboat *Breck Marshall* (1986.10) and the Gil Smith catboat *Anitra* (1988.10) followed by a series of Chaisson dory tenders. The research and construction involved with *Nelson B.* revealed much about Rangeley building techniques. Special tricks were discovered, like the need to set up the molds with some rocker, something not done on this boat, with the result that her hull has a slight hog. Due to lack of natural crooks for the boat's outer stem, the Boat Shop researched and applied the art and science of compression bending with steam. *Nelson B.*, named for J. Henry Rushton's foreman and master builder Nelson Brown, is now a popular member of the Museum's livery fleet.

STATUS: Excellent condition, in use.

DONOR: Mystic Seaport-built

FURTHER READING (in addition to citings for 1974.1007):

McClave, Edward. "Bending Stems at Mystic Seaport." *WoodenBoat* 33, Mar/Apr, 1980.

McGuire, Paul. "The Rangeley Tradition." *WoodenBoat* 39, Mar/Apr, 1981.

ACCESSION NO. 1978.165

Plans for 1978.165/1974.1007 are available from Mystic Seaport's Watercraft Plans Collection.

Rangeley Lake boats under construction in Mystic Seaport's Small Boat Shop in 1978. (Photo: Mary Anne Stets, Mystic Seaport 1978-7-111)

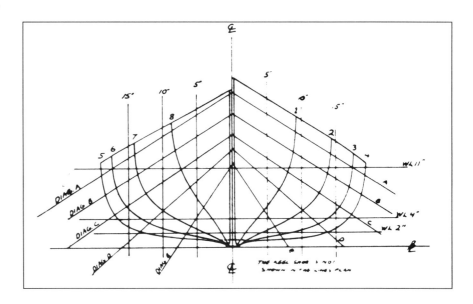

Transom-sterned Rangeley Lake boat 1991.11
(Photo: Mary Anne Stets, Mystic Seaport 1991.11D)

RANGELEY LAKE BOAT BY COLLINS

17' 1" x 4' 0"   ca. 1938

This is the classic Rangeley model from the pre-outboard, square-stern era, even though it was built well into the time of the outboard motor. The original Rangeleys were patterned after a boat from Ogdensburg, New York, brought to Maine in the early 1870s by a member of the Oquossoc Angling Association, a fishing club founded in 1869. The Ogdensburg boat was most likely an early version of the St. Lawrence River skiff. Rangeley boats evolved into their final form sometime before the turn of the century, losing the decks of the St. Lawrence skiff and departing in construction and shape as well.

Ultimately they could be found all over the big lakes of western Maine at fishing clubs, hotels, and private camps. They could be rowed all day at a fly-casting pace by a well-conditioned guide with two sports aboard, and a typical trip could cover as much as 20 miles in a day, starting with a run to the south in early morning before the prevailing southwesterly breeze came up.

The Barretts of Rangeley were the dominant builders in the years from 1888 to 1929. This boat was built by S.A. Collins, who started building Rangeley boats around 1935. He'd taken over from Fred Conant who set up shop around 1909, having learned his trade from Hod Loomis, one of the Barrett family's early competitors. Besides a builder's plate, this boat also has a plate identifying a former owner: "James T. Trumpbour, Rangeley, ME. Tel Rangeley 63"–most likely a guide with his local telephone.

STATUS: Fair condition, some missing pieces.

DONOR: Colin Dinwoodie, in memory of Ernest "Buddy" Kruger

FURTHER READING:
(Same as for 1974.1007 and 1978.165)

ACCESSION NO. 1991.11

Lake-type double-ended pulling boat, 1978. (Photo: Maynard Bray, Mystic Seaport 1978-2-58)

PULLING BOAT, LAKE-TYPE

18' 6" x 3' 6"

While the designer and builder of this sleek double-ender are not known, they must have been inspired somewhat by the Rangeley Lake boat and perhaps the St. Lawrence River skiff. This boat's planking method derives from yet a third well-known boat type, the Adirondack guide boat. The planks form a smooth skin inside and out; yet their edges are bevelled and fastened along the laps making what is commonly called a guideboat seam. There is no indication of her ever having had a centerboard, but she was rigged for sailing at one time. Her mast partner is a rather fancy affair made of bronze and pivoted to open so the mast can be more easily stepped.

STATUS: Original, frames broken and rotted in many places, poor condition.

DONOR: Joel M. White

ACCESSION NO. 1977.257

The 14' Rushton pulling boat in 1978. (Photo: Ken Mahler, Mystic Seaport 1975.440 (132a))

PULLING BOAT BY RUSHTON

14' 1" x 3' 2"   1888

J. Henry Rushton's boatshop in Canton, New York, produced this boat and she was purchased as a birthday gift for the donor's great aunt, Miss Catherine Kitchell, when she turned ten. First used at the family summer place on Lake George, New York, the boat went eventually to Lake Memphremagog in Vermont. The Rushton catalog of 1887 shows a similar

boat as No. 109. There is no doubt that Rushton built wonderful boats; yet he did his share of "puffing up" his products. His catalog claims that by 1887 he had received more than 75,000 letters, apparently most of them from satisfied customers. These letters were the basis for his statement that 99-1/3% of his customers "expressed unqualified approval of our work."

STATUS: Refinished by donor, mostly original, good condition.

DONOR: Gordon K. Douglass

FURTHER READING:

Manley, Atwood. *Rushton and His Times in American Canoeing.* Syracuse, New York: Syracuse University Press for The Adirondack Museum, 1968.

Promotional catalog describing and illustrating the boats by Rushton. Privately printed, dated 1887. A copy is in the library at Mystic Seaport.

ACCESSION NO. 1975.440

A.L. Rotch in 1975. (Photo: Maynard Bray, Mystic Seaport 1975-5-240)

A.L. Rotch

PULLING BOAT BY RUSHTON

14' 1" x 3' 0"   ca. 1888

This boat was fresh from the Rushton shop when the Rotch family bought her. We believe she is a standard version (Rushton called it his Grade B construction) of the above boat (1975.440). Not only is only is her

shape (except for a minor variation in beam) the same as 1975.440, but her oarlock sockets, gudgeons, and bow eyes match perfectly to those shown in Rushton's illustrated catalog.

Although she lay idle for about 50 years before coming to Mystic Seaport in 1960, she was carefully kept in covered storage by the family who had always owned her.

STATUS: Mostly original, good condition.

DONOR: Arthur Rotch

FURTHER READING:
(Same as for 1975.440)

ACCESSION NO. 1960.261
Plans for 1960.261 are available from Mystic Seaport's Watercraft Plans Collection.

200

PULLING BOAT BY JOYNER

14' 0" x 3' 1"   ca. 1890

The Schenectady, New York, shop of Fletcher Joyner and Sons built this boat and advertised it as a standard model called a "cedar hunting and ladies boat." Joyner was a well-known competitor of J. Henry Rushton in that wonderful era of high-quality lightweight wooden small craft produced by North Woods boatshops. She is smooth-planked over closely spaced frames and has outrigger-type oarlocks to permit the use of longer oars. The design of her hinged backrest is particularly neat and could be

Joyner-built pulling boat in 1978. (Photo: Maynard Bray, Mystic Seaport 1978-2-50*)*

adapted to fit the thwart of most any small boat.

STATUS: Original, good condition.

DONOR: John C. Gehrig

FURTHER READING:
F. Joyner & Son's Photographic Catalog and Price List for 1884. Glens Falls, New York. A copy is in the library at Mystic Seaport.

ACCESSION NO. 1975.459

ROWING CANOE BY GERRISH

15' 9" x 4' 1"   ca. 1920

Evan (Eve) H. Gerrish, a guide from Brownville, Maine, moved to Bangor, Maine, in 1875 and opened a small shop where he experimented with canvas-covered wood canoes. Family tradition maintains that he got the idea during a canoe trip, when he repaired a leaking bark canoe by covering it with canvas. By 1878 he was turning out 18 wood-canvas canoes a year; by 1884, when he earned a gold medal at the New Orleans World's Fair, he was producing 50 a year. By 1895 he was the largest canoe-builder in Maine, with a staff of ten

turning out 150 a year. Gerrish's only known catalog, issued in 1898, shows that he had diversified by adding a rowing "canoe" to his line. Other canoe-builders, including Rushton and Joyner, had done the same thing, making good use of their production and marketing skills.

Gerrish's rowing canoes were especially popular among the fishing guides who worked the salmon pools on the Penobscot River. As his boats grew wider they became known as salmon canoes or salmon peapods. In 1909, Gerrish retired and sold his business to Herbert D. Walton, who moved production to Costigan, Maine, where this boat was built. Walton focused on

the salmon canoes and remained active through the 1910s. Business declined in the 1920s, and the shop burned in the early 1930s.

This boat came into the donor's family sometime in the 1920s and was used on Webster Lake near Dudley, Massachusetts. (See 1991.150.2)

STATUS: Good. Restored while owned by donor.

DONOR: Andrew J. Bates

FURTHER READING:
Stelmok, Jerry, and Thurlow, Rollin. *The Wood & Canvas Canoe.* Gardiner, Maine: The Harpswell Press, 1987.

ACCESSION NO. 1991.150

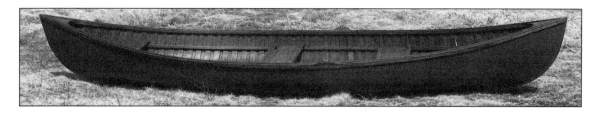

The Gerrish rowing canoe. (Photo: Maynard Bray, Mystic Seaport 1991.150.1A*)*

PULLING BOAT WITH CANOE-LIKE ENDS

15' 0" x 3' 5"

Nothing is known about the origin or history of this canoe-like rowing boat except that she was last used in Maine. Certainly the quick sheer at her ends along with the profiles of her bow and stern show that she descended from the open Indian canoe. Perhaps another feature of the Indian canoe, its flat frames, should have been used in this

Pulling boat 1976.65 in 1976. (Photo: J. Deupree, Mystic Seaport 1976-5-127*)*

boat as well, because the small square frames with which she was built have nearly all broken.

STATUS: Original, fair condition.

DONOR: William C. Page

ACCESSION NO. 1976.65

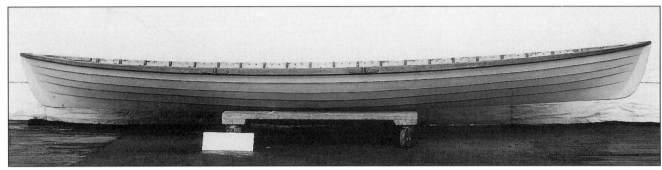

John Gardner's modified version of a slim Francis Herreshoff-designed pulling boat. (Photo: Mary Anne Stets, Mystic Seaport 1982-2-119)

The Green Machine

PULLING BOAT BY GARDNER/HERRESHOFF

17' 2" x 3' 9"   1980

For lack of a better name, this boat was dubbed "The Green Machine" by the people who first used her at Mystic Seaport's Small Boat Workshop in 1980. John Gardner based his design on the L. Francis Herreshoff pulling boat design which first appeared in his book *Common Sense of Yacht Design*. Gardner gave the boat more flare in the sides and ends. "What I have attempted to do here is add buoyancy and lift but without slowing down the boat by spoiling Herreshoff's fine entrance at the load line." Her building allowed John to experiment with using non-marine exterior plywood lapstrake planking up to the sheer strake, laminated guideboat-style frames, and a guideboat-style building setup.

A number of these pulling boats have been built and in recent years. *The Green Machine* has represented the high-performance end of Mystic Seaport's boat livery. Fitted with the temporary decks at either end as John had suggested for rough-water use, she won her class in the demanding Howard Blackburn Memorial Race, 20 miles around Cape Ann. *The Green Machine* has folding thwarts and was originally designed to be rowed as a single in one direction and as a double in the other. Some builders have selected one end as the bow, however, and have trimmed some area from the external stem and added a small skeg to her stern. This eliminates her sometimes nasty habit of broaching when running down a steep chop. Users always remark on her oars, designed by Andy Steever and built by Val Danforth. They are St. Lawrence River skiff-style, but have been modified for conventional oarlocks and carefully counterweighted on their inboard ends to lighten the weight in hand.

STATUS: In use, excellent condition.

DONOR: Built at Mystic Seaport

FURTHER READING:

Building Classic Small Craft, Volume 2. Camden, Maine: International Marine Publishing Co., 1984. Chapter One discusses the 17' Francis Herrshoff double-ended rowing boat.

Steever, Andrew B. *Oars For Pleasure Rowing, Their Design and Use.* Mystic: Mystic Seaport Publications, 1993.

ACCESSION NO. 1981.11

Young Mystic Seaport volunteer Eddie Murphy gets The Green Machine *ready for a summer of livery service. (Photo: Sharon Brown)*

J. Henry
PULLING BOAT BY RUSHTON
15′ 0″ x 3′ 2″   ca. 1900

Built in the J. Henry Rushton shop sometime in the waning years of the nineteenth century, this boat managed to find her way to Cape Cod, where Captain R.D. "Pete" Culler rescued her from the dump. She was one of Rushton's "Iowa" recreational rowing boats, Model No. 6, a B or C grade, offered at either $75 or $64 in Rushton's 1903 catalog. She was upgraded with a set of 8″ folding outriggers at $5.00. These fancy oarlock fittings as well as most of Rushton's other fittings were furnished by M.E. Blazier Mfg. Co. of Utica, which also made fittings for other builders of canoes, guideboats, and St. Lawrence River skiffs. When found, she was a wreck and Pete substantially rebuilt her. He added a lateen sailing rig and a leeboard as well as two pairs of his oars. Completing the outfit are a ditty box with sail twine and needles, a fid, and a small tallow bucket. Pete named her for her builder, and painted the boat a fine shade of lavender. "I always wanted a purple boat," he said.

Rushton-built pulling boat (rigged for sail by Pete Culler) in 1978.
(Photo: Mary Anne Stets, Mystic Seaport 1978.101)

STATUS: Rebuilt, good condition.
DONOR: Mrs. R.D. Culler
FURTHER READING:
Crowley, William. *Rushton's Rowboats and Canoes.* Camden, Maine: International Marine Publishing, 1983.

Manley, Atwood. *Rushton and His Times in American Canoeing.* Syracuse, New York: Syracuse University Press for The Adirondack Museum, 1968.

ACCESSION NO. 1978.101

Pentimento
DOUBLE-ENDED WHERRY
BY BAKER
17′ 8″ x 3′ 6″   1980

This boat, designed and built for the donor, shows the elegance that Robert H. Baker of Westport, Massachusetts, could bring to boatbuilding by careful choice of materials and styles. As such, she is worth careful study. *Pentimento* has a Herreshoff-type sheer strake and carefully selected and proportioned seat knees and breasthooks of apple and cherry. Seats and risers are beaded, and the aft seat is caned to save weight. The Baker Boat Works signature star, along with the boat's name, are carved into the backboard. Oil has been used for the bright interior finish and sheer strake to save maintenance. Careful attention has

been paid to saving weight throughout, and *Pentimento* is fast but somewhat less stable and wetter in a chop than the donor had anticipated. She would be ideally suited for a single rower covering serious miles on a sheltered river. Her shape is such that, like *The Green Machine* (1981.11), she needs to be down by the stern to track well. A small

experimental skeg added after she was built made tracking much more certain.

STATUS: Excellent condition.

DONOR: Kevin Sheehan

ACCESSION NO. 1981.69
Lines and offsets are available from Anne Baker, 29 Drift Rd., Westport, Massachusetts 02790.

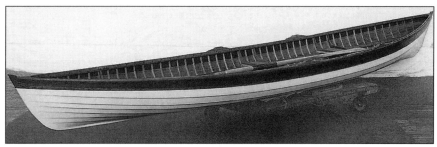

The light wherry designed and built by Bob Baker.
(Photo: Mary Anne Stets, Mystic Seaport 1982-2-118)

Starlight

YACHT TENDER
REPRODUCTION

10' 0" x 4' 0"   1979

Under the tutelage of John Gardner, his assistant Julia Rabinowitz measured and built a reproduction of *Brilliant*'s original Nevins-built tender (discussed below) in 1979. A study of the wear in the original produced some small changes, notably slackening the bilges a bit to keep frames from breaking, and substituting hackmatack for the original bent-wood and bronze-strapped breasthook and quarter knees. This boat has been displaced from her normal spot between the masts on *Brilliant*'s deck by the need to carry liferafts there as required by the Coast Guard for *Brilliant*'s use as a passenger-carrying vessel.

STATUS: Excellent.
DONER: Museum-built reproduction by Julia Rabinowitz
ACCESSION NO. 1979.114

Starlight *chocked up on* Brilliant's *deck in 1979. (Photo: Gene Myers,* Mystic Seaport 1979-7-7)

Brilliant's *Nevins-built tender from 1932. (Photo: Maynard Bray,* Mystic Seaport 1980.13A)

BRILLIANT'S
YACHT TENDER
BY NEVINS

10' 0" x 4' 0"   ca. 1932

This lapstrake cedar-on-oak tender is the same model as *Comet* on the next page with some modernizing changes. She was retired due to frame breakage suffered in her 40 years of work. Study of the breaks helped in understanding stresses on this boat and led the way to the construction changes mentioned above. Her oars and floorboards were transferred to her replacement, *Starlight*. The fancy stern sheet support and metal knees were characteristic of Nevins tenders. The elongated horseshoe stern seat allows four persons to be carried, two in the stern and one on each rowing bench. By 1932, the Nevins shop was recognizing outboards by adding an outboard-motor mount, a board on the inside of the transom into which the transom knee was let. This tender also has skids on her bottom and a coved rubrail to accommodate a laced-on fender.

STATUS: Fair, seat back and oarlocks missing, some frame breakage.
DONOR: Briggs S. Cunningham
ACCESSION NO. 1980.13

Comet *in storage in 1975. (Photo: Maynard Bray, Mystic Seaport 1975-10-91)*

Comet

YACHT TENDER
BY NEVINS

10' 0" x 4' 0"   ca. 1920

This little boat's overall length was probably dictated by the stowage space on board one of the many yachts built by the Nevins yard at City Island, New York. She is too short for good rowing and really a bit small to carry more than three persons. But being able to take the tender or dinghy aboard is a distinct advantage, and the sacrifice in performance was oftentimes judged to be a worthwhile compromise.

STATUS: Some repair, mostly original, fair condition.

DONOR: Isaac B. Merriman, Jr.

FURTHER READING:
Taylor, William H. "Henry B. Nevins, Master Yacht Builder." *Yachting*, April, 1950.

ACCESSION NO. 1964.632

Madelon

YACHT TENDER
BY LAWLEY
HULL #1571

9' 3" x 3' 8"   ca. 1920

The donor used *Madelon* into the 1970s as the tender for his 31' Victory-class sloop of the same name. Lawley's, as the yard of George F. Lawley & Sons, at Neponset just south of Boston, was called, built numbers of yacht tenders each year to have on hand for outfitting its large yachts and to sell individually. John Harvey ruled the boatshop and demanded perfection from his men; his small boats were put together with the same exacting fits, superior woods, and fine finish for which the Lawley yard was famous in the production of elegant large yachts. Everyday use is hard on these delicate little shells and in time, even with reasonable care, which this one probably had, weaknesses begin to show up. For example, the screw fastenings holding lower planking against the stem have pulled out and in the process have caused the planks themselves to split. Perhaps a heavier stem of oak rather than hackmatack would have served better.

STATUS: Damaged as noted above, finish in poor shape, original, good condition.

DONOR: Francis H. Chafee, M.D.

FURTHER READING:
Gardner, John. "Small Craft Wizardry at Lawley's." *National Fisherman*, September, 1977.

ACCESSION NO. 1977.254

Madelon *in storage in 1978. (Photo: Maynard Bray, Mystic Seaport 1978-2-22)*

YACHT TENDER BY LAWLEY
HULL #1710

12' 2" x 4' 3"   ca. 1920

Following the custom of Lawley's, this larger tender is carvel-planked rather than being lapstraked like *Madelon*. Her teak trim was probably special, since mahogany was usually used to enhance the basic cedar-on-oak hull. There is no record of her early history, although chances are she was part of some elegant Lawley-built, teak-trimmed yacht's outfit. Bronze lifting eyes fore and aft enabled her to be hoisted aboard on the larger yacht's davits when not being used. Special bronze castings also form the seat knees, quarter knees, and the breasthook. A few years ago, this tender was used as a plug from which the fiberglass-hulled "Harbormaster" dinghies were molded.

STATUS: Outside of hull covered with fiberglass, finish is quite weathered, original, good condition.

DONOR: James F. Steele

FURTHER READING: Gardner, John. *Building Classic Small Craft, Vol. 2.* Camden, Maine: International Marine Publishing, 1984. Includes a chapter that discusses the 12' Lawley tender.

ACCESSION NO. 1977.253

Lawley yacht tender #1710 in 1978. (Photo: Maynard Bray, Mystic Seaport 1978-2-20)

YACHT TENDER, PROBABLY BY LAWLEY

12' 1" x 4' 5"   ca. 1932

The donor ordered this husky lapstrake boat with a specific purpose in mind: he wanted a lifeboat to tow behind his New York 50, *Midnight Sun*. Although she was never needed as a rescue craft, she was certainly modeled with that in mind, for she is very burdensome and has unusually high freeboard. Construction features indicate she was probably built by the Lawley yard at Neponset, Boston, Massachusetts.

STATUS: Refinished 1974, original, excellent condition.

DONOR: Warner Eustis

ACCESSION NO. 1972.929

The Warner Eustis tender in 1974. (Photo: Ken Mahler, Mystic Seaport 1974-11-134)

Tamasese II
YACHT TENDER BY LAWLEY
HULL #1614

11' 2" x 3' 11"   1929

In the late 1920s, the Lawley yard in Neponset, like many of its competitors, began to build stock cruisers. The first Lawley 38, designed by Walter McInnis, was on display at the New York Boat Show in January of 1926. One of these boats, *Tamasese II*, was bought by the Mitchell family later that year for their Nantucket summer home. While each

boat was delivered with a 9' tender like *Madelon* shown on page 205, the Mitchells must have replaced theirs with this 11-footer built in 1929 for another Lawley yacht. The new price on these tenders was $250. *Tamasese II* gave way to an American Car and Foundry 38-footer in 1934, but the family kept the tender. She is a carvel-planked cedar-on-oak boat, with a mahogany sheer strake and the characteristic details found on small boats from the Lawley shop, such as the cast-bronze breasthook and quarter knees found on later tenders.

STATUS: Good condition, two partial sister frames.

DONOR: Estate of Christel T. Mitchell

FURTHER READING:

"Fifty Years of Yacht Building." *Yachting*, May, 1915. A brief history of George Lawley and his firm to 1915.

Gardner, John. "Small Craft Wizardry at Lawley's." *National Fisherman*, September, 1977.

The address of the Lawley Boat Owners Association is P.O. Box 242, Gloucester, Massachusetts 01931

ACCESSION NO. 1986.18

The Tamasese II *tender in 1986. (Photo: Maynard Bray,* Mystic Seaport 1986.18A)

Riptide
YACHT TENDER BY LAWTON

10' 2" x 3' 10"   ca. 1931

Charles A. Lawton of Marblehead built this tender for *Grenadier*, a 60' schooner designed by John Alden and built at Lawley's in 1931. This boat could have replaced an original Lawley tender. More likely, *Grenadier*'s first owners, Henry and Charles Morss, knew Lawton's work and considered it superior to even that of the famed Lawley boatshop. Certainly John Gardner, who worked with Lawton at the James E. Graves yard in Marblehead, felt Lawton's work to be as good or better than the Lawley shop's. At that time Lawton was approaching 90, having spent 70 years in boatbuilding, specializing in building tenders. Lawton was a St. John, New Brunswick, native who had come down to Boston to go to work building canoes, St. Lawrence River skiffs, and other fancy boats for the Partelow Company in the 1890s. When Lawton retired at 90, he gave John Gardner molds, patterns, and lines, among which were the molds to build his 10' tender. These were checked against this boat and found to be an exact match.

Despite years of use the Lawton tender shows no broken frames, split planks, or failing joints. Her detailing is elegant. Shallow U-shaped stern sheets are supported by both an ornamental beam and a pair of turned posts. Similar posts support both rowing thwarts, and the seat riser is double-beaded. Floorboards are beaded as well. Natural crooks are used for the single seat knees and the quarter knees. The floorboards, fastened in place, have a rowing heel brace. The backboard still bears the gold-leafed name *Grenadier*, but at some point, probably after she was separated from her parent, the tender got the name *Riptide*.

STATUS: Excellent original condition, noticeable wear.

DONOR: Ray Burns, Jr.

FURTHER READING:

Carrick, Robert W., and Richard Henderson. *John Alden and His Yacht Designs*. Camden, Maine: International Marine Publishing Co., 1983, has material on *Grenadier*.

Gardner, John. *Building Classic Small Craft, Vol. 2*. Camden, Maine: International Marine Publishing Co., 1984. His chapter on "Yacht Tenders" discusses Lawley and Lawton and has lines for Lawley's 12' tender as well as Lawton's 10-footer, and it makes specific reference to this boat. It is an updated version of columns he published in *National Fisherman* in 1977, 1978, and 1980.

ACCESSION NO. 1980.70

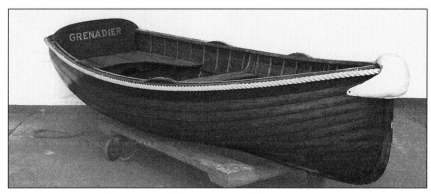

The Grenadier *tender in 1981. (Photo: Maynard Bray,* Mystic Seaport 1981-2-93)

TENDER FOR THE PASSENGER STEAMER
SABINO

12' 0" x 4' 4"   1978

It seemed most appropriate, once *Sabino*'s restoration was complete, for Mystic Seaport's Small Boat Shop to build a suitable boat to be carried onboard the little passenger-carrying steamboat as a tender. In response, John Gardner drew plans that he based on the lapstrake yacht tenders once produced by the Lawley yard in Neponset, Massachusetts–a type always held in high regard. Since the boat normally sits cradled on *Sabino*'s canopy top, there's little opportunity for using her. But even in this rather static mode she serves to enhance the appearance of an already authentic and eye-catching vessel. (See page 310 for more on *Sabino*.)

STATUS: In use, good condition.

DONOR: Mystic Seaport-built by Barry Thomas

ACCESSION NO. 1978.82

The Sabino *tender designed by John Gardner. (Photo Mary Anne Stets, Mystic Seaport 1978-3-15)*

Seafarer

YACHT TENDER
BY HERRESHOFF
HULL #1-485

10' 3" x 4' 3"   1926

Charlie Sylvester built this tender and figures that, with few exceptions, all the dinghies and tenders from the Herreshoff yard between 1920 and when he left its employ in 1942 were personally built by him. Such experience, together with a keen memory for detail, made Charlie the prime information source for Barry Thomas's monograph on building a similar boat. She is a bit more burdensome than the Herreshoff Columbia lifeboat model and was developed in 1915 for the new Herreshoff 40' (waterline) one-design sloops of the New York Yacht Club. Records show that these boats were built as late as 1927, some lengthened by as much as two feet. Origin of the name *Seafarer* is uncertain; it was on her stern when she came to Mystic Seaport and was probably the name of the yacht she last served.

STATUS: Restored 1970, mostly original, good condition.

DONOR: Roberts Parsons

FURTHER READING:

Herreshoff, L. Francis. *The Common Sense of Yacht Design*. New York: The Rudder Publishing Company, 1948. Chapter XIX, entitled "Small Craft,"

gives the background of the Columbia model tender.

Thomas, Barry. *Building the Herreshoff Dinghy*. Mystic, Connecticut: Mystic Seaport Publications, 1977. Gives a detailed description of building a similar boat.

ACCESSION NO. 1965.389

Herreshoff yacht tender #1-485. (Photo: Ken Mahler, Mystic Seaport 1974-11-105)

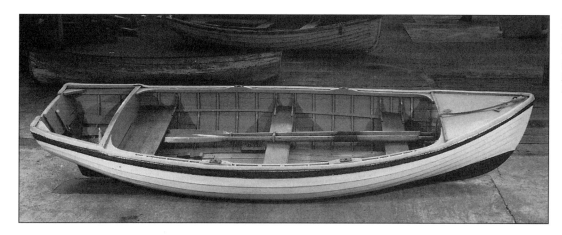

*The 12'5"
Columbia lifeboat
model tender.
(Photo: Maynard
Bray, Mystic Seaport
1978-2-23)*

YACHT TENDER
BY HERRESHOFF,
COLUMBIA LIFEBOAT MODEL

12' 5" x 4' 10"   1929

"...soon after 1900 he (Nathanael Herreshoff) brought out a model which we in the rowboat shop used to call the Columbia lifeboat model. The first of these was the racing boat on the deck of the cup boat *Columbia*,...and a very great many similar ones were built. Perhaps my father modeled ten rowboats of varying proportions after the Columbia lifeboat model, but he never departed radically from this shape. This is the best model for a

tender I have ever seen. They row well, sail well, and are good dry sea boats, and will tow through anything...a short deck over the stern very much increases their value as a lifeboat, as they can be easily and quickly launched stern first from the yacht without being partially swamped. In the case of a man overboard or a fire, the delay in bailing out a partly swamped tender may be most serious..." L. Francis Herreshoff, *The Common Sense of Yacht Design.*

To add even more to her ability as a lifeboat, she has a watertight compartment under her foredeck. According to the donor, who at the time was president of the Herreshoff Manufacturing Company, this boat was

used on the America's Cup defender *Enterprise* or the cup contender *Weetamoe.*

STATUS: Fiberglass-covered outside, stern compartment cover missing, original, good condition.

DONOR: R.F. Haffenreffer 3rd

FURTHER READING:

Herreshoff, L. Francis. *The Common Sense of Yacht Design.* New York: The Rudder Publishing Company, 1948.

Thomas, Barry. *Building the Herreshoff Dinghy.* Mystic, Connecticut: Mystic Seaport Publications, 1977. Gives detailed description of building a similar boat.

ACCESSION NO. 1975.454

*Yacht tenders abuilding at the Herreshoff Manufacturing Company in 1926.
(Photo: Courtesy of Sidney Herreshoff, Mystic Seaport 1975-7-127)*

Dixie

YACHT TENDER
BY HERRESHOFF

18' 7" x 5' 6" ca. 1910-20

When Commodore George P.P. Bonnell bought the 89-foot Herreshoff power yacht *Comfort* in the middle of the Depression, there were two boats aboard. Since then both have become part of Mystic Seaport's watercraft collection by different paths. (The other is *Cormorant Rose*, a 17' power launch, 1975.466.) *Comfort*, which had been built in 1909 as *Enaj*, perished in the 1938 hurricane but her boats were both rescued. For a while, until old age got the best of her and she was returned to him, this boat was loaned by Bonnell to Mystic Seaport as a tender for the schooner *Brilliant*. To

our knowledge three others have been built recently using this hull for measurements and details, but all three were smooth-planked rather than lapstraked. Joel White's yard in Brooklin, Maine, produced two, one for *Brilliant* and one for the Hudson River sloop *Clearwater*. When the first of these was lost at sea from *Brilliant* a few years ago, Barry Thomas built the third boat, *Afterglow*, to replace her.

Herreshoff referred to this model and even to her smaller sisters as lifeboats, which for that time was surely true. But today, considering how boats of this type are most often used and to avoid any confusion with the standard ship's lifeboat, it seems appropriate to use the term tender.

STATUS: Fiberglass tape on plank laps, original, fair condition.
DONOR: Robert Florin
FURTHER READING:
(Same as for Columbia lifeboat, 1975.454)
ACCESSION NO. 1974.995

Dixie in storage in 1978. (Photo: Maynard Bray, Mystic Seaport 1978-2-51)

Afterglow

TENDER FOR
THE SCHOONER *BRILLIANT*

18' 10" x 5' 9" 1976

Because she is too large to carry on deck, this boat spends much of her sea time on the end of *Brilliant*'s towline–thus her name. A big, husky, seaworthy rowboat that tows as well as this one answers the schooner's needs perfectly–so perfectly, in fact, that over the many years that *Brilliant* has operated from Mystic Seaport she has gone through three tenders of the same model. *Dixie*, the boat discussed above, was the first, and she was just worn out. The second, built by Joel White's Brooklin Boat Yard as her replacement, was lost at sea. Barry Thomas built *Afterglow* in 1976 in the Museum's Small Boat Shop. So perfectly proportioned is this boat that when seen all by herself it is difficult to judge her size. When people are aboard it's easy to see that she's a bigger than usual rowboat–too large, really, for a

single rower. On *Brilliant*'s cruises, however, there is an abundance of willing hands, and with four rowers manning four oars, and several more passengers that are aboard, *Afterglow* flourishes as a safe, handsome,"proper" yacht tender.

STATUS: In use, good condition.
DONOR: Mystic Seaport reproduction by Barry Thomas of a Herreshoff Manufacturing Company original
ACCESSION NO. 1980.15

Afterglow under construction at Mystic Seaport. (Photo: Ken Mahler, Mystic Seaport 1975-4-169)

YACHT TENDER
BY DYER
HULL #42-799

12' 0" x 4' 7"   1942

This lapstrake tender, designed by William Dyer and built at The Anchorage in Warren, Rhode Island, clearly shows the influence of outboard motors on small-boat design. Compared with earlier rowing tenders from Herreshoff, Lawley, Nevins, and the like, this one is beamier and has a wider, more burdensome stern equipped with wooden and bronze pads for an outboard. To get the additional beam, she is built with 12 planks per side, two more than are usually found on rowing tenders of similar size. Sturdy bronze seat knees with inset T-shaped ends help reinforce the boat. For all that, she does have enough rocker and a small skeg to make rowing both practical and pleasurable.

STATUS: Structurally good condition with some sister frames.
DONOR: Dr. & Mrs. Robert M. Jung
ACCESSION NO. 1980.151

Dyer tender #42-799 in 1981. (Photo: Ken Mahler, Mystic Seaport 1981-2-94)

YACHT TENDER
BY OLD TOWN
HULL #21-100

9' 4" x 3' 11"

The Old Town Canoe Company added tenders to their canvas-covered canoe line in the first few years of the new century, hiring B.B. Crowninshield to design them. The 9-footer in the 1910 catalog cost $45 more than the company's best canoes, and weighed 82 pounds. By the time this tender was built, the design had been widened a bit and the stern had been modified for use with an outboard. A line to the outboard motor ran around the boat's inside so that the boat could be steered no matter where you sat.

STATUS: Good Condition.
DONOR: Estate of Ann Kenyon Morse
FURTHER READING:
Audette, Susan, with David E. Baker. *The Old Town Canoe Company: Our First Hundred Years.* Gardiner, Maine: Tilbury House, 1998.

ACCESSION NO. 1991.165.2

The 9' 4" Old Town yacht tender with transom designed for outboard power. (Photo: Maynard Bray, Mystic Seaport 1991.165.2A)

YACHT TENDER
BY OLD TOWN
HULL #132931

14' 0" x 4' 8"   1941

As early as 1902 the Old Town Canoe Company began entering other markets which could use light boats. They hired naval architect B.B. Crowninshield to design their first yacht tenders, which were 9' and 11' 6". The 14' model appeared in 1926. These wood-canvas tenders became popular and were imitated by other builders of cedar canoes with canvas hull covering. Many of these builders added, as did Old Town, a range of outboard runabouts to their product lines in the 1920s. By 1941, when this boat was built, Old Town offered a range of wood-canvas rowing boats from 7-1/2' and 100 pounds to this 14' boat at 225 pounds. Built for inventory, these 14-footers took about a week of carpentry and another seven days for the various steps of filling canvas and painting. This one was sold for use at a summer camp on Norway Lake, Maine, but spent most of her life in a barn until 1977 when she was bought by the donor and used for three seasons at Biddeford Pool, Maine.

STATUS: Excellent, original condition.

DONOR: John R. Deupree

FURTHER READING:
Audette, Susan, with David E. Baker. *The Old Town Canoe Company: Our First Hundred Years.* Gardiner, Maine: Tilbury House, 1998.

ACCESSION NO. 1980.139

The 14' Old Town Canoe Company tender from 1941. (Photo: Maynard Bray, Mystic Seaport 1980.139A)

YACHT TENDER
BY DION

11' 0" x 4' 2"   ca. 1927-28

This round-bottom "set work" or carvel-planked tender was built by Frederick J. Dion at his Salem, Massachusetts, yacht yard and may have been built to the lines of a Lawley tender. One of the men who worked for him, Charles Chandler, had worked for Lawley and copied the tender molds. He gave them to Dion, and John Gardner later drafted lines to the 12' Lawley tender based on these mold tracings. Length variations on these tenders were created by changing the spacing of the molds. This tender is an open-gunwale boat with natural-crook knees. Materials are of good quality, but the boat is plainly finished, without the beading that many tenders sported. Her paint scheme of a painted interior to the riser, then bright finish to the rail, is a good way of finishing a boat to get the durability of paint with a hint of the look of varnish.

STATUS: Fair condition, sister frames on starboard side.

DONOR: Robert Dion

FURTHER READING:
Gardner, John. *Building Classic Small Craft, Vol. 2.* Camden, Maine: International Marine Publishing Co., 1984.

——. *Wooden Boats to Build and Use.* Mystic, Connecticut: Mystic Seaport Publications, 1996. Includes a chapter on the 11'10" Dion tender.

ACCESSION NO. 1990.152

The 11' Fred Dion yacht tender in 1990. (Photo: Judy Beisler, Mystic Seaport 1990.152B)

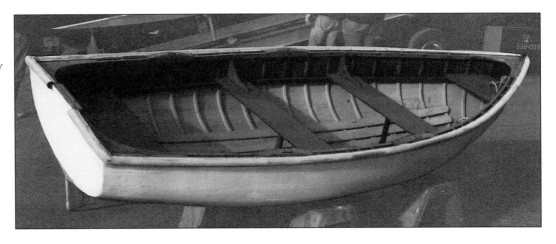

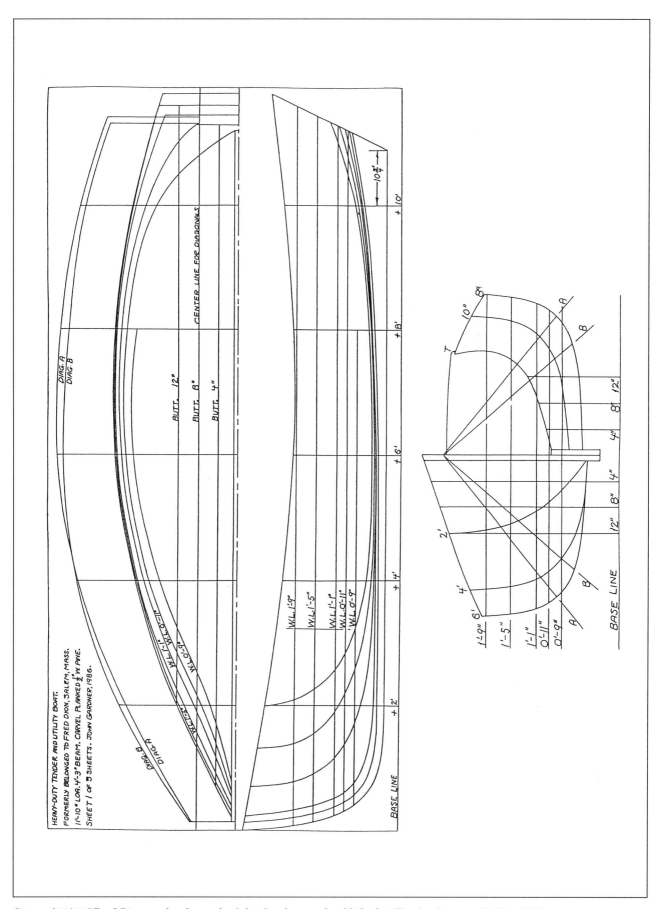

Lines of 11′ 10″ Fred Dion tender drawn by John Gardner and published in Wooden Boats to Build and Use, *a Mystic Seaport publication.*

YACHT TENDER
BY LUDERS MARINE
CONSTRUCTION COMPANY
HULL #326

10′ 1″ x 4′ 1″   ca. 1930

In 1908 A.E. Luders, who had started as a draftsman for the large-yacht design firm of Tams, Lemoine, and Crane, established his yard in East Port Chester, Connecticut, moving it to Stamford in 1912. There the yard flourished for six decades, with his son Bill Luders (A.E., Jr.) taking it over in the 1960s. In the pre-World War II days, Luders built primarily large power yachts to his designs and to the designs of others, developing a reputation for fine construction. This lapstrake cedar tender upholds the reputation. Her thin frames and tiny rivets, together with other light scantlings, are more delicate than those of any other tender in Mystic Seaport's

collection. Despite such ultralight construction, this boat was used for at least 25 years around Morgan Point, Connecticut, by her owner Richard Smith.

The Luders yacht tender at Mystic Seaport in 1993.
(Photo: Maynard Bray, Mystic Seaport 1993.42A)

STATUS: Good condition, some split planks.
DONOR: Richard Smith
ACCESSION NO. 1993.42

Yacht tender from Northeast Harbor, Maine, in 1980.
(Photo: Mary Anne Stets, Mystic Seaport 1980-2-34)

YACHT TENDER
FROM MAINE

9′ 2″ x 3′ 11″   pre-1915

It seems likely that this small tender was built in Maine, since she was originally owned by the donor's father in Northeast Harbor before being moved to Long Island in 1916, and some of her features are characteristic of low-volume boatbuilding. She is sturdier by comparison with the fancy tenders from the shops of Nevins, Lawley, or Herreshoff, and she has carefully selected natural-crook knees, doubled at the seats, with elongated quarter knees running to the stern-post. Breasthook and stern knee are also sturdy natural crooks. Efforts have been made to put beads in the right places. Her stern seat is a long U-shape that overlaps the after rowing thwart. More normal in a boat built to serve a large vessel, she has a rubrail at the lower corner of her sheer strake. She has relatively full lines, delivering more carrying capacity than is usual for her size.

STATUS: Fair original condition, well worn, some repairs.
DONOR: Prescott B. Huntington
ACCESSION NO. 1979.219

Old Lace
ROWING AND SAILING TENDER
10' 3" x 3' 7"

This lapstrake tender does not appear to be one of the "manufactured tenders" produced as identical stock boats for inventory by the Herreshoff Manufacturing Company and its competitors. Her history indicates use on Narragansett Bay but that is all. This boat is narrower than most of her type and has a wineglass stern. Fitted are stretchers for two rowing positions and a mast step and partners, but no centerboard trunk. She has closed gunwale construction with beads cut into the bottom of the inwale and the top of the riser, and a backboard and tiller yoke. She is built lightly but well, and the builder seems to have made an effort to make her look light wherever the eye hits.

STATUS: Good condition.
DONOR: Frank Mauran
ACCESSION NO. 1985.6

Old Lace *in storage in 1985.*
(Photo: Deborah Bates,
Mystioc Seaport 1985.6A)

Fly
CHAISSON-STYLE TENDER
10' 0" x 4' 0"   1994

Built during the winter of 1993-94 at Mystic Seaport by 14-year-old Forest Lowrie under the supervision of Barry Thomas and Bill Sauerbrey, *Fly* has been part of the Museum's boat-livery fleet since the summer of 1995. George L. Chaisson of Swampscott, Massachusetts, was building dory-skiff yacht tenders like *Fly* as early as 1916, and produced them in two grades: either bright-finished with copper fastenings, or paint-finished with galvanized fastenings.

STATUS: In use, excellent condition.

Fly *in boat-livery use at Mystic Seaport.*
(Photo: Mary Anne Stets, Mystic Seaport 1988-11-30)

YACHT TENDER
10' 2" x 4' 0"

This riveted-lapstrake tender shows evidence of substantial rebuilding, with new frames, floorboards, and even a new top to her transom. She served the donor as a tender to the *Alerion* replica that was built by Seth Persson in his boatyard on the Connecticut River.

STATUS: Good condition, heavily and nicely rebuilt, fitted with two pair of oars and oarlocks.
DONOR: Paul Snyder
ACCESSION NO. 1987.145

The 10' 2" lapstrake tender in 1989. (Photo: Maynard Bray, Mystic Seaport 1987.145A)

Breezy

YACHT TENDER
BY ALONZO EATON

14' 3" x 4' 1"   1978

This carvel-planked tender is the last boat built by Alonzo Eaton of Castine, Maine, who learned his trade from his father. At the age of 12, Alonzo's father had borrowed $3 for materials and built a peapod with some help from his father, who helped him get out the planks by setting up a "saw pit" in the family barn, using the loft. This pod put the Eatons in the boatbuilding business. Alonzo then continued the business, establishing Eaton's Boatyard in Castine. Over the years he built more than 75 boats, including a pair of 35' cruisers, a fleet of 22 eighteen-foot sailboats, and many tenders like *Breezy*. Alonzo's son Kenny continues to run the boatyard, where the *Breezy* building molds are stored. *Breezy* is the type of tender that Maine builders evolved from peapods, using the bow half of a pod, and from amidships aft extending fair lines to a transom. Local materials were used: the cedar, oak, and apple knees all came from within 30 miles of Castine. *Breezy* has two rowing stations, one for pulling while sitting and facing the stern, and the other for standing and pushing–an arrangement common to working peapods.

STATUS: Excellent condition.
DONOR: C. Thomas Clagett, Jr.
ACCESSION NO. 1986.90

The 14' 3" Alonzo Eaton tender when it was acquired in 1986. (Photo: Maynard Bray, Mystic Seaport 1986.90A)

YACHT TENDER
BY SPURLING

11' 8" x 4' 3"   ca. 1946

Although he lived on an island off the beaten path, Arthur Spurling gained a following for the small boats he built for natives and summer folks in the Mt. Desert region of the Maine coast. Little Cranberry Island, lying to the south of the big island of Mt. Desert, was where Spurling lived and built his boats. They were lovely little things, and summer residents of the region became Spurling's loyal customers. This boat, which the donor bought new for $125, served as tender for his Northeast Harbor B-Class sloop, and at other times was used for a variety of on-the-water amusements. In spite of her long use, good care prevailed as evidenced by the brightness of her varnished interior.

STATUS: Original, good condition.
DONOR: Charles L. Sheppard, Jr.
FURTHER READING:
Gardner, John. *Building Classic Small Craft, Vol. 1.* Camden, Maine: International Marine Publishing Co., 1977. Chapter 12 discusses the Spurling yacht tenders.

ACCESSION NO. 1985.79

Spurling yacht tender at Mystic Seaport in 1986. (Photo: Maynard Bray, Mystic Seaport 1985.79B)

Cleopatra's Barge
YACHT TENDER
16′ 6″ x 5′ 0″   ca. 1930

Thomas Davidson of New Castle, New Hampshire, built this boat for the Warren family to go with the 60′ sloop *Valiant*. Both boats were designed by Charles Drowne, also of New Castle. A small outboard was sometimes used on the tender, and with her rather large stern it appears that she was modeled with that idea in mind.

STATUS: Original, good condition.
DONOR: Mrs. Richard F. Warren
ACCESSION NO. 1975.432

Richard Warren rowing Cleopatra's Barge *in the 1940s. (Photo: Courtesy of Mrs. Richard Warren,* Mystic Seaport 1988.37.1.290*)*

Cleopatra's Barge *at Mystic Seaport in 1975. (Photo: Maynard Bray,* Mystic Seaport 1975.10.77*)*

YACHT TENDER BY PENN YAN
9′ 0″ x 3′ 10″   ca. 1950

This Aerolight dinghy was the smallest of Penn Yan's yacht tender offerings in the years after World War II. Beginning in 1923, and building boats "For Every Purse & Purpose," the Penn Yan Boat Company came to specialize in adapting wood-canvas canoe construction to larger boats and in building strip-planked inboards and outboards. But canoes, tenders, sailboats, and motorboats continued to be part of the company's line. In 1956, Penn Yan began building fiberglass outboard boats, but continued to build plywood lapstrake runabouts and utilities well into the 1960s.

STATUS: Good original condition with a few cracked frames.
DONOR: Ed Hildreth
FURTHER READING:
Speltz, Robert. *The Real Runabouts, Vol. III*. Albert Lea, Minnesota: Robert Speltz, 1980.
ACCESSION NO. 1984.145

Penn Yan Aerolight wood-and-canvas tender. (Photo: Maynard Bray, Mystic Seaport 1984.145A*)*

Over Flow

YACHT TENDER
BY PENN YAN
HULL # TD753

10' 0" x 4' 3"   1958

Once a suitable yacht tender is acquired, a yacht owner often keeps it through a succession of larger boats.

This was the life of *Over Flow.* One of Penn Yan's Yachtsman-model tenders, introduced in 1951, she was bought for $700 to serve a 55' motor yacht. Subsequently she served various sailboats ranging from a Flying Scot on a lake near Mansfield, Ohio, to 36' sailboats in Los Angeles and on Lake Erie. New York's Penn Yan Boat Company built her using wood-canvas

canoe construction methods adopted earlier by canoe builders in Maine. A lightweight and always watertight hull is the result.

STATUS: Excellent, professionally recanvassed and refurbished.
DONOR: Truman B. Clark
ACCESSION NO. 1983.85

The Penn Yan Yachtsman tender Over Flow. *(Photo: Maynard Bray, Mystic Seaport 1983.85A)*

YACHT TENDER
BY LAWLEY

10' 2" x 4' 1"   pre-1938

This tender came out of the Lawley boatshop sometime before the hurricane of 1938, which it barely survived at Edgartown, Massachusetts,

with major structural damage. George Lauder purchased the boat from a friend of his sister's and repaired her to serve his collection of yachts in Watch Hill, Rhode Island. Paint helps hide the little dinghy's repairs, but the interior shows that almost every frame in the boat needed sistering.

STATUS: Good condition, heavily rebuilt.
DONOR: George Lauder, Jr.
FURTHER READING:
"Fifty Years of Yacht Building." *Yachting,* May, 1915. A brief history of George Lawley and his firm to 1915.

ACCESSION NO. 1987.75.7

Lawley-built 10' 2" yacht tender. (Photo: Judy Beisler, Mystic Seaport 1987.75.7E)

DINGHY
BY RUSHTON

12' 0" x 4' 0"   ca. 1900

As the market for pleasure boats expanded beyond lightweight rowboats and canoes, so did J. Henry Rushton's offerings. He experimented without much success with small motorboats, finally dropping out and boasting that he built no motorboats of any kind. Dinghies like this one were one way that customers who might have moved up from a cruising canoe to a small sailing

yacht that needed a tender could still own a Rushton product. They ranged in size from 9' to 15'. Capacity of the 10-1/2' model was rated at six people, perhaps a few more than would be permitted today. This Model 195 (offered from 1892 to 1903) cost $100 in Grade AA. A 60-square-foot sail, Radix folding centerboard, and air tanks for additional buoyancy were offered as sailing-model options for an extra $60. This boat has the circular Rushton nameplate used from 1895 until 1903.

STATUS: Seats broken or missing, some repair, generally good condition.

DONOR: Paul Shuttleworth

FURTHER READING:

Crowley, William, ed. *Rushton's Rowboats and Canoes: The 1903 Catalog in Perspective*. Blue Mountain Lake, New York: The Adirondack Museum, and Camden, Maine: International Marine Publishing Co., 1983.

Manley, Atwood. *Rushton and His Times in American Canoeing*. Syracuse, New York: Syracuse University Press, 1968.

ACCESSION NO. 1980.158

J. Henry Rushton dinghy from the turn of the century. (Photo: Ken Mahler, Mystic Seaport 1981-2-79*)*

Rhythm
DINGHY BY SHEW
& BURNHAM

12' 0" x 4' 3"

Dick Shew and Cecil Burnham were working at a Maine shipyard in 1968 when they decided to become partners in a wooden-boat shop at South Bristol. After building a number of larger boats they settled on a line that included a Boston Whitehall, an 8' Herreshoff

dinghy, and a 12' rowing and sailing dinghy designed by Shew.

Keeping their operation small, they survived the changing fortunes of wooden-boat builders, and remained in business long after the failure of the shipyard where they once worked. They claimed John Gardner as their inspiration, and the revival of interest in wooden boats that he fostered in the *National Fisherman* and at Mystic Seaport for their success.

The quality of their boats, as represented by this cedar-on-oak beauty with mahogany transom and trim, certainly contributed as they brought the quality standards of the past into the present.

STATUS: Excellent condition.

FURTHER READING:

Getchell, David R., Sr. "A Living from Small Boats?" *WoodenBoat* 77, July/Aug, 1987.

Rhythm at Mystic Seaport. (Photo: Dennis Murphy, Mystic Seaport*)*

YACHT TENDER

12' 9" x 4' 5"   ca. 1925

The delicate, high-quality construction of this boat and the lifting eyes which are fitted fore and aft indicate that she

The 12'9" Bradshaw yacht tender from the 1920s. (Photo: Maynard Bray, Mystic Seaport 1978-2-26)

was once a tender for a larger yacht. She came upon hard times afterwards, however, and one of her later owners fitted her out with heavy and rather crude guard rails, seats, and seat knees. She has been abused and

certainly has seen more rugged service than originally intended. She has a natural-crook hackmatack stem and oak frames which run from rail to rail across a plank-type keel.

STATUS: Repaired and modified, approximately 80% original, poor condition.
DONOR: Forrest and Katherine Bradshaw
ACCESSION NO. 1975.456

YACHT TENDER BY QUINCY ADAMS

10' 2" x 4' 0"   ca. 1932

Builder's plates, like the oval one attached to the transom of this boat, were one way a proud builder could promote his work. It was common for some builders to make use of such a device, as it still is. Builder's plates are also keepers of a boat's pedigree. This boat for example, is "Boat No. 157"

from the Quincy Adams Yacht Yard of Quincy, Massachusetts–a builder known for turning out high quality work. An examination of this varnished tender shows first-rate boatbuilding, with items such as cast bronze knees and breasthook, nicely fitted backrest, and a rudder with yoke. Reinforcing pads each side of the transom knee, along with a full underwater shape near the stern, show that she was designed

with an outboard motor in mind in addition to oars.

STATUS: Original, fair condition.
DONOR: Atherton Loring, Jr.
FURTHER READING:
Somer, Jack A. *Ticonderoga, Tales of an Enchanted Yacht.* New York: W.W. Norton Co., 1997.
ACCESSION NO. 1977.261

CONCORDIA YACHT TENDER BY ABEKING & RASMUSSEN HULL #5109

8' 6" x 3' 11"   1955

Every one of the 99 Concordia yawls built by Abeking & Rasmussen of Lemwerder, Germany, was furnished with one of these rowing prams. All these prams had a mast step and a mast hole in the forward thwart as a way to cut import duties—boats that sailed were taxed half as much as boats that didn't.

Based on traditional Scandinavian tenders – "Eka" boats"–these were called Concordia Båtekas, and the sales brochure that described them attracted non-Concordia owners as well: "She rows easily, steadily and dryly in the manner of a first-class rowboat of longer dimensions. She carries her way in rough water, or smooth, with a crew of one or four. She tows unbelievably

The Concordia Båteka tender. (Photo: Maynard Bray, Mystic Seaport 1986.46A)

well, without appreciable drag and without shipping water even in extreme rough conditions."

The construction of these Concordia Båtekas is a fine example of the meticulous workmanship that made Abeking & Rasmussen world-famous. This example was acquired by Percy Chubb II, a friend and sailing companion of Waldo Howland, president of the Concordia Company.

STATUS: Fair condition, one side chewed; gunwale guard missing.
DONOR: Corrine (Mrs. Percy) Chubb
FURTHER READING:
Howland, Waldo. *A Life in Boats: The Concordia Years.* Mystic, Connecticut: Mystic Seaport Publications, 1988.
ACCESSION NO. 1986.46

ADIRONDACK GUIDEBOAT
BY PARSONS & ROBERTS
HULL # 1908-118

16' 0" x 3' 4"   1908

Riley Parsons learned to build guideboats from Dwight Grant and set up a competing shop in Old Forge, New York, in 1890, together with another Grant carpenter named Seeber. The Parsons guideboats have the same flared bow shape developed by Grant, but with two underdeck frames instead of one, a thinner stem band, and half-lapped seat joints. The Parsons numbering sequence varies from when Riley changed business partners and when his sons Ben and Ira took over after his death in 1904. The shop was known as Parsons & Seeber from 1890 to 1896; then Parsons & Co. from 1897 to 1904; Parsons & Roberts from 1904 to 1909, with Riley's sons in partnership with John E. Roberts; and finally Parsons Brothers from 1910 to 1945. This boat has the typical dark blue hull popular with guides and fishermen, and fancy nickel-plated "scroll-pattern" oarlock plates that were supplied to builders by special hardware makers like the M.E. Blazier Manufacturing Co. of Utica, New York. Blazier also furnished hardware to St. Lawrence River skiff builders and canoe builders.

STATUS: Excellent original condition; this boat's carrying yoke and seat are from different boats.

DONOR: H. Danforth Miller, Jr.

FURTHER READING:

Bond, Hallie E. *Boats and Boating in the Adirondacks.* Blue Mountain Lake, New York: The Adirondack Museum; Syracuse, New York: Syracuse University Press, 1995.

Comstock, Edward, Jr., ed. *The Adirondack League Club, 1890-1990.* Old Forge, New York: The Adirondack League Club, 1990.

Durant, Kenneth and Helen. *The Adirondack Guide-Boat.* Blue Mountain Lake, New York: The Adirondack Museum; Camden, Maine: International Marine Publishing Co., 1980.

M.E. Blazier Manufacturing Company. *Boat, Yacht and Marine Hardware,* Catalog Number 15. Utica, New York, 1907.

Stephens, Robert W. "The Evolution of the Adirondack Guide Boat." *WoodenBoat* 130, May/June, 1996.

ACCESSION NO. 1986.79

The 16' Parsons-built guideboat. (Photo: Maynard Bray, Mystic Seaport 1986.79A)

Guideboats served visitors to the Adirondacks in many ways, including rowing recreation. (Photo: Courtesy of the Adirondack Museum, Mystic Seaport 1975-1-52)

The native guide and his client, the city sportsman, are shown here with a pair of guideboats. Their combined skill, good taste, and money, brought these craft to a high degree of refinement. (Photo: Courtesy of the Adirondack Museum, Mystic Seaport 1975-1-55)

With the yoke in place, one man could carry a lightweight guideboat overland between lakes, as shown here. (Photo: Courtesy of the Adirondack Museum, Mystic Seaport 1975-1-56)

Arbutus
ADIRONDACK GUIDEBOAT

16' 0" x 3' 2"   ca. 1900

Once the common means of transportation in the Adirondack region of New York State, these exquisite craft were regularly used by guides taking sportsmen on camping and fishing trips. Rivalry–keen among the guides –produced a highly refined boat, ideal for its intended use. Construction was commonly thin white cedar planking on fine ribs of spruce root, with fastenings of clenched nails. The boats were carried upside down on the guides' shoulders when portaging to the next lake; a contoured carrying yoke made the operation comfortable. The Adirondack Museum at Blue Mountain Lake, New York, which specializes in collecting, exhibiting, and studying guideboats, should be visited by anyone wishing to know more about them. *Arbutus*, built for Anna Hyatt Huntington, the sculptress and daughter-in-law of railroad mogul Collis P. Huntington, was used at the family "summer camp" in the Adirondacks, also named Arbutus.

STATUS: Original, including the painted finish, good condition.

DONOR: Thomas L. Cheney

FURTHER READING:

Durant, Kenneth. *Guide-Boat Days and Ways*. Blue Mountain Lake, New York: The Adirondack Museum, 1963.

Evans, Cerinda W. *Anna Hyatt Huntington*. Newport News, Virginia: The Mariners' Museum, 1965.

Ford, Howard. "Building the Adirondack Guide Boat." *WoodenBoat* 18, Sept/Oct, 1977.

Gardner, John. "Adirondack Guide Boat." *National Fisherman*, April, 1963.

——. "Adirondack Guide Boat." *Outdoor Maine*, August-September, 1959.

Manley, Atwood. *Rushton and His Times in American Canoeing*. Syracuse, New York: Syracuse University Press for The Adirondack Museum, 1968.

ACCESSION NO. 1975.429

Arbutus at the 1971 Small Craft Workshop before being given to the Museum. (Photo: Ken Mahler, Mystic Seaport 1971-6-467)

ADIRONDACK GUIDEBOAT

11' 0" x 3' 0"

"Raiders" were the names given to the smallest of the Adirondack guideboats, for their ability to be carried in to fish tiny, hard-to-reach ponds. This example was found by the donor abandoned on Fresh Pond, Hitherhills State Park, Long Island, a long way from the North Woods.

STATUS: Fair, mostly original, some repairs.

DONOR: Kenneth Steinmetz

ACCESSION NO. 1979.153

The small guideboat 1979.153. (Photo: Maynard Bray, Mystic Seaport 1979.153A)

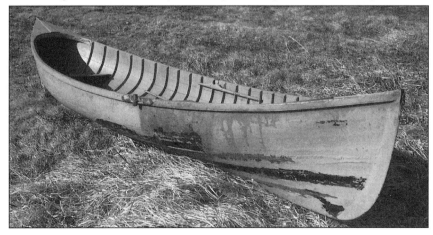

ADIRONDACK GUIDEBOAT
15' 8" x 3' 3"

This is a Long Lake-style guideboat with tumblehome in the stems. Like most of the guideboats, it carries no builder's identification, and only the initials A.P.S. are visible under a layer of paint. This boat was exported to an estate in western Massachusetts called Shadowbrook on the Stockbridge Bowl owned by Anson Phelps Stokes, a yachtsman and New York Yacht Club Vice Commodore. Stokes brought the boat down from his camp in the Adirondacks on Upper St. Regis Lake.

STATUS: Fair condition, needs new stem. Boat designated for use and awaiting restoration.
DONOR: Henry H. Williams, Jr.
ACCESSION NO. 1987.52

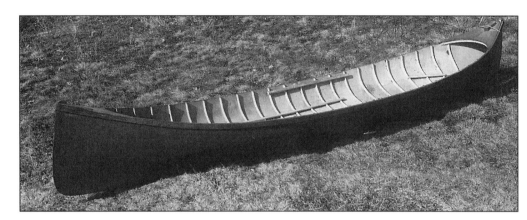

The 15' 8" Long Lake-style guideboat. (Photo: Maynard Bray, Mystic Seaport 1987.52A)

The Grant-built guideboat with oars and seat in place. (Photo: Maynard Bray, Mystic Seaport 1985.84A)

ADIRONDACK GUIDEBOAT BY GRANT
#1905-9
15' 1" x 3' 3"   1905

Thanks to meticulous records and other shop artifacts, which are preserved at the Adirondack Museum, and thanks to a boatbuilding business that spanned more than half a century between 1880 and 1934, the Grants of Boonville, New York, are perhaps the best-known guideboat builders of the Adirondacks. Part of this was due to a distinctive and functional style of boat developed by Dwight Grant, a boat with a raking bow instead of the tumblehome bow generally used by the central Adirondack builders. Part was due to special planes that allowed the Grants to make a lapped plank with a shoulder rather than with the more common and weaker feather edge. It was also due to a steady demand for boats from the members of the Adirondack League Club, where guideboats remained popular long after motorboats had made them less fashionable in other areas of the mountains. Another contributing factor was the club's banning of motors on two of its lakes. Both Dwight Grant and his son Lewis were well known at the Adirondack League Club, where they served as managers for many years.

W.D. Baldwin, head of the Otis Elevator Company, bought this boat for his daughter Louise in 1905, the year before Dwight Grant died. That same year Baldwin bought three additional Grant boats for his Bisby Lake camp, doubling the size of its Grant guideboat fleet.

STATUS: Excellent, in use until given to Mystic Seaport.
DONOR: Mary Louise Deupree (Mrs. James Y.), in memory of Louise Baldwin Vanderhoef
ACCESSION NO. 1985.84

ADIRONDACK GUIDEBOAT, PROBABLY BY AUSTIN OR COLE

13' 4" x 3' 2"   ca. 1890

One of the reasons this boat is still in existence is that she has been in storage since 1907 after being slightly damaged. The donor states that she was never actually used by a guide but rather for family recreation.

STATUS: Original, good condition.

DONOR: Given in memory of Bertram A. Redington by Elizabeth H. Webster, Nancy V. Webster, and Caroline V. Corwin

FURTHER READING:
(Same as 1986.79 and 1975.429)

ACCESSION NO. 1975.377

Guideboat 1975.377 in storage at Mystic Seaport. (Photo: Mary Anne Stets, Mystic Seaport 1975-10-105)

Adirondack guideboat variants by Salisbury–1974.461 to the left, 1974.460 to the right. (Photo: Maynard Bray, Mystic Seaport 1975-4-280)

ADIRONDACK GUIDEBOAT VARIANTS BY SALISBURY

14' 4" x 3' 0" and 14' 4" x 3' 3"

The same man appears to have built both of these boats, although only one of them (1974.460) carries a builder's nameplate: H.L. Salisbury & Bro., Long Lake, New York. They differ from the true guideboat in that they have keels rather than bottom boards. Number 1974.461 is fitted for rowing.

STATUS: Some repair, mostly original, good condition.

DONOR: Mr. and Mrs. James C. Smith

FURTHER READING:
(Same as 1986.79 and 1975.429)

ACCESSION NOS. 1974.460 and 1974.461

Annie

ST. LAWRENCE RIVER SKIFF BY A. BAIN & COMPANY

17' 9" x 3' 3"   ca. 1885

Annie is one of the finest extant St. Lawrence River skiffs. At 140 pounds and 39" beam, she is both narrower and lighter than the typical 17' skiff. The usual standard was 200 pounds and 42". Like all skiffs she is finer aft than forward, something that improved tracking in a cross wind. When rowed alone, her stern became the bow and needed some weight in the opposite end to give proper trim. She has the typical single tholepins of most skiffs, a design that allows the oars, which are pierced by the pins, to trail when fishing, and provides solid placement of the oars when pulling hard. Such fixed oars, of course, cannot be feathered.

Xavier Colon probably supervised *Annie*'s building or built her himself. One of the original and best builders on the river, his work attracted the attention and the capital of dentist and summer resident Alexander Bain. In 1873, Bain and Colon became partners, and by 1887 Bain had found additional investors, including Charles Emery, owner of Calumet Island, and the original owner of *Annie*. A large factory was built in Clayton, New York, and the following year Emery removed Bain as manager and renamed the company the St. Lawrence River Skiff, Canoe, and Steam Launch Company. In 1894 the operation moved downriver to Ogdensburg, after being bought by Spalding Sporting Goods. J.G. Fraser bought the company around the turn of the century and moved it to Long Island, first as the Whitestone Hollow Spar and Boat Company, then as the Fraser Hollow Spar and Boat Company of Greenport, Long Island.

Annie spent her working life on Calumet Island, near where she was built, and won the 1974 Skiff Class award at the annual antique and classic boat gathering in Clayton after cosmetic reconditioning by the St. Lawrence Restoration shop.

STATUS: Excellent condition, almost all original materials.

DONOR: Mrs. H.B. Cox

FURTHER READING:

Keats, John. *The Skiff and The River*, Nantucket, Massachusetts: The Herrick Collection, 1988.

Steever, Andrew. "Native to the Thousand Islands." *WoodenBoat* 20, 21, Jan/Feb, and Mar/Apr, 1978.

Annie's plans were drawn in 1977 by Andrew Steever, were published in *WoodenBoat*, and are available from The Antique Boat Museum in Clayton, New York. Unpublished research material and catalogs are also part of the collection of The Antique Boat Museum.

ACCESSION NO. 1980.76

Plans for 1980.76 are also available from Mystic Seaport's Watercraft Plans Collection.

Annie *in storage at Mystic Seaport in 1981. (Photo: Mary Anne Stets,* Mystic Seaport 1981-2-52)

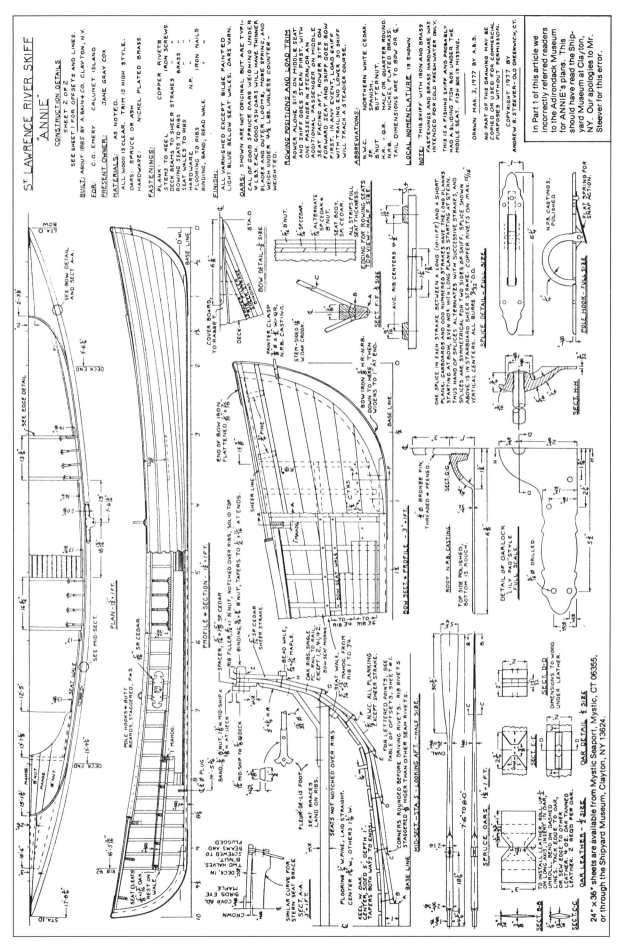

Annie's construction details are clearly shown in this drawing by Andrew Steever; the complete set of Steever drawings is available from Mystic Seaport or The Antique Boat Museum in Clayton, New York.

227

ST. LAWRENCE RIVER SKIFF
BY SPALDING

17' 1" x 3' 6"   ca. 1895

"The St. Lawrence River Skiff, so highly praised by all who have used it, is the outgrowth of certain conditions and local surroundings and...is specially good for its destined use.

"The boats are used everywhere about the Thousand Islands (upstate New York) for fishing, rowing and sailing, to the exclusion of all other small boats. They are handled by professional boatmen who show the greatest skill in their handling." So said *Forest and Stream* in its issue for April 25, 1889.

This boat was built by the Spalding St. Lawrence Boat Company of Ogdensburg, New York. Her construction is lapstrake with white cedar planking fastened with copper rivets and clinch nails. The Hudson River near Rhinebeck rather than the St. Lawrence was her home, perhaps explaining why a rudder and regular oarlocks were fitted. These skiffs usually had their oars mounted on fixed pins, a convenience when landing a fish as the oars could simply be dropped without fear of their slipping overboard, but frustrating indeed to the pleasure rower accustomed to feathering his oars.

STATUS: Restored 1972, original, excellent condition.
DONOR: Mrs. Frank B. Washburn
FURTHER READING:
(Same as for skiffs 1980.76 and 1973.31)
ACCESSION NO. 1971.382

St. Lawrence River skiff from Spalding St. Lawrence Boat Company. (Photo: Maynard Bray, Mystic Seaport 1975-5-205)

Barkis
ST. LAWRENCE RIVER SKIFF

19' 1" x 3' 6"   ca. 1894

Barkis in storage at Mystic Seaport. (Photo: Maynard Bray, Mystic Seaport 1975-10-107)

Like many St. Lawrence River skiffs, this one is fitted for a mast, enabling her to sail downwind. Some of these boats were fitted with "Radix" fan-type centerboards as well, but rarely with rudders: that would spoil the excitement of rudderless sailing, a skiff owner's refined but sometimes wet sport.

STATUS: Rig missing, original, good condition.
DONOR: Edward L. Crabbe
FURTHER READING:
(Same as for skiffs 1980.76 and 1973.31)
ACCESSION NO. 1972.570

Tub

ST. LAWRENCE RIVER STYLE SKIFF

15' 10" x 3' 9"   ca. 1890

In the 1890s St. Lawrence River skiffs were widely sold to areas other than the St. Lawrence as their fame was spread by articles in *Forest and Stream*, *Harper's*, and *The Rudder*, whose founder, Thomas Fleming Day, was the New York agent for St. Lawrence River skiffs. Thus this skiff, whose home was Lake Canandaigua in the Finger Lakes region farther south, could have come from the St. Lawrence or have been built by a Finger Lakes builder. Her folding oarlocks could have been made by Utica's Blaisdell Manufacturing Company, which furnished hardware to canoe and skiff builders. These oarlocks were not typical of skiffs used on the St. Lawrence. *Tub* also came with a complete sailing rig–a gaff sail stepped in the bow, catboat-style–and four spoon oars that carried the name of the boat's first owner: "H.W. Riley, Ithaca, N.Y."

STATUS: Good original condition.
DONORS: Ralph and Harriet Simmons
FURTHER READING:
(Same as for skiffs 1980.76 and 1973.31)
ACCESSION NO. 1991.184

The St. Lawrence River skiff-type from Lake Canandaigua. (Photo: Maynard Bray, Mystic Seaport 1991.184A)

ST. LAWRENCE RIVER SKIFF BY ANDRESS

16' 1" x 3' 6"   1911

St. Lawrence River skiffs were built on both sides of that great river. This one came from Gananoque on the Canadian side and was built for Mrs. George P. Douglass to use in the waters around the American Canoe Association's base at Sugar Island. The Douglass family were enthusiastic canoeists, with Mr. Douglass the A.C.A.'s Commodore in 1907. Their son, Gordon K. Douglass, was a champion canoe sailor and designer of the Thistle, Highlander, and Flying Scot one-design sailboats. Because this St. Lawrence River skiff was also used in Maryland on the open waters of the Chesapeake, it was not set up with the usual pin oarlocks of the river, but had feathering oarlocks and spoon oars. She was built by Raymond Andress of Gananoque, father of William E. Andress, whose son Elmer was the last of the skiff builders with nineteenth-century roots. The Andress family continued to use the same molds for three generations, molds which produced boats with fuller ends than those of their racier New York cousins.

STATUS: Good, recently refinished with a few missing pieces.
DONOR: Alan K. Douglass
FURTHER READING:
(Same as for skiffs 1980.76 and 1973.31)
ACCESSION NO. 1982.76

The 16' 1" Andress-built skiff. (Photo: Maynard Bray,
Mystic Seaport 1982.76A)

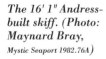

Two sports and a guide fish from a St. Lawrence River skiff. (Photo: Courtesy of the Antique Boat Museum, Mystic Seaport 1975-3-112)

Guideboats and St. Lawrence River skiffs on Big Moose Lake. (Photo: Courtesy of the Adirondack Museum, Mystic Seaport 1975-1-50)

A recreational excursion aboard a St. Lawrence River skiff in the 1890s. (Photo: Courtesy of the Antique Boat Museum, Mystic Seaport 1975-3-111)

ST. LAWRENCE RIVER SKIFF BY SHELDON

14′ 0″ x 3′ 2″   ca. 1900

The nameplate on this skiff reads "O. Sheldon & Co., Boat Builders, Boston, Mass." Although smaller than the usual St. Lawrence River skiff, this boat has a beautiful hull shape and exhibits some first-class workmanship.

STATUS: Some fittings missing, hull has been stripped to bare wood, original, fair condition.
DONOR: William B. Dodge
FURTHER READING:
(Same as for skiffs 1973.31 and 1980.76)
ACCESSION NO. 1975.177

The Sheldon & Co. skiff in 1975. (Photo Maynard Bray, Mystic Seaport 1975-4-146*)*

ST. LAWRENCE RIVER SKIFF FOR HUNTING

18′ 0″ x 4′ 9″

Obtained for study only, John Gardner brought this boat from Clayton, New York, home of The Antique Boat Museum. At that museum, examples of preserved skiffs, canoes, launches, and mahogany speedboats have promoted a revival of local historic boat types through the annual Antique Boat Show.

Chances are that this boat was originally a hunting vehicle used where a fancy finish wasn't needed, and most likely used by a hunter who made his living directly from nature instead of as a guide.

STATUS: Relic, poor condition.
DONOR: John Gardner
FURTHER READING:
Gardner, John. *Building Classic Small Craft.* Camden, Maine: International Marine Publishing Co., 1977.

Haxall, Boling W. "St. Lawrence Skiffs." *WoodenBoat* 11, Jul/Aug, 1976.

Simpson, Dwight S. "The St. Lawrence River Skiff." *Forest and Stream* 93.

Additional information on these boats is contained in *The Rudder*, July and September, 1890 and March and April, 1891. There is more in *Yachting*, November, 1969.

ACCESSION NO. 1973.31

The hunting skiff in storage in 1975. (Photo: Maynard Bray, Mystic Seaport 1975-10-95*)*

ST. LAWRENCE RIVER
SKIFF TYPE

17' 2" x 3' 9"   ca. 1900

This skiff has the general shape and size of a St. Lawrence River skiff but is carvel-planked, rather than lapstrake, and has open gunwales. She also does not have the characteristic metal seat braces, and in fact may be one of the St. Lawrence River skiff types built by Sheldon, Partelow, and others in the 1890s after these boats became popular in resorts outside the North Country. Her color scheme, red anti-fouling bottom paint with white topsides, show her adaptation to salt water where she was used for many years. She has had a sailing rig and centerboard trunk added.

STATUS: Good, paint peeling, possibly not original finish.
DONOR: Captain John E. McDonnell
FURTHER READING:
(Same as for skiffs 1980.76 and 1973.31)
ACCESSION NO. 1976.78

The 17' 2" St. Lawrence River skiff-type in 1978.
(Photo: Maynard Bray, Mystic Seaport 1978-2-55)

The 17' 10" W. E. Andress skiff in storage at Mystic Seaport.
(Photo: Maynard Bray, Mystic Seaport 1978-2-54)

ST. LAWRENCE RIVER SKIFF
BY W. E. ANDRESS

17' 10" x 3' 6"   ca. 1930

In the 1930s, the skiff shop of W. E. Andress was in full swing at Gananoque on the Ontario side of the St. Lawrence, and with a crew of six could produce 25 boats each winter. Andress alone could do the woodwork on a skiff in two weeks; finishing would take another two, and the boat would go out the door priced at $200. Such boats were very like this one, which migrated to Great Neck, Long Island. By the 1930s and 1940s W. E. was moving into building outboards and larger cruisers, launches and inboard runabouts, as well as building docks and cabins in the summer. His son Elmer continued the family's business until he retired in the mid-1970s.

STATUS: Good condition.
DONOR: Jack R. Aron
FURTHER READING:
(Same as for skiffs 1980.76 and 1973.31)

ACCESSION NO. 1977.133

Peapods in use at Deer Isle, Maine, in the 1880s. (Photo: Courtesy of The Hudson Collection, Mystic Seaport 1967-2-8)

PEAPOD, PROBABLY FROM DEER ISLE, MAINE

16' 0" x 4' 5"   ca. 1900

Distinctive double-enders, peapods are believed to have originated in "lobster country"– Penobscot Bay, Maine – and most were used for just that purpose. Standing up and facing forward, his oars in "raised up" oarlocks, the lobsterman rowed his pod from trap to trap, each being marked by a cedar buoy of his own particular color scheme. Planking was either lap or smooth and centerboards were fitted in many pods to make long passages easier by sailing.

STATUS: Restored, approximately 75% original, good condition.

DONOR: Robert S. Douglas (by exchange)

FURTHER READING FOR PEAPODS:

Brooks, Alfred A. "The Boats of Ash Point, Maine." *The American Neptune*, October, 1942.

Chapelle, Howard I. *American Small Sailing Craft.* New York: W.W. Norton & Co., 1951.

Gardner, John. *Building Classic Small Craft.* Camden, Maine: International Marine Publishing Co., 1977.

——. *Classic Small Craft You Can Build.* Mystic, Connecticut: Mystic Seaport Publications, 1993.

——. "Maine Peapods." *Maine Coast Fisherman*, September, October, 1951.

——. *Building Small Boats for Oar and Sail.* Camden, Maine: National Fisherman, 1971.

Goode, George Brown, ed. *The Fisheries and Fishery Industries of the United States.* Washington, D.C.: U.S. Government Printing Office, 1887.

Van Ness, C.W. "A Maine Peapod." *Yachting*, February, 1932.

ACCESSION NO. 1959.1472
Plans for 1959.1472 are available from Mystic Seaport's Watercraft Plans Collection.

Peapod 1959.1472 on display at Mystic Seaport. (Photo: Maynard Bray, Mystic Seaport 1975-6-80)

Red Star

SAILING PEAPOD FROM DEER ISLE BY NATE EATON

14' 11" x 4' 5"   ca. 1920

Sheldon Torrey, *Red Star's* original owner, used to sail her from his home waters on the Benjamin River in Sedgwick, Maine, mostly for pleasure, although she was used by a later owner for clamming in the same part of the Maine coast. She was built in the Mountainville region of Deer Isle by Nate Eaton, and in later years was used as a yacht tender by the donor. A spritsail, rather than the leg-o-mutton sail shown here, was fitted originally.

STATUS: Mostly original, good condition.

DONOR: Mrs. Albert B. Hunt

Red Star *as she appeared in 1975 at Mystic Seaport. (Photo: Maynard Bray, Mystic Seaport 1975-6-84)*

Red Star *under sail on Eggemoggin Reach, Maine. (Photo: Courtesy of Mrs. Albert B. Hunt, Mystic Seaport 1971-6-127)*

FURTHER READING:
(Same as for 1959.1472)
White, Joel. "Peapods for Sailing." *WoodenBoat* 27, Mar/Apr, 1979.

ACCESSION NO. 1970.638
Plans for 1970.638 are available from Mystic Seaport's Watercraft Plans Collection.

The Beano

PEAPOD FROM LITTLE DEER ISLE BY MACE EATON

14' 0" x 4' 2"   ca. 1914

In Maine, smart summer people turn to a local boatbuilder when they need a small boat for errands or recreation. When the family of the donor needed a boat for their summer cottage on Little Deer Isle, they contracted with Mace Eaton, whose shop was then on Blastow Cove, for a 14' seven-plank lapstrake pod with mast step for $20.

Eaton, in his late teens, agreed to a very low price, probably because part of the contract was to use cedar from another summer resident's woods (which had to be selected, cut, planed, and milled) rather than prefinished lumber. After finishing, the builder asked for and got another $20. The boat was used for picnics, fishing, exercise, and general utility. The donor's mother and uncle rigged her for sailing, with only an oar over the stern as a rudder and a rock in the bow for ballast. *The Beano* also played a romantic role in 1922, when the donor's father proposed to his future bride aboard her.

STATUS: Good condition, recently painted, largely original.
DONOR: J. Devereaux deGozzaldi, in memory of his father, Jake deGozzaldi

FURTHER READING:
(Same as for 1959.1472 and 1970.638)

ACCESSION NO. 1982.36

Peapod 1982.36 in use on the coast of Maine. (Photo: Courtesy of J.D. deGozzaldi, Mystic Seaport 1982.36.2)

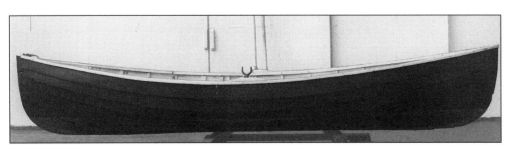

The Beano *at Mystic Seaport, freshly painted. (Photo: Maynard Bray, Mystic Seaport 1982.36)*

PEAPOD BY ASA COOPER
13' 5" x 4' 4"   ca. 1932

It was this boat that Havilah Hawkins used as the model for the peapods he built in the 1950s and early '60s, and Jim Steele still uses the same shape for the "Downeast Peapods" he turns out. Of these, Jim has built well over a hundred. It's little wonder that the Cooper pod has been so well received; compared to most working peapods, this one is not only prettier but better adapted to recreational use. Rather than the flattish midsection and hard

bilges that working pods need in order to be stable with a lobster trap on the gunwale, this one has more deadrise and a correspondingly narrower waterline. You can bet that she rows much, much easier–especially with a light load when wetted surface is at a minimum.

This peapod remained with one family for 50 years. The donor's grandfather, Earl Carter, bought it brand-new in the early 1930s for $25 after Cooper built it as a high school shop project. Asa Cooper went on to build three more similar peapods, all

of which he sold to local lobster fishermen or clam harvesters.

STATUS: Outside sheathed in fiberglass, poor condition.

DONOR: Christopher E. Carter

FURTHER READING:
Bray, Maynard. "Improving the Building Process." *WoodenBoat* 77, July/Aug, 1987.

ACCESSION NO. 1984.26

The Asa Cooper peapod in 1984. (Photo: Maynard Bray,
Mystic Seaport 1984.26A)

PEAPOD BY JAMES F. STEELE
13' 6" x 4' 6"   1967

In 1967, Charles & Phaeton Matthews ordered two peapods for their steel passenger schooner *Mystic Whaler*. This is one of that pair, which served as tenders for 15 years. This one went on to hang from another schooner's davits–those of the *Mystic Clipper*–for three additional seasons until its ownership passed to Quentin Snediker, who donated it to Mystic Seaport in 1991.

Jim Steele has been building peapods since he took over from Havilah Hawkins in 1964, averaging three to five boats a year, with peak annual production occasionally hitting

as many as twelve. Building peapods has always been a part-time affair–a kind of antidote to building houses. Now in semiretirement, Jim continues turning out these exquisite double-enders on a small-scale, production-line basis. To date, 169 "Downeast Peapods" have rolled out of Jim Steele's shop in Brooklin, Maine, and there are doubtless more to come.

After milling out all the pieces for several pods, including keels, stems, planking, frames, seats, and seat knees, Jim begins by assembling the backbone and cutting the four stem rabbets with his ingenious, router-based automatic cutting machine–a device he built himself. He sets the completed backbone, followed by the

steam-bent oak frames, atop an inverted building "trap" that can be raised or lowered to a convenient height for hanging the cedar planking. The remaining pieces go in after the hull is turned right-side up.

STATUS: Fair, with original planking and 80% of original frames. In need of striping, repainting, and breasthook repair.

DONOR: Quentin Snediker

FURTHER READING:
Getchell, David R., Sr. "A Living from Small Boats?" *WoodenBoat* 77, July /Aug, 1987.

Henry Wall, lobstering from his peapod off Vinalhaven. Notice the long-shanked oarlocks for rowing while standing. (Photo: Courtesy of Jerry Rooney, <small>Mystic Seaport 1982-6-10</small>)

PEAPOD FROM VINALHAVEN BY GUSTAVSON

15' 6" x 4' 3"   ca. 1950

The Walls, father and son, were possibly the last lobstermen on Vinalhaven Island in Maine to depend on oar-powered boats for a livelihood. The boat, built by Harold Gustavson, was already about 20 years old when the Walls began to use her for lobstering. Henry, the father, painted this locally built peapod bright yellow during the 1970s when he owned her. The color matched his pot buoys. Son Richard

favored gray–the boat's present color–when he took over after Henry died. Both men had the same operating technique, however. They kept the boat on a haulout in front of their house and always worked her in the mornings before the wind came up. The route was alongshore and the distance was not great–at most four or five miles in the course of a day. Special long-shanked oarlocks were fitted, and the rowing was done standing up and facing forward, except when pulling against a strong and unexpected headwind when you "had to put your back into it" as

well as reduce the windage by sitting down. Unfortunately the oars didn't come with the boat. They were a historical record in themselves; through use, the oarlocks had worn them to a fraction of their original diameter. The smell of bait, decayed crabs, periwinkles, and starfish is still with the boat (as are some of the causes). We are fortunate that this peapod passed directly to the Museum from her lobstering days, and consider the aroma as verification.

STATUS: Original, fair condition.

DONOR: Mystic Seaport purchase

FURTHER READING:
(Same as for 1971.237)

ACCESSION NO. 1978.222

Peapod from Vinalhaven showing wear from lobstering work. (Photo: Maynard Bray, <small>Mystic Seaport 1978.222A</small>)

PEAPOD BUILT AT MYSTIC SEAPORT

14' 2" x 4' 5"   1971

With more deadrise and easier bilges than most working pods, this one was modeled to row easily rather than to be stiff while lobster traps were hauled over her rail. She was designed by John Gardner and built in 1971 by Sylvester Costelloe of Mystic Seaport's Small Craft Lab. Her plans appear in Gardner's *Building Classic Small Craft*.

In their shape, peapods are a lot like St. Lawrence River skiffs, and these two types of small craft are compared by John Gardner in the book noted above. Although unheralded as a rudderless sailboat, peapods probably

perform that way as well as their freshwater cousins. In Brooklin, Maine, where Jim Steele's shop turns out a standard traditionally built pod, peapods rigged with boomless spritsails have been sailed with great success in recent years, sans both rudders and centerboards.

STATUS: In use, excellent condition.

DONOR: Mystic Seaport-built reproduction

FURTHER READING:
(Same as for 1959.1472)

ACCESSION NO. 1971.237
Plans for 1971.237 are available from Mystic Seaport's Watercraft Plans Collection.

Mystic Seaport-built peapod in 1975. (Photo: Maynard Bray, <small>Mystic Seaport 1975-6-85</small>)

PEAPOD FROM NORTH HAVEN BY WHITMORE

14' 2" x 4' 4"   ca. 1929

Shortly after boatbuilder Alton Whitmore moved his shop from the nearby island of North Haven to Rockport, he built this "double-ender" for a local lobster fisherman who used her for about ten years. Subsequently, the boat was owned by Captain Allison Ames of Camden, from whom John Gardner bought her about 1966. John used her off and on at Mystic Seaport after he joined the staff to set up the Museum's several small-craft programs in 1969. Those who worked her have special praise for this boat: one fisherman "claimed she didn't blow about and held steadier in a wind than any boat he had ever used."

Whitmore built this carvel-planked pod without molds, using pre-bent frames. He seems to have used the same technique and possibly the midship-section shape to build the transom-sterned recreational rowboats he began to turn out after lobster fishermen abandoned peapods for engine-powered lobsterboats.

STATUS: Good; some frames sistered, some plank chafe suffered in Hurricane Gloria.

DONOR: John Gardner

FURTHER READING:
Gardner, John. *Classic Small Craft You Can Build.* Mystic, Connecticut: Mystic Seaport Publications, 1993. Chapter 6 discusses this boat.

——. "Building the North Haven Peapod." *National Fisherman*, Jan-Feb, 1986.

ACCESSION NO. 1985.135
Plans for 1985.135 are available from Mystic Seaport's Watercraft Plans Collection.

Alton Whitmore, right, with brother Gus. (Photo: Courtesy of Una Ames)

The Whitmore pod in storage at Mystic Seaport. (Photo: Maynard Bray, Mystic Seaport 1985.135)

NORTH HAVEN PEAPOD REPRODUCTION

14' 2" x 4' 4"   1984

Peapods were to be featured at the Museum's annual Small Craft Workshop in 1984, so at the conclusion of that winter's boatbuilding classes, John Gardner and his assistant Bill Mills set to work to build a reproduction of John's pod and have it well underway for the June event. This reproduction differs in construction from the original in that conventional molds were used with the frames bent inside the ribbands. Bronze screws were used instead of hot-dipped galvanized boat nails. Two features that set this boat off from many other pods and make her more durable are a heavy, wide rockered oak plank keel and continuous seat risers that are joined together and to the stems as well by blocks that act as lower breasthooks.

While Alton Whitmore's pod has been retired, this reproduction has joined Mystic Seaport's boat livery where Museum visitors get to try her out.

STATUS: Excellent, in use.

DONOR: Museum-built by John Gardner and Bill Mills

FURTHER READING:
(Same as for 1959.1472 and 1985.135)

ACCESSION NO. 1985.136

The North Haven peapod built at Mystic Seaport by John Gardner. (Photo: Maynard Bray, Mystic Seaport 1985.136)

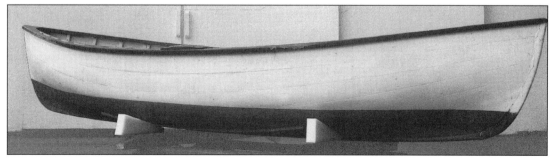

DOUBLE-ENDED DINGHY, POSSIBLY BY LAWLEY

11' 2" x 3' 10"   ca. 1918

Much like a Maine peapod, but with different provenance, this diminutive double-ender is said to have been built by Fred Lawley around 1918–or to have come out of the Lawley shops in Neponset on Boston harbor. If so, she is one-of-a-kind, built for someone who insisted on having a double-ended tender (and not mentioned in the Lawley building record). She is nicely built, with grown knees used in her carvel-planked and riveted construction. Her hull is asymmetrical, beamier aft than forward. A coved-out rubrail to take a fender indicates that she was intended as a tender, but not a very capacious one. She must have given good service, as the donor's family used her steadily from the 1920s.

STATUS: Fair; has had some reframing. Fiberglass covering, worn and weathered paint.
DONOR: Davis Taylor
ACCESSION NO. 1981.48

Peapod-type tender possibly by Fred Lawley. (Photo: Maynard Bray, Mystic Seaport 1982-2-125*)*

PEAPOD FROM CAPE SPLIT, MAINE

16' 2" x 4' 2"   ca. 1880

Crudely built at or near Harrington, Maine, this peapod is finer-lined than most. She was used for lobstering until the end of her career when the donor experimented with her, writing up his results in the February 1962 issue of *National Fisherman.*

STATUS: Relic, some repair, poor condition.

DONOR: Benjamin B. Drisko
FURTHER READING:
(Same as for 1959.1472)

ACCESSION NO. 1967.302
Plans for 1967.302 are available from Mystic Seaport's Watercraft Plans Collection.

The Cape Split peapod on her arrival at Mystic Seaport in 1967. (Photo: Louis Martel, Mystic Seaport 1967.302*)*

Els-Har-Chris-Robyn-David
PEAPOD FROM MID-COAST MAINE

15' 10" x 4' 0"

This pod was found in front of a lumber company in Maine in 1956; she had been used at a camp on Randell Pond near Belfast, and that is all anyone knew. She was taken home to Marblehead and used with enthusiasm by the family that discovered her–so much so that everyone wanted to be part of the name. A careful look at her shape shows a boat with finer lines and more deadrise than found in the usual working peapod, and she had a mast step as well–features that would make a superior recreational boat. Her framing with flat frames is similar to boats built in Nova Scotia. She is galvanized-fastened with a lapped oak sheer strake, then smooth cedar or spruce planking.

STATUS: Fair structural condition, cosmetically rough.
DONORS: Wardwell A. Ratcliff and Ben Lufkin
ACCESSION NO. 1980.160

The peapod from mid-coast Maine in 1980. (Photo: Maynard Bray, Mystic Seaport 1981-2-86*)*

SAILING PEAPOD

12' 0" x 4' 1"   ca. 1945

Little is known about this pod, other than a report that she was built somewhere in Maine. She is on the small side for a peapod and quite heavily built. With some changes to reduce her weight, she would make a fine little tender for a larger boat. An unusual feature is the way in which her seat knees fay against the edges instead of the tops of her seats.

STATUS: Original, poor condition.
DONOR: John A. Knauth
FURTHER READING:
(Same as for 1959.1472 and 1970.638)
ACCESSION NO. 1975.457

Peapod with centerboard and sailing rig in storage at Mystic Seaport. (Photo: Mary Anne Stets, Mystic Seaport 1975-10-174)

Tattlededdy
PEAPOD BY FRANK SMITH

16' 4" x 4' 5"   pre-1930

Frank P. Smith built this peapod at his West Jonesport, Maine, boatyard for Frank Dobbins, the donor's father. She was set up to sail when the wind served, being built with a forward mast thwart. Father and son used her for clamming, lobstering, and gunning. When the donor was a boy, he used her to tend a string of lobster pots within sight of the family kitchen, loading her deep with "cuttings"–fish heads and tails–from the Underwood processing plant in Jonesport. The family called her *Tattlededdy*, a name they got from Frank Dobbins's Coast Guard C.O., who named the pod for a boat built of straw. Hunting was on the mind of the donor's brother, who painted duck silhouettes on the boat when she was last used in the 1950s. Like the Cape Split peapod (1967.302), Smith's hull design sacrificed the flat-floored, hard-bilged shape and the initial stability of a lobster pod like Whitmore's (1985.135) for easy rowing. *Tattlededdy* has clench-nailed cedar planks on flat bent-oak frames in the Nova Scotia style, similar to the Museum's Cape Sable boat (1989.113, page 276). She has had three rowing thwarts, so she could be balanced depending on load and crew. In normal use, a single rower would have stood and pushed. She now has only one rowing thwart along with a mast thwart.

STATUS: Cosmetically rough with indications of various repairs.
DONOR: Millard J. "Buzz" Dobbins
ACCESSION NO. 1993.49.1

The Frank Smith pod on her arrival at Mystic Seaport. (Photo: Judy Beisler, Mystic Seaport 1993.49.1)

SHIP'S BOAT (STOREBAAD) FOR *JOSEPH CONRAD*

21' 6" x 6' 5"   1980

Lines for this boat came from Burmeister & Wain in Copenhagen, builder of the *Joseph Conrad*, ex-*Georg Stage*. Details, however, were lacking. To fill in the gaps, Museum shipwright Willits Ansel used a period British book by Ernest Blocksidge about ships' boats, together with examination of a British ship's boat then in the Museum collection. Some of this boat's details are uncommon in American small-craft construction: a keel and sternpost half-lapped and riveted, and nibbed and riveted plank scarfs. This one is built lapstrake, has ports for 10 oars, would be rowed double-banked, and can set two low-peaked spritsails.

STATUS: Excellent condition, in use.
SOURCE: Museum-built

FURTHER READING:
Ansel, Willits. "A Ship's Boat for the *Joseph Conrad*." *WoodenBoat* 43, Nov/Dec, 1981.

Blocksidge, Ernest Walter. *Ship's Boats: Their Qualities, Construction, Equipment and Launching Apparatus.* London: Longmans, Green & Company, 1920.

ACCESSION NO. 1980.149
Plans for 1980.149 are available from Mystic Seaport's Watercraft Plans Collection.

The Joseph Conrad *ship's boat hung in davits aboard the larger vessel. (Photo: Ken Mahler, Mystic Seaport 1981-6-97)*

QUARTER BOAT (JOLLE) FOR *JOSEPH CONRAD*

20' 0" x 6' 10"   1982

For a second *Conrad* boat, Museum shipwright Willits Ansel altered the lines used for ship's boat 1980.149, and, with Tom Jannke, built this one in 1982. Her size is based on the boats that were known to be carried on the ship. Both boats are used to teach rowing technique in various educational programs based aboard the former sail-training ship *Joseph Conrad*. They each have bluff bows, round bilges, and are quite deep. Light, they float high and feel tender, yet they come into their own when loaded with a full crew and passengers.

STATUS: Excellent condition, in use.
SOURCE: Museum-built
ACCESSION NO. 1984.15

The quarter boat being built at Mystic Seaport in 1982. (Photo: Mary Anne Stets, Mystic Seaport 1982-5-80)

The Race Point surfboat outside the New Shoreham (Block Island) Life-Saving Station, now on the grounds of Mystic Seaport. (Photo: Maynard Bray, Mystic Seaport 1975-6-101)

RACE POINT SURFBOAT, USCG HULL # 24311

24' 7" x 6' 1"   ca. 1940

Although most Race Point surfboats were built before the turn of the century for the old U.S. Life-Saving Service and came out of private boatshops on Cape Cod, this boat and some others like her were produced much later by the Coast Guard's Curtis Bay, Maryland, shipyard. In 1930, when the Coast Guard started building them, the Race Point model was only in limited use, having been replaced in most stations by the self-bailing "standard service" surfboat. Nevertheless, before the end of World War II, Curtis Bay had turned out 62 boats like this one, mostly for use along the coasts of New England and Long Island. Only three more were built after the war and they came out in 1958.

For a light boat that would hold together in spite of rough use, yet was a match for whatever screeching gale came along, the Race Point boat was hard to beat. Coastal stations of the U.S. Life-Saving Service began using them back in 1894, mostly along the outer shore of Cape Cod. It is likely that the inspiration for their design came from the surfboats of the privately run Massachusetts Humane Society. They take their name from the headland at the tip end of Cape Cod, near Provincetown.

STATUS: Restored 1975, approximately 90% original, good condition.

DONOR: Anonymous

FURTHER READING:
MacArthur, Keith R. "The Research Behind the Restoration: Mystic's Life Saving Craft." *Wooden Shipbuilding & Small Craft Preservation*. Washington, D.C.: The Preservation Press, 1976.

Shanks, Ralph, and Wick York. *The U.S. Life-Saving Service*. Petaluma, California: Costaño Books, 1996.

Wilkinson, William D. "Surfboat Authority Sheds Light on Race Point Type." *National Fisherman*, November, 1972.

ACCESSION NO. 1947.1982
Plans for 1947.1982 are available from Mystic Seaport's Watercraft Plans Collection.

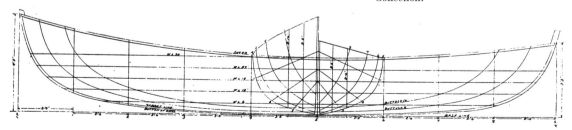

These lines of the Coast Guard's Race Point surfboat, by naval architect Ralph Winslow, appeared in The Rudder *for August, 1926.*

Massachusetts Humane Society surfboat in 1973 after restoration. (Photo: Mary Anne Stets, Mystic Seaport 1973-11-103)

SURFBOAT FROM MASSACHUSETTS HUMANE SOCIETY

28' 8" x 6' 8"   ca. 1900

Starting with the country's first coastal life-saving station (Cohasset, 1807) the Massachusetts Humane Society continued as a volunteer organization throughout the more than one hundred years of its existence. But with the expansion of the U.S. Life-Saving Service after the 1870s, the need for such an organization began to diminish. By the time the U.S. Coast Guard was formed in 1915 (by combining the Life-Saving Service with the U.S. Revenue Cutter Service) only a few of the old Humane Society stations were still active.

This boat was built for the society's Marblehead station by the celebrated Graves boatyard of Marblehead. She was used in the twilight years of the society's existence, mostly for boat-handling practice and competitive rowing against the boats of other

Horses got surfboats to the beach where stranded vessels' crews could be rescued. (Photo: Mystic Seaport 1974-2-137)

Massachusetts Humane Society surfboat with crew at practice. (Photo: Courtesy of Marblehead Historical Commission)

stations. She was modeled after the previous boat, which was damaged beyond repair in a rescue the year before, and was commanded by James Frost, father and son, until she was given up sometime before World War II. Later on, under a subsequent owner, she was fitted with an inboard engine and still later was abandoned ashore. A complete restoration was in order when Mystic Seaport acquired her. Some of the details and thinking that went into her restoration are reported in the Preservation Press publication listed below.

STATUS: Restored 1975, approximately 80% original, excellent condition.

DONOR: Mystic Seaport purchase

FURTHER READING:

Howe, M.A. DeWolfe. *The Humane Society of the Commonwealth of Massachusetts–An Historical Review, 1785-1916*. Boston, Massachusetts: The Riverside Press, 1918.

MacArthur, Keith R. "The Research Behind the Restoration: Mystic's Life-Saving Craft." *Wooden Shipbuilding & Small Craft Preservation*. Washington, D.C.: The Preservation Press, 1976.

ACCESSION NO. 1972.901

The Massachusetts Humane Society surfboat before its restoration at Mystic Seaport. (Photo: Maynard Bray, Mystic Seaport 1972.901A)

243

Tycho Brahe
CONVERTED GOVERNMENT SURFBOAT

25' 7" x 7' 5" ca. 1942

When, after World War II, Dr. Frederic Tudor wanted a boat for cruising, he found this lapstrake government-surplus surfboat in her original undecked configuration, bought it for approximately $200, and had suitable alterations made. These included a cabin, an outboard motor well, pulpits fore and aft, and basic interior accommodations. Tudor, who in his youth had cruised extensively with his father, W. Starling Burgess,

considered the self-righting *Tycho Brahe* (named after the famous Danish astronomer) an especially safe craft in most any weather. In his words, "she is so very sea-easy, we felt the necessity of using a harness, especially standing at

the tiller in the narrow stern, sometimes 6-8 feet above the water."

STATUS: Alterations removed, fair condition.
DONOR: Dr. Frederic Tudor
ACCESSION NO. 1979.197

Dr. Frederic Tudor's surfboat returned to her original open-boat configuration. (Photo: Mary Anne Stets, Mystic Seaport 1980-2-26)

METAL LIFE SAVING CAR
10' 6" x 4' 0"

Getting the crew and passengers safely ashore from stranded vessels was once a job for the men of U.S. Life-Saving Service, founded in the 1870s and a precursor of the U.S. Coast Guard. While most rescues could be accomplished with a surfboat, extreme conditions forced the life-savers to rig a high line from the shore to the ship. Some sort of rescue vehicle was then suspended to shuttle back and forth from the ship to shore. The metal life saving car was one such vehicle, invented by Joseph Francis of Massachusetts in 1838 and perfected nine years later. It was essentially a covered, double-ended lifeboat with rings for attachment to the high line. Later on, the better-known breeches

buoy came into widespread use, although chances are it did not give such a dry ride.

The builder's plate indicates that this car was built by T.F. Rowland, Continental Works, Brooklyn, New York. It was last in service at the Watch Hill, Rhode Island, Coast Guard Station.

DONOR: U.S. Coast Guard

FURTHER READING:
Bennett, Robert F., Cmdr., USCG. *Surfboats, Rockets, and Carronades.* Washington, D.C.: Department of Transportation, U.S. Coast Guard, 1976.

Francis, Joseph. *History of Life-Saving Appliances.* New York: Slater, 1885.

Shanks, Ralph, and Wick York. *The U.S. Life-Saving Service: Heroes, Rescues and Architecture of the Early Coast Guard.* Petaluma, California: Costaño Books, 1996.

ACCESSION NO. 1950.3086

The life-saving car in 1975. (Photo: Maynard Bray, Mystic Seaport 1975-10-78)

The Hankins New Jersey skiff. (Photo: Maynard Bray, Mystic Seaport 1975-10-94)

Lavallette
Beach Patrol
SEA BRIGHT SKIFF BY HANKINS

16' 3" x 5' 0" 1964

Waves, sometimes born of a savage Atlantic storm, sometimes kicked up by a summer sea breeze, pound New Jersey's exposed coast. Penetrating these breakers by boat in either direction calls for balance, strength, and a feel for the task; one also needs a good boat under him. Shore fishermen back in the 1850s had to conquer the same surf as New Jersey lifeguards do today. Both used the Sea Bright skiff or "dory surf boat," as one builder called them. That builder was Charles Hankins & Son, whose Lavallette shop has been in the business since 1906 and is still at it. According to Peter Guthorn in his book *The Sea Bright Skiff and Other Jersey Shore Boats*: "(Their) design and scantlings are almost identical to those built more than a century ago, except that they are no longer equipped with a centerboard or sails." Demand for new boats from the Hankins shop certainly hasn't been hurt by the state law requiring an available surfboat at all recreational beaches, or by spirited surf-boat competitions among lifeguards each year. Although New Jersey sand is easier on a sea skiff's bottom than Maine rocks are on a wherry's, the surf is much worse and requires a bow-first launching.

Structurally a Sea Bright skiff is a lot like a wherry. Both are lapstrake-planked and have planked-down skegs. They are both bottom-board boats and even look a little alike. Most sea skiffs have steam-bent frames rather than sawn frames, and those in the skeg area pass over and are fastened to "codwads," or floor timbers connecting them to the bottom board.

STATUS: Original, very good condition.

DONOR: Charles E. Hankins

FURTHER READING:

Bouchal, Gerald. "Surfing Sea Bright Style." *WoodenBoat* 17, July/Aug, 1977. First-hand account of handling these boats in the surf by a New Jersey lifeguard.

Chapelle, Howard I. *American Small Sailing Craft*. New York: W.W. Norton & Co., 1951.

Gardner, John. *Building Classic Small Craft*. Camden, Maine: International Marine Publishing Co., 1977.

Goode, George Brown. *The Fisheries and Fishery Industries of the United States*. Washington, D.C.: U.S. Government Printing Office, 1887.

Guthorn, Peter J. *The Sea Bright Skiff and Other Jersey Shore Boats*. New Brunswick, New Jersey: Rutgers University Press, 1971.

ACCESSION NO. 1972.571

YANKEE SKIFF

22' 8" x 6' 2"

For tonging oysters in the bays and inlets of Staten Island and northern New Jersey, skiffs built like the Maine salmon wherries and Sea Bright skiffs (but far prettier than either) were used. As far as can be determined, not one of these so-called Staten Island or Raritan Bay oyster skiffs survived, but thanks to Martin Erissmann, who carefully measured a boat and drew up her plans in 1909, we have a good record of what one looks like. The 22' 8" Yankee skiff in Mystic Seaport's collection, shown here, is very similar to the boat in Erissmann's drawings. She was acquired in 1976 from The Mariners' Museum, and her designer, builder, and location of use are not known. Remarkably, this boat is about the same as the Yankee skiff of Chesapeake Bay, a boat also nearly extinct, and like southern variants of the New Haven sharpies a migrant from New England. These boats were ceiled inside over their frames for ease in shoveling out the oysters, and when in use were fitted with culling boards astride their gunwales. Another of the Yankee skiffs is on exhibit at The Mariners' Museum, Newport News, Virginia.

The 22' 8" Yankee skiff in storage at Mystic Seaport. (Photo: Maynard Bray, Mystic Seaport 1978.2.62)

STATUS: Modified for inboard engine, relic, poor condition.

DONOR: Mystic Seaport purchase through The Mariners' Museum

FURTHER READING:

Gardner, John. *Classic Small Craft You Can Build*. Mystic: Mystic Seaport Publications, 1993.

Guthorn, Peter J. *The Sea Bright Skiff and Other Jersey Shore Boats*. New Brunswick, New Jersey: Rutgers University Press, 1971. The chapter on the Raritan Bay oyster skiffs is good and includes Erissmann's plans.

Kochiss, John M. *Oystering from New York to Boston*. Middletown, Connecticut: Wesleyan University Press for Mystic Seaport, 1974. Good information on Staten Island oystering, including material quoted from contemporary sources.

ACCESSION NO. 1976.4

Staten Island oyster-men use a similar Staten Island skiff to tong for oysters in Prince's Bay in this illustration from Ballou's Pictorial Drawing Room Companion, September 29, 1855. (Mystic Seaport 1993-2-32)

The Lincolnville salmon wherry on display at Mystic Seaport in 1975. (Photo: Maynard Bray, Mystic Seaport 1975-6-19)

SALMON WHERRY FROM LINCOLNVILLE, MAINE

13' 4" x 4' 4"   1892

The Maine salmon wherry, the New Jersey Sea Bright skiff, the Adirondack guideboat, some dories, and probably the early peapods, were structually alike even though different in outward appearance. They were lap-fastened bottom-board boats with softwood frames sawn from natural crooks. This was an old-time way of boatbuilding that had a lot going for it, although getting good framing stock today might be difficult. Boats so built sit upright while on land, and if the bottom board is of hardwood, as it is in the wherries, the heels of the frames have a secure landing and good fastening into it. Installing a strong centerboard trunk is easy, and if the bottom board is protected on its outside with a sacrificial false bottom, beaching out in a hard-chance landing place like Lincolnville is no problem.

Afloat and in use the salmon fisherman knelt in the bow while tending his weir, taking aboard whatever fish were caught up in it. Thus the wherries were full forward and, being launched stern first off the beach, were fine-lined aft. This was the boat of Robie Ames, a Lincolnville fisherman, whose fish house, its entire contents, and his wherry are in Mystic Seaport's collection.

STATUS: Original, fair condition.

DONOR: The Adirondack Historical Association in exchange for a Mystic Seaport-built reproduction.

FURTHER READING:

Brooks, Alfred A. "The Boats of Ash Point, Maine." *The American Neptune*, October, 1942.

Gardner John. *Building Classic Small Craft.* Camden, Maine: International Marine Publishing Co., 1977. Contains the plans of this boat as well as much other information about wherries. A prime source.

——. "14' 'Reach Boat' is Obvious Maine Wherry Kin." *National Fisherman*, July 1974. Good comparison of wherry and Reach boat characteristics, including the known history of each.

——. "The New England Wherry." *The Log of Mystic Seaport*, Winter, 1970.

Goode, George Brown. *The Fisheries and Fishery Industries of the United States.* Washington, D.C.: U.S. Government Printing Office, 1887. Gives good description of the salmon weir-fishing process.

Simmons, Walter. "The Lincolnville Wherry." *WoodenBoat* 2, Nov/Dec, 1974.

ACCESSION NO. 1971.239

Members of the Wade family pose on the beach at Lincolnville with their wherries and a couple of sizable Atlantic salmon, ca. 1920. A hook of nets dries on poles in the background. (Photo: Courtesy of Osbourne Wade, Mystic Seaport 1972-6-373)

SALMON WHERRY REPRODUCTION

13' 6" x 4' 3"   1975

Two of these wherries were built at Mystic Seaport during the 1970s as close copies of the boat on the previous page. Willits Ansel built this one in more or less the old-time way; that is, he first set up the backbone (stem, stern, and bottom board) then planked her up over a few molds set in place to give the right shape. Finally he scribed in the frames and fastened them into position. Being familiar with the shape the planks had to be to give him the boat he wanted, the old-time builder would doubtless have gotten by with fewer molds, perhaps only one at the mid-point would have sufficed. This wherry, like the other Mystic Seaport reproductions, was built to be put overboard each year and used. People rowing one of these boats will find that, although they move along easily under oars, they are tiddlish when light (much like a banks dory), while at the same time high freeboard makes rowing in a breeze a bit of a chore. For recreational rowing there are better boats than this one, and unless one plans on going salmon fishing in the traditional way, another model would be the better choice.

STATUS: In use, excellent condition.
DONOR: Mystic Seaport-built reproduction
FURTHER READING:
(Same as for 1971.239)
ACCESSION NO. 1975.438

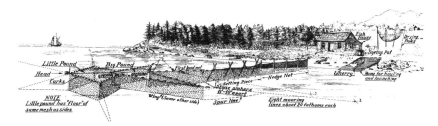

John Leavitt's sketch depicts the arrangement of a "hook of nets" and shoreside facility for salmon fishing in the Lincolnville area. (Photo: Mystic Seaport, 1975.338*)*

The 1975 reproduction salmon wherry. (Photo: Maynard Bray, Mystic Seaport 1975-6-77*)*

SALMON WHERRY BY GARDNER

13' 5" x 4' 6"   1971

This is a reproduction of Mystic Seaport's Lincolnville wherry (1971.239), built by John Gardner for the Adirondack Museum shortly after he came to Mystic. For many years it was part of that museum's Adirondack guideboat exhibit as an example of related boats. It has since been returned to Mystic Seaport's Watercraft Collection.

STATUS: Excellent condition.
DONOR: The Adirondack Museum
FURTHER READING:
(Same as for 1971.239)
ACCESSION NO. 1994.38

The reproduction salmon wherry built by John Gardner for the Adirondack Museum. (Photo: Judy Beisler, Mystic Seaport 1994.381*)*

The St. John, New Brunswick, wherry. (Photo: Russell Fowler, Mystic Seaport 1971-12-11)

WHERRY FROM ST. JOHN, NEW BRUNSWICK
21' 9" x 5' 10"

A boat of unknown origin, this one has many of the same features as the smaller Robie Ames salmon wherry from Lincolnville, Maine, including the fully planked skeg area where no deadwood is used. A gasoline engine was installed at one time.

STATUS: Pieces missing, mostly original, fair condition.
DONOR: Mystic Seaport purchase
FURTHER READING:
(Same as for 1971.239)
ACCESSION NO. 1971.246

The 12' 8" Moosabec Reach boat. (Photo: Maynard Bray, Mystic Seaport 1974.978C)

MOOSABEC REACH BOAT
12' 8" x 4' 4"

"The Maine Reach boats, which are extensively used in the coast fisheries of Maine, are also, to some extent, employed in lobstering. They range in length from 10' to 18', but the most common length is about 14'. They are sharp in the bow, round bilged, keeled, clinker or lap-strake, and have a square, heart, or V-shaped stern, with two or three thwarts, according to their size; they are as a rule entirely open, fore and aft, rarely having any wash-boards. They are well adapted both for rowing and sailing and all but the smallest usually carry one or more sprit-sails." (Quote from *The Fisheries and Fishery Industries of the United States*, pages 670-71.) Apparently Reach boats were common back in 1887, but as far as can be determined this is one of only a few that have survived. When this boat was acquired by Mystic Seaport in 1974, John Gardner reported that she was the only Reach boat he knew of that fit the description from Goode's *Fisheries* quoted above. Shortly after, John learned of another Reach boat, described on the next page. But, as John pointed out in the July, 1974, *National Fisherman*, there seems to be conflicting information as to what a Reach boat looks like and how it was built. Lawrence

Crowley of Addison, Maine, owned this boat; thus it is assumed that she took her name from the nearby Moosabec Reach.

STATUS: Relic, mostly original, poor condition.

DONOR: Mystic Seaport purchase

FURTHER READING:

Chapelle, Howard I. *American Small Sailing Craft*. New York: W.W. Norton & Co., 1951.
Gardner, John. "14′ 'Reach Boat' is Obvious Maine Wherry Kin." *National Fisherman*, July, 1974.

Goode, George Brown. *The Fisheries and Fishery Industries of the United States*. Washington, D.C.: U.S. Government Printing Office, 1887.
Mitman, Carl W. *Catalog of the Watercraft Collection*, U.S. National Museum No. 127. Washington, D.C.: U.S. Government Printing Office, 1923.

ACCESSION NO. 1974.978

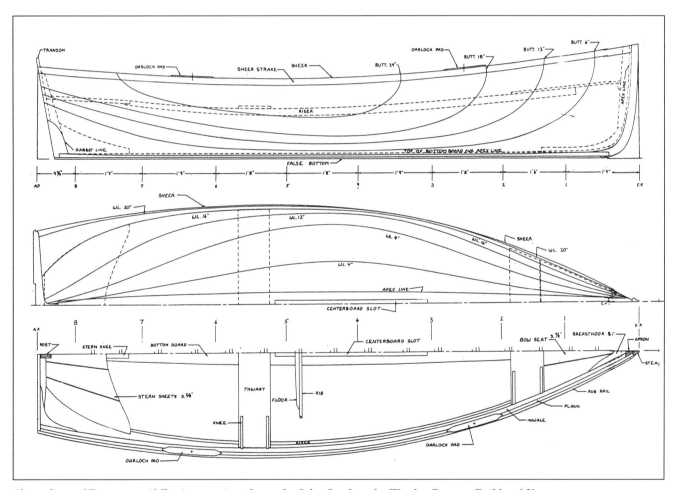

Above, lines of Temporary *(following page) as drawn by John Gardner for* Wooden Boats to Build and Use.

Moosabec Reach boat
Temporary.
(Photo: Judy Beisler,
Mystic Seaport 1994.17G)

Temporary

MOOSABEC REACH BOAT

14' 3" x 4' 9"   pre-1900

Temporary was bought by the donor, Andrew Chase, from Nathaniel French, owner of the Bucksport Alamoosook Island Camp where the boat had been used as the "temporary" replacement for a tender for the camp's schooner. French had first seen her being rowed by a fisherman in Castine in the 1920s and bought her about 1950. Chase acquired the boat in the early 1970s, and soon after brought her to Mystic Seaport. Chase measured and repaired her under the supervision of John Gardner. After taking the boat back to Maine, Chase added a centerboard and rig, using the plugged trunk hole in her bottom board as a guide, and also replaced other pieces. Like the smaller Lincolnville wherries, this boat floats high and is a

bit tiddly under oars if light, but handles a load well. She has a much finer entry than the salmon wherries, and this would make her quicker if less burdensome. As a sailboat, her freeboard and shape, stable when heeled, works nicely. Chase rigged her to be able to be sailed as a cat or cat ketch. Most boats built using this bottom-board construction are lapstrake (e.g. the salmon wherries, the New Jersey skiffs, and the other known reach boats). This one is unusual in her carvel construction. She was lightly built using apple for floors, breasthook, and quarter knees, with yellow birch for bottom board, transom, and stern framing. In recent years, with the new construction of several small wherry and Sea Bright skiff types, this bottom shape has proven a superior rowing shape. Among its advantages are increased stern buoyancy, compared to finer Whitehall-based shapes, lessening

squatting when driven to hull speed. Maine Maritime Museum has a Freeman Beal, Beals Island, Reach boat of about the same size, in addition to a larger one built at Popham Beach, Maine, and a small 1890 boat built in Machiasport.

STATUS: Fair condition—sister frames; floor timbers, thwarts, stern seat, sheer strakes, inwales, rubrails, and breasthook replaced; centerboard trunk added. With spars and rudder.

DONOR: Andrew Chase

FURTHER READING:
Gardner, John. *Wooden Boats to Build and Use*. Mystic, Connecticut: Mystic Seaport Publications, 1996. A chapter in this book is devoted to this boat and the history of the type, and includes plans.

ACCESSION NO. 1994.17
Plans for 1994.17 are available from Mystic Seaport's Watercraft Plans Collection.

New and used seine boats for the mackerel fishery lie at Higgins & Gifford's Gloucester, Massachusetts, boatshop in this 1912 photograph by Henry D. Fisher. (Photo: Mystic Seaport 1976.208.376)

Pedro

SEINE BOAT REPRODUCTION

36′ 0″ x 8′ 6″   1975

Encircling a school of mackerel by rowing around them while heaving out a purse seine called not only for an experienced crew, but also for a fast and maneuverable boat, one large enough to hold the 200 fathoms or so of seine twine. This boat was reproduced from photos, descriptions, and sketches, since no originals survive today. Derived from whaleboats in the 1850s, seine boats were built in large numbers by Higgins & Gifford at Gloucester between 1870 and 1920. They were towed to the fishing grounds by schooners like Mystic Seaport's *L.A.*

Dunton or occasionally taken aboard if the weather was bad. The boats had positions for nine oarsmen, space for the seine aft, and a bilge pump to deal with water brought aboard as the seine was pursed to capture a school of thousands of mackerel. *Pedro* is used in Mystic Seaport's youth training program for rowing instruction.

STATUS: In use, excellent condition.

DONOR: Mystic Seaport-built reproduction

FURTHER READING:

Ansel, W.D. "A Seine Boat to Save and Study." *National Fisherman*, September, 1975.

Church, Albert Cook. *American Fishermen*. Text by James B. Connolly. New York: W.W. Norton & Co., 1940.

Garland, Joseph E. *Down to the Sea*. Boston: David R. Godine, 1983.

German, Andrew W. *Down on T Wharf*. Mystic, Connecticut: Mystic Seaport Publications, 1982.

Goode, George Brown. *The Fisheries and Fishery Industries of the United States*. Washington, D.C.: U.S. Government Printing Office, 1887.

McFarland, Raymond. *The Masts of Gloucester*. New York: W.W. Norton & Co., 1947.

Pierce, Wesley G. *Going Fishing*. 1934; reprint, Camden, Maine: International Marine Publishing Co., 1989.

Smith, Edward W., Jr. *Workaday Schooners*. Camden, Maine: International Marine Publishing Co., 1975. Wonderful photographs of seine boats and fishing schooners coming and going from Newport, Rhode Island, in the 1890s.

ACCESSION NO. 1975.453

Pedro with a fresh coat of paint after she was built by Will Ansel. (Photo: Maynard Bray, Mystic Seaport 1975-10-108)

A seine boat crew paying out the seine. (Photo: From Goode, Mystic Seaport 1972-9-16)

A striker boat and purse boats of the menhaden steamer Promised Land *in Long Island Sound in 1949.*
(Photo: ©Mystic Seaport, Rosenfeld Collection, 124000F)

MENHADEN STRIKER BOAT

11′ 11″ x 4′ 8″

Large schools of menhaden on the Atlantic and Gulf coasts have attracted commercial fishermen since the mid-1800s. The fish are rendered into oil or fertilizer or fish meal, and are caught with purse seines. A boat like the one shown here, manned by the "striker" who rowed her, preceded two larger net-carrying purse boats to the school of menhaden and helped them encircle it without the fish getting away. Uncommonly heavy, a boat like this was built to hold her own with the operation's larger boats at sea, where flat calms don't last long. Ringbolts fore and aft enable hoisting her aboard the big fishboat, which is home to all hands while on a trip. This boat was last used in Gardiners Bay at the east end of Long Island.

STATUS: Original, poor condition.

DONOR: The Smith Meal Company, Inc.

FURTHER READING:

Frye, John. *The Men All Singing: The Story of Menhaden Fishing*. 2nd ed. Virginia Beach, Virginia: The Donning Co., 1999.

Goode, George Brown. *The Fisheries and Fishery Industries of the United States*. Washington, D.C.: U.S. Government Printing Office, 1887.

Greer, Rob Leon. "The Menhaden Industry of the Atlantic Coast." *Report of the Commissioner of Fisheries*, 1914. Washington, D.C.: U.S. Government Printing Office, 1915.

ACCESSION NO. 1970.390

The Striker Boat when donated in 1970.
(Photo: Louis Martel, Mystic Seaport 1970-10-82)

NEWPORT SHORE BOAT

11' 4" x 4' 8"   ca. 1860

With one man to a boat, these craft fished along the rocky shores of Newport, Rhode Island, and could be rowed, sailed, or sculled. Setting out in the early morning calm, under oars, the fisherman doubtless planned his route to return under sail before the afternoon sou'west breeze, thus not needing windward ability and the complications of a centerboard. He operated from aft with his catch contained amidships by parting boards under the seats. The anchor could be let go and hauled up from aft with the rode running over a sheave at the stemhead.

STATUS: Restored 1972, approximately 80% original, good condition.

DONOR: Robert H. Baker

FURTHER READING:
LaFarge, C. Grant. "Button Swan." *Scribner's Magazine*, October, 1921. Vol. 70, Reprinted in *The Catboat Association Bulletin* 46, March, 1975.

Leavens, John M. "Unusual Boat Type (Newport Beach) Confined to a Single Rhode Island Cove." *National Fisherman*, June, 1975.

ACCESSION NO. 1954.1482

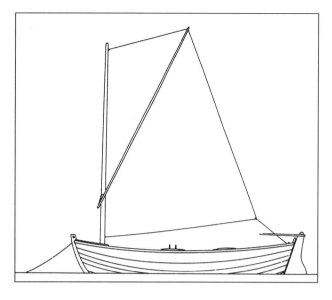

The simple spiritsail rig of a Newport Shore Boat.

The Newport Shore Boat on display in 1975. (Photo: Maynard Bray, Mystic Seaport 1975-6-11)

Shore fishermen and boats in front of the old stone boathouse, Newport, Rhode Island, about 1860. (Photo: Mystic Seaport 1982.84.89)

WESTPORT SMACK

12' 4" x 5' 0"   ca. 1880

Damaged in the 1954 hurricane, this so-called smack was repaired and used for awhile by the donor, who purchased her from Howland Ballard for whose uncle she was built. She was originally used in Buzzards Bay at Westport, Massachusetts, as a one-man shore fishing boat, like the Newport Shore Boat on the previous page. She is unusually well-modeled and when new was exquisitely constructed.

STATUS: Relic, mostly original, poor condition.
DONOR: Robert H. Baker
ACCESSION NO. 1974.312

The Westport Smack in 1974. (Photo: Ken Mahler, Mystic Seaport 1974-3-236)

RHODE ISLAND HOOK BOAT

15' 9" x 5' 6"   ca. 1910

Putting to sea through the shallow inlets on Rhode Island's south coast often compelled fishermen to row through several steep breaking waves before reaching fishing grounds in open water. And on the return, if it had "come on to blow," one might find matters fearfully worse. A double-ended boat invariably has proved best for such service since, with equal buoyancy at each end, its actions are more predictable than a transom-sterned craft. Two men, facing each other with one pushing on his oars and the other pulling, rowed this boat. Although the man who push-rowed could not reach full effectiveness in that position, his value as a lookout more than made up for it. Steve Peckham built this boat and several others like her. Used at Quonochontaug Inlet, she is a typical shore boat having lapstrake planking and steam-bent frames which notch or "joggle" over the laps.

STATUS: Restored in 1969, approximately 90% original, good condition.
DONOR: George W. King
FURTHER READING:
Goode, George Brown. *The Fisheries and Fishery Industries of the United States.* Washington, D.C.: U.S. Government Printing Office, 1887.

ACCESSION NO. 1967.201

The Rhode Island Hook Boat in storage. (Photo: Maynard Bray, Mystic Seaport 1975-10-98)

Patience

TARPON SPRINGS
SPONGE BOAT

11' 11" x 4' 2"   pre-1930

Racing sailor Cornelius Shields first saw *Patience* in 1932 at the Larchmont Yacht Club. She was owned by F. Slade Dale, who bought her in Tarpon Springs, Florida, from Greek sponge fishermen and used her as a tender to his schooner *Emma C. Berry* (page 98). Dale lent her to Shields, and Shields had the Kretzer Boat Yard of City Island, New York, rig the boat for improved sailing, giving her a free-standing centerboard trunk. Shields also replaced her lateen sail with a taller mast and a sail from a frostbite

dinghy. Dale sold Shields *Patience* for the same $85 he paid for her. Built like a little ship (and weighing 400-450 pounds), the boat's heavy planks are nailed to frames sawn from crooks, with floor timbers joining each pair of frames over the top of the keel. She is a sharp boat with a high wineglass stern, and looks to have been lively under sail. Corny Shields thought highly of her. As he testified, "Sailing *Patience* is sheer joy. She has the most wonderful motion in a sea you can imagine."

Unrigged boats like *Patience* were descended from Bahamian and Greek boats used for "hooking" sponges, and became tenders to sail–and engine-powered sponge boats when hardhat diving became the normal method of harvesting sponges.

STATUS: Good condition, one sprung plank, missing seats. Rig, rudder, and tiller intact.
DONOR: Cornelius Shields, Jr.
FURTHER READING:
Moore, H.F. "The Commercial Sponger and the Sponge Fisheries." *Bulletin of the Bureau of Fisheries* 28 (1908): 403-511.

Shields Cornelius. *Cornelius Shields on Sailing*. Englewood Cliffs, New Jersey: Prentice-Hall, 1964.
ACCESSION NO. 1990.138

Patience after her donation to Mystic Seaport. (Photo: Maynard Bray, Mystic Seaport 1990.138A)

DOUBLE-ENDED
PULLING BOAT
FROM FISHERS ISLAND, N.Y.

12' 4" x 3' 10"   ca. 1880-1900

Reputedly built by Ebenezer Morgan Stoddard, this 12' double-ender is unfamiliar as a type and quite possibly one-of-a-kind.

STATUS: Mostly original, fair condition.
DONOR: Mrs. H. Lee Ferguson, Jr.
ACCESSION NO. 1972.300

The Fishers Island double-ender in 1975. (Photo: Maynard Bray, Mystic Seaport 1975-10-101)

FOUR-OARED RACING SHELL
43' 9" x 1' 11"

While not as spectacular as the very large eight-oared shells used in college rowing competition, the proportions of this ultra-slim 43'9"–long shell are nevertheless impressive.

STATUS: Original, good condition.
DONOR: Riverside Boat Club
FURTHER READING:

Gardner, John. "Early Days of Rowing Sport." *The Log of Mystic Seaport*, Winter, 1971.

Kelley, Robert F. *American Rowing: Its Background and Traditions*. New York: G. P. Putnam's Sons, 1932.

Mendenhall, Thomas C. *The Harvard-Yale Boat Race, 1852-1924*. Mystic, Connecticut: Mystic Seaport Publications, 1993.

ACCESSION NO. 1963.27

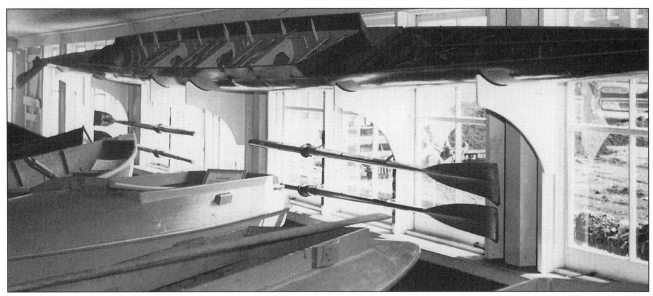

The four-oared shell on display at Mystic Seaport. (Photo: Louis Martel, Mystic Seaport 1963.27)

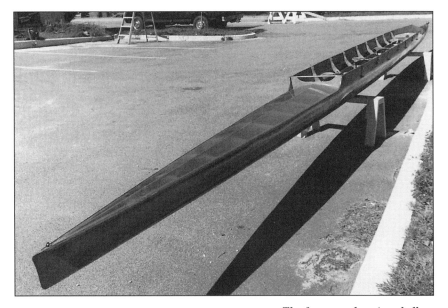

The four-oared racing shell Cookie Jar *at Mystic Seaport. (Photo: Judy Beisler, Mystic Seaport 1994.114.11)*

Cookie Jar
FOUR-OARED RACING SHELL BY POCOCK
39' 6" x 1' 10"   1964

By 1964 George Pocock's Seattle-based Pocock Racing Shell Company was the premier builder of racing shells in the U.S. The business was started by Pocock and his brother Richard when they moved to Canada in 1911, and then to Seattle the following year. The Pococks had trained at Eton School in England, where their father ran the Eton boathouse. After a 1916-22 stint at Boeing, Richard left to become the boatbuilder for Yale, and George reestablished his business in a shop on the University of Washington campus. *Cookie Jar* was built two years after George moved off campus to a shop under a freeway bridge. Pocock used two matched pairs of 11/64" red cedar veneers in building these shells. The fine veneers are bent over the frame and keel after all the internal bracing is in place. The technique represented the best in shell-building before glued planks and fiberglass skins came along. *Cookie Jar* raced at the New York Athletic Club for two years, chiefly with high-school rowers like later Olympian Jim Dietz. Fred Emerson of the Blood Street Sculls bought her in 1966 and brought her to Lyme, Connecticut. There she was raced primarily by the women's crew. Her first victory, in the 1967 Riverside Sculls in Boston, was the defeat of the Philadelphia Girls Rowing Club by a crew of Old Lyme High School sophomores. *Cookie Jar* could be rigged as a coxed sculling boat or as a sweep boat.

STATUS: Excellent condition.

DONOR: National Rowing Foundation in memory of Fred Emerson

FURTHER READING:

Dodd, Christopher. *The Story of World Rowing*. London: Stanley Paul, 1992.

Green, T.M. "George Pocock Racing Shells, Inc. *WoodenBoat* 21, Mar/Apr, 1978.

Newall, Gordon. *Ready All? George Yeoman Pocock and Crew Racing*. Seattle: University of Washington Press, 1987.

ACCESSION NO. 1994.114.1

Mary Thrulesen
DOUBLE SHELL BY POCOCK
31' 9" x 1' 6"   1970

The *Mary Thrulesen* was last used by the Blood Street Sculls of Lyme, Connecticut. The Blood Street Sculls founder, Fred Emerson, helped start many successful scholastic rowing programs in the Northeast.

George Pocock built this boat in 1970 as a "pair without," for two rowers without a coxswain. By adding or subtracting outriggers, the rowers can use either two sculling oars or one sweep apiece.

The boat has always been well cared for and is a prize example of the wooden-hulled shell prior to the shift to fiberglass, kevlar, and carbon-fiber construction.

STATUS: Excellent condition.

DONOR: National Rowing Foundation

FURTHER READING:
(Same as for shell 1994.114.1)

ACCESSION NO. 2000.136.2

SINGLE SCULL SHELL BY DAVY
30' 0" x 1' 0"   ca. 1890

Boston's Charles River would be where one might expect to use a shell, particularly one built in nearby Cambridge by W.H. Davy. Yet Dr. Charles Weld took this one to his beloved North Haven, Maine, where the Fox Island Thoroughfare's shelter was nearly as good as the Charles's and the scenery breathtaking. At least Dr. Weld thought so, for he was one of that Maine island's first summer settlers and had a big hand in convincing other well-heeled Bostonians to build there. This shell, obviously cherished and carefully taken care of over the years, was passed down through the family for awhile, but eventually became the possession of Charles P. Williamson, a summertime neighbor who continued to use and enjoy her in the same waters.

STATUS: Minor repair, mostly original, very good condition.

DONOR: Given in memory of Charles P. Williamson by Mrs. Charles P. Williamson

FURTHER READING:
(Same as for shell 1963.27)

ACCESSION NO. 1974.450

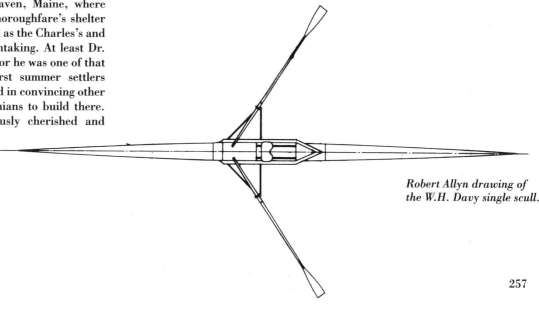

Robert Allyn drawing of the W.H. Davy single scull.

SINGLE SCULL SHELL
BY HAGERTY

25' 10" x 1' 5"   ca. 1950

Francis Hagerty, an MIT-trained engineer and rower, used his experience building radomes from molded wood during World War II to begin building molded-plywood racing shells after the war. He took over W.H. Davy and Sons of Cambridge, a shell-builder that had been in business since 1870, and moved the company to Cohasset where he set up under his own name. The Hagerty shell was built using two long lengths of two-ply veneer bent around removable molds. The only structure needed was an inner keel piece and two sheer clamps or stringers. The use of several layers of veneer or plywood kept the sides from splitting, a common problem with the older single-layer shells like 1974.450. Hagerty later sold his shell business to Joe Garafalo of the Worcester Oar and Paddle Company and went on to start the Cohasset Colonial Furniture Company.

STATUS: Good, some repairs; fitted with oars and carrying equipment.
DONOR: Dr. Steward King
FURTHER READING:
(Same as for shell 1963.27)

And also:
Martin, Arthur. *Life in the Slow Lane.* Portsmouth, New Hampshire: Peter E. Randall, Publisher, 1990.
ACCESSION NO. 1986.29

The Hagerty single scull. (Photo: Deborah Bates, Mystic Seaport 1986.29F*)*

Detail of Hagerty single scull with sliding seat and riggers. (Photo: Deborah Bates, Mystic Seaport 1986.29C*)*

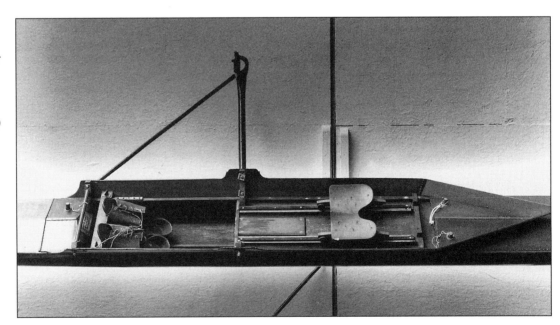

Barrier
SIMS SINGLE

26' 5"   ca. 1960

Barrier is one of a matched pair of boats built by the internationally famous George Sims, Ltd. of Eel Pie Island, Twykenham on the Tideway, England, for the Bermuda Olympic Committee to train scullers. Due to unfavorable water conditions the boat was given to the Kent School in Connecticut, where it was used only sparingly before being sold to a school alumnus. Given in turn to the National Rowing Foundation, *Barrier* is a pristine example of the ultimate development of traditional wooden shell building just prior to the introduction of synthetics in the early 1960s.

Barrier was named for a historic mark on the Thames River race course of the Henley Royal Regatta.

STATUS: Excellent condition.
DONOR: National Rowing Foundation
ACCESSION NO. 1995.89.1

SINGLE SHELL
BY VAN DUSEN

26' 6" x 1' 2"   1982

Competitive rowing has seen its periods of intense development. The mid-1800s saw the development of the fixed outrigger (1830s), smooth-skinned shell construction (1840s), and the sliding seat (1860s). A little more than a hundred years later, hulls of glass-carbon fiber-honeycomb and epoxy resins were introduced (1972), producing boats that are now stiffer, stronger, more durable, more easily repaired, and that require less maintenance than boats built of wood.

For years, designers had been trying to eliminate the porpoising caused by a rower's moving center of gravity when using a sliding seat. In 1981, Empacher Bootswerft of Eberbach, Germany, successfully developed a technology featuring a fixed seat with movable outriggers and foot braces. Without the drag caused by porpoising, boats so equipped were approximately 10 percent faster, on average, than boats with the older technology, and Empacher singles won the World Championship in 1981, '82, and '83.

In 1982, Ted Van Dusen of Composite Engineering in Concord, Massachusetts, responded by designing and building his own fixed-seat, movable-rigger boats. One of six ultralight hulls built of kevlar and fiberglass, the boat won a Bronze medal in the 1982 World Championship, rowed by John Biglow, and in 1983, rowed by Tiff Wood. The last owner, Peter Mallory, gave the boat to the National Rowing Foundation in 1997.

After the 1983 Worlds, FISA, the governing body of competitive rowing, outlawed the movable outrigger, claiming that it was more expensive than the sliding seat and that it made fixed-outrigger, sliding-seat boats obsolete.

STATUS: Excellent condition.
DONOR: National Rowing Foundation
FURTHER READING:
Dodd, Christopher. *The Story of World Rowing*. London: Stanley Paul and Company, 1992.

Mendenhall, Thomas C. *A Short History of American Rowing*. Boston: Charles River Books, ca. 1980.

ACCESSION NO. 2000.136.4

The Van Dusen single at Mystic Seaport. (Photo: Dennis A. Murphy, Mystic Seaport 2000.136.41*)*

A detail of the sliding outrigger and fixed seat of the Van Dusen single. (Photo: Dennis A. Murphy, Mystic Seaport 2000.136.4F*)*

UNION BOAT CLUB PRACTICE WHERRY

19' 6" x 2' 1"   ca. 1920

Whiffs, wherries, funnys, gigs, galleys, skiffs, tubs, barges: the training and exercise world of the rigger rower is a confusion of names and types. This four-plank lapstrake sculling boat has a small transom stern and a steel frame that strengthens her in the "engine room," the area of the riggers, the sliding seat, and the rower. This boat is shorter and wider than a racing single scull or "Best boat." Originally owned by Eric Verrill, she was given to his club, the Union Boat Club of Boston, and played a role in the Regatta Productions film *Ned Hanlon, World Racing Champion 1872*. Although very old, this boat does not appear in the listing that was published as part of the Union Boat Club's 60th-anniversary history in 1913. It is likely that she was built for Eric Verrill around 1920.

STATUS: Fair, except for damage to sheer clamp and one plank forward. Fabric deck sheathing has been removed.

DONOR: Union Boat Club

FURTHER READING:

Sixty Years of the Union Boat Club. Boston: The Union Boat Club, 1913.

Dodd, Christopher. *The Story of World Rowing*. London: Stanley Paul, 1992.

ACCESSION NO. 1985.17.1

The Union Boat Club practice wherry. (Photo: Judy Beisler, Mystic Seaport 1985.17.1C)

POCOCK PRACTICE WHERRY

21' 5" x 2' 2"

This elegant boat was built by George Pocock of University Station, Seattle, Washington, as a boat in which competitive rowers would take practice sessions. It is shorter by 4 to 5 feet and wider by a foot than most competitive single sculls. Nevertheless, it is lightweight, built with a veneer skin, and reinforced with a hogging member under the sliding seat and metal strapping.

STATUS: Good, minor repairs.
DONOR: National Rowing Foundation
ACCESSION NO. 1999.19.1

A detail of the outrigger, sliding seat, and fixed shoes of this beamy Pocock practice wherry. (Photo: Judy Beisler, Mystic Seaport 1999.19.1A)

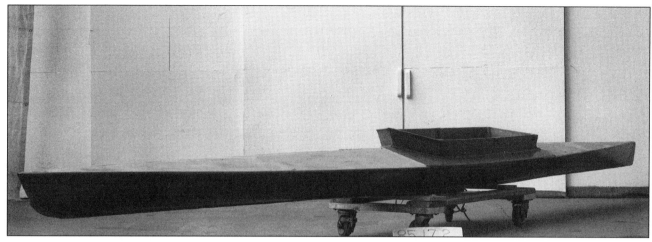

Union Boat Club cruising scull 1985.17.2. (Photo: Deborah Bates, <small>Mystic Seaport 1985.17.2D</small>)

UNION BOAT CLUB
CRUISING SCULLS

23' 0" x 2' 7"   ca. 1920

After the Charles River was dammed in 1908, to the great improvement of rowing, the Union Boat Club built a new clubhouse. However, club members still needed boats to tour Boston Harbor after locking down, in order to continue the club's long tradition of cruising under oar and paddle. The result was a fleet of touring boats like this one, basically enlarged wherries, clinker-built with 4" wash boxes onto which the riggers were mounted. These boats served the purpose well, able to live amongst the steamer and tug wakes of what was then an active shipping harbor. In the early 1970s, before the advent of the modern ocean shell, boats like this were used in several races around Cape Ann.

STATUS: 1985.17.2– fair condition, with damage to keel. 1985.17.3 – good condition; has been fiberglassed.

DONOR: Union Boat Club

ACCESSION NOS. 1985.17.2 and 1985.17.3

Union Boat Club cruising scull 1985.17.3. (Photo: Deborah Bates, <small>Mystic Seaport 1985.17.3D</small>)

PRACTICE WHERRY
22' 2" x 2' 3"

Primarily an exercise boat for collegiate rowing competitors, the greater beam of a practice wherry makes her more stable than a shell, and being shorter she is more easily transported and stored.

STATUS: Relic, poor condition.
DONOR: Martha Fuller
FURTHER READING:
(Same as for shell 1963.27)
ACCESSION NO. 1972.1112

Practice wherry 1972.1112.
(Photo: Claire White-Peterson,
Mystic Seaport 1972.1112)

The Williams Racing
Shell Boat Yard prac-
tice wherry.
(Photo: Ken Mahler,
Mystic Seaport 1975-9-111)

PRACTICE WHERRY BY WILLIAMS
20' 0" x 2' 0"   ca. 1934

The term wherry used out of context can be misleading, as may be seen by contrasting this lightweight exercise boat with the husky salmon wherries described on page 246. To be under-stood, one must specify exactly what kind of wherry he is talking about, as there are others besides the two mentioned. There are, for example, the big freight-carrying Norfolk wherries of England.

The Williams Racing Shell Boat Yard of Foxboro, Massachusetts, built this wherry, according to her name-plate. She has had little use and arrived at Mystic Seaport in like-new condition, crated, and completely equipped.

STATUS: Excellent original condition.
DONOR: Harry D. Deutschbein
FURTHER READING:
(Same as for shell 1963.27)
ACCESSION NO. 1975.313

WILLIAMS WHERRY

17' 0" x 2' 0"   1932

"William" Williams was one of a number of English boatmen and shell builders who emigrated to the U.S. after World War I to build boats for American and Canadian competitive rowers. According to shell- and oar-builder Joe Garafalo of Worcester, Massachusetts, who worked for Williams from 1935 to 1938, Williams moved to the U.S. from England in the early 1930s and worked briefly for the Herreshoff Manufacturing Company in Bristol, Rhode Island, before setting up on his own in Foxboro, Massachusetts, to build shells for the

Boston market. An excellent craftsman, but not a good businessman, Williams needed help from a benefactor to move his shop to Worcester's Lake Quinsigamond in order to be on hand for the 1932 Olympic trials. Williams stayed on at Worcester until around 1939, when he moved to New Orleans to build shells for a school's new rowing program.

Because this wherry is too lightly built to be a training boat for a school program, Garafalo believes it was probably built for an individual who wanted something which was a step up from the general rowing boat of the time. Built in early 1932 during Williams's Foxboro period for around

$50, Garafalo says it couldn't be replaced today for anything less than $10,000.

Spanish cedar planks are rivetted to bent oak frames, and cleverly designed outriggers fold inboard when not in use. Bright finished, the boat has always been well cared for and is in mint condition.

STATUS: Excellent.

DONOR: National Rowing Foundation

ACCESSION NO. 2000.136.3

The 1871 crew of the Massachusetts Agricultural College poses in this shell or its predecessor on the Connecticut River. (Photo: Courtesy of the University of Massachusetts)

SIX-OARED SHELL

48' 9" x 2' 0"   ca. 1870

This six is widely held to be the shell used by the Massachusetts Agricultural College (now the University of Massachusetts) to defeat Harvard and Brown in March of 1871 in a race held at Ingleside on the Connecticut River, near Springfield, Massachusetts. This competition was the first true intercollegiate competition and was

held under the auspices of the new Rowing Association of American Colleges. The boat may, however, be a 1872 replacement for the original, said to have been burned in a fire.

STATUS: A dry and limber relic, only the hull planking, frames, and deck covering remain. The seats, foot stretchers, outriggers and sweeps are missing.

DONOR: National Rowing Foundation

FURTHER READING:

Kelley, Robert F. *American Rowing.* New York: G.P. Putnam's Sons, 1932.

Mendenhall, Thomas C. *The Harvard-Yale Boat Race 1852-1924 and the Coming of Sport to the American College.* Mystic, Connecticut: Mystic Seaport Publications, 1993.

ACCESSION NO. 2000.136.1

LADIES GIG

23' 3" x 2' 2"   ca. 1875

An outrigged boat fitted for a single sculler and passenger was frequently called a ladies gig in the 1870s. This is an exceptionally nice one. Its lack of a sliding seat hints that it predates 1875, by which time sliding seats had become common. This is a delicately built, transom-sterned lapstrake boat with a flagpole socket and rudder gudgeons. The beaded sheer strake, along with beveled backrest and rigger and seat support frames, show the care taken in her building. She may have been rowed out of the Monmouth Boat Club, founded in 1878 on the Shrewsbury River in New Jersey, and was found in a house purchased from the La Marche family, owners of a munitions firm in the years before the First World War.

STATUS: Good original condition, planks with some checks, missing outriggers, rudder, and footrest.
DONOR: J. Sheppard Poor
ACCESSION NO. 1990.133

The 23' 3" circa-1875 ladies gig. (Photo: Mary Anne Stets, Mystic Seaport 1990.1331)

ALDEN OCEAN SHELL #1 BY ARTHUR MARTIN

16' 0" x 2' 0"   1970

This is the prototype for the boat that created a new type of recreational rowboat: boats that combined the power of rowing on a sliding seat with durability and stability. In the late 1960s naval architect and ardent rower Arthur Martin designed and built several kayaks. His third, a 13½-footer, had a beautiful bow, sharp below the waterline and flaring above, but was too fine aft. To solve this, Martin cut the stern off and attached a stern that came out of the mold he was using for his 15' kayak. This gave him a 16' hull. It also gave him food for thought. "As I stood contemplating the result of the crude graft, it suddenly occurred to me that

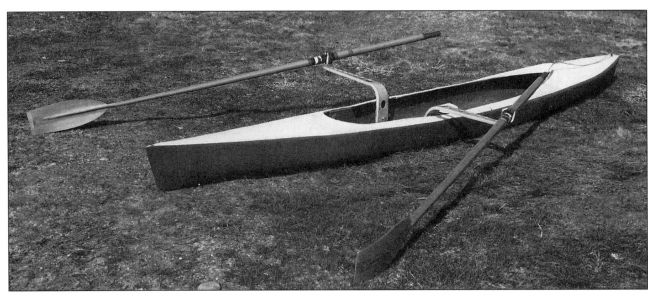

The first Alden Ocean Shell. (Photo: Maynard Bray, Mystic Seaport 1989.50A)

the boat could be rowed with a sliding seat, like a shell, a concept I had dreamed of but never followed through." He bought a portable sliding seat from Old Town. "When I first tried rowing the unusual combination, I felt like shouting "Eureka." The sensation was nothing short of breathtaking." Arthur's wife Marjorie wanted one, too, and he used the prototype to make a mold and the second boat. In the spring of 1970 both boats were brought to Mystic Seaport's first Small Craft Workshop and attracted considerable attention.

That same year Martin started

work in the brokerage and insurance section of the John Alden design office in Boston. There he met the owner, Neil Tillotson, who had another business building small boats in fiberglass in partnership with Everett Pearson. They expressed some interest in building the shells, but asked Arthur to cover the tooling costs if fewer than 20 were sold. Based on the boat's attraction to traditionally oriented rowers at Mystic's workshop, and after careful thinking about the world of the sliding-seat competitor, Martin decided to risk his slim savings. The boats were built by Tillotson-Pearson, marketed under the

Alden name, and were introduced at the Boston Boat Show in 1971. The first year ended with 165 boats sold, and the Alden Ocean Shell was on its way.

STATUS: Good, equipped with a replacement Oarmaster rig.
DONOR: Arthur E. Martin
FURTHER READING:
Lee, Madeline. "Common Sense and the Energy 48." *WoodenBoat* 47, Jul/Aug, 1982.
Martin, Arthur. *Life in the Slow Lane.* Portsmouth, New Hampshire: Peter E. Randall, Publisher, 1990.
ACCESSION NO. 1989.50

John Gardner
ALDEN 16 OCEAN SHELL
16'   ca. 1989

Arthur & Marjorie Martin
ALDEN 18 OCEAN SHELL
18'   ca. 1989

In 1989, Arthur and Marjorie Martin donated two of their boats to Mystic Seaport's Williams College-Mystic Seaport undergraduate studies program for student and staff use on the Mystic River. The Alden 16 is the most popular recreational shell in the world. The Alden 18 can be rowed as a single or double. Both use removable

drop-in frames that hold outriggers and sliding seats, which Arthur Martin called Oarmasters. This keeps the boats light and easy to lift onto roof racks.

STATUS: Excellent condition; used regularly.
DONOR: Arthur & Marjorie Martin

The Post board boat in the Mystic River ca. 1945, set up with outriggers and sliding seat. (Photo: Mystic Seaport 1987.58.119)

BOARD BOAT BY FRANKLIN G. POST & SON
15' 4" x 11"   ca. 1945

What do you call a "boat" designed to be rowed, paddled, or propelled by pedals? Taking advantage of plywood and thinking about an increased boating market after World War II, Ernie Post designed this board to do all of the above. It was probably the smallest "boat" that ever came out of the Mystic, Connecticut, shop of

Franklin Post, where small inboard fishing boats and yachts were the normal products. Franklin Post set up his shop in 1914, after working as a machinist for the Lathrop Engine Company. There is no record that this was anything more than an experimental prototype. It was perhaps a bit before its time: boating in the 1940s was only on the verge of becoming watersports. It would be the Alcort Company with its Sailfish that established the popularity of board

boats, beginning in 1948. Not until 1970 did the Alden Ocean Shell create the recreational market for sliding-seat boats, and not until the 1980s did sea kayaking and sit-on-top paddling become popular.

STATUS: Good, unrestored condition.
DONOR: Mr. & Mrs. Robert P. Anderson, Jr.
ACCESSION NO. 1990.32

Brant

DUCK BOAT

10' 3" x 4' 7"   1894

This duck boat was owned by Charles Ferguson of Groton, Connecticut, a boatbuilder by trade, who probably built her as well. She has a low profile and could be made quite inconspicuous, but it is doubtful if she ever ventured far from shore. She was built neither for seaworthiness nor for ease of rowing. She's truly a special-purpose boat. Her construction is of unusually high quality.

STATUS: Mostly original, good condition.
DONOR: The family of Charles F. Ferguson
ACCESSION NO. 1957.917
Plans for 1957.917 are available from Mystic Seaport's Watercraft Plans Collection.

Duck boat Brant *from Groton, Connecticut.*
(Photo: Maynard Bray, Mystic Seaport 1975-5-55)

SCULL FLOAT BY DAVIES

10' 1" x 4' 0"   ca. 1900

Thomas Davies built this scull float just prior to 1900 for his own waterfowling on the Connecticut River near Saybrook Point at the mouth of the river. His son, William Davies, also gunned from it before giving it to the donor's father, Philip C. Fairbank, shortly after World War II. Fairbank was a state senator and onetime head of the Connecticut Fish and Game Commission, and he had the privilege of often gunning with Oliver LaPlace, the legendary guide and railbird hunter of Essex, Connecticut. A Fairbank family story has it that Oliver, using a pump gun, once had six dead birds in the air at one time.

In the 1950s the boat was fiberglassed below its gunwales and painted white for wintertime use. Despite its unusually high-crowned foredeck, the boat probably looked much like an ice cake when the gunner sculled downriver toward a raft of ducks. The cross-planked bottom is flat except for a slight rise in the last two feet, and the sides are brought straight back from amidships. The gunner sat quite far aft when rowing or sculling. The canvas covering the foredeck and sides down to the gunwales is still in good condition.

STATUS: Unrestored, good condition.
DONOR: Philip Fairbank
ACCESSION NO. 1986.70

Connecticut River scull float by Thomas Davies.
(Photo: Deborah Patterson, Mystic Seaport 1986.70C)

DUCK BOAT FROM GREAT BAY, NEW HAMPSHIRE

14' 8" x 3' 4"

Without fuss, duck-hunting boats like this could sneak within range of their prey. The duck boat would be covered with brush that nearly concealed the hunters as well as the craft. Hidden also was the upper part of the sculling oar contained within an open-ended well aft of the transom. Scull float was an alternate name for these boats because of their propulsion.

STATUS: Original, good condition.

DONOR: Philip S. Drake

FURTHER READING:

Ansel, Willets. "Duckboat Job Has Builder a Bit Skeptical." *National Fisherman*, December, 1975. Brief write-up about the building and trials of a reproduction of this boat.

Chapelle, Howard I. *American Small Sailing Craft*. New York: W.W. Norton & Co., 1951.

ACCESSION NO. 1961.559

Plans for 1961.559 are available from Mystic Seaport's Watercraft Plans Collection.

The Great Bay, New Hampshire, duck boat.
(Photo: Maynard Bray, Mystic Seaport 1975-5-65)

DUCK BOAT FROM GREAT SOUTH BAY, NEW YORK

16' 3" x 3' 9"   ca. 1900

If a low profile was the builder's objective he certainly succeeded with this boat. She is almost like a surfboard as her deck is joined directly to her bottom. The open rail which completely encircles the deck is interesting and must have been a big help in securing the brush used to help hide her from wary ducks. Of interest also is her fantail stern which, although quite handsome, does not permit the convenient use of a sculling oar. For watertightness, her bottom has been covered with fabric.

STATUS: Some repair, mostly original, poor condition.

DONOR: R. Nelson Rose

FURTHER READING:
Chapelle, Howard I. *American Small Sailing Craft*. New York: W.W. Norton & Co., 1951.

ACCESSION NO. 1976.79

The Great South Bay, Long Island, duck boat. (Photo: Maynard Bray, Mystic Seaport 1978-2-49)

DUCK BOAT BY BARTLETT

14' 2" x 3' 1"   1959

Before starting work on this boat, at age 92, Capt. Howard Bartlett had the experience of building about 45 others like her. This was to be his last boat, as sickness forced him to turn her over to a friend, Myron Cowden, for finishing. The Warrens of York Harbor, Maine, for whom Capt. Bartlett had been a long-time professional yacht skipper, commissioned her building.   She is planked with mahogany and covered on the outside with fiberglass.

STATUS: Original, excellent condition.
DONOR: Mrs. Richard F. Warren

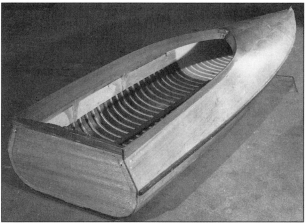

The Howard Bartlett duck boat. (Photo: Maynard Bray, Mystic Seaport 1975-10-76)

FURTHER READING:
Chapelle, Howard I. *American Small Sailing Craft.* New York: W.W. Norton & Co., 1951.

ACCESSION NO. 1975.431

Duck boat 1979.28 built by Brooks Boat Co. (Photo: Maynard Bray, Mystic Seaport 1979.28A)

LAING-WHEELER SCULL FLOAT BY BROOKS BOAT COMPANY

15' 1" x 4' 0"   ca. 1870

This scull float was owned at different times by Albert Laing (1811-1886) and Charles "Shang" Wheeler (1872-1949), two of the "big three" of the Stratford, Connecticut, school of waterfowl decoy carvers. It was built by the Brooks Boat Company of nearby New Haven, Connecticut, sometime between the end of the Civil War and the early 1880s.

Stratford-area gunners, besides hunting in the marshy Nell's Island area at the mouth of the Housatonic River, often gunned in the river itself or outside on Long Island Sound. For good stability in swift current or choppy waters they needed a boat with a relatively deep-V, or deadrise, midship section, which the Brooks Boat Company was glad to provide.

These conditions also required a different sort of decoy. In the 1860s, Albert Laing altered the existing hollow decoy model by giving it a more seaworthy high, upswept breast, non-ferrous fastenings, and life-like conformations. This model is still used today. Laing, a gentleman gunner, strongly influenced Ben Holmes (1843-1912), a professional guide and carver, who then influenced "Shang" Wheeler, sometime state senator, shellfisherman, and conservationist. Birds by these Stratford school carvers demand top dollar in today's decoy market.

Donor Charles Welles gunned in this boat with Wheeler in the Stratford area and at the mouth of the Connecticut River. In the early 1980s, this boat was reproduced in fiberglass. In a video of these reproductions in use on Long Island Sound, each boat is attached to a line, one end of which is anchored close to the set or "stool" of decoys, the other end anchored away from the set. The boat's position could be adjusted along this line. The original boat has both raised rowlocks and a scull hole.

STATUS: Fair to good.
DONOR: Charles Welles
FURTHER READING:

Barber, Joel. *Wild Fowl Decoys.* New York: Dover Publications, 1954.

Chitwood, Henry, with Thomas C. Marshall and Doug Knight.

Connecticut Decoys, Carvers and Gunners. West Chester, Pennsylvania: Schiffer Publishing, 1987.

Dixon, Merkt, MacD. *Shang.* Spanish Fork, Utah: Hillcrest Publications, 1984.

Mackey, William J., Jr. *American Bird Decoys.* New York: Bonanza Books, 1965.

ACCESSION NO. 1979. 28

CONNECTICUT RIVER DUCK BOAT

12' 5" x 3' 5"

Used for bird shooting, this boat has a centerboard trunk and mast step so it could be sailed to and from the hunting area.

STATUS: Unrestored, original, good condition, rig missing.
DONOR: George P.P. Bonnell
ACCESSION NO. 1959.208
Plans for 1959.208 are available from Mystic Seaport's Watercraft Plans Collection.

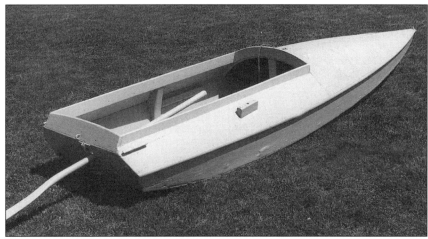

The 12' 5" duck boat from the Connecticut River. (Photo: Maynard Bray, Mystic Seaport 1975-5-59)

TYLER LINE SKIFF

14' 1" x 4' 0"   1874

In the days of large waterfowl flocks, prior to 1900, one way of gunning involved the pre-dawn anchoring of a number of gunning skiffs in a line across a known flyway, an activity known as line shooting. The locations chosen would be where birds would pass at dawn to their feeding grounds along a relatively narrow band of water—perhaps between two islands or an island and the mainland. The boats would be spaced two gunshot lengths apart, and it was important to assemble enough boats to span the waterway and prevent "endruns." This made for quite a social occasion, with anywhere from a few to more than 50 boats involved. Plenty of ribald comments would be passed on the performances of other gunners. There was a gentleman's agreement that no shots be fired in another boat's direction, but the excitement of the moment often meant that a boat got peppered with shot.

Competition for high bag was stiff. Point positions were often determined by draw, and sometimes a gunner would trail decoys behind his skiff to swing birds over his point in the line. Gunners would cast off their buoyed anchor lines to pick up downed birds or chase cripples. Who actually killed a bird was often a matter of "discussion" when a cash pool was awarded to the high bag. Although any gunning skiff could be used, the skiff needed to row well; a gunner might have to row five or ten miles to be in place. Playing the tides was important.

This 14' line skiff was built in 1874 at Branford, Connecticut, by John Tyler, the donor's grandfather, for George Blackstone, who used it for line shooting and gunning over decoys at nearby Sachem Head. Blackstone gave the boat to the donor in the 1920s when he could no longer use it. Elmer Tyler stored the boat in the family boatyard at Summer Island from 1937 until 1985 when he gave it to Mystic Seaport. Considering its age, the boat is in good structural condition. The canvas is gone from the half deck forward but is still evident on the cockpit cover. This cover was lockable and allowed for secure storage of oars, decoys, etc. when the boat was left unattended. With a cross-plank bottom, straight up-and-down sides, and a simplicity of construction dictated by economy, the boat has the good looks of an object that fulfills its purpose.

STATUS: Structure good but cosmetically rough.
DONOR: Elmer Tyler
ACCESSION NO. 1985.5

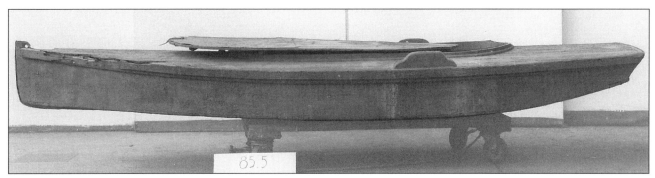

The Tyler line skiff in storage at Mystic Seaport. (Photo: Deborah Bates, Mystic Seaport 1985.5D)

*The Long Point Company
duck-hunting punt.
(Photo: Maynard Bray,*
Mystic Seaport 1980.71A)

DUCK-HUNTING PUNT
BY REEVES

15′ 4″ x 3′ 5″   ca. 1930

In 1886 the Long Point Company bought most of Long Point, a 25-mile-long sand spit running east into Lake Ontario off its north shore. There the members established a private hunting camp and opened it for six weeks each year during the duck season. Each member had his own cottage, along with a punt and decoy rig. Each morning at breakfast the company's head keeper would supervise a drawing by the members for their gunning spots. The member and his guide, or punter, would set out the decoy rig at their designated spot and then back the boat into the marsh grass. They'd disguise the boat from the view of incoming ducks by "grassing" it. This consisted of stuffing quill reeds or cattails carefully cut and placed in elastic bands around the skiff and across a temporary fence, or bulkhead, amidships. The member would do his gunning while sitting on a swivel stool forward while the punter crouched back aft. The essential thermos and lunch pail were never far from reach. The punter would move the boat in deep water by using a combination pole-paddle, and in shallow water by wading in the water and pushing on a flipped-up bracket mounted on the aft deck. It was chilly work.

In good weather, when there were no ducks to shoot, the members sailed and raced their skiffs. A movable leeboard, slipped over the gunwale at the balancing point, provided lateral resistance, and the pole-paddle was used to steer. The rig consisted of a lateen sail of about 35 square feet, often of the same color as the member's school colors, hung on a short mast.

This Long Point Company boat was built by Jack Reeves of Port Rowan, Ontario, about 1930. Jack was the third generation of the Reeves family to be head keeper for the company. The Reeves family is also well known for their decoys, prized by collectors.

STATUS: Good, unrestored condition.
DONOR: Henry S. Morgan
FURTHER READING:
Crandell, Bernard W. "The Reeves of Long Point Company." *Decoy* magazine, Summer, 1976. A copy of this article is in the Registrar's files at Mystic Seaport.
ACCESSION NO. 1980.71

WATERFOWL GUNNING FLOAT

17' 7" x 3' 7"

Family tradition has it that this boat was built by a Carter on Long Island.

Construction is straightforward with a cross-planked bottom, single-plank sides, and straight planked deck, all painted a "dull duckboat drab"–a brownish khaki in color.

Absence of rowlocks or sailing rig indicate that this boat was probably towed into position and then anchored, amid a set of decoys, using lines through the ring bolt aft and the stem hole forward. Once in position the gunner would "grass" the boat to hide its outline. This "grass" was straw sewn to a 17"-wide canvas strip, which was laced to a rail that extended full-length along each side.

Shelves for shotgun shells exist on both sides under the side deck and a loop for receiving the barrel of a shotgun is on the starboard side. A rack for carrying decoys rests on the afterdeck. The cockpit hatch is missing.

STATUS: Excellent.
DONOR: John Robinson
ACCESSION NO. 1997.107

A bow-on view of the gunning float, showing the lashing rail for "grassing" the boat and the decoy rack on the after deck. (Photo: Mystic Seaport 1997-6-119A)

KIDNEY GREEN BAY HUNTING BOAT

16' x 3' 8"

In the early 1870s, young Dan Kidney moved west from Buffalo, New York, to work in the lumber and shipbuilding industries of DePere, Wisconsin. Soon he was spending most of his free time on the marshes of the nearby Fox River, gunning for waterfowl. He sold his first gunning skiff, and orders for more developed into a flourishing business. By 1920 he was able to claim he had sold 27,000 "small launches, row and hunting boats, special rowboats for outboard motors and canoes" to owners all over the world. His Green Bay Hunting Boat was his most popular model, with sales of over 6,000 since it was introduced in 1885.

It's easy to see why it was popular. Well-built, it was light and strong, had a large carrying capacity, moved easily under oar, paddle, and push pole, and had a very shallow draft. It was built with white cedar (later, pine) lapstrake planking clench nailed to oak frames, which were bent in on the flat, had canvas covered decks, and galvanized fastenings. White oak knees supported the narrow side decks and married the deck, side planking, and keel together as one unit. Although 3" coamings–a Kidney trademark–made the boat quite safe in a chop, you could request extra-high topsides by ordering an optional fifth plank per side.

The 16' Kidney Green Bay Hunting Boat, showing the cap of one of the pipe "anchor holes" for anchoring the boat with a push pole. (Photo: Maynard Bray, Mystic Seaport 1987.60A)

Kidney built a vertical pipe into both the fore and aft decks through which you could shove a push pole down into the marsh bottom, effectively anchoring the boat. Called "pole wells" by some, Kidney called his "anchor holes." The boat came equipped with a portable seat, one pair of 6' oars, one 10' push pole, and a 5' paddle. Kidney offered this model in lengths from 12 to 18 feet.

The Museum's boat is sixteen feet long and would have weighed 130 pounds when built. You would have paid $57 for it if you bought it in 1920.

STATUS: Unrestored, good.
DONOR: John Phalen
FURTHER READING:
Beno, Mike. "The Dan Kidney-A Midwestern Classic." *Ducks Unlimited Magazine*, 1984.

Ducks Unlimited, One Waterfowl Way, Memphis, Tennessee 38120-2351.

ACCESSION NO. 1987.60

RAILBIRD SKIFF

15' 3" x 3' 0"

This boat, with its slightly rockered flat bottom, was ideally suited for going in over the flooding tidal marshes after rail or other waterfowl. Paddled or pushed with a pole, this symmetrical double-ended skiff could glide over the clinging grasses or escape the grasping mud with ease. The builder was a skilled artisan. Lapstrake planking is clench-nailed to light frames bent in on the flat, and three sets of equally spaced overlapping sawn frames give the boat additional stiffness. The gunner could anchor this skiff to the bottom by shoving his push poles through "pole wells"–vertical watertight pipes installed through the fore and aft decks.

STATUS: Unrestored, good condition.
DONOR: Philadelphia Maritime Museum (Independence Seaport Museum)
ACCESSION NO. 1984.29

Railbird skiff 1984.29. (Photo: Maynard Bray, Mystic Seaport 1984.29C)

RAILBIRD SKIFF
ATTRIBUTED TO LaPLACE

15' 1" x 4' 4"   ca. 1930

Family tradition holds that Oliver LaPlace built this boat in Essex, Connecticut, in the late 1920s. It was used at the mouth of the Connecticut River, to hunt railbirds, then ducks as the rail population dwindled.

A powerboat would be used to tow a number of these boats to the vicinity of the marshes. Each boat would then set off up a creek with the guide push-poling the boat from a raised platform aft, while the sport sat on a stool forward. As the tide rose, the guide would go in over the grassy flats and a colorful marker would be thrown for each downed bird. As the tide receded, the markers and the hard-to-see birds would be retrieved.

This boat was built of lightweight materials with a bottom that is slightly rockered, both fore-and-aft and sideways. These qualities kept the boat from being captured by the suction of the mud or by the clinging grass.

The construction is unique. The bottom is single-planked fore-and-aft with a spline between each plank. The bottom and sides both set into rabbets in the chine log.

STATUS: Good.
DONOR: E.E. Dickinson Company
FURTHER READING:
Scott, John. "Rail Shooting on the Connecticut River." *Sports Afield*, October, 1953.
Crawford, Rebecca. "Oliver LaPlace." *Gray's Sporting Journal*, Fall, 1980.
Chitwood, Henry, with Tom Marshall. *Connecticut Decoys.* West Chester, Pennsylvania: Schiffer Publishing, 1987.

ACCESSION NO. 1982.9

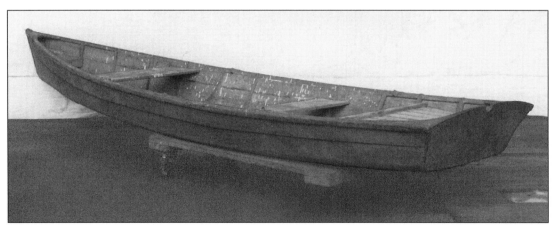

Railbird skiff attributed to Oliver LaPlace. (Photo: Mary Anne Stets, Mystic Seaport 1982.9D)

RAILBIRD SKIFF

14' 4" x 2' 9"   pre-1930

It's hard to believe that a flat-bottomed, flat-sided boat could be as graceful and attractive as this one. According to the donor, Jessica Stevens Loring, this boat was built sometime before 1930 for her father, C. Leigh Stevens. This model of a railbird skiff was then in use in the marshy areas around Lake Muskegon, Michigan. Lightly but carefully put together, the skiff is built entirely of spruce, with the exception of the oak stems, and is fastened with iron nails. The boat lacks chines; dory-like sawn frames are joined to floors, which support the two sections of floorboards. There is a hatch in the aft deck that gives access to a watertight space used to stow birds. A double-bladed paddle or a push pole would have moved this light boat very efficiently. Leigh Stevens used this double-ended skiff and its near replica, the boat described below, for waterfowl gunning on the Combahee River in Beaufort County, South Carolina.

STATUS: Good Condition.
DONOR: Jessica Stevens Loring
ACCESSION NO. 1981.70

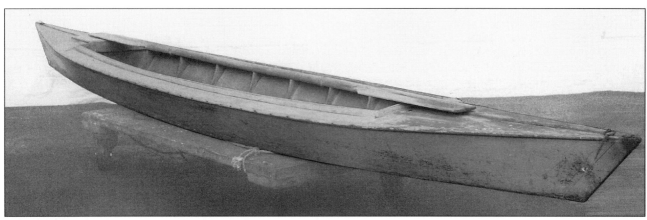

Lake Muskegon railbird skiff. (Photo: Mary Anne Stets, Mystic Seaport 1982-2-83)

RAILBIRD SKIFF

15' 10" x 3' 1"   ca. 1948

This railbird skiff was built by Leonard Tallman at the Chester A. Crosby Yacht Yard in Osterville, Massachusetts. It was to be a roughly 10-percent-larger version of another railbird skiff also owned by C. Leigh Stevens and used by him on the Combahee River in South Carolina. That skiff, 1981.70, is discussed above. Like its inspiration, this boat is nearly symmetrical end for end, but the decks are made of plywood, not spruce, and fastenings are bronze.

STATUS: Good condition.
DONOR: Jessica Stevens Loring
ACCESSION NO. 1981.71

Slightly larger version of railbird skiff 1981.70. (Photo: Mary Anne Stets, Mystic Seaport 1982-2-80)

DELAWARE DUCKER
15' 0" x 4' 0"

Known also as railbird boats, rail gunning skiffs, reed bird skiffs, push skiffs, and pole skiffs, these altogether delightful little boats were judged by Howard I. Chapelle to be the most able of all gunning skiffs for use in rough water. Some were fitted for sail, and not a few of them, beautifully built, came out of high-class boatshops near Philadelphia. Marshes south of that city and further down Delaware Bay abounded with small birds known as rail. Market-gunners and sports alike used these boats for their pursuit.

After sailing and rowing from shore, two men—one poling from the stern, the other poised to blast away up forward—hunted during a brief two-hour high tide period when the railbirds were flooded out of their hiding places. Then, as Ed Sandys tells us, "The amount of shooting to be obtained largely depends upon the height of the tide and the skill of the boatman. But whether the gun is kept busy for hours or mostly rests upon its owner's knees, the experience is a pleasant one. Properly propelled, the light draught boat steadily glides through or over the yielding cover; a rail flutters up within a few yards and goes wobbling away, its feet hanging as if reluctant to leave their accustomed footing; the flush is indicated by the pusher's automatic cry of 'Mark,' and the squib of the light charge punctuates a kill or a miss—usually the former if the sportsman possesses a moderate amount of skill. The performance may be repeated until from twenty to one-hundred shells have been exploded and the outgoing waters have uncovered so much lush growth that the rail cannot be compelled to rise. It is an easy, restful form of sport, with just enough of sunshine, of the salt strength of the marshes and of mild excitement to do a tired man a great deal of good."

The hulls of these boats, being symmetrical, pushed with equal ease in either direction. In profile they were

John B. York's Delaware ducker. (Photo: Maynard Bray, Mystic Seaport 1975-10-166)

much like a sailing canoe; but, as a shooting platform for two standing men when on location, greater beam was needed. Three or four wooden prongs on the dirty end of the push pole (crow's foot) kept it from sticking too far into the mud. The Chesapeake Bay Maritime Museum at St. Michaels, Maryland, and Philadelphia's Independence Seaport Museum have fine examples of these boats, and interested persons would do well to examine them. This was John B. York's boat and was given to Mystic Seaport fully equipped, even to an awning and tent for her cockpit, by his grandson.

STATUS: Original, good condition.

DONOR: John J. York, Sr.

FURTHER READING:

Chapelle, Howard I. *American Small Sailing Craft.* New York: W.W. Norton & Co., 1951.

Fuller, Benjamin A.G. "The Delaware Ducker." *WoodenBoat* 48, Sept/Oct, 1982.

——. "Fishtown Tricks: The Delaware River's 15' flyers." *WoodenBoat* 148, May/June, 1999.

Guthorn, Peter J. *The Sea Bright Skiff and Other Jersey Shore Boats.* New Brunswick: Rutgers University Press, 1971.

Sandys, Ed. W. "Rail and Reed Bird." *Outing*, September, 1896.

Cover of Outing *magazine, September, 1896, showing railbird shooting from a Delaware ducker. (Photo:* Mystic Seaport 1978-2-96*)*

Stephens, W.P. *Canoe and Boat Building.* New York: Forest and Stream Publishing Co., 1889.

ACCESSION NO. 1969.821

Plans for 1969.821 are available from Mystic Seaport's Watercraft Plans Collection.

Delaware ducker 1969.98 in 1975. (Photo: Maynard Bray, Mystic Seaport 1975-5-171*)*

DELAWARE DUCKER FROM DELAWARE BAY

14' 10" x 3' 10"

Unlike the other two boats of this type in Mystic Seaport's watercraft collection, this boat is not rigged for sail, and perhaps this is why she needed no side decks or coamings. It is this boat that Peter Guthorn pictures in his book on the Sea Bright skiff, page 184, and which he says was found at Cape May, New Jersey, in 1968 by the donor.

STATUS: Original, fair condition.

DONOR: John Dubois

FURTHER READING:

(Same as for 1969.821)

ACCESSION NO. 1969.98

Plans for 1969.98 are available from Mystic Seaport's Watercraft Plans Collection.

The Delaware ducker Oriole in 1975. (Photo: Maynard Bray,
Mystic Seaport 1975-5-11)

Oriole
DELAWARE DUCKER
15' 1" x 3' 8"

The product of an unidentified builder, this boat has an unusually long foredeck, with the dagger board trunk passing through it. The flat sheer indicates that she was designed for rough-water use.

STATUS: Original, fair condition.
DONOR: Samuel W. Burgess
FURTHER READING:
(Same as for 1969.821)
ACCESSION NO. 1969.208

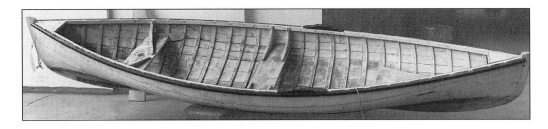

The 14' 9" Cape Sable gunning skiff. (Photo: Judy Beisler,
Mystic Seaport 1989.113B)

CAPE SABLE GUNNING SKIFF
14' 9" x 4' 3"

Found throughout Shelburne County, Nova Scotia, these gunning skiffs resemble the peapods of Maine. They are not as specialized for duck hunting as some gunning boats, as they served for lobstering very near shore and also as harbor tenders. They were generally turned out by builders of larger boats on speculation during slack times. They share the wide and relatively flat frames commonly found in other round-bottom Nova Scotia boats. They have iron clench nails as fastenings, have two seats (but only one rowing station), and a low stern platform with a storage locker and drain plug underneath. The forward seat is set up as a partner for a mast so that the user could carry a small spritsail when the wind favored. These boats have a much more asymmetrical shape than do peapods, a generally lower sheer, pronounced knuckles at the stems, and a curve of stern lower than the bow. This boat was found in upstate New York and has been measured and replicated. She makes a fast, stable rowing vehicle for one person.

STATUS: Good original condition.
DONOR: The Rockport Apprenticeshop, which was given the boat by Bob and Mary Sutter
ACCESSION NO. 1989.113

DUCK-HUNTING PUNT
8' 7" x 3' 6"

Although simplicity and shallow draft are achieved in this punt, she would be hard to conceal when in use because of her high sides. The fact that she has such a small deck makes camouflage with brush difficult.

STATUS: Original, good condition.
DONOR: Isaac B. Merriman, Jr.
ACCESSION NO. 1961.393

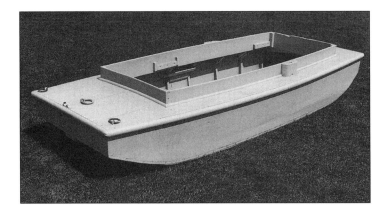

The 8' 7" duck-hunting punt—a floating box with space for one or two gunners. (Photo: Maynard Bray, Mystic Seaport 1961.393)

PORTABLE EXTENSION BOAT BY FENNER

9' 6" x 2' 9" (extended),
23" x 33" x 22" (closed)   ca. 1875

The Fenner folding boat frame, with components in position.
(Photo: Mary Anne Stets, Mystic Seaport 1972.279)

Many kinds of folding devices were manufactured by the C.A. Fenner Company of Mystic River, Connecticut, from 1869 until Charles Fenner sold the business in 1883. The company advertised its folding boat as especially suitable for traveling sportsmen. Fenner's catalog describes this boat as follows:

"(Folded up), a strong trunk is thus formed which contains the canvas cover of the boat, with room enough left for tent or clothing. It may be enclosed in a box, trunk, or canvas trunk-cover, or may be carried without any protection as the case may require. The largest size occupies a space only one foot wide, two feet high, and three-and-a-half feet long, the smaller sizes proportionally less.

"This frame (can be) drawn out in an instant to eleven times (its folded) length. In order to obtain this sudden extension, the frame is made in the form of lattice-work with a rivet at each intersection upon which the joints move easily and accurately. Great strength also is secured, as may be seen in the ordinary railway bridge built upon the same general principle. Longitudinal pieces lock the whole firmly and stiffly in place. No tools nor ingenuity are required to set it up, nor even the assistance of a second person.

"The cover is made of heavy seamless duck, stouter than the usual thickness of birch bark or cedar in canoes. The value of this material for boat coverings has been too well proven to need defense. These are woven to order for this special use, and are waterproof. They are then treated by a special process which preserves the fibre, prevents mildew, and renders every part impervious to water. The cover is quickly and easily attached to the frame in a way to secure the least delay and the greatest strength. The boat can, without difficulty, be made ready for the water in five minutes. The best materials are used throughout, selected ash and hickory for the frame, with brass joinings and fastenings, making a thoroughly safe and reliable boat. A pair of jointed paddles, with

rowlocks, are packed inside each boat, with extra seats according to its carrying capacity. A sail, with jointed mast, can also be used. Air-tight compartments can be furnished to place under the end seats, thus making a life-preserving boat, which can be carried in the form of a serviceable trunk by travelers upon the water. For yachts it saves taking a boat in tow, and for steamers and sailing vessels it is the best of life-boats, as it occupies little room, and is set up in a few minutes.

"The inventors of this boat offer it with the confidence which comes from a practical knowledge of watercraft, and of the needs of sportsmen and travelers for a boat which can be carried and checked as an ordinary trunk, and therefore occupying no space, at the same time capable of being made ready for the water in a few minutes, and as quickly put up compactly for conveyance again. When not in use it

can be stored in the house. To sportsmen going from our cities and towns by rail or stage into the wilderness, or by wagon over the game regions of the West and South with their frequent lakes, and to tourists in general, it will be found to be a convenient and available companion in many ways."

Mystic's noted photographer, E.A. Scholfield, owned this boat and doubtless found her convenient for his business. He was the donor's father.

STATUS: Original, complete with all pieces, excellent condition.
DONOR: Everett E. Scholfield
FURTHER READING:

C.A. Fenner Co. *The Fenner Portable Extension Boat.* Mystic, Connecticut: C.A. Fenner Co., 1876. An illustrated catalog.
ACCESSION NO. 1972.279 (Separate pieces numbered 1972.279.1 through .7)

Mystic photographer E.A. Scholfield depicted this boat on the Mystic River, ca. 1875. (Photo: Mystic Seaport 1976-12-94)

POWER
Chapter One
Inboard-Powered

Nellie on exhibit in Mystic Seaport's North Boat Shed. (Photo: Louis Martel, Mystic Seaport 1956.1085)

Nellie
(ex-Glory B., Old River, Clermont)

STEAM LAUNCH

30' 10" x 5' 1"   1872

Nellie (her original name) is believed to have been the first propeller-driven boat on New Hampshire's Lake Winnipesaukee. The Atlantic Works built her at East Boston, and she was used at Portsmouth, New Hampshire, before going to the lake. Sheltered waters must have been favored, for in a seaway she probably was cranky in behavior and certainly very wet. A passing glance shows that most of the best space is taken up by her boiler and engine, explaining why so few of these small steam-powered launches were built. It wasn't until the compact naphtha and gasoline engines were on the market that the small power launch came into common use.

STATUS: Mostly original, good condition.

DONOR: George Lauder

ACCESSION NO. 1956.1085

Plans for 1956.1085 are available from Mystic Seaport's Watercraft Plans Collection.

George Lauder with Nellie *under full steam at Indian Harbor, Connecticut. (Photo: Courtesy of Robert Holbrook)*

Lillian Russell
(ex-Helen G.)

NAPHTHA LAUNCH

21' 3" x 5' 1"   ca. 1904

The engine that powers *Lillian Russell* makes her unique. Frank Ofeldt of Newark, New Jersey, patented the naphtha engine in 1883, a small-boat powerplant in which naphtha serves not only as fuel but recirculates as a heat transfer fluid through the engine, condenser, retort (boiler), and other parts of the power system–much the same as steam does in a steam plant. Its operation was simple compared to steam, and no license was needed to run it. Compared to the gasoline engines that came along early in the twentieth century it was trouble-free and quiet. Naphtha launches proliferated in sizes up to 50' during the years from 1885 (when the first one was built) to around 1903 when there were more than 3,000 in use. Production dropped off with the coming refinements in gasoline engines, but it is notable that one company, the Gas Engine and Power Company of Morris Heights, New York, held the patent rights to the naphtha engine and was the exclusive builder of naphtha launches and engines. It is also interesting that this company, under its later name of Consolidated, went on to design and build some of the finest power yachts ever produced in the U.S.

Lillian Russell is one of the standard naphtha launches and spent much of her life in storage before being reactivated by John Haln, who also gave her the present name. The lifting shackles fore and aft would lead one to believe she was a tender to a larger yacht early in her career and was hoisted out on davits when not in use.

STATUS: Mostly original, engine restored 1973, good condition.

DONOR: Purchased for Mystic Seaport by P.R. Mallory

FURTHER READING:

Chapman, Wilbur R. "Early American Launches." *Steamboat Bill*, Spring, 1959.

Durant, Kenneth. *The Naphtha Launch.* Blue Mountain Lake, New York: The Adirondack Museum, 1976.

Hiscox, Gardner D. *Gas, Gasoline and Oil Vapor Engines.* New York: Munn & Company, 1901.

Kunhardt. C.P. *Steam Yachts and Launches.* New York: Forest and Stream Publishing Company, 1887.

MacDuffie, Malcolm. "Naphtha Launch. The Missing Link." *National Fisherman,* May, 1971.

McConnell, Chrystie. "The Redoubtable Naphtha Launch." *The Ensign,* 1967.

"New American Industry." *Forest and Stream,* December 8, 1887.

"The Naphtha Launch." *The Rudder,* July, 1890.

"Where Naphtha Launches Grow." *The Rudder,* December, 1898.

A promotional catalog describing and illustrating its boats, entitled *Yachts, Launches and Their Propellers,* was printed by Gas Engine and Power Company, Chas. L. Seabury & Company, Consolidated, and dated 1909. A copy is in the library at Mystic Seaport.

ACCESSION NO. 1953.3071
Plans for 1953.3071 are available from Mystic Seaport's Watercraft Plans Collection.

Lillian Russell in a Mystic Seaport exhibit in 1975. (Photo: Maynard Bray, Mystic Seaport 1975-5-425)

THE NAPHTHA ENGINE IN THE LAUNCH.

HOW TO START ENGINE.

TURN Air Valve (*B*) from left to right; give Air Pump (*E*) sufficient number of strokes (2 to 5) to force gas from tank, through outlet pipe to burner, and ignite by match introduced through hole in base (*A*), and so heat retort by means of the flame, which is kept up by using the Air Pump. Use air pump one to two minutes in warm weather; but in cold weather much longer, as gas then generates very slowly in the tank. Open wide Naphtha Valve (*D*) and give 10 to 20 quick strokes with Naphtha Pump (*F*), which pumps Naphtha from tank in bow to Retort on top of Engine, and if Retort has been sufficiently heated, the pressure will at once be indicated on gauge. Then open Injector Valve (*C*) which supplies fuel to burner, and keeping the Damper (*I*) partially closed, especially if there be much wind blowing; after which, by the Handwheel (*G*), which is the starting and reverse wheel combined, turn the Engine over several times, both forward and back, by turning the wheel from right to left, and from left to right, during which operation the fire will go down, unless prevented by four or five strokes of the Naphtha Pump (*F*), as often as necessary to keep the fire going and the pressure at about 20 pounds, until the Engine starts itself. Should fire go out, it is important to shut off Injector Valve and light by using Air Pump, as before, opening Injector immediately thereafter. If Engine starts or turns over hard, block open Safety Valve, and keep using Naphtha Pump; this allows the pressure to go through the Engine, and blows out condensed Naphtha that is on top of piston To go ahead, turn Wheel (*G*) to the left; to back, turn to the right.

Now the Engine takes care of itself.

Use 76° Deodorized Naphtha.

(3)

Engine and instructions from a Gas Engine and Power Company catalog of 1909. (Photo: Mary Anne Stets, Mystic Seaport 1978-1-103)

Panhard I *on exhibit at Mystic Seaport in the 1950s.* (Photo: Louis Martel, <small>Mystic Seaport 1953.3072A</small>)

Panhard I

GASOLINE RACING LAUNCH

31' 2" x 4' 7"   ca. 1904

Built by the Electric Launch Company of Bayonne, New Jersey, this torpedo-boat-like craft was exhibited at the 1905 New York Boat Show to promote marine use of the Panhard & Levassor automobile engine, which powered her. Her photograph appears on the cover of *The Rudder* for February, 1905.

The early gasoline engines were hard to start and quite unreliable compared to either naphtha or steam, and they were noisy as well. But they were cheap, attainable by persons of moderate means, easily installed in boats, and quickly surpassed all other forms of small-craft propulsion, even traditional working sail. The first decade or two of the twentieth century was overrun with small gasoline engine builders, as a look at any contemporary boating magazine will confirm, each one claiming that his model was the best, when in fact there were few engineering differences among any of them.

STATUS: Loose diagonal planking, mostly original, engineless, fair condition.

DONOR: D. Cameron Peck

FURTHER READING:

Fostle, D.W. *Speedboat*. Mystic, Connecticut: Mystic Seaport Museum Stores, 1988.

Fuller, Benjamin A.G. "The Coming of the Explosive Engine, 1885-1910." *The Log of Mystic Seaport*, Autumn, 1993.

ACCESSION NO. 1953.3072

Plans for 1953.3072 are available from Mystic Seaport's Watercraft Plans Collection.

Panhard I *under way in 1904, a photograph published in* The Rudder.
(Photo: Mary Anne Stets, <small>Mystic Seaport 1959-11-24</small>)

Papoose *on exhibit at Mystic Seaport in 1975. (Photo: Maynard Bray,* Mystic Seaport 1975-5-431*)*

Papoose
AUTOBOAT

14' 9" x 3' 1"   1908

Papoose was built in Kennebunkport, Maine, by Clement Clark to the specifications of Atwater Kent, Sr., the radio pioneer. Her hull is canvas-covered and she is powered by a Roberts one-cylinder "jump-spark" engine. Not surprisingly, her ignition coil is manufactured by Atwater Kent.

STATUS: Restored 1972, mostly original, excellent condition.

DONOR: A. Atwater Kent, Jr.

FURTHER READING:

Fostle, D.W. *Speedboat.* Mystic, Connecticut: Mystic Seaport Museum Stores, 1988. Chapters 5 and 6 discuss autoboats.

ACCESSION NO. 1963.879

Plans for 1963.879 are available from Mystic Seaport's Watercraft Plans Collection.

This view shows the simple boxy lines and arrangement of this small autoboat. (Photo: Maynard Bray, Mystic Seaport 1975-5-431*)*

POWER TENDER FROM YACHT
Quill II

12' 2" x 3' 10"   ca. 1905

On a different scale and in a more elegant way, this boat served the same purpose as the yawlboat from the *Mertie B. Crowley* (1956.1137), for the 38' yawl *Quill II* had no power for much of her life. Little is known about this nicely built boat except that she was towed rather than hoisted aboard when not in use, hence her big towing eye low on the stem and her somewhat cut-away forefoot. *Quill II* was designed by B.B. Crowninshield and built by Hodgdon Bros. in East Boothbay, Maine. She was built in 1905, and her power tender appears to be of that same vintage. The tender carries a single-cylinder, "make-and-break" engine.

STATUS: Restored 1975, approximately 75% original, excellent condition.
DONOR: Robert Eaton
FURTHER READING:
The plans and a commentary for *Quill II* are contained in *The Rudder*, November, 1905.
ACCESSION NO. 1970.802

The Quill II *tender prepared for an exhibit in 1975. (Photo: Maynard Bray,* Mystic Seaport 1975-11-28*)*

Cormorant Rose

HERRESHOFF MANUFACTURING COMPANY MOTOR LAUNCH

17' 8" x 5' 0"   1909

For their motor launches, the Herreshoff Manufacturing Company relied on engines built by others. In this launch, a tender for the 1909 steam yacht *Enaj*, plans called for a 2-hp Buffalo. Replacement of that engine with a snappier one meant that the boat went faster, and the occupants got wet, so the bow's foredeck was raised to help keep passengers dry. The work was done skillfully (but not by the Herreshoff Manufacturing Company) and it takes close observation to see that it was an addition. The new raised foredeck was made from first-class materials that matched the original boat; the new cockpit coaming came out of a mahogany plank that had to be two feet wide. The current engine, a Hallett Aero-Motor Company 4-cylinder model, was probably installed in the late 1920s, when that company was briefly in business. Mystic Seaport also owns the other tender (1974.995) that came from *Enaj*, both rescued from the yacht after she (as *Comfort*) was wrecked in the 1938 hurricane. *Cormorant Rose* served her owner as a tender to get out to his ketch *Compass Rose* from his summer home on Cormorant Point, Block Island. She is not as pretty now as she was when she was built, but her passengers around Block Island would have been dry and happy.

STATUS: Good condition, structurally and cosmetically.
DONOR: Commander Joseph Wadsworth
ACCESSION NO. 1975.466

Cormorant Rose *in storage at Mystic Seaport.*
(*Photo: Maynard Bray,* Mystic Seaport 1975.466A)

Yankee

GASOLINE LAUNCH BY LOZIER

21' 11" x 5' 6"   ca. 1904

During his ten-year association with the Lozier Motor Company, Frederick Miller designed boats of all types and sizes, and it is safe to say that he designed *Yankee*. The boat was no doubt built in Plattsburgh, New York, or in Bascom, Ohio, where Lozier had its boatbuilding factories. As its name implies, the Lozier organization built engines (and automobiles as well), and a Lozier engine was installed in *Yankee*

when she left the plant. Unfortunately, it is no longer with her. The Lozier catalog for 1901, and presumably for other years near the beginning of the century, lists models from 12-1/2' to 36' and gives a very detailed description of how the launches were put together. There is little doubt, after reading the catalog, and after examining *Yankee*, that there was truth in the Lozier statement that "they are built in one grade, which is the best, and no expense is spared to render them durable, safe and speedy."

There are Lozier launches in the collections of the Adirondack Museum

in Blue Mountain Lake, New York, and the Antique Boat Museum in Clayton, New York, and, as these boats are more indigenous to New York State, both of these organizations are better prepared for research by those interested in Lozier boats and engines than is Mystic Seaport.

STATUS: Original, some equipment missing, good condition.
DONOR: Herbert R. and Harold O. Reif
ACCESSION NO. 1961.1167
Plans for 1961.1167 are available from Mystic Seaport's Watercraft Plans Collection.

Yankee *in storage in 1978. (Photo: Maynard Bray,* Mystic Seaport 1978-2-53)

Resolute

LAUNCH BY HERRESHOFF MANUFACTURING COMPANY

26' 2" x 6' 6"   ca. 1917

Five of these double-cockpit launches were built after they were designed by Nat Herreshoff for possible use by the U.S. Navy during the First World War. Legend has it that because the Herreshoffs wouldn't allow other builders the use of their design, the navy went elsewhere after obtaining

only one boat. Two boats that were built to this design by the Herreshoff Manufacturing Company ended up at the Seawanhaka Corinthian Yacht Club on Long Island, this one having served beforehand as a tender for the America's Cup defender *Resolute*. Year after year, *Resolute*, this boat that took on its name for obvious reasons, and *Emerald*, her sister club launch, shuttled between shore and the moored fleet carrying club members and their guests. Now both boats are in museums–*Emerald* at the Herreshoff Marine Museum on the site of the

Bristol, Rhode Island, yard that built her. Arriving weathered and worn from her many years of service, *Resolute* has been thoroughly and beautifully restored by Mystic Seaport's shipyard staff. She is once again operational and carries paying passengers along the Museum waterfront.

STATUS: Restored, operating, excellent condition.

DONOR: Purchased from SCYC

ACCESSION NO. 1980.133

Resolute in use at Mystic Seaport. (Photo: Mary Anne Stets, Mystic Seaport 1993-9-316B)

LAUNCH FROM INDIAN HARBOR YACHT CLUB BY PALMER

26' x 6' 6"   1893

According to the records of the Indian Harbor Yacht Club, this launch was built by the Palmer Brothers at Cos Cob, Connecticut, in 1893 and given a naphtha engine. This preceded by two years the first Palmer gasoline engine, which went into a 15' Whitehall. The Palmers would have obtained this launch's original naphtha apparatus from the Gas Engine and Power Company of Morris Heights, New York. George Lauder, who bought the launch in 1976, thought that the Palmers were building boats before they were building engines, which might be the reason they were able to easily produce both once the engine business was solidly established. The boat was repowered with a two-cylinder Palmer about 1903 and was repowered as needed in her career as a hard-working yacht club launch. Lauder found and installed a 1927

The Indian Harbor launch shortly after she was acquired from George Lauder. (Photo: Mary Anne Stets, Mystic Seaport 1987-8-72)

Palmer T-head two-cylinder engine of 18 horsepower, which he figured was as close to a period engine as he could get. This boat is ruggedly built, with cedar planking on bent oak frames, a teak deck (not original), and varnished mahogany trim and interior. She steers with a side staff, which, after one learns to use it, is a quick and convenient way to handle a boat if maneuverability is important. The launch also has useful features like

twin towing bitts and concealed boat-hook stowage. Lauder considered her to be one of the "easiest, nicest and driest" boats he had ever run.

STATUS: Good condition.

DONOR: George Lauder

FURTHER READING:
Gribbins, Joseph. "George Lauder's Nautical Garden." *Nautical Quarterly* 23, Fall, 1983.

ACCESSION NO. 1987.75.4

Isabel (ex-Active)

LAUNCH BY HERRESHOFF MANUFACTURING COMPANY HULL #277

29' 6" x 7' 6"   1911

Few boats can claim to have been owned twice by the same museum; but when *Isabel* arrived as a donation in 1987, in a manner of speaking she was returning to one of her former homes. Her stay this time would be permanent. It was a quick stop she made back in 1955 when the Museum accepted her for a fund-raising resale. *Active* was her name then, but as soon as he bought her George Lauder gave her back her original name of *Isabel*. Lauder took wonderful care of this lovely launch. He generally kept her and the rest of his fleet of vintage yachts up in a corner of the harbor at Watch Hill, Rhode Island, and stored them winters at the Frank Hall Boatyard in nearby Avondale where he, his dedicated professional skipper Ray Thombs, and the yard crew could work on them. In hull shape and general layout somewhat like *Resolute*, previously discussed, *Isabel* not only is larger but a good deal more elegant, with her double planking and teak trim. At various times *Isabel* served as crew launch for the J-Class America's Cup contender *Weetamoe*, and the Indian Harbor Yacht Club used her as one of its club launches in Greenwich, Connecticut.

STATUS: Original, good condition.
DONOR: The estate of George Lauder
ACCESSION NO. 1987.75.1

Isabel under way on the Mystic River. (Photo: Lisa Brownell, Mystic Seaport 1987-7-37)

Zenith (ex-Haddock II)

MOTOR LAUNCH BY SHIVERICK

20' 8" x 6' 10"   1933

George W. Shiverick of Kingston, Massachusetts, built this launch in 1933 for his son Roger. Seaworthiness and seakindliness are the chief features of the design, with a watertight cockpit and heavy semi-displacement hull. *Zenith* had a two-cylinder Red Wing engine her first year, which due to oil leaks was replaced by a four-cylinder Graymarine. After three years with the Shivericks she was sold to Mrs. Thurber of Pine Hill, Duxbury, Massachusetts, renamed *Haddock II*, and used on shopping expeditions to Plymouth. In 1940, she passed to a nephew on Lake Champlain and was later sold to a boys camp. In 1958 she returned to Duxbury, where she passed through the hands of several owners, until purchased by the donor who had her restored in 1978 and repowered with a Universal Atomic 4. He used her for several years around Vinalhaven, Maine, before donating her to Mystic Seaport. Shiverick's launch design must have been a success for this boat to have had such a record of good care and active use by her owners. For those content with an economical speed of eight or ten knots, achievable comfortably in virtually all weather, this type of launch has much to recommend it.

STATUS: Restored, excellent condition.
DONOR: David C. Fogg
ACCESSION NO. 1985.80

Zenith in storage in 1985. (Photo: Maynard Bray, Mystic Seaport 1985.80)

FISHING LAUNCH
BY SHIVERICK

25' 0" x 8' 5"   ca. 1930

The Shiverick fishing launch when she was acquired in 1991. (Photo: Judy Beisler, Mystic Seaport 1991.70A)

George W. Shiverick established his Kingston, Massachusetts, shop in November of 1895, moving from East Dennis where he had set up in May, 1892. Shiverick began his training in 1888, building yawl boats for schooners at the shop of Harwichport boatbuilder Charles Jenkins, then spent three winters with the famous catboat builder C.C. Hanley of Monument Beach. By 1926, the Shiverick shop had built 228 boats ranging from dories to a 41' sloop. George Shiverick did not just build catboats and recreational launches, he also turned his hand to fishing boats. These were boats that planed easily and evenly and did not slam coming down off a wave. They were rough-water boats designed to handle the short steep chop off Chatham, Massachusetts, and they were influenced by sailing workboats. Like the powered lobster boats that developed in Noank, Connecticut, from Noank sloops, these easy-running semi-displacement power boats were developed by Shiverick and other south shore and Cape Cod builders from boats like the local Kingston lobster boats. This one is the

earliest of three built from about 1929 to 1934, among the last boats Shiverick built. She cost Allie and Ralph Hunter $1,250 without an engine, and passed through two other owners before going to the donor. These boats were used for whatever fishery was in season: lobstering, long-lining, or flounder dragging.

The Shiverick fishing launch was originally built as an open boat, then a deckhouse was added, which has since been removed and replaced with a cuddy. The current engine is a flathead Ford V-8 from the mid-1930s. She has been redecked with plywood, raising it

to make the working area self-draining. Her gear is not with the boat, but there are marks for davits or gallows on the starboard side. Despite heavy use, the boat has her shape; some 30-40 frames have been sistered out of a total of 52.

STATUS: Poor condition, rebuilt extensively.
DONOR: Russell H. Clark
FURTHER READING:
Schwind, Phil. *Cape Cod Fisherman.* Camden, Maine: International Marine Publishing Co., 1974.
ACCESSION NO. 1991.70

Dr. Livingston
MOTOR LAUNCH
BY DYER

14' 0" x 5' 8"   1955

Dr. Livingston in storage in 1980. (Photo: Mary Anne Stets, Mystic Seaport 1980-2-58)

When James Farrell, Jr., needed a launch to get out to his 56' Sparkman & Stephens yawl *Impala*, or to go striper fishing, or do other things a nice inboard power launch can do in a harbor like Edgartown on Martha's Vineyard, Massachusetts, he turned to William Dyer and his boatbuilding company, The Anchorage of Warren, Rhode Island. The result was a seaworthy lapstrake launch that served until 1970. The boat was so successful it became the prototype for Dyer's well-known fiberglass Glamour Girl line of inboard launches. *Dr. Livingston's*

original power was a Universal Atomic 4 gas engine. When the Farrells owned the boat, they had the transom, foredeck, engine box, and thwarts replaced with mahogany.

STATUS: Good condition.
DONOR: Mrs. James A. Farrell, Jr.
ACCESSION NO. 1980.12

POWER TENDER
FROM YACHT
JANE ANNE

14' 0" x 4' 8"   1920

In 1910, William H. Johns of Bayside, Long Island, had a 72' steam yacht built at George F. Lawley's yard in South Boston and named her *Welcome*. When she went back into the yard in 1920, under new ownership and renamed *Jane Ann*, she emerged with a big Palmer six-cylinder gasoline engine and with this small motor launch in her davits. George Lauder took the little lapstrake launch, engineless, in trade for some work at his Fairfield Boat Works in the late 1930s. He gave her a new engine, an 18-hp, four-cylinder Red Wing, and used her on a lake near his Connecticut home until he brought her to join his Watch Hill fleet. She has a painted canvas foredeck under which the engine hides. Otherwise she is built like a big lapstrake tender. Wet in a chop, she would nevertheless have been handy for ferrying passengers and supplies out to the big yacht.

STATUS: Good condition.
DONOR: George Lauder
FURTHER READING:
Gribbins, Joseph. "George Lauder's Nautical Garden." *Nautical Quarterly* 23, Fall, 1983.
ACCESSION NO. 1987.75.3

Two views of Jane Anne's *power tender in storage at Mystic Seaport in 1987.* (Photos: Judy Beisler, Mystic Seaport 1987.75.3C and 1987.75.3B)

My Home
MOTOR LAUNCH
ATTRIBUTED TO MATTHEWS

11' 1" x 4' 0"   pre-1923

In 1923 Andrew Bates was given this small inboard launch to putt around a Massachusetts lake. Originally, the boat probably hung in the davits of a larger motor yacht, and the Bates family installed davits on a lakeside float so that *My Home* could be hoisted out of the water between outings. Her two-hp engine would push her close to five mph, faster than rowing, especially with a picnic or fishing party aboard. She was fancily built, reputedly by the Matthews Company of Port Clinton, Ohio, as a tender for a large Matthews powerboat. Details such as the gas tank hidden by wood staving, and fancy metal seat knees, bespeak a small boat built for a high-priced market and indicate this could be true. Her Arrow engine dates from the 1916-24 period, and matches the boat's style. The Matthews Company was founded in 1890, and from 1898 to 1904 built launches sold under the Lozier name. Matthews built cruisers and motor yachts in wood from before 1910 until the 1960s, then built in fiberglass until bankruptcy in 1974.

STATUS: Excellent original condition.
DONOR: Andrew J. Bates
FURTHER READING:
Rohr, Frank. "Diamond Jubilee at Port Clinton." *Motor Boating*, January 1965.
"Scott Matthews Motor Boats." *Motor Boat*, April 10, 1929.
ACCESSION NO. 1991.150.2

My Home *when she was acquired in 1991. (Photo: Maynard Bray,* Mystic Seaport 1991.150.2A)

Posse at Mystic Seaport in 1965. (Photo: Louis Martel, Mystic Seaport 1965.803)

Posse
LAUNCH BY FERGUSON
18' 4" x 5' 7"   ca. 1910

It is unfortunate that so little remains of *Posse*, because she must have been a good-looking little boat with her strong sheer and oval coaming. The shop of Charles Ferguson, where she was built, was on the Groton side of the Thames River, not more than seven miles from Mystic Seaport. The Museum is fortunate in having a number of Ferguson's half models in its collection as well, since he was a well-known and prolific builder in the early years of this century.

STATUS: Relic, poor condition.
DONOR: Paul V. Donahue
ACCESSION NO. 1965.803

Delphine in storage at Mystic Seaport in 1992. (Photo: Maynard Bray, Mystic Seaport 1992.7A)

Delphine (ex-*Yankee, Yankee Girl*)
LAUNCH BY ELDREDGE
20' 8" x 7' 2"   ca. 1902

Although now a relic, *Delphine* was once a lovely open launch of eye-catching proportions. Webster Eldredge's Noank shop, located only about three miles south of Mystic Seaport, generally turned out workboats for local fishermen, but he'd occasionally build a pleasure craft. *Delphine*, known later as *Yankee* and *Yankee Girl*, was one of them. Gasoline engines were just beginning to proliferate when he built *Delphine*, and her first powerplant would have been small, heavy for its horsepower, slow-turning, and driving a big propeller. *Delphine*'s hull is shaped to push easily, but because it has very little bearing aft, it squats and drives with increasing difficulty if overpowered. Owners of such boats at the turn of the century were relieved at not having to row, and satisfied running at near-rowboat speeds. Launches like *Delphine* suited them perfectly.

STATUS: Relic, poor condition.
DONOR: Holt C. Vibber
ACCESSION NO. 1992.7

MOTOR LAUNCH ATTRIBUTED TO PALMER

17' 0" x 4' 9"   ca. 1905

To improve sales of their gasoline engines, early engine-builders like Palmer added boats to their product line, using their own shops or subcontracting. This enabled them to offer complete boat-engine packages. The Palmer Engine Company, which began in 1895 in Cos Cob, Connecticut, added a boatshop to its new plant in 1901, but by the time of World War I the engine-builder had dropped boatbuilding. By then there were plenty of boatbuilders to provide hulls for motors. This boat was collected by Bob Baker in Colchester, Connecticut, and because it looked like Palmer's catalog offerings, he believed it to be a genuine Palmer. Whatever the provenance, this was a handsome boat with fantail stern, oval cockpit coaming, and beaded decks.

STATUS: Fair, has been fiberglassed and partially repaired.
DONOR: Anne (Mrs. Robert H.) Baker
FURTHER READING:
Day, Richard A., Jr., and Barbara B. *Operating Instructions* (for various Palmer engines, 1895-1940). Severna Park, Maryland: Heritage Engine Collection, 1984, 1985, 1987.
Fostle, Don. *Speedboat*. Mystic, Connecticut: Mystic Seaport Museum Stores, 1988.
Grayson, Stan. *Old Marine Engines*. Marblehead, Massachusetts: Devereux Books, 1998.
———. *Engines Afloat*. Marblehead, Massachusetts: Devereux Books, 1999.
Staff of *Motor Boat*. "The Palmers of Cos Cob." *Motor Boat*, April 10, 1929.
The G. W. Blunt White Library at Mystic Seaport has a collection of microfilmed Palmer catalogs.
ACCESSION NO. 1990.141.2

Launch 1990.141.2 in 1990. (Photo: Maynard Bray, Mystic Seaport 1990.141.2A)

The Bessey-built launch in 1990. (Photo: Maynard Bray, Mystic Seaport 1990.141.3A)

MOTORIZED CAT-RIGGED BOAT BY BESSEY

12' 4" x 4' 11"   ca. 1930

A Westport, Massachusetts, builder named Bessey built a number of these boats. This is one of a pair that were fitted with small engines and fished off Westport (Horseneck) Beach in the 1930s. Both were tossed ashore in the hurricane of '38. This boat is especially simply built, with a V-bottom and single-strake sides, construction similar to that of the flat-bottomed skiffs and sharpies that were popular around Westport. Bob Baker, with his eye for a good boat, added her to his collection–for fifty cents.

STATUS: Good original condition, no engine.
DONOR: Anne (Mrs. Robert H.) Baker
ACCESSION NO. 1990.141.3

The Mullins Leader launch in 1992. (Photo: Maynard Bray, Mystic Seaport 1992.106A)

Charles & Arthur

TORPEDO-STERN LAUNCH BY MULLINS HULL #7885

18' 1" x 5' 0"   1926

By 1926, the W.H. Mullins Company of Salem, Ohio, had been building pressed-steel motor boats for 22 years. This Leader model cost Arthur H. Dayton of Naugatuck, Connecticut, $675 with a 12-hp Universal four-cylinder engine. She was shipped by rail and then truck to Nicatous Lake in Maine, where the Daytons had a camp on Harwood Island. There she worked hard, transporting people and gear from the roadhead at the lake's dam to the island, towing canoes to a stream mouth for fishing trips, and towing other objects such as rafts and logs. For

60 years, she served the family as its chief picnic, wildlife-watching, and sunset-watching boat. She was quiet and capacious, but never did more than 10 knots. *Charles & Arthur* is nicely laid out with two side benches forward and a steering wheel on center as well as lever steering alongside the engine box. A locker under an athwartship stern seat provides access to a storage area under the after deck, while the gas tank is hidden forward under the foredeck.

The W.H. Mullins Company used wooden frames to help a metal boat like this hold its shape, as they did in their pulling boats (see 1984.175). Originally powered with engines the company subcontracted, Mullins boats by the time of this one were fitted with off-the-shelf engines. The company itself was the Mullins Body Corporation by the 1920s, with its chief product

automobile bodies (which they had started making in 1902). The company manufactured metal boats until 1939.

STATUS: Good operable condition. The current engine (a U.S. Motor Company Hercules) was installed in 1949, and a new engine box built.

DONORS: Arthur B. Dayton, Jr., and Charles B. Dayton

FURTHER READING:
Mullins catalogs for 1907, 1919, and 1926 are in the collection of the G.W. Blunt White Library at Mystic Seaport.

Speltz, Robert. *The Real Runabouts, Volume III*. Albert Lea, Minnesota: Robert Speltz, 1980.

Staff of *Motor Boat*. "Mullins Adds Motorboats." *Motor Boat*, December 25, 1904.

ACCESSION NO. 1992.106

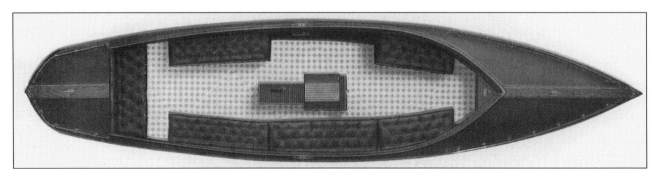

Deck and interior view of Leader launch from a Mullins catalog. (Photo: Kathleen Ramey-Gilman, Mystic Seaport 2000-11-9)

Spray
RUNABOUT
BY LAUDER AND DENNING
22' 0" x 5' 6"   1928

In 1927, George Lauder, then a senior in high school, decided he needed a boat that rode easier at speed than his family's 22' Chris-Craft. Accordingly, he went to the Stamford, Connecticut, office of young naval architect Arthur Doane. Doane had been publishing plans in *The Rudder* since 1923, and had a line of build-it-yourself plans. Lauder chose one for an engine-

forward runabout, figuring that sitting aft of the engine would give a smoother ride than sitting in the forward cockpit of a boat like the Chris-Craft with the engine amidships. During the winter of 1927-28, Lauder built her in the shop of the New England Boat Works in Mianus, helped by Jerry Denning, one of the yard's carpenters. They lowered the chine forward for a bit more displacement to carry a bigger engine, but otherwise followed the plan. This attractive speedboat has batten-seam topsides and a straight planked bottom with mahogany planking on oak frames. Doane's design created a boat

higher, beamier, and fuller in the bow than similar 1920s speedboats. A Ford 165-hp V-8 engine replaced her original Graymarine straight 8, and with this engine she will do an easy 30 mph. *Spray* suited George Lauder, and he kept her as part of his fleet until she came to Mystic Seaport after his death.

STATUS: Good condition.
DONOR: Estate of George Lauder
FURTHER READING:
Gribbins, Joseph. "George Lauder's Nautical Garden." *Nautical Quarterly* 23, Fall, 1983.
ACCESSION NO. 1987.75.2

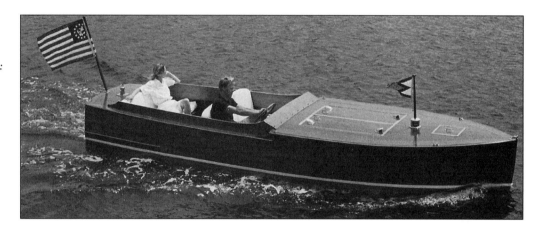

George Lauder's Spray *on the Mystic River in 1987. (Photo: Lisa Brownell,* Mystic Seaport 1987-7-37*)*

POWER DORY BY TOPPAN
21' 2" x 6' 8"   ca. 1912

Of all the many companies in the power dory business from 1905 until the fad died out around the time of World War I, Toppan Boat Mfg. Company of Boston was most prolific. "The best boat for the price in the world," they boasted. And perhaps for its type it was, made so by combining the newly-perfected small gasoline engine (Toppan

made their own) with an already popular hull that lent itself to the economies of mass-production. Hundreds of these "tomboy sorts of boats," as Malcolm MacDuffie called them, were bought by middle-class people caught up in the power craze. Only a handful of power dories survive today. Nearly all were built in Massachusetts, with Boston's Haverhill Street being the center of things.

This dory had an engine aft in a

separate compartment, which was the standard arrangement for her type.

During its heyday, the power dory was widely promoted, and anyone interested in the type would do well to look through contemporary copies of boating magazines such as *The Rudder* and *Yachting*. Sales circulars were printed by major builders which, if they can be located, yield additional information.

STATUS: Considerable repair, no engine, poor condition.
DONOR: Timothy J. McDonnell
FURTHER READING:
MacDuffie, Malcolm. "A Special Feeling For Power Dories." *National Fisherman*, March, 1971. Delightful account of power dory history by a man who remembers it.
ACCESSION NO. 1976.57

The Toppan power dory in 1978. (Photo: Maynard Bray, Mystic Seaport 1978-2-59*)*

401

POWER DORY BY CAPE COD POWER DORY COMPANY

20' 0" x 5' 6"   ca. 1907

Simply called "401" by her owner, the Pine Island Camp of Belgrade Lakes, Maine, this boat spent a 50-year working life shuttling campers, staff, and supplies. She seems to have been one of her Wareham, Massachusetts, builder's "Special Dory Launches" designed by Charles S. Gurney.

According to the later Cape Cod Shipbuilding catalog, "It is considered to be the best and safest little sea-going boat built." At Pine Island this boat was considered to be wetter than the older lapstrake power dory she replaced. Toward the end of her career, she sank with regularity despite the efforts of various non-boatbuilders to keep her going. Most Cape Cod Specials were equipped with Lathrop or Ferro engines of about 4 hp and sold for $987. This boat has a U.S. Motors Company four-stroke engine, Model V-1-K.

STATUS: Fair, much interior structure missing and many repairs.

DONOR: Penobscot Marine Museum, which received it from Eugene L. Swan, Jr., in 1968

ACCESSION NO. 1981.50

401's engine compartment in 1982. (Photo: Mary Anne Stets, Mystic Seaport 1982-2-108)

The Cape Cod power dory in 1982. (Photo: Mary Anne Stets, Mystic Seaport 1982-2-108)

POWER DORY

20' 2" x 5' 3"   pre-1907

The oval builder's plate was removed from this carvel-planked power dory sometime after she was brought to Maine's Kezar Lake in 1907, where she served to tend Sidney Peterson's camp, so there is some mystery about who built her. Her original single-cylinder engine was replaced in 1937 with a two-cylinder engine. In 1951 she was given to Bill Vinton, who installed a Wisconsin air-cooled engine of 10-12 hp. The builder was probably one of the "big four": Gerry Emmons of

Swampscott who was just finishing his career, or Cape Cod of Wareham, Atlantic of Amesbury, or Toppan of Boston. All of these builders started building power dories around 1905. This boat is nicely built, of yacht quality with natural frames, two bent frames in between the sawn ones, and largely copper-fastened.

STATUS: Good condition, minor repair.

DONOR: Vinton Family Trust via the Maine Maritime Museum

FURTHER READING:

Gardner, John. *Building Classic Small Craft*, Vol. 2. Camden, Maine: International Marine Publishing Co., 1984. A chapter in this book, "Boston Power Fishing Dories," discusses these boats.

Motor Boat, The Rudder, and *Yachting* published plans and advertisements of these builders beginning around 1905 and continuing until about World War I, when more modern launches able to handle bigger engines became more popular. Mystic Seaport has catalogs for Emmons, Atlantic, Toppan, and the Cape Cod Company.

ACCESSION NO. 1991.103

Power dory 1991.103 in 1991. (Photo: Judy Beisler, Mystic Seaport 1991.103A)

POWER DORY BY A.R. TRUE
22' 8" x 6' 2"   ca. 1920

Amesbury, Massachusetts, builder A.R. True is best known for his line of small "tabloid" sailing cruisers, primarily the True "Rocket," still in production in the 1960s. Like many boatbuilders from the North Shore of Massachusetts Bay and the bottom of the Merrimack River, he apparently got his start building dories, and in roughly 1905-06, along with other builders, began to install early gasoline engines in them. This power dory was built near the end of the popularity of the type. She was originally powered by a Hubbard engine, which was replaced with a Universal, both of which came with the boat. By the time this boat was built in roughly 1920, faster and flashier boats from Midwestern builders like Chris-Craft were about to dominate the series-built markets. Some companies such as the Cape Cod Power Dory Company of Wareham, Massachusetts, adapted by changing the product line, and so did A.R. True. True obviously saw that the demand for power dories was slowing, and that there was considerable competition in power launches. True also saw that there was a market for inexpensive pocket sailing cruisers. The Museum has one of True's later outboard-powered dory-skiffs (1996.81.1).

STATUS: Fair condition.
DONOR: Scott Nason
ACCESSION NO. 1991.24.1

The A.R. True power dory in 1991. (Photo: Maynard Bray, Mystic Seaport 1991.24.1A)

Patti Carol

SEDAN CRUISER BY CHRIS-CRAFT
HULL #S-22-341

22' 0" x 7' 5"   1952

After World War II, Chris-Craft and other powerboat builders adopted nautical versions of automotive-inspired "streamline" design. A good example is this 22' Chris-Craft Sedan Cruiser introduced in 1948. The low rounded cabin had much in common with the window-and-roof lines of postwar cars, and details such as the steering wheel were just like an automobile's. Automotive design influence would reach its peak in the 1950s when cars–and boats–grew fins. This boat was based in Norwich, Connecticut, and made an ideal Thames River cruiser. Her original 158-hp gasoline engine could drive her to 36 mph, making a short run of a trip to New London or Gales Ferry, or even out to Fisher's Island on a calm day. In 1954, the last year of this model's production, it would have cost $5,630, with something extra for the bright finish on its mahogany double-planked hull.

STATUS: Good original unrestored condition, with original engine (MCLR 302481) six-volt electrical system, and cushions.

DONORS: Walter and Irene Maciejka
FURTHER READING:
Gribbins, Joseph. *Chris-Craft–A History–1922-1942.* Marblehead, Massachusetts: Devereux Books, 2001.

Rodengen, Jeffrey L. *The Legend of Chris-Craft.* Fort Lauderdale, Florida: Write Stuff Syndicate, 1988.

Savage, Jack. *Chris-Craft.* Osceola, Wisconsin: MBI Publishing, 2000.

The principal archive of Chris-Craft records, catalogs, and photographs is at The Mariners' Museum, Newport News, Virginia.

ACCESSION NO. 1994.93

The Chris-Craft Sedan Cruiser on arrival at Mystic Seaport. (Photo: Judy Beisler, Mystic Seaport 1994.93)

Maynard Bray

WORK GARVEY FOR MYSTIC SEAPORT

19' 0" x 6' 4"   1976

Tending to outside work on the larger vessels at Mystic Seaport is best done from the water, and this garvey was built with that purpose in mind. Weather permitting, she sets out each day to wash down, pump out, and clean the other floating watercraft at the Museum. A gasoline-driven pump is part of her outfit. She is equipped with a towing bitt, has hefty fenders for coming alongside other boats without damaging them, and is heavily built for her own well-being.

STATUS: In use, excellent condition.
DONOR: Mystic Seaport-built by Willits Ansel and Keith MacArthur
ACCESSION NO. 1976.92

Shown here in 1976 with outboard power, Maynard Bray *is now driven by a Westerbeke diesel inboard. (Photo: Ken Mahler, Mystic Seaport 1976-8-99)*

Dorothy D.

MOTORIZED CONNECTICUT RIVER SHAD BOAT BY CHAMPION

17' 11" x 6' 5"   ca. 1890

This shad skiff is similar to others of her type in Mystic Seaport's collection. However, it is unclear whether she ever had a sailing rig. Her history is murky. She is alleged to have been built by a man named Champion for a man named Darling, for whose daughter she was named. She was based at the Steamboat Dock in Essex, and was bought by her donor from George B. Czikowsky. Her high bow kept her dry in the wind-against-current chop found on the Connecticut River, and an inboard engine, no longer installed, helped her work her drift nets. Some of her steam-bent frames were kerfed, uncommon in smaller craft. Her shape is graceful, and it is easy to see why she was not chopped up or burnt when her working life was over.

STATUS: Poor condition; interior missing; planking mostly original, about 50% of remaining structure original.
DONOR: Jane C. Lange, in memory of John F. Lange
ACCESSION NO. 1986.88

Dorothy D. *in 1986. (Photo: Deborah Patterson, Mystic Seaport 1986.88E)*

Analuisa on exhibit in 2000. (Photo: Judy Beisler, Mystic Seaport 2000-10-1)

Analuisa
CUBAN FISHING LAUNCH
20′ 1″ x 7′ 7″   1959

Most boats in Mystic Seaport's collection have stories to tell; but only a few have a story as dramatic as *Analuisa*'s. She was launched in 1959 by fisherman/boatbuilder Luciano Cuadras Fernández at Mariel, Cuba, as the first boat in the Cuadras and Fernández family fishery to have an engine. In August, 1994, *Analuisa* left Mariel with 19 members of the family aboard, bound for Key West and a new life in the U.S. On the second day of the passage they were taken aboard a Carnival Cruise Line ship, abandoning the 20′ *Analuisa*. In the same waters another small Mariel fishing boat, *Carmencita*, was at the mercy of the Gulf Stream with a stalled engine and four people aboard. Then a miracle happened. The *Carmencita* refugees saw *Analuisa* on the horizon, rowed to her, got aboard, started the 1-hp engine, and powered to Key West. *Analuisa* is a V-bottom launch characteristic of fishing vessels from Cuba's northwest coast. Her engine is a Russian-made copy of a Briggs and Stratton engine.

STATUS: Fair condition, on exhibit.

DONOR: The U.S. Coast Guard

FURTHER READING:
Roorda, Eric. "The Voyage of the *Analuisa.*" *The Log of Mystic Seaport*, Summer, 1997.

ACCESSION NO. 1994.130.1
Plans for 1994.130.1 are available from Mystic Seaport's Watercraft Plans Collection.

Crystal
SEA SKIFF BY VERITY
28′ 3″ x 8′ 0″   1948

The box-keel and flat-bottom structure found in the lapstrake beach boats of New Jersey and Long Island was easy to adapt to engine power. The engine could be low with the shaft run straight back. Fishing craft, pleasure yachts, and fast rumrunners were all created using the same construction method. As engines got bigger, the "keel" got wider, and eventually merged into a flat bottom at the transom, ideal for fast planing. Charles Verity of Freeport, Long Island, built this sea skiff in 1948; later owners put a raised-deck cabin on the boat. The Veritys had a great reputation for sea skiffs on Long Island; but the New Jersey builders popularized the type as pleasure boats during the 1950s and 1960s.

Crystal in storage in 1992. (Photo: Maynard Bray, Mystic Seaport 1992.8A)

STATUS: Hull only, fair condition, no equipment.

DONOR: Pat Nelson

FURTHER READING:
Guthorn, Peter J. *The Sea Bright Skiff and Other Jersey Shore Boats.* New Brunswick, New Jersey: Rutgers University Press, 1971.

Hendrickson, Ray. "Sam Verity's Skiff." *Nautical Quarterly* 18, Summer, 1982.

ACCESSION NO. 1992.8

YAWLBOAT FROM SCHOONER
Mertie B. Crowley
25′ 7″ x 7′ 11″   ca. 1907

Cargo schooners such as the six-masted *Mertie B. Crowley* almost never had auxiliary power and depended upon their yawlboats to push them around in crowded berths and keep them going in calm weather. During an offshore passage, the yawlboats were hoisted on davits, well clear of the water. The *Crowley* was one of the giant schooners launched after 1900 to carry coal to New England from ports further south, such as Newport News, Baltimore, and Philadelphia. In January of 1910, less than three years after leaving her builder's yard in Rockland, Maine, she came to grief on Wasque Shoal, near Martha's Vineyard, Massachusetts. Her yawlboat was rescued and eventually purchased by the Cromwell family who used the boat to hunt swordfish for many years. The donor took her over in 1954 and gave her to Mystic Seaport shortly thereafter. The Museum also has the nameboard and a masthead pennant from the *Crowley* in its collection.

STATUS: Restored 1961, approximately 60% original, fair condition.

DONOR: Robert S. Douglas

FURTHUR READING:

Bunting, W. H. *Portrait of a Port: Boston 1852-1914.* Cambridge, Massachusetts: The Belknap Press of Harvard University Press, 1971.

——. *Steamers, Schooners, Cutters, and Sloops.* Boston, Massachusetts: Houghton Mifflin Company, 1974.

Goold, Allen O. "Handy Motor Tenders of Commerce." *Yachting*, January, 1913.

Leavitt, John F. *Wake of the Coasters.* Middletown, Connecticut: Wesleyan University Press, 1970, and Mystic Seaport Publications, 1984.

Parker, W.J. Lewis. *The Great Coal Schooners of New England, 1870-1909.* Mystic Connecticut: The Marine Historical Association Inc., 1948.

ACCESSION NO. 1956.1137
Plans for 1956.1137 are available from Mystic Seaport's Watercraft Plans Collection.

The *Mertie B. Crowley* *yawlboat on exhibit in 1956.*
(Photo: Louis Martel, Mystic Seaport 1956.1137A*)*

Fully laden with coal, and under full sail, the Mertie B. Crowley *dwarfs the 25-foot yawlboat hoisted at her stern. (Photo: Courtesy of the Peabody Essex Museum, Salem, Massachusetts)*

POWER
Chapter Two
Outboard-Powered

Toy

OUTBOARD RACING HYDROPLANE

11' 0" x 4' 0"   1930

Outboard racing began in the mid-1920s when outboard motors were powerful enough to make a little boat plane. By the season of 1930-31 there were outboard races all over the U.S., class divisions had been created, and five manufacturers of outboard motors—Lockwood, Caille, Elto, Evinrude, and Johnson—were producing specialized racing engines. Boats were also lighter and more sophisticated single-step hydroplanes–this one with a shoe-shaped underbody forward, which carried the hull at speed on just its after edge. *Toy* had especially successful seasons in 1930 and 1931, becoming national champion in Class B (piston displacement not more than 20 cubic inches) and setting a speed record for the class of 44 mph. The 150-pound boat was designed by Ernest Way and built by the Frank Harrison Boat Yard of Essex, Connecticut, for Elliott Spencer. Spencer's Johnson racing outboard was rated for 16 hp.

STATUS: Excellent unrestored condition.

DONOR: Elliott Spencer, Jr.

FURTHER READING:

Hunn, Peter. *The Golden Age of the Racing Outboard*. Marblehead, Massachusetts: Devereux Books, 2000.

Milkofsky, Brenda. *Golden Afternoons: Yachting in the Connecticut River, 1840-1940*. Essex, Connecticut: The Connecticut River Museum, 1991.

ACCESSION NO. 1987.137.1

*Toy in 1989.
(Photo: Maynard Bray, Mystic Seaport 1983.137.1A)*

Dry Run

CLASS A/B UTILITY OUTBOARD RACING BOAT #86-N

10' 9" x 4' 2"   1956

By 1952 outboard racing had grown popular enough to warrant its own magazine, *Boat Sport*, which captured the excitement of the revitalized, postwar sport. Outboard motor builders caught up with the World War II pent-up demand for general-purpose engines and began to build special racing models. Marine and aircraft plywood was much more affordable and available than before the war. There was a boom in boat designing and building for stock outboard racing. These little boats became floating "hot-rods," a tinkerer's delight; but even in 1955 there were only about 6,000 stock-outboard racers, a small market for engine makers.

This was the second racing boat built by John Willhardt to a design by Hal Kelley. Built of Honduras mahogany plywood on sawn frames for the A/B Class, 86-N could be powered by either a 15- or 20-cubic-inch engine. Willhardt preferred Class A, with its smaller engines, using a 7.5-hp Mercury KG4H Rocket Hurricane with a Quicksilver racing lower unit (donated to the Museum with the boat), built in 1952 and tuned as much as possible within the class limits. These little engines could drive the boats well over

Dry Run *in 1989.*
(Photo: Maynard
Bray, Mystic Seaport
1989.33.1A)

40 mph in competition. Willhardt raced the boat frequently in the New York-New Jersey area, winning 34 trophies, including a first in the Manhattan Marathon, twice around Manhattan Island.

Outboard racing in single-hull runabouts and sponson-supported hydroplanes still has a loyal but limited following, with perhaps a thousand American Powerboat Association licensed racers. The boats are generally home-built wooden boats, "grass-roots" racing at its best.

STATUS: Excellent unrestored condition, with two engines, parts, and trophies.

DONOR: John A. Willhardt

FURTHER READING:

Bowman, Hank Wieand. *The Encyclopedia of Outboard Motor Boating.* New York: A.S. Barnes and Co., 1955.

Gribbins, Joseph. "Stock Outboards–Simple, Sophisticated." *Nautical Quarterly* 17, Spring, 1982.

Hunn, Peter. *The Old Outboard Book.* Camden, Maine: International Marine Publishing Co., 1991.

——. *The Golden Age of the Racing Outboard.* Marblehead, Massachusetts: Devereux Books, 2000.

Spectre, Peter H. "Float Like a Butterfly, Sting Like a Bee: A Weekend of Grass-roots Outboard Speedboat Racing." *Woodenboat* 80, Jan/Feb, 1988.

ACCESSION NO. 1989.33.1

Mr. Willhardt also donated the Hal Kelley plan for this boat, which is in Mystic Seaport's Watercraft Plans Collection.

With the donor at the wheel of his first Kelley design, Class A/B Utility Outboard 2-N competes at the Delaware Water Gap in the 1950s. (Courtesy John A. Willhardt, Mystic Seaport 1989-6-107)

HICKMAN SEA SLED FOR OUTBOARD MOTOR

13′ 2″ x 4′ 1″   ca. 1925

Sea Sleds were the invention of Albert Hickman, and with their boxlike planing hulls were not unlike the Boston Whalers of today. They were mass-produced in sizes ranging from 13′ outboard tenders to high-powered inboards of 32′. Hickman also produced custom Sea Sleds for military use and for service as water taxis for 1920s Florida hotels. They were well made and beautifully finished, becoming one of the many coveted "toys" of the wealthy in those halcyon days before the Great Depression. At one time there were two large production plants in southeastern Connecticut, one in Groton and one in West Mystic at the present site of Mystic Shipyard, Inc.

Although the company "failed up" a few years after the crash of 1929, it is surprising that there are not more survivors from the many boats produced. A number of pieces of hardware, some photos, and salesmens' brochures were left behind when the plants closed, and most of this material has been donated to Mystic Seaport. The sales literature makes much of Hickman's "surface propellers," which at rest were partly above the water, but when underway drove the hulls with unusual efficiency, much like Howard Arnesen's contemporary surface-drive systems. These inboard Sea Sleds were fast: a 26-footer powered with two 200-hp Hall-Scott engines was guaranteed to do 45 mph and had an advertised top speed of 50 mph. Early in their development, the Sea Sled people furnished a 55-footer with four engines to the U.S. Navy, which used it as a take-off platform; it ran along at over 50 mph with a 10,000-pound bomber aboard ready to take to the air.

STATUS: Original, poor condition.

DONOR: Edwin Pugsley

FURTHER READING FOR 1965.393, 1984.108, AND 1984.56:

"Launching Airplanes From Motor Craft." *Motor Boating*, July, 1919.

Feature article, *The* (New London) *Day*, September 16, 1972.

Seidman, David. "Damned by Faint Praise: The Life and Hard Times of Albert Hickman." *WoodenBoat* 100, May/June, 1991.

Speltz, Robert. *The Real Runabouts*, Vols. III, IV. Albert Lea, Minnesota: Robert Speltz, 1980, 1982.

ACCESSION NO. 1965.393

Sea Sleds underway. The 13′ outboard model in the foreground is similar to 1965.393.
(Photo: Edwin Levick, courtesy of J.R. Hellier, Mystic Seaport 1975.273.117)

HICKMAN SEA SLED
MODEL 13

13' 2" x 3' 8"   ca. 1925

The 13' Sea Sleds were the Hickman Company's smallest model. This one has had some repairs but came with equipment such as cushions (needed to help make the ride more comfortable) and oarlocks (useful when the motor was stubborn). This craft was built shortly after the West Mystic plant opened in 1925, and was little used during her first 30 years. In the mid-1950s she went to Fortune Rocks in Maine where, powered by a 15-hp engine, she was found to ride hard in open water. This was before the commonly accepted stable-but-punishing ride of the Sea Sled's descendent, the Boston Whaler. During production, the 13' Sea Sled could be had for as little as $150. Some were used for racing, and in 1928 a Model 13 won in stock outboard races on courses ranging from 35 miles around Staten Island to a 260-mile marathon from New York to Boston. One of the Model 13s was the only boat to finish of 38 starters in that year's Catalina Ocean Sweepstakes in California. The Hickman plants in West Mystic and Groton built over 6,000 boats while in operation from 1925 to 1934.

STATUS: Good, various repairs and reinforcements.
DONOR: S.M. Rust, Jr.
FURTHER READING:
(Same as for 1965.393)
ACCESSION NO. 1984.108

13' Hickman Sea Sled 1984.108. (Photo: Mystic Seaport 1984.108B)

HICKMAN SEA SLED,
MODEL 16

15' 11" x 4' 7"   1929

This largest of the outboard-motor Sea Sleds had the same inverted-V hull shape that Hickman had patented in 1914. When running, air confined under the hull caused it to lift slightly and increase its speed over a conventional V-bottom or flat-bottom planing hull for a given amount of power. Non-tripping chines were also a feature. The ride, while hard, was much softer than that of other planing hulls of the era, and in fact was not improved on until the high-power, deep-V's originated by Ray Hunt came out in 1957. A year later Hunt designed the Boston Whaler as a modification of the Sea Sled. At 340 pounds, this Model 16 Sea Sled was rated to handle the largest outboards then available: motors like the 32-hp Johnson YR-45. When

The Model 16 Hickman Sea Sled, showing the inverted-V hull shape. (Photo: Mary Anne Stets, Mystic Seaport 1984.56)

purchased in 1929, this boat was fitted with a Johnson V-45, rated for 26 hp. This Sea Sled was bought as a college graduation gift for Richard Keppler and was used on Schroon Lake in the Adirondacks, where, in 1972, she was found by the donor and restored.

STATUS: Excellent, restored; missing some cushions.

DONOR: Edgar S. Lawrence

FURTHER READING: (Same as for 1965.393)

ACCESSION NO. 1984.56

As the largest outboard-powered Sea Sled, the Model 16 had two cockpits. (Photo: Maynard Bray, Mystic Seaport 1984.56A)

OUTBOARD MOTORBOAT BY EVINRUDE MOTOR COMPANY
MODEL X1B, SERIAL #3308
16' 0" x 4' 0"   ca. 1916

To provide boats suitable for its "Detachable Row Boat Motor," the Evinrude Motor Company began building boats sometime after Ole Evinrude sold his share to his partner in 1913. Evinrude boats were built from about 1915 into the 1920s, by which time there were plenty of other builders providing boats suitable for outboards. The 62 pounds of motor,

together with the operator, in the stern of a fine-lined rowboat of that era would make the boat squat considerably unless there was a passenger in the bow. In the design of this boat, however, the stern has been widened and strengthened, and the bottom has been flattened, all changes that were precursors of features on today's outboard skiffs. This example, a fancy round-bottom Sea Pup model, sold for $80 in 1916. Its engine, of 2- to 4-hp, would be sold separately. Although a sister craft made the run from New York to Boston in 52 hours, this particular boat led a quieter life on

New Hampshire's rivers and lakes, where it was in use up to 1956.

STATUS: Good structural condition, some wear and cosmetically poor.

DONOR: Leon Cote, Jr., and Celia Dingee, in memory of Leon Cote, Sr.

FURTHER READING:

Hunn, Peter. *The Old Outboard Book.* Camden, Maine: International Marine Publishing Co., 1991.

Rodengen, Jeffrey. *Evinrude, Johnson, and the Legend of OMC.* Fort Lauderdale, Florida: Write Stuff Syndicate, 1993.

ACCESSION NO. 1984.59

The Evinrude outboard motorboat in 1984. (Photo: Judy Beisler, Mystic Seaport 1984.59B)

THOMPSON SEA SKIFF SPECIAL

14' 0" x 5' 4"   1955

In 1955 Warren Rubery bought this Thompson Sea Skiff Special for $480 from Apponaug Marine Supply in Rhode Island and powered it with a Johnson Fastwin 15-hp engine. It was a quality-conscious choice. Thompson Boats of Peshtigo, Wisconsin, had been in business since 1904 and had built a quarter of a million boats. Warren's boat was one of 258,000 outboard boats sold in 1955 into a recreational fleet that numbered around five million. The fleet is now well over 12 million, thanks to the introduction of fiberglass. A fiberglass Thompson was available in 1955, but it was the builder's first year with the material, and the boat–a tail-finned Starfire "playboat"–wasn't very practical.

The Thompson family rode the 1920s boom in recreational small craft. Beginning by building flat-bottom skiffs and wood-canvas canoes as something to do in the winter on their farm, they initially sold to resort owners in the Wisconsin Lakes region. By 1920 canoes were still important, but outboard motor boats were beginning to dominate their production. Seven years later, they set up an additional factory in New York and added racing outboards to their line, also offering trailers and a choice of outboard motors. During the wooden days, their construction methods varied by model: canvas-covered, cedar-strip, and lapstrake hulls like this boat were all part of the line. The company set the standard for the outboard industry.

STATUS: Excellent restored condition.
DONOR: Warren E. Rubery
FURTHER READING:
Speltz, Robert. *The Real Runabouts*, Vol. IV. Albert Lea, Minnesota: Robert Speltz, 1982.
ACCESSION NO. 1988.80

The Thompson Sea Skiff Special in 1988. (Photo: Maynard Bray, Mystic Seaport 1988.80A)

The outboard work garvey in storage in 1984. (Photo: Maynard Bray,
Mystic Seaport 1984.153A)

WORK GARVEY FOR OUTBOARD BY BOYCE

14' 10" x 4' 3"   1951

The shapely scows called garveys developed as sailing craft in the New Jersey bays as early as 1750, shifting to power in the 1900s. With an upswept bow, hard chine, and wide bottom for carrying a load on a shallow draft, they were well suited for fishing, clamming, oystering, and gunning in the bays and marshes inside the barrier beaches from New Jersey to Chesapeake Bay. Harry

OUTBOARD DORY-SKIFF BY A.R. TRUE

14' 1" x 4' 8"

Boatbuilder A.R. True of Amesbury, Massachusetts, widened the traditional dory-skiff to accept an outboard motor. This postwar example would have been pushed by a motor of 5 hp or less. By the time she was built, dory clips to hold the bottom to a boat's sawn frames were widely used. Her stern-seat arrange-ment, with seats in each corner, was clearly set up with the knowledge that the driver would sit to one side of the outboard while steering with the tiller arm. The transom was also more vertical than in True's earlier dory-skiffs, and the bottom was wider. The owner built up the transom to take an upside-down rolling rig for moving the boat on land, which meant that he needed to use a long-shaft outboard.

STATUS: Good, used condition.
DONOR: R. Patricia Schoppe
ACCESSION NO. 1996.81.1

The A.R. True dory-skiff for outboard power. (Photo: Judy Beisler, Mystic Seaport 1996.81.1G)

B. Boyce of Longport and Pleasantville, New Jersey, built this garvey for his daughter in 1951. Born in 1880, Boyce was a bayman, hunter, and decoy carver who built garveys and sneakboxes for his boat-rental business. Since he worked in the boat shop at the Philadelphia Navy Yard during both world wars, he knew what he was doing, and this cedar-planked garvey, with a transom notched for an outboard motor, is a nice example of this regional type.

STATUS: Good condition, loose thwarts and skeg.

DONOR: Harry McConnell

FURTHER READING:

Chapelle, Howard E. *American Small Sailing Craft*. New York: W.W. Norton & Co., 1951.

——. "Some American Fishing Launches." *Fishing Boats of the World*, Part 1, Jan-Olof Traung, ed. London: Fishing News (Books) Ltd., 1955.

Gardner, John. *Building Classic Small Craft*. Camden, Maine: International Marine Publishing Co., 1984, 1997.

ACCESSION NO. 1984.153

J & D (ex-Jim and Debbie)

OUTBOARD MOTOR LAUNCH BY STEPHENS

19' x 6"   1985

The 19' outboard motor launch *J & D* was designed and built by Robert Stephens in 1985. A naval architect, Mr. Stephens is an alumnus of the Williams College-Mystic Seaport undergraduate maritime studies program. The vessel serves as a workboat and research platform for students in the program's marine science classes. Construction was funded by Williams-Mystic alumni. *J & D* is a hard-chine design, built of fir marine plywood on white oak keel and frame. This boat is powered by a 25-hp outboard motor.

STATUS: Good condition, in the water each year.

DONOR: Museum purchase (Williams College-Mystic Seaport Program Alumni Fund)

Ben Fuller and Sharon Brown aboard the launch J & D *in the Mystic River. (Photo: Claire White-Peterson, Mystic Seaport 1998-6-303)*

Elwood

OUTBOARD SKIFF BY WILLITS ANSEL

14′ 2″ x 5′ 2″   1981

When Mystic Seaport's shipyard work skiff *Ram* (1972.326) wore out, shipwright Willits Ansel built this near-reproduction. Like the original, she is cross-planked on the bottom with three planks making up each of the sides. She's been strengthened in the way of the thwarts to better resist being pinched between ships and wharves or floats, and is sheathed with sheet copper along her waterline to keep from being cut by the winter's skim ice, an old Chesapeake waterman's trick. She's named for veteran Mystic Seaport shipwright Elwood Bogue. She proved her worth year-round as the principal small boat in use during several winters spent constructing the granite seawall that borders the Museum's waterfront.

STATUS: Excellent, in use.
DONOR: Mystic Seaport-built reproduction
ACCESSION NO. 1981.158

Elwood is a near-reproduction of the work skiff Ram, *shown here in the 1970s. (Photo: Ken Mahler,* Mystic Seaport 1972.326)

Bob Allyn

WORK SKIFF FOR OUTBOARD MOTOR

14′ 6″ x 5′ 0″   1986

Shipwrights Willits Ansel and David Snediker took the basic measurements off Mystic Seaport's Noank-built outboard skiff *Ram* (1972.326) and built another one a few years after *Elwood* (above). They stiffened her up a little and put sheet copper around her waterline so she could work in the light ice common on the Mystic River in winter. Comparing her shape to the various cross-planked rowing skiffs in the collection, it is easy to see how these boats were adapted to outboard power by increasing their beam a foot and taking most of the rocker out of the stern. This plain, rugged skiff does her work year-round on the Museum's waterfront.

STATUS: Excellent condition, in use.
DONOR: Mystic Seaport-built reproduction
ACCESSION NO. 1986.78

Builder Willits Ansel starts the motor while naval architect Bob Allyn prepares for a ride in his namesake boat. (Photo: Nancy d'Estang, Mystic Seaport 1986-11-204)

POWER
Chapter Three
Larger Vessels

Sabino (ex-Tourist)

PASSENGER STEAMBOAT
OFFICIAL NO. 205213

57' 1" x 23' 0"   1908

When W. Irving Adams launched her from his shipyard in East Boothbay, Maine, *Tourist* was one of countless coastal steamers; today she is one of the last coal-fired passenger steamers in operation in the U.S. Each summer Mystic Seaport visitors may ride her, see her compound steam engine work (still the original), and watch her engineer fire the boiler and respond to bell signals from the captain, who has neither throttle nor shift lever in his pilothouse. Over the years her appearance has changed, due mainly to a larger upper deck and canopy, sponsons (watertight chambers on each side of her hull to make it more stable),

and a wider deckhouse. *Sabino,* as she was renamed in 1921, spent most of her life in Maine running on the Damariscotta River (1908-19), the Kennebec River (1922-27), and Casco Bay (1927-61). When sold by Casco Bay Lines for $500 in 1961, she was quite run down and her new owners worked six years refurbishing her for operation on the Merrimac River. That was still her route when Mystic Seaport acquired her in 1973. The *Sabino* was declared a National Historic Landmark in 1992.

STATUS: In use, considerable alteration and rebuilding, including new bottom planking in 1976 and a new deck and hull framing in 1978, original Paine engine rebuilt in 1991, good condition.

DONOR: Purchased for Mystic Seaport by John and Jean Deupree

FURTHER READING:

Dunn, William W. *Casco Bay Steamboat Album.* Camden, Maine: Down East Enterprise, Inc., 1969.

King, George III. *A Steamboat Named Sabino.* Mystic, Connecticut: Mystic Seaport Publications, 1999.

Lang, Constance Rowe. *Kennebec–Boothbay Harbor Steamboat Album.* Camden, Maine: Down East Enterprise, Inc., 1971.

Millinger, Jim. "The Steamer *Sabino* on Casco Bay, 1927-1961." *The Log of Mystic Seaport,* Autumn, 1995.

Perkins, James E. and Jane Stevens. *One Man's World, Popham Beach, Maine.* Freeport, Maine: The Bond Wheelwright Company, 1974.

Richardson, John M. *Steamboat Lore of the Penobscot.* Augusta, Maine: Kennebec Journal Print Shop, 1941.

Ryan, Allie. *Penobscot, Mount Desert and Eastport Steamboat Album.* Camden, Maine: Down East Enterprise, Inc. 1972.

ACCESSION NO. 1973.187

The Sabino *makes hourly trips, carrying passengers along the Museum's waterfront, from spring to fall. (Photo: Nancy d'Estang, Mystic Seaport 1992-9-276)*

As shown in this postcard view at Damariscotta, Maine, ca. 1908, the boat's original configuration as Tourist *was narrow and largely open. (Photo: Courtesy of John L. Lockhead Collection, Steamship Historical Society,* Mystic Seaport 1994-11-20*)*

The sponsors, added in 1927-28 to make the Sabino's hull wider and more stable, are clearly visible in this bow-on view. (Photo: Ken Mahler, Mystic Seaport 1980-9-284)

In this configuration, the Sabino operated on the Kennebec River between Bath and Popham Beach from 1922 to 1927. (Photo: W.H. Ballard Collection, courtesy of Diane Ballard Michael)

With a good number of passengers, the Sabino *backs out of her berth at Portland for a run on Casco Bay in the 1950s. (Photo: Jim Giblin,* Mystic Seaport 1991-12-226*)*

Kingston II

HARBOR TUG
OFFICIAL NO. 236134

44' 1" x 13' 9"   1937

Kingston II is thought to be one of the earliest all-welded vessels. Designed by Electric Boat's yard manager E.B. Wheeler and naval architect Robert C. Simpson, she was built by apprentice welders using scrap steel. What they learned on her was put to good use in constructing U.S. Navy submarines. For more than 40 years she attended at launchings and guided submarines into and out of their berths at the Electric Boat plant in Groton, Connecticut.

Life changed dramatically for this steel-hulled tug when she arrived at Mystic Seaport in 1980, a gift from General Dynamics Corp. Her new role–more leisurely, perhaps, but no less exacting–was to move the Museum's larger historic vessels around. She also was to play a vital role in the dock-building operation that completely re-bulkheaded Mystic Seaport's waterfront in granite. In other waterfront work, *Kingston*, made up tightly to one end of the crane-carrying barge *Gingerly*, moves the rig from one location to another. And sometimes during the boating season one can find *Kingston* on the starting line of a race, patrolling Mystic Seaport's annual Antique and Classic Boat Rendezvous, or escorting a deep-draft visiting vessel like the Danish training ship *Georg Stage* upriver or down. Power is a big GM 12V-71 diesel, and although General Dynamics submarines may have dwarfed *Kingston* in her previous role, she has come to better terms with scale here in semi-retirement.

Sitting on the Museum's lift dock, Kingston II *shows off the shape of her welded steel hull. (Photo: Nancy d'Estang,* Mystic Seaport 1990-10-96*)*

Kingston II, *working along the Mystic Seaport waterfront. (Photo: Ken Mahler,* Mystic Seaport 1979-5-79*)*

Doing the work she was designed for, Kingston II *maneuvers a nuclear submarine in the 1970s. (Photo: Courtesy General Dynamics,* Mystic Seaport 1979-10-45*)*

Roann

EASTERN-RIG DRAGGER
OFFICIAL NO. 253099

60' 1" x 16' 9"   1947

Roann is one of the last surviving examples of the fishing vessels that replaced sailing schooners like Mystic Seaport's *L.A. Dunton*. The eastern-rig draggers originated in the 1920s; indeed, Thomas McManus, who designed the *L.A. Dunton*, was influential in their development. Draggers completed the revolutionary advance from sail to engine, and from hooks to nets, in New England fishing technology. Powered by a diesel engine, and dragging a large conical fishnet called an otter trawl along the seabed, *Roann* and her crew of three could catch cod and haddock twice as fast as dorymen from a vessel like the *L.A. Dunton* could with their baited hooks. Draggers also were the first to catch large quantities of flounder.

As an "eastern-rig" vessel, *Roann* has her helm aft and her working deck amidships like schooners and like the big British-style, steam-powered steel trawlers that introduced the technology in eastern New England just after 1900. "Western-rig draggers" of Connecticut and Rhode Island, like Mystic Seaport's

Florence (1982.118), which grew out of the local fishing-sloop tradition and worked in more protected waters, had pilothouses forward and working decks aft.

Albert E. Condon (1887-1963) designed *Roann* in 1944 for Roy W. Campbell. A native of Friendship, Maine, Condon worked as a boatbuilder before taking night classes in naval architecture and becoming a draftsman and later a shipyard supervisor. In the 1940s, while

superintending the Pierce and Kilburn yard in Fairhaven, Massachusetts, Condon was a leading designer of New England fishing vessels. His plans, including *Roann*'s, are part of Mystic Seaport's Watercraft Plans Collection.

Three years after Condon completed the design, *Roann* was built by Newbert & Wallace of Thomaston, Maine, a company that built dozens of draggers and was well-known and respected for the quality and durability of its construction. Master builder

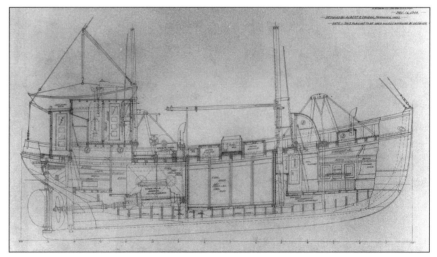

Roann's inboard profile was drawn by Albert Condon on May 16, 1944, three years before the vessel was built. Her fish hold could accommodate 55,000 pounds of iced fish. (Photo: Jennifer M. Stich, Mystic Seaport Watercraft Plans Collection, 35.22*)*

Roann underway in 1997, at the end of her fishing career. (Photo: Jennifer M. Stich, Mystic Seaport 1997-6-219)

Leroy Wallace, a protege of Condon's, opened his yard about the beginning of World War II and remained in business for 30 years.

At 60', *Roann* is on the small end of the spectrum for eastern-rig draggers, but she is a hard-working, seaworthy vessel that survived 50 years of use without major alterations. Roy Campbell of Vineyard Haven, Massachusetts, fished *Roann* from Martha's Vineyard, dragging local waters for flounder, cod, and haddock. Her second owner, the late Chet Westcott, fished *Roann* from Point Judith, Rhode Island, as did her last owner, Tom Williams, and his sons.

The eastern-rig dragger had been around for more than 20 years when *Roann* joined the fleet, and the type remained the standard New England

fishing vessel into the 1970s. Since then, however, wooden eastern-rig draggers have virtually disappeared, replaced by larger, more efficient steel-hulled stern trawlers like the one Tom Williams bought to replace *Roann*. These have their pilothouses forward and use net reels and stern ramps to fish more safely and even more productively.

STATUS: Largely original, with good documentation on repairs and alterations. Good condition.

DONOR: Mystic Seaport purchase

FURTHER READING:

Dunne, W.M.P. *Thomas F. McManus and the American Fishing Schooners: An Irish-American Success Story.* Mystic, Connecticut: Mystic Seaport Publications, 1994. See 317-22 for discussion of the early McManus draggers.

Edwards, Morry. "The Fisherman's Sea Tractor." *WoodenBoat* 79, Nov-Dec, 1987.

Finn, William. *The Dragger.* Boston: Little, Brown, 1970.

German, Andrew W. "Otter Trawling Comes to America: The Bay State Fishing Company, 1905-1938." *The American Neptune,* Spring, 1984.

Ludwig, Leslie G. "*Roann.*" *The Log of Mystic Seaport,* Autumn, 1997.

Matteson, George. *Draggermen: Fishing on Georges Bank.* New York: Four Winds Press, 1979.

Symonds, Ralph F. and Henry O. Trowbridge. "The Development of Beam Trawling in the North Atlantic." *Transactions of the Society of Naval Architects and Marine Engineers,* 1947.

ACCESSION NO. 1997.137.1

Plans for 1997.137.1 are available in the Albert E. Condon Collection, catalog no. 35.22, in Mystic Seaport's Watercraft Plans Collection.

First owner Roy W. Campbell and his first wife Annie pose at Roann's *bow just before her launch at the Newbert & Wallace yard in 1947. The vessel's name is derived from their names. (Photo: courtesy of Rod Cook,* Mystic Seaport 1998-4-94)

Tom Williams (at the trawl winch) and his son Tom handle the otter trawl during Roann's *last day of fishing in May, 1997. (Photo: Mary Anne Stets,* Mystic Seaport 1997-6-55A)

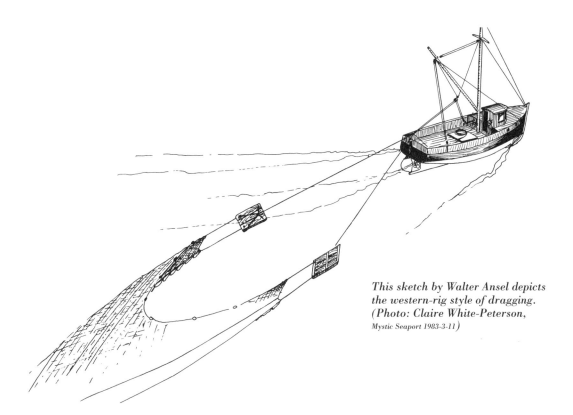

*This sketch by Walter Ansel depicts
the western-rig style of dragging.
(Photo: Claire White-Peterson,*
Mystic Seaport 1983-3-11*)*

Florence

WESTERN-RIG DRAGGER
BY POST
OFFICIAL NO. 225298

39′ 8″ x 12′ 10″   1926

When a boat is restored as carefully as
was *Florence*, the files soon fill up with
all kinds of information as her history
becomes known. Fortunately, *Florence* is
of recent enough build so that there were
many people familiar with the boat and
eager to contribute to this store of
information. And because *Florence* was
locally built and used, research was
convenient. As a "western-rig" dragger,
with pilothouse forward and working
deck aft, she's a powered descendant of
the fishing sloops and catboats of
southern New England.

The Franklin G. Post yard, located
less than a mile downriver from Mystic
Seaport, built *Florence* for Morris
Thompson, a brother of artist and writer
(and draggerman as well) Ellery
Thompson. Post turned out yachts as
well as working craft, but draggers were
always one of the yard's standard
offerings. The two-foot-longer *Betzy C.*,
for example, was built over the same

molds as *Florence*. For more than half a
century, *Florence* dragged for flounder,
hunted swordfish, and sometimes chased
mackerel–the roles for which Post had

built her–and, afterwards, harvested
quahogs by water-jet dredging. She wore
out several engines. Her first one,
logically, was a 6-cylinder Lathrop gas

Florence *looked like this when the Museum acquired her in 1982. (Photo: Claire
White-Peterson,* Mystic Seaport 1983-8-2*)*

315

engine of 65 hp. (The Lathrop Engine Co. shops were a stone's throw away on the opposite side of the Mystic highway bridge from the Post yard.) She received her present engine–a Gray Marine 6-71 diesel–during the extensive rebuilding made necessary by damage from the 1954 hurricane. Overhauled as part of the restoration, and reinstalled until a proper Lathrop turns up, the 6-71 remains with *Florence* and powered her from Mystic Seaport to nearby Stonington to help celebrate the 1992 blessing of that town's fishing fleet as well as her own restoration.

STATUS: Restored, good condition.
DONOR: Mystic Seaport purchase
FURTHER READING:
Ansel, Walter. "The Dragger *Florence*." *The Log of Mystic Seaport*, Winter, 1985.
Thompson, Ellery. *Draggerman's Haul.* New York: Viking Press, 1950.
ACCESSION NO. 1982.118

Rigged for swordfishing with a topmast and pulpit, Florence was photographed at Newport in 1937. (Photo: Courtesy of Karsten Kristianson, Mystic Seaport 1989-9-6)

Rafted alongside the Emma C. Berry, *her local antecedent, a restored* Florence *displays her original configuration, with pilothouse to starboard. (Photo: Nancy d'Estang,* Mystic Seaport 1996-6-65)

Barracuda, (ex-*Zan Tee*)
MOTORSAILER BY HOLMES
34' 3" x 8' 0"   1911

In 1932, Walter M. "Doc" Swazey pulled *Barracuda* into his Falmouth Harbor, Massachusetts, boathouse declaring that he would not relaunch her until Franklin Delano Roosevelt was out of the White House. (Yankees took politics seriously in those days.) Doc had spotted the boat under construction in 1911 at the Holmes Motor Company in West Mystic, Connecticut, but she was under contract to author Booth Tarkington, who named her *Zan Tee* after his wife Suzannah. The boat was rigged to carry either a Marconi or gaff main, but the sails saw little use. Booth Tarkington used her from his Kennebunkport, Maine, summer home. Doc Swazey kept track of the boat and in 1920 found Tarkington willing to sell after he had been beaten in a race. Doc had a faster boat built for Tarkington and traded that to him along with

$1,000 for *Zan Tee*, which he renamed *Barracuda*, in 1922. Doc used her up and down the coast, wearing out the original engine, replacing it with a Kermath V-8. When Howard Williams got the boathouse and boat in the early

1970s *Barracuda* was still in good shape, her only problem being the rusted-out engine, which he removed. When the boat was given to Mystic Seaport, it was relaunched amid considerable fear of sinking. With

Barracuda emerges from her boathouse, on her way to Mystic Seaport in 1988. (Photo: Nancy d'Estang, Mystic Seaport 1988-6-280)

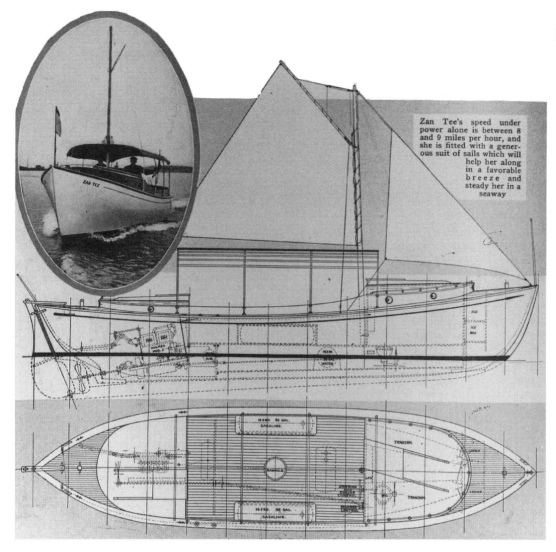

Zan Tee's speed under power alone is between 8 and 9 miles per hour, and she is fitted with a generous suit of sails which will help her along in a favorable breeze and steady her in a seaway

Barracuda, as depicted in the January 1916 issued of Motor Boating, *when she was still owned by Booth Tarkington and named* Zan Tee.

pumps standing by, it was towed across the harbor. *Barracuda* leaked about a gallon.

West Mystic's Holmes Motor Company shifted into small motorboat building in 1903 (changing its name from the Holmes Shipbuilding Company). By 1911 the yard was well-known for motor lifeboats built for the U.S. Life-Saving Service, and had adapted that design to create a line of economical seaworthy powerboats. In 1915 they were advertising these as Holmes Life Boat Cruisers, just prior to the retirement of manager and designer Charles D. Holmes and the dissolution of the company. The Holmes Company prided itself on its line of unique "get-at-able" engines–four-stroke engines with open crankcases that looked like steam engines.

STATUS: Good, unrestored condition.

DONOR: James G. DiCostanzo

FURTHER READING:

Bray, Maynard, and Paul Lipke. "Selective Documentation: A Guide to Quick Measuring." In Lipke, Paul, Peter Spectre, and Benjamin A.G. Fuller, eds. *Boats: A Manual for Their Documentation.* Nashville, Tennessee: American Association for State and Local History, and Mystic, Connecticut: Museum Small Craft Association, 1993. This boat is used as an example and has notebook information and photo details.

ACCESSION NO. 1988.82

Barracuda in 1988. (Photo: Claire White-Peterson, Mystic Seaport 1988-6-208*)*

Wallace B.

NOANK LOBSTER BOAT BY WHITTAKER

34' 3" x 11' 0"   1953

This Noank-style lobster boat was built towards the end of the era when these boats were built in Noank by Robert Whittaker. He learned his trade from Webster Eldredge, starting in 1927, at Eldredge's shop at the foot of Spring Street in Noank, and took over the shop after Eldredge died in 1942. There he worked, building his last boat, a sharpie, in the mid-1990s. The shop's location allowed an unusual launching method: shoving a boat off a platform over the water at high tide. *Wallace B.* was built at another shop on the west side of Noank, as the Spring Street shop wasn't rebuilt after the Hurricane of 1938. The boat's owners, Raymond and Wallace Chapman, Jr., named her for

their father and fished her out of Baker's Cove, Groton, setting traps for lobster in summer, hook-and-lining for blackfish in fall. A bit bigger than *Star* (1976.231)–the sportfishing version of this type–*Wallace B.* was in use into the 1990s. Her original small shelter cabin, on the starboard side, was replaced by a full-width shelter cabin in the 1960s by Seaport Marine. Like *Star*, she has a wet well into which the self-bailing cockpit can drain in addition to draining into freeing ports in her sides. Her 6-cylinder Lathrop was replaced by a Model M265 International 150-hp engine built by Palmer. In Noank lobster-boat style, the rudder is transom-hung.

STATUS: Poor condition, deck shelter cabin removed by donor in 1992.

DONOR: Paul Bates

FURTHER READING:
Stubing, Paul, with Maynard Bray and Meg Maiden. "From Sail to Power: The Evolution of the Noank Lobsterboat." *WoodenBoat* 69, Mar/Apr, 1986.

ACCESSION NO. 1993.23

Wallace B. arrives at Mystic Seaport in 1993. (Photo: Peter Fix, Mystic Seaport 1993 1 18)

Star

NOANK FISH AND LOBSTER BOAT
OFFICIAL NO. 260030

34' 0" x 10' 8"   1950

Star was built as a swordfish and tuna boat by Robert Whittaker in Webster Eldredge's shop in Noank, Connecticut. She was modeled by Eldredge to be like most of the contemporary boats from that area, many of which fished from Block Island, Point Judith, Greenport, Fishers Island, and other ports near to Noank. *Star* was Capt. Jack Wilbur's boat from when new until he sold her to Jim Giblin in 1969. She still has her original wet well and Lathrop LH-6 engine, and is now used as a workboat on Mystic Seaport's waterfront. The building molds for *Star* and several similar Webb Eldredge boats are in Mystic Seaport's collection.

Star in 1976. (Photo: Ken Mahler, Mystic Seaport 1976.231)

STATUS: The basic boat is largely original, but there have been changes to her top-hamper; for example, her swordfishing pulpit and lookout mast have been removed. Good condition.

DONOR: Mystic Seaport purchase
FURTHER READING:
Thompson, Ellery. *Draggerman's Haul.* New York: Viking Press, 1950.

ACCESSION NO. 1976.231

Mactan

RUMRUNNER

31' 4" x 9' 2"   1919

In the years between the wars, fast powerboats were much narrower than those we see today. Great attention was given to making them as light as possible, yet still able to handle the much heavier engines of the era. This boat has light steam-bent frames and copper-riveted planking, an arc-shaped "hogging girder" on each side to help hold her shape, and heavy engine beds capable of supporting an engine such as the big Liberty surplus aircraft engine of World War I. The hull is semi-displacement, with hard bilges and a narrow flat bottom aft, tapering forward. *Mactan* was built by Ryder and Leiblen at Great Eastern Boatworks, Long Island, for rumrunning in 1919, or so the story goes. She looks a lot like the later rumrunners, but the real business did not get started until later in the 1920s, when well-known designers and builders such as William Hand, William Deed, Walter McInnis, and Fred

Lawley were building "express freight" boats or "fast fishermen" whose business was delivering alcoholic refreshment from schooners and other large vessels anchored beyond the three-mile limit.

STATUS: Hull only, fair condition, engine and gear removed.
DONOR: Pat Nelson

FURTHER READING:
Fostle, D.W. *Speedboat.* Mystic, Connecticut: Mystic Seaport Stores, 1988. Plans of the Lawley 36' launch illustrated in *Speedboat* are very similar to *Mactan.*

Gribbins, Joseph. "Rumboats." *Nautical Quarterly* 3, Spring, 1978.

Willoughby, Malcolm. *Rum War at Sea.* Washington, D.C.: U.S. Government Printing Office, 1964.

ACCESSION NO. 1991.182

Mactan in storage. (Photo: Maynard Bray, Mystic Seaport 1991.182A)

CANOES
Chapter One
Paddling Canoes

Sailing canoes and double-paddle decked canoes fill the Hudson River in this Milton Burns illustration, "Spring Meeting of the Hudson River Canoe Clubs," from Harper's Weekly, June 13, 1885. (Mystic Seaport 1976.184)

Canoes:
From Work to Pleasure

Summer vacations, the privilege of the few in 1870, had reached the clerks by 1900.–Samuel Eliot Morison, *The Oxford History of the American People.*

When Europeans arrived in North America, they found a thriving Native American culture of skin, dugout, and bark working boats. Perfected over centuries of local use, these watercraft survived among the native cultures and were adapted, first for work, then for pleasure, by Euro-Americans.

With the increase in leisure for urban Americans, it didn't take long for journalists, advertisers, professional sportsmen, and manufacturers to promote new leisure activities. Inspired by the writings of John MacGregor, who told wonderful tales of cruising inland and coastal Europe and the Middle East in his lightweight Rob Roy traveling canoes, many Americans joined the canoe craze. Beginning in the 1870s, and pursued in boats that imitated the fine-lined skin boats of the Inuit and the dugouts and bark canoes of Native Americans, canoeing ranged from Sunday-afternoon interludes on nearby rivers and ponds to long cruises through the wilderness.

The competitive American spirit, coupled with the era's propensity for "joining," soon saw widespread formal canoe racing under sail and paddle sponsored by newly organized clubs, which the American Canoe Association unified into a national association. Racing and cruising paralleled each other in refinement of boats and gear with sliding seats, "Radix" centerboards, cam cleats, cockpit tents, and further development of what became "the poor man's yacht." In magazines such as *Forest and Stream* and in books like W.P. Stephens's *Canoe and Boat Building*, canoe chroniclers

expounded at length. Interest in these boats led to an interest in small cruising yachts that could be sailed by the owner without crew and captain.

While the canoe fad lasted, essentially up through the 1930s, hundreds of skilled builders in dozens of shops like J. Henry Rushton's in Canton, New York, were at work fashioning these delicate little boats. From Northern New York came the all-wood lapstrake canoe. In the Peterborough area of Ontario, Canada, builders invented batten-seam and strip-built canoe methods using local Indian dugouts as a form. By 1900, with the diversion of a craze for bicycling and increasing competition from less-expensive canvas-covered Indian-type canoes developed in Maine's Penobscot River valley, the age of exquisitely crafted, cedar-planked decked canoes with their piano-like finishes came to a close. In the new century, the canvas-covered wood canoe, built by shops using efficient series-production, became the canoe of choice.

These single-paddle, Indian-type open canoes, made of canvas-covered wood, were the first truly successful high-volume, mass-market boats. After World War II, canoes made of new materials—aluminum, fiberglass, and polyethylene—gained ground each year, bring boating to tens of thousands, and showing larger boatbuilders the way. The near indestructibility of these last-named materials has made widespread whitewater canoeing possible in recent years. Sailing canoes continued to be refined as well, with the sport becoming highly organized and international in scope. Equipped with sliding seats and other specialized gear, the sailing canoe is considered one of the fastest single-hull craft in the world.

The King Island qajaq (1965.903, left) and two-hole qajaq (1938.312) in 1975. (Photo: Maynard Bray, Mystic Seaport 1975-5-24)

KING ISLAND *QAJAQ*

15' 1" x 2' 4"   ca. 1890

European explorers of northern North America found a vital working boat culture among the Inuit. Their wood-frame skin boats varied according to purpose and local environment. Animal skin sewn over a wooden frame forms the hull of these craft. Decks are also skin-covered with only small one-man cockpits, so that the paddler, fitted with a waterproof jacket drawn tight over the cockpit rim, becomes almost part of his kayak. So outfitted, it is perhaps the most seaworthy boat of its size anywhere, and with a properly manipulated double paddle it can be righted after a capsize. Sealskin, waterproofed with animal oil and fat, is usually used for the covering because of its resilience and availability. This, along with the resilience of the framework itself, makes these little boats very resistant to ice damage.

This *qajaq* (kayak) came from King Island in the Bering Strait off Alaska. King Island boats are the best-made and strongest of the Bering Strait types,

according to Dr. David W. Zimmerly who identified this craft for Mystic Seaport. Its upswept bow and well-peaked decks kept it dry in the normally rough water. King Islanders hunted and traveled across the Strait in these boats, and they could carry cargo or even an additional crew member under deck or back-to-back in the cockpit. Driven with a single (*anguun*) or double-bladed (*pautik*) paddle, these boats were maneuverable and could be rolled if

needed. The type became familiar to New England whalers, who frequented the Bering Strait and Arctic Ocean from the mid-1800s. A whaleman may have brought this boat back to New England.

STATUS: Extensive repairs have been made to frame, good condition.
DONOR: Estate of Dr. Alexander Forbes
ACCESSION NO. 1965.903

Using handlines from their baidarkas, Aleuts fish for cod in this 1872 sketch by Henry Elliott, published as plate 36 in George Brown Goode's Fisheries and Fishery Industries of the United States *(1887).*

KING ISLAND TWO-HOLE *QAJAQ*

18′ 0″ x 2′ 5″   ca. 1920

Common in the Aleutians and among the Gulf of Alaska Inuit were two- and three-hole *baidarkas*, as the Russians called them. Russian fur hunters, who arrived in the middle of the eighteenth century, "industrialized" native sea otter hunting, organizing fleets of hundreds of hunters and exporting the pelts to China. Two-hole craft were commonly used, and longer boats with three holes were used to carry the nonpaddling Russians. Under this influence the style spread north to the King Islands, but only four of these craft are known to have been built. This one was brought back by a Chicago sportsman who was interested in having Old Town duplicate it.

Remarkably, three of these Bering Strait two-hole kayaks are still around. Besides this one, there is a similar boat in the Southwest Museum of Canada and one in the Mariners' Museum at Newport News, Virginia. Plans of the latter are included in Dr. Zimmerly's paper, "Kayaks: Their Design and Use." The skin coverings of these boats were removed each winter and their bare frames were stored outside, but kept high enough to be safe from damage by prowling animals. The coverings were usually renewed completely each year. Mystic Seaport has a number of kayak models in its collection, some of them very well built.

STATUS: Very good condition.

DONOR: Old Town Canoe Co.

FURTHER READING:

Adney, Edwin Tappan, and Howard I. Chapelle. *The Bark Canoes and Skin Boats of North America*. Washington, D.C.: U.S. Government Printing Office, 1964.

Arima, E.Y., ed. *Contributions to Kayak Studies*. Hull, Quebec: Canadian Museum of Civilization, Canadian Ethnological Service, No. 122, 1991. Includes a paper by John D. Heath on the King Island kayaks.

Boyne, Dan. "To Build a Baidarka." *WoodenBoat* 143, July/Aug, 1998.

Brink, Wolfgang. *The Aleutian Kayak*. Blacklick, Ohio: Ragged Mountain Press/McGraw Hill, 1995.

Dyson, George. *Baidarka*. Edmonds, Washington: Alaska Northwest Publishing Co., 1986.

Inuit Kayaks in Canada: A Review of Historical Records and Construction Based Mainly on the Canadian Museum of Civilization's Collection. Hull, Quebec: Canadian Museum of Civilization, Canadian Ethnological Service, No. 110, 1987.

"Preliminary Kayak Bibliography No. 2." (unpublished) dated September, 1975. A copy of this comprehensive work is on file in Mystic Seaport's library. Others may be obtained from the Canadian Ethnology Service, National Museum of Man, Ottawa, Canada.

Roberts, Kenneth G., and Philip Shackleton. *The Canoe: A History of the Craft from Panama to the Arctic*. Camden, Maine: International Marine Publishing Co., 1983. This is the best single-volume canoe history.

Zimmerly, David W. *Qajaq: Kayaks of Siberia and Alaska*. Juneau, Alaska: Division of State Museums, 1986.

——. "Kayaks: Their Design and Use." *Wooden Shipbuilding & Small Craft Preservation*. Washington, D.C.: The Preservation Press, 1976.

The Baidarka Historical Society of Port Moody, British Columbia, publishes occasional papers, including Lubischer, Joseph. "The Baidarka as a Living Vessel." May 1988.

ACCESSION NO. 1938.312

Natives of Cook's Inlet, Alaska, harpoon a beluga whale from their baidarka in this sketch by Henry W. Elliott, published as plate 201 in George Brown Goode's Fisheries and Fishery Industries of the United States *(1887).*

Using their baidarkas, Aleuts hunt a school of humpback whales in the Bering Sea in this sketch by Henry W. Elliott, published as plate 202 in George Brown Goode's Fisheries and Fishery Industries of the United States *(1887).*

LABRADOR KAYAK FRAME
19' 0" x 1' 10"

Much of the strength of a kayak was in its gunwales, as is indicated by this frame, which was once the property of Admiral Byrd. This kayak is in the Eastern Canadian style, most likely from Labrador, a long narrow kayak which emphasized speed more than carrying capacity.

STATUS: Bottom has been reinforced by a mounting board, mostly original, good condition.

DONOR: Mystic Seaport purchase

FURTHER READING:

Arima, E.Y., ed. *Contributions to Kayak Studies*. Hull, Quebec: Canadian Museum of Civilization, Canadian Ethnological Service, No. 122, 1991.

Inuit Kayaks in Canada: A Review of Historical Records and Construction Based Mainly on the Canadian Museum of Civilization's Collection. Hull, Quebec: Canadian Museum of Civilization,

Canadian Ethnological Service, No. 110, 1987.

"Preliminary Kayak Bibliography No. 2." (unpublished) dated September, 1975. A copy of this comprehensive work is on file in Mystic Seaport's library. Others may be obtained from the Canadian Ethnology Service, National Museum of Man, Ottawa, Canada.

Roberts, Kenneth G., and Philip Shackleton. *The Canoe: A History of the Craft from Panama to the Arctic.* Camden, Maine: International Marine Publishing Co., 1983.

ACCESSION NO. 1964.1562

Attached to a mounting board, this Labrador kayak frame shows the delicate structure of these seaworthy craft. (Photo: Maynard Bray, Mystic Seaport 1975-10-170)

UMIAK FROM DIOMEDE ISLANDS
31' 4" x 6' 7"   ca. 1930

Cross an American whaleboat with a Western Arctic umiak and this boat is the result. In it, the Inuit adopted the round, bent-frame bottom of whaleboats, which they began taking in trade from American whalers. They combined it with the best features of their own hard-chine, flat-bottom umiaks: their extreme lightness, durability, and repairability using local materials. Hundreds were built between 1880 and 1950. To donor John

Bockstoce's knowledge, only two survive. This one was used regularly in trade between Siberia and Alaska. Bockstoce bought the boat frame in 1970, covered it with skins as the Inuit did, and used the boat for coastal surveying, looking for evidence of New England whalers on the north coast of Alaska.

In 1980, Bockstoce completed his survey by bringing the boat through the Northwest Passage to Baffin Bay. This was about the twentieth known surface transit of the Northwest Passage, and the first open boat to make the trip. For this work the umiak was ideal, being

perhaps the only large boat that could be carried by six people onto the ice, or onto land, where she could be left safely to winter over until the next season.

STATUS: Good condition.

DONOR: Dr. John Bockstoce

FURTHER READING:

Bockstoce, John. "Arctic Odyssey." *National Geographic*, July, 1983.

——. *Arctic Passage.* New York: Hearst Books, 1991.

Snaith, Skip. *Umiak: An Illustrated Guide.* Eastsound, Washington: Walrose & Hyde, 1997.

ACCESSION NO. 1981.156

With its skin covering still laced on, the Umiak arrives at Mystic Seaport in 1981. (Photo: Claire White-Peterson, Mystic Seaport/1981.156)

In the design of his wooden Rob Roy canoes, John MacGregor was inspired by the native canoes and qajaqs he had seen. MacGregor used this canoe for a trip through the Shetland and Orkney Islands off Scotland in 1872. (Photo: Maynard Bray, Mystic Seaport 1975-5-179)

DECKED CANOE, ROB ROY TYPE BY SEARLE & CO.

12' 0" x 2' 4"   ca. 1872

In 1865, with a 90-pound, 15' canoe much like this, barrister, philanthropist, and adventurer John "Rob Roy" MacGregor began traveling the lakes, rivers, and canals of Europe. For this, MacGregor developed a special boat: one that could be either paddled or sailed, would survive rough seas, and yet be light and rugged enough for dragging overland. The bark canoes of Native Americans, seen in Canada in 1858, and the skin-covered kayak of the Inuit, seen

a year later in Kamchatka, were his inspiration. He took his idea to Searle & Co., Thames River boatbuilders. His series of Rob Roy canoes was the result.

The success of his creation may be measured by the many Rob Roys built following the publication of his first book, *A Thousand Miles in a Rob Roy Canoe*. For cruising, as MacGregor did it, his Rob Roy was hard to beat. Her oak bottom planks could withstand being dragged over beaches and ledges; short length kept her weight down and also allowed her to fit railroad cars and wagons for shoreside traveling. And she sailed reasonably well, her paddle being

used in lieu of a rudder and her full-length keel timber resisting leeway so that a centerboard wasn't needed. MacGregor planned the sailing rig to be far forward so as not to interfere with the pleasure of the man in the cockpit, and he made this rig small enough so it would store underneath the forward deck when not being used.

This is either MacGregor's fifth or seventh Rob Roy, used for an 1872 cruise in the Shetlands and Orkneys. She was given to the New York Canoe Club in 1920 by MacGregor's widow, through the offices of explorer and journalist Poultney Bigelow, who met the

Paddling 1,000 miles across Europe in 1865, MacGregor attracted thousands curious to see his unusual double-paddle canoe, ultimately inspiring many of them to take up the new sport of canoeing. (Illustration from MacGregor's A Thousand Miles in a Rob Roy Canoe (1866), Mystic Seaport 1972-4-35)

MacGregors before paddling down the Danube and writing about it in 1892. This boat is shorter than the 14' generally preferred by MacGregor, but light weight made her easier to hand carry at less than 75 lbs. Unlike the early Rob Roys, this one carries two masts and a rudder, and her cockpit is longer than the 32" MacGregor considered ideal in his early writings. Her framing is typical Thames: floor timbers up to the turn of the bilge, and frames that run from sheer to the garboard without attachment to keel or floors. In rough weather, protective aprons of cloth or India rubber covered the cockpit and were snugged around the torso of the paddler. This canoe's coaming has a provision for such an apron. The first Rob Roy in Australia, the *Evangelist*, was an 1877 copy of this boat.

STATUS: Refinished 1972, no paddle, seat, or rig, original, excellent condition.

DONOR: New York Canoe Club and North Shore Yacht Club

FURTHER READING:

Baden-Powell, Warrington. *Canoe Traveling*. London: Smith, Elder & Co., 1871.

Bond, Hallie E. *Boats and Boating in the Adirondacks*. Blue Mountain Lake New York: The Adirondack Museum, 1995.

Gardner, John. "Sailing Canoes Once Held Brief Place in Sun." *National Fisherman*, June, 1977.

Hoffman, Ronald C. "The History of the American Canoe Association 1880-1960." Dissertation, Springfield College, 1967.

Hodder, Edwin. *John MacGregor*. London: Hodder Brothers, 1894.

Kemp, Dixon. *A Manual of Yacht and Boat Sailing*. 6th ed. London: Horace Cox, 1888.

MacGregor, John. *A Thousand Miles in a Rob Roy Canoe*. London: Low, Marston and Co., 1866.

——. *The Rob Roy on the Baltic*. London: Low, Son and Marston, 1867.

——. *The Rob Roy on the Jordan*. London: John Murray, 1869. It is unclear how many "Rob Roys" MacGregor had built. The first trip used a 15-footer, the second a 14-footer, and the trip on the Jordan another 14-footer. This boat is in the National Maritime Museum in Greenwich, England. After the 1868-69 Jordan trip, MacGregor took two more, one in 1871 to Holland and one to the Shetland and Orkney Islands in 1872, before his marriage in 1873, when he gave up long paddling trips. Each trip required a new boat.

Schoettle, Edwin J., ed. *Sailing Craft*. New York: The MacMillan Company, 1928. Has a good chapter on the history of sailing canoes by Maurice Witt.

Stansfield-Hicks, C. *Yachts, Boats, and Canoes*. New York: Forest and Stream Publishing Co., 1888.

With a spray cloth to seal his cockpit, MacGregor challenges the Baltic in one of his Rob Roy canoes. (Illustration from MacGregor's The Rob Roy on the Baltic *(1867),* Mystic Seaport 1972-4-2*)*

Stephens, W. P. *Canoe and Boat Building*. New York: Forest and Stream Publishing Co, 1889. This book together with its pack of 50 canoe plans went through several editions after its first publication in the early 1880s.

——. *Traditions and Memories of American Yachting*. New York: Hearst Magazines, 1945, and WoodenBoat Publications, 1989.

Waters, Balch & Co. *The Annual Illustrated Catalogue and Oarsman's Manual for 1871*. Troy, New York: Waters, Balch & Co., 1871. This extensive catalog deals at length with the Rob Roy canoe as first conceived by MacGregor. This company laid up its boats out of laminations of thin paper, much the way fiberglass boats are built nowadays, and their catalog gives some interesting information about the process.

Vine, P.A.I. *Pleasure Boating in the Victorian Era*. Shopwyke Hall, Chicester, Sussex: Phillimore & Co. Ltd., 1983.

ACCESSION NO. 1958.1286

MacGregor could rig a simple sail on the Rob Roy, steering with a paddle blade, and even attempt to catch his dinner as he cruised along. (Illustration from MacGregor's The Rob Roy on the Baltic *(1867),* Mystic Seaport 1972-4-4*)*

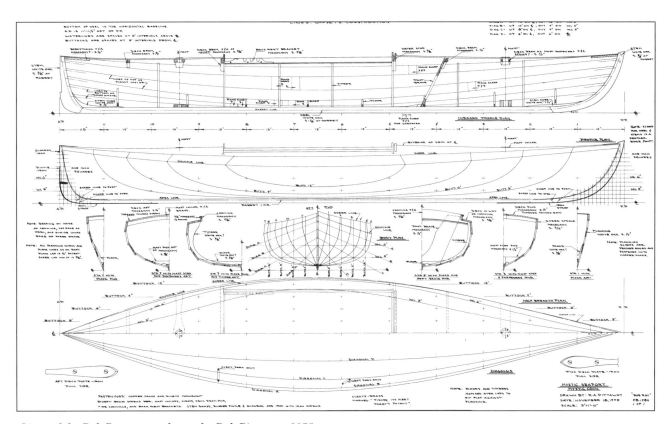

Lines of the Rob Roy canoe, drawn by Rob Pittaway, 1975.

Chic

DECKED CANOE

16' 10" x 2' 5"   ca. 1900

Once the sport of canoeing gained momentum, many variations of MacGregor's Rob Roy double-paddle canoes came into being, and some confusion reigned in the matter of how to classify them. In the United States, at the meeting in Lake George, New York, where the American Canoe Association was founded, a special classification committee, including leading builders J. Henry Rushton and W. P. Stephens, sorted these canoes into five classes: Class I paddling canoes, Class II sailable paddling canoes, Class III sailing and paddling canoes, Class IV paddleable sailing canoes, and Class V sailing canoes.

Chic, since she is not fitted to sail, would belong in Class I. Further class-ification beyond this into an easily recognizable type is nearly impossible. Some would call *Chic* a latter-day Rob Roy, a name that hung around for a long time and was pinned on a number of canoes. J. Henry Rushton built a model almost like *Chic*, which he called an American Traveling Canoe, one of which is in the Adirondack Museum's collection. *Chic* is a typical American double-paddle canoe, built with cedar-on-oak lapstrake construction and outfitted with copper buoyancy tanks.

STATUS: Refinished 1971, seat missing, original, excellent condition.
DONOR: James P. Stow
FURTHER READING:
(Same as for canoe 1958.1286)
ACCESSION NO. 1961.262

Chic in 1972. (Photo: Russell A. Fowler, Mystic Seaport 1972-3-40)

DECKED PADDLING AND SAILING CANOE

15' 2" x 2' 9"   ca. 1900

Oliver Lathrop bought this lapstrake canoe before he graduated from Harvard in 1904. He paddled it on the Charles River, in Boston Harbor, on the Concord River, and on the Winchester Lakes. Later, on vacations from his medical practice, he took the boat on trips to Lake Winnipesaukee and to the Rangeley Lakes. Unfortunately, no builder's plaque or other identification is evident. This is a fine example of a tandem Rob Roy-style canoe, with a forward air compartment, good hardware, excellent materials, and fine detail. Dr. Lathrop added a set of leeboards made from paddles because the original simple lateen rig was, like those of MacGregor, designed only for an assist when the wind favored. In big seas an apron went around the coaming.

Able to handle almost any sea conditions, this is the kind of boat that L. Francis Herreshoff was designing and building in the 1930s (see 1971.245) and that many paddlers would do well with today.

STATUS: Excellent original condition, with sails and a boat cart.
DONOR: Oliver A. Lathrop, Jr.
ACCESSION NO. 1986.98

Lathrop's decked paddling and sailing canoe in 1986. (Photo: Maynard Bray, Mystic Seaport 1986.98A)

Oliver Lathrop and a companion sail the canoe on the upper Charles River, ca. 1900. (Photo: Courtesy of Oliver A. Lathrop, Jr., Mystic Seaport 1986.98.1)

Stiletto

KAYAK BY GEORGE GUEST

17' 0" x 1' 11"   ca. 1897

This canvas-covered, carvel-planked kayak has a radically rockered bottom and raking ends. Loosely based on Greenland-style Inuit designs, *Stiletto* is a highly sculptural boat built by New London sculptor and artist George Guest. Besides his sculpture, with creations as varied in size as the John Winthrop statue in New London and the Indian Head five-dollar gold piece, Guest was a fine boatbuilder, frequently working on the Yale College shells. On the Thames, Guest organized an informal club for young people called the Rambler Boat Club, originally located near the present State Pier, then moved to the east side of the river. There he built a combination club, studio, and residence that looked like "two chests of drawers back to back with some of the lower drawers pulled out." He built a number of kayaks, including two for the F.H. Chappell family, which operated the Thames Towboat Company. *Stiletto* was owned by Thomas H. Chappell, who paddled her on the Thames and Mystic Rivers.

STATUS: Excellent condition.
DONOR: Frank H. Chappell, Jr.
ACCESSION NO. 1989.61.1

Stiletto is identical to this Guest kayak. (Photo: Maynard Bray, Mystic Seaport 1985.27)

DECKED CANOE BY L. FRANCIS HERRESHOFF

16' 4" x 2' 6"   ca. 1927

Marblehead, Massachusetts, saw a brief revival of the double-paddle canoe in the early 1930s when L. Francis Herreshoff, Norman Skene, W. Starling Burgess, and some others became interested in the sport. Herreshoff was very enthusiastic about them and produced a number of different designs. His plan for this canoe shows a two-man 18-footer, one of which was built. However, this craft and one other, although using the same plan, were shortened when they were built by Henry Vincent of Warren, Rhode Island. Vincent had worked for the Herreshoff Manufacturing Co. in Bristol, and the high standards of that

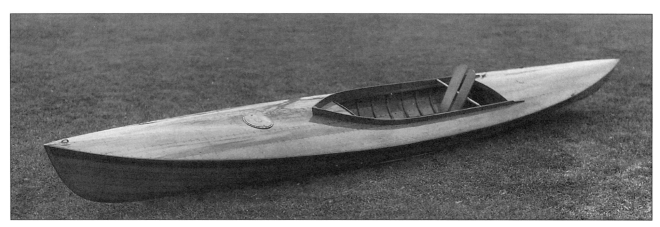

The L. Francis Herreshoff decked canoe. (Photo: Mary Anne Stets, Mystic Seaport, 1973-1-155)

The canoe, ready for use by L. Francis Herreshoff, ca. 1931. (Photo: Courtesy of Mrs. Muriel Vaughn, Mystic Seaport 1973-3-593)

Decked canoes in Marblehead Harbor, ca. 1930. An 18' two-person canoe is in the foreground. W. Starling Burgess (with hat) is in the canoe in the background. One of the smaller canoes may be the canoe now at Mystic Seaport. (Photo: Courtesy of Mrs. Muriel Vaughn, Mystic Seaport 1973-3-511)

yard were carried over into the construction of this boat. She is exquisitely built of cedar and oak and has teak trim. Francis Herreshoff used this canoe for a number of years–his story of spending a night on the dry breakers ledge originated from one of his trips in her. Later she came to be owned by his long-time friend, Starling Burgess. In chapter 1 of his *Common Sense of Yacht Design,* Herreshoff claimed that this canoe was the most seaworthy craft for her freeboard with which he had ever had personal experience. Between 1927 and 1934 "she was kept where she could be easily launched–she was paddled almost every pleasant day that the thermometer was over 40 during the winter."

STATUS: Refinished 1972, original, excellent condition.

DONOR: Dr. Frederic Tudor

FURTHER READING: (See also 1958.1286)

Herreshoff, L. Francis. *The Compleat Cruiser.* New York: Sheridan House, 1956.

——. "The Dry Breakers." *The Rudder,* April, 1948, and reprinted in *The Log of Mystic Seaport,* Fall, 1974.

——. *Sensible Cruising Designs.* Camden, Maine: International Marine Publishing Co., 1973. Chapter 1, which gives instructions and plans for building another canoe of his design, contains valuable data on paddles, backrests, and footbraces as well as some information on the sport of paddling.

ACCESSION NO. 1971.245

"DUGOUT" DECKED CANOE BY L. FRANCIS HERRESHOFF

17' 11" x 2' 4"   ca. 1930

The swelling and shrinking of wood was a fascination of Mr. Herreshoff's. This canoe, glued up of 1-1/2" cedar "lifts" without frames, has the wood grain running all one way; thus it can shrink and swell without opening seams or straining fastenings. The shell thickness averages about half an inch, being thicker on the bottom and thinner at the deck. Great care was taken in lofting this boat and in gluing up the lifts, both operations being done at the Geo. F. Lawley Yard by Herreshoff's good friend Bror Tamm. It was then up to Herreshoff himself to smooth her up and finish her. Although the process of building a boat in this way takes longer, the result in some cases may be worth it–at least in terms of durability and adaptability to unusual shapes. In the 1970s copies of this boat, in fiberglass, were built commercially by Graves Yacht Yard of Marblehead. By today's standards these are fast, quite heavy, and track like the boat was on rails.

STATUS: Original, excellent condition.

DONOR: Mrs. Muriel Vaughn

FURTHER READING: (See also 1958.1286)

Bray, Maynard. "The Incredible Herreshoff Dugout." *WoodenBoat* 14, Jan/Feb, 1977. Contains a first-hand account of how this boat was built by Bror Tamm as well as a more complete history of her.

Herreshoff, L. Francis. *The Common Sense of Yacht Design.* New York: The Rudder Publishing Co., 1946. Chapter III on cabin arrangement says of this boat: "A cuddy only eighteen inches high under a tight deck is nice to crawl into under some circumstances. Figure 59 (which shows this canoe) shows a cabin cruiser I own at the present time with a deck designed to sleep under."

ACCESSION NO. 1973.100

The Herreshoff dugout canoe underway in 1973. (Photo: Mary Anne Stets, 1973-3-568)

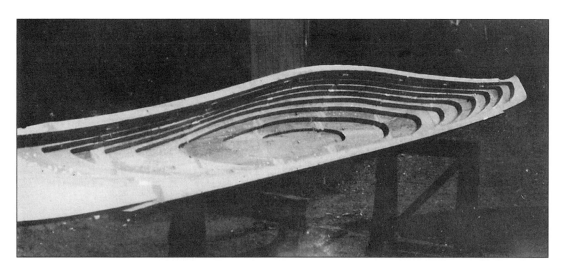

Half the hull of the Herreshoff dugout canoe, showing the inside (above) and outside of the glued-up "lifts." Bror Tamm lofted, cut, and glued the two halves. L. Francis Herreshoff then faired and smoothed them into a thin wooden hull. (Photos: Courtesy of Mrs. Muriel Vaughn, Mystic Seaport 1973-3-512, 1973-3-514)

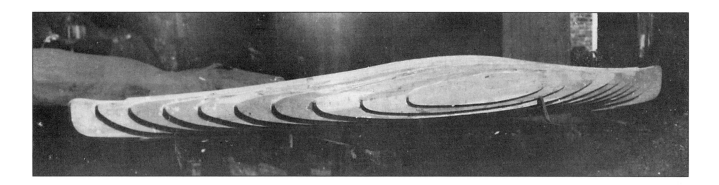

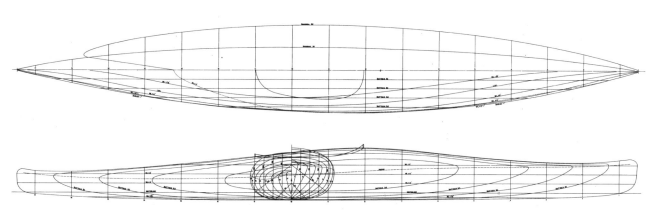

Lines of the L. Francis Herreshoff dugout canoe, traced by Robert Allyn, 1973.

Sprig

DECKED CANOE, DORY TYPE, BY L. FRANCIS HERRESHOFF AND BROR TAMM

16' 0" x 2' 9"   1948

L. Francis Herreshoff's designs published in *The Rudder* haunted many a seafarer's off-watch fantasies during World War II and in the lean years following. And so it was for LeRoy Kramer, Jr. Despite dreaming about large boats, realities of work and family called for something more modest. When L. Francis published his 1933 dory-style kayak in 1947, Kramer wrote the designer for a builder recommendation. Herreshoff directed Kramer to a good friend and consummate craftsman, Bror Tamm, who, after working for Lawley's for 34 years, was struggling to find a living after the yard closed. "Tammy" brought to the pair of canoes that he built for the Kramers, the same workmanship he'd given to projects ranging from the mast for the J-Boat *Whirlwind*, to laying down some 260

yachts at Lawley's (where he was yard superintendent and assistant general manager). Bror Tamm charged the Kramers $265 each for the boats; shipping added another $36 to each bill. Worried about damage in shipping, Tammy built crates for the boats, and apologetically charged $72 for the pair of crates, as they took him 16 hours each.

Roy Kramer and his wife were delighted. She named hers *Wisp*, he chose *Sprig*. The boats were a new experience for Kramer, who was an expert sailor in larger yachts. "When my wife and I come down the river, they [users of other craft] stop, look, take a second look, and stand very far away thoughtfully–not saying a word–and get a faraway look in their eyes," he wrote Tamm. During the boats' careers they made the trip, in the shipping crates, from Chicago to Northern Michigan regularly, then were stored and used at camps on the Manitou Islands, and finally at Harbor Springs, after the National Park Service made it impossible for the Kramers to keep their camp on South Manitou.

After 40 years of use, a stroke suffered by Mrs. Kramer forced the couple to sell the canoes, but only to the right buyer. Through the generosity of Mystic Seaport supporter Tom Clagett, the Museum was able to purchase one of the boats, with the other going to canoe historian David Baker who arranged their transport in furniture vans.

This canoe type has been one of the most popular of L. Francis Herreshoff's designs. *Sprig* shows how a master builds, and how a loving user cares.

STATUS: Excellent condition.
DONOR: Leroy Kramer, Jr.
FURTHER READING:
Herreshoff, L. Francis. *Sensible Cruising Designs.* Camden, Maine: International Marine Publishing Co., 1973.
Howland, Llewellyn III. "A Farewell to Bror Tamm." *WoodenBoat* 46, May/June, 1982.
ACCESSION NO. 1990.59.1
Plans for 1990.59.1 are available from Mystic Seaport's Watercraft Plans Collection.

Sprig in 1990. (Photo: Maynard Bray, Mystic Seaport 1990.59.1A)

L. Francis

DECKED CANOE, DORY TYPE, BY KELLEY

16' 0" x 2' 9"   1970

An interpretation of the L. Francis Herreshoff dory-style kayak model used for *Sprig* (1990.59.1), this was an early venture of George Kelley's, who was to become an experienced amateur

boatbuilder and great friend of the late R.D. Culler. He built this boat in 1970, and shortly afterward called on L. Francis Herreshoff and received a guided tour of his Marblehead home, "The Castle," as Bror Tamm dubbed it. George changed one detail: he gave *L. Francis* round hatches instead of square. After he apologized to the designer for this detail, L. Francis said "I thought it should have round hatches but thought

they would be too difficult for amateurs to make." George designated this canoe "for use" so that people who visit Mystic Seaport's Boathouse boat livery can try out a classic double-paddle decked canoe.

STATUS: Excellent, in use.
DONOR: George B. Kelley
ACCESSION NO. 1990.147

Batten-seam kayak in 1981. (Photo: Maynard Bray, Mystic Seaport 1981.107A)

KAYAK WITH BATTEN SEAMS

16' 8" x 2' 6"   ca. 1930

When is a kayak a kayak? When is it a double-paddle, decked canoe? Both are propelled sitting down, facing forward, by a double-bladed paddle. Perhaps the best way to tell the difference is that kayaks more nearly resemble the Inuit craft they came from. They generally rely on the skill of the paddler for stability when the sea is up. They almost always need a spray skirt of some type to keep the water out. The paddler of a kayak is part of the craft. The double-paddle canoe or decked canoe user sits in the boat, and the boat can be left to take care of itself. By this definition, this is a wooden kayak.

Boats often come with stories attached, stories that may be documented fact or wishful thinking. With this boat came the tale that she was built by N.G. Herreshoff, but there is no evidence to support it. She does resemble some of the racing designs of L. Francis Herreshoff but does not match any of them. She spent most of her life on Upper St. Regis Lake in the Adirondacks, and went into guideboat builder Willard Hanmer's boatshop around 1962 for a rebuild. After that she was never used. Her three-plank batten-seam construction was common in wooden smooth-planked canoes; but her fancy stripped deck is unusual and may have been a Hanmer reconstruction. It is like the decks he put on his guideboats. No matter who built her, she must have been delightful, moving along easier and faster than walking in the cool mist of an Adirondack morning.

STATUS: Excellent condition, refinished ca. 1962.

DONOR: Robert D. Huntington

ACCESSION NO. 1981.107

FOLDBOAT BY KLEPPER

16′ 8″ x 2′ 9″   1936

The path to fame came to Munich tailor Johannes Klepper in 1907, when he bought the design of a folding kayak invented by a young Munich architect named Alfred Heurich. Klepper started a company that had put thousands on the water by the 1930s. The 1936 Olympics even saw a 10,000-meter race for both single and double "faltboats." The "faltboat" was brought into England by J. Kissner in 1933, starting the "Folboat" company, which he moved to the United States in 1935. Through his promotional work, the folding boat caught on. Paddlers organized foldboat trains, similar to the ski trains of the era, ran rivers that were previously considered unnavigable, and set up foldboat clubs.

This Klepper Super T-6 Wander Zweier was brought back from Germany in 1945. After World War II interest in these craft continued, especially for river touring and whitewater, until superseded by fiberglass boats in the early 1960s. Foldboats are still quite popular for specialized applications where portability is paramount.

STATUS: Fair condition, missing sailing rig.

DONOR: James Crocker in the name of Frederick Crocker

FURTHER READING:

Kissner J. ed. *Foldboat Holidays*. Flushing, New York: Repro Art Co., 1940.

Vesper, Hans Egon. *50 Years of the International Canoe Federation*. Florence, Italy: International Canoe Federation, 1974.

ACCESSION NO. 1982.72

The Klepper Super T-6 Wander Zweier, with its fabric skin laid out next to the folding frame, viewed from the stern. (Photo: Maynard Bray, Mystic Seaport 1982.72A)

CRUISING KAYAK BY STRUER

16′ 7″ x 2′ 1″   ca. 1965

Struer, a small Danish town, became synonymous with molded-veneer plywood kayak building, thanks to two canoe racers, Gerhard Sorensen and Helge Kobburup. These craftsmen, having read about the wooden DeHavilland Mosquito fighters of World War II, applied the technology to canoes and kayaks. Around 1960, designer Jørgen Samson was added to the team, and he, with English paddler Alex Moulton, designed a modern touring Rob Roy-style kayak to be built by the Kirk and Stogaard Kano og Kajakbyggeri in Struer. This boat was imported by Competition Canoes of Niles, Michigan, and retailed for $360 around 1965. Samson's molded wood boats are still built and are highly competitive with boats built of kevlar and graphite on the Olympic racing circuit.

STATUS: Excellent condition.
DONOR: Frank Bissel
FURTHER READING:
Anderson, Fletcher. "Championships for Struer." *WoodenBoat* 82, May/June, 1982.
ACCESSION NO. 1990.127

Struer cruising kayak in 1990.
(Photo: Maynard Bray, Mystic Seaport 1990.127A)

The Perception Jib in Mystic Seaport's Native Legacy exhibit, 1999. (Photo: Mark Starr)

WHITEWATER PLAYBOAT
BY PERCEPTION
JIB MODEL

6' 8" x 2' 0"   1999

Today's recreational kayaks come in all shapes and sizes. Perception's Jib is the epitome of a modern whitewater playboat: maneuverable, agile, suited to cartwheels, enders, and surfing. Bottom and edges are surfboard-like. With these boats, rivers become three dimensional gravity-fed playgrounds.

Like Inuit *qajaqs* (kayaks), modern boats are designed to fit paddlers. "Fun comes in all sizes. And now innovation is available in a boat that's custom-tailored for paddlers under 140 pounds. The Jib is a hip-hop freestyler that gives new meaning to the world of playboating for the smaller paddler. Aaron Phillips along with the Perception R&D team, designed this boat to be amazingly responsive and aggressively agile," as the catalog says.

Founded by Bill Masters in 1975, Perception started building rotationally molded polyethylene boats in 1977. Masters pioneered the creation and changing of the complex tools needed to produce these boats so that many models can be built for well under the price of fiberglass and wood, and in shapes impossible to achieve in any other way.

To get a production model, Perception made several prototypes and modified them. Starting with a plug of wood, foam, and fiberglass, they made a fiberglass mold. They used it with their polyethylene rotomolded machine to make some boats. These boats went to the river for testing and were modified by cutting and heat-welding together, with the addition of foam and plastic where needed. After more testing, another mold was made, and, another boat for further testing. Production boats can go through dozens of changes and several molds before the final design. Testing and modification is what makes these boats work.

STATUS: New, unused.
DONOR: Perception, Inc.
ACCESSION NO. 2000.13

OPEN HUNTING CANOE
BY RUSHTON

13″ x 2′ 9″   ca. 1885-93

J.H. Rushton of Canton, New York, was one of the first American boatbuilders to take advantage of the public interest in canoeing generated by John "Rob Roy" MacGregor's writings. Starting in 1873 as a builder of light hunting canoes and rowing craft for the Adirondacks, he built Rob Roy-style canoes in 1876 for a couple of Kentuckians who paddled them to the Philadelphia Centennial Exposition from upstate New York. Publicity from this and other voyages put Rushton on the national map, and he became one of the American Canoe Association founders in 1880.

This lapstrake canoe is like the first canoes that Rushton built, designed for hunting in the Adirondacks, before he began to build for the national market. It matches the dimensions of a Model 120 in Rushton's 1887 catalog, and her builder's plate is one used from 1885 to 1893. Prices varied from $55 for an A grade to $45 for a C; the folding Radix centerboard (patented in 1885) and mast step were extras, making this a sailing and paddling Model 154. Rushton's description claims "for a hunting canoe this had no superior." At 40 to 45 pounds without the rig, she would have been easy to carry, but probably a bit crowded with two aboard, the way these were set up, for a paddler and a gunner. This boat came to the donor from Lake George, New York.

Rushton open hunting canoe in 1990. (Photo: Maynard Bray, Mystic Seaport 1990.141.1A)

STATUS: Fair condition, board and parts missing, some checks in planks.
DONOR: Anne (Mrs. Robert H.) Baker
FURTHER READING:
Bond, Hallie E. *Boats and Boating in the Adirondacks*. Blue Mountain Lake, New York: The Adirondack Museum; Syracuse, New York: Syracuse University Press, 1995.

Crowley, William. *Rushton's Rowboats and Canoes: The 1903 Catalog in Perspective*. Blue Mountain Lake, New York: The Adirondack Museum, 1983.

Manley, Atwood. *Rushton and his Times in American Canoeing*. Syracuse: Syracuse University Press for Adirondack Museum, 1968.

Rushton, J.H. *Rushton's Portable Sporting Boats and Canoes*. Canton, New York: J.H. Rushton, 1887.

ACCESSION NO. 1990.141.1

OPEN DOUBLE-PADDLE
CANOE BY RUSHTON
NESSMUK MODEL

10′ 5″ x 2′ 5″   ca. 1905

George Washington Sears–"Nessmuk"– was one of America's first writers to preach the gospel of do-it-yourself travel in the woods. He wrote frequently for sporting periodicals of the 1880s and published the first handbook for the "outers," called *Woodcraft and Camping*. He preached: "Go light; the lighter the better so that you have the simplest materials for health, comfort and enjoyment." His needs in canoes matched his words. The first one that Rushton built for him weighed 18 pounds; two subsequent ones were lighter still. Nessmuk's writing helped popularize Rushton's work. Nessmuk's canoes were designed for efficient double paddling with the paddler sitting in the bottom. Beginning in 1881, Rushton offered Nessmuk's first canoe as the "Nessmuk" Model. At $27.50 in 1903, it was a little less expensive than his cheapest wood-canvas canoe, but it was not for everyone. They needed careful treatment, and this one has had thwarts added to strengthen it.

STATUS: Good; some breaks in planks and unfairness in way of thwarts.
DONOR: Bruce F. Kingsbury

FURTHER READING:
Sears, George Washington. *Canoeing the Adirondacks with Nessmuk: the Adirondack Letters of George Washington Sears.* Edited by Dan Brenan with revisions by Robert L. Lyon and Hallie E. Bond. Blue Mountain Lake, New York: Adirondack Museum, 1993.

——. Nessmuk [pseud.]. *Woodcraft.* New York: Dover Publications, Inc., 1963.

Reprint of book first published in 1884 by Forest and Stream Publishing Co.

ACCESSION NO. 1986.25.1

Nessmuk model canoe in 1986. (Photo: Maynard Bray, Mystic Seaport 1986.25.1A)

Iola

OPEN CANOE BY RUSHTON

15′ 8″ x 2′ 1″   ca. 1900

Iola is one of what Rushton called his "racing paddler" when first brought out in 1892. He had started building Canadian-style open canoes in 1891. However, he used the smooth-skin lapstrake construction of Adirondack guideboats, with 1/4″-thick planking. This meant many more hours of work and higher-grade materials than his Canadian competition. His boats were twice as expensive as both the Canadian wooden canoes and the wood-canvas canoes from Maine.

The "Arkansas Traveler" model, which is what they were called from 1903 to 1915, is five inches narrower than most canoes and was sold as a racing boat. The wide gunwales stiffen *Iola* so she does not need thwarts, making it easy to paddle her with a double-blade paddle from a movable seat, or with a single-blade paddle from a high kneeling, racing position.

STATUS: Refinished and minor repairs made 1971, mostly original, excellent condition.

DONOR: Edward J. Ludwig III

FURTHER READING:
Crowley, William. *Rushton's Rowboats and Canoes: The 1903 Catalog in Perspective.* Blue Mountain Lake, New York: Adirondack Museum; Camden, Maine: International Marine Publishing Co., 1983.

Gardner, John. *Building Classic Small Craft.* Camden, Maine: International Marine Publishing Co., 1984, 1997. Has write up and plans.

Manley, Atwood. *Rushton and His Times in American Canoeing.* Syracuse: Syracuse University Press for Adirondack Museum, 1968.

ACCESSION NO. 1963.1514

Iola, an open canoe by Rushton, in 1975. (Photo: Maynard Bray, Mystic Seaport 1975-5-160)

Mignon

OPEN CANOE BY J.R. ROBERTSON

17' 1" x 2' 11"   1898

John Ralph Robertson established his shop in 1881 on the Merrimack River at Lawrence, Massachusetts. By 1892 he had moved to Auburndale, on the Charles, where he could take advantage of the booming interest in canoeing. He may have learned canoe-building in the Rushton shop, as he was born in Canton, New York, Rushton's hometown. Robertson's first catalog (in partnership with a Holmes), in 1884, was lifted directly from the Rushton catalog. The 1892 American Canoe Association *Year Book* had a full-page advertisement showing his shop and how to reach it on the Boston trolleys. By 1908, after his return from helping establish Old Town Canoe Company, Robertson had been elected commodore of the association and his shop had grown to 8,000 square feet. His Riverside boathouse could house 900 canoes and included a boat livery.

Mignon was lapstrake-built. She was built for the Damon family and paddled out of the Newton Boat Club on the Charles until the 1940s when she went to Cape Cod. In addition to her cushions and backrests, she sports two eagle-headed flag poles for the American flag and the Newton Boat Club pennant.

STATUS: Excellent structural condition.

DONOR: Lawrence B. Damon

FURTHER READING:

American Canoe Association. *Year Books.* Rochester, New York: American Canoe Association, 1890-1909.

Audette, Susan T. with David E. Baker. *The Old Town Company: Our First Hundred Years.* Gardiner, Maine: Tilbury House, 1998. A good description of canoeing on the Charles and Robertson setting up his business and later relationship with Old Town.

Robertson, J.R. *Catalogue of Boats and Canoes Designed and Built by J.R. Robertson, Auburndale, Massachusetts.* Auburndale, Massachusetts: J.R. Robertson, ca. 1881-1895.

ACCESSION NO. 1988.79

Mignon, *an open canoe by Robertson, in 1988.*
(Photo: Maynard Bray, Mystic Seaport 1988.79A)

OYSTER-TONGING DUGOUT FROM FAIR HAVEN, CONNECTICUT

27′ 1″ x 3′ 2″   ca. 1824

Dugout canoes, hollowed from logs large and small, are among the earliest boats. European settlers adopted several types, and their steel tools made it easier for both Native and Euro-Americans to build them. Throughout North America, native peoples produced characteristic designs: large, deep white-pine dugouts by northeastern cultures like the Pequot and Wampanoag; graceful, shallow, cypress pirogues by the southeast Seminole; and long, highly decorated steam-spread dugout cedar canoes of the northwest.

In size and design, this oystering dugout would be close to the craft that could carry from eight to fifty, used by the Pequots and others on Long Island Sound. It shows how native designs continued long after the period of initial contact, as long as building materials could be found.

Durability and shallow draft kept large dugouts popular among the Connecticut oystermen well into the 1800s. Builders had to travel to the headwaters of the Connecticut and into the Finger Lakes area of New York to find large enough white pine trees. Records say that this dugout was built at Cayuga Lake, New York, by John Smith about 1824. If that information is correct, this craft and the one following are the oldest in Mystic Seaport's entire collection. There is little reason to doubt that these go back that far since the new Erie Canal (completed in 1825) opened vast areas of wilderness to timber harvesting. The big white pine trees needed for these dugouts had become scarce even at the head of the long Connecticut River. According to historian W. P. Stephens, the local builders went up the Hudson to the inland lakes, bringing down a fleet of 20 to 30 canoes every spring.

The only "European" refinements were a small sail, a leeboard, and a long sculling oar over the stern; yet these basic boats served the oyster tongers a good long time. Possibly after their bottoms were worn out from shoveling out oysters, these dugouts were given flat

The restored oyster-tonging dugout in 1975. (Photo: Maynard Bray, Mystic Seaport 1975-10-96)

bottoms by nailing short boards athwartships. This long, narrow, cross-planked structure may have given rise to the cross-planked skiff and sharpie designs that seem to have originated in mid-coast Connecticut in the mid-1800s. Increasing scarcity of big trees, convenient access to sawmills, availability of metal fastenings, and a need to go further offshore for oysters all contributed to the dugout's replacement by the sailing sharpie (see 1947.597 and 1974.1031).

STATUS: Restored 1968, bottom replanked, approximately 50% original, good condition.

DONOR: F. Mansfield & Son

FURTHER READING FOR 1946.643 AND 1946.644:

Gardner, John. "Native Dugout Canoes." *The Log of Mystic Seaport*, June, 1969.

Hall, Henry. *Report on Shipbuilding Industry in the United States.* Washington, D.C.: U.S. Government Printing Office, 1884.

Kochiss, John. *Oystering from New York to Boston.* Middletown, Connecticut: Wesleyan University Press for Mystic Seaport, 1974.

Morris, E.P. *The Fore and Aft Rig in America.* New Haven: Yale University Press, 1927.

ACCESSION NO. 1946.643

Several dugouts, a sharpie, and a sharpie skiff, photographed in the Quinnipiac River at Fair Haven, Connecticut, in the 1890s. (Photo: Mystic Seaport, 1978.152.494)

OYSTER-TONGING DUGOUT FROM FAIR HAVEN, CONNECTICUT

30' 8" x 3' 7"   ca. 1824

Much like the restored dugout (1946.643, previous page) and having the same history, this one still has much of her original bottom, a part of the log itself. The length of all oyster dugouts probably varied some, being whatever the tree would make. Their long life was made possible, at least in part, by having the wood grain running all in the same direction, so it could shrink and swell without damage, and by having no metal fastenings to rust or corrode. Radial checking around the heart of the tree at the bow and stern was probably troublesome, particularly if the craft were allowed to dry out in the hot summer sun, but the tongers no doubt had some effective way of minimizing this.

STATUS: Original, poor condition.
DONOR: Ernest E. Ball
FURTHER READING: (Same as for 1946.643)
ACCESSION NO. 1946.644

The unrestored oyster-tonging dugout on exhibit in 1975. (Photo: Maynard Bray, Mystic Seaport 1975-10-164)

DUGOUT CANOE FROM THE MIRAMICHI RIVER

28' 1" x 2' 3"   ca. 1930

STATUS: Original, good condition.
DONOR: Henry Bradford
ACCESSION NO. 1975.245

Miramichi River dugout in 1975. (Photo: Maynard Bray, Mystic Seaport 1975-10-74)

Even in the birchbark canoe belt, natives built dugouts. Micmacs from New Brunswick in Canada built this canoe from a single pine log for fishing on the Miramichi River. Slim and elegant, she is a far cry from the heavier dugout canoes. Several natural crook hackmatack frames reinforce the hull.

Similar lightweight, shorter dugouts of the Mississauga, from Ontario's Rice Lake area, were petite craft suited to navigating complex lake marshes. After arriving in the early 1800s, European settlers borrowed and built dugouts for hunting and fishing on lake waters. By the 1850s, racing was popular. Settlers strove for lighter and leaner dugouts. In 1857, Peterborough's John Stephenson steam-bent frames over an existing dugout, then nailed wide, thin basswood planks to them. With that, the Canadian canoe and a canoe-building industry was born.

OPEN CANOE
BY THE PETERBOROUGH
CANOE COMPANY
MODEL 64

16' 2" x 2' 7"   1908

In the 1860s, canoe-builders from Ontario's Peterborough area invented a construction method that called for battens covering the seams between three or four wide basswood boards. Light dugouts that they had learned to build from the local Mississauga Indians of Rice Lake served both as inspiration and as molds. These canoes, built by several companies, came to be called "Peterboroughs," and their export to Europe made "Canadian Canoes" the international name for open canoes. The Peterborough Canoe Company was established first as the Ontario Canoe Company in 1879, then renamed the Peterborough Canoe Company in 1892 after a disastrous fire.

In the year 1908, 16-year-old Roger Batchelor of Milwaukee got this four-board Peterborough canoe which he liked so well that he left it to his children.

It was built by Canada's Peterborough Canoe Company, successor to the shop and company established by the inventor of the dugout-based canoe, John Stephenson. Batchelor's family paid about $39.00 for his present, a good bit of money when salaried workers averaged about $1,000 a year and a wage worker earned $600. But it is a bargain in today's dollars when the equivalent buys a nice fiberglass canoe, and an all-wood boat would be at least twice that amount. Roger's boat was a slim boat for two and not much gear, narrower and sportier than almost any double canoe that you can buy today.

STATUS: Good, original condition, unrefinished.

DONOR: Dr. Roger P. Batchelor, Jr.

FURTHER READING:

Jennings, John, Bruce W. Hodgins, and Doreen Small. *The Canoe in Canadian Cultures*. Toronto: Natural History Books, 1999.

Raffan, James. *Bark, Skin and Cedar, Exploring the Canoe in Canadian Experience*. Toronto: Harper Collins Publishers. Ltd., 1999.

Raffan, James and Bert Horwood eds. *Canexus: The Canoe in Canadian Culture*. Toronto: Betelguse Books, 1988.

Stephenson, Gerald F. "John Stephenson and the Famous 'Peterborough' Canoes." Occasional paper #8 published by the Peterborough Historical Society, November, 1987, reprinted in *Wooden Canoe* 51, 1992.

During the last fifteen years Canadians have been studying and writing about both their First People and Euro-Canadian canoe heritage. This has culminated in the creation and opening of the Canadian Canoe Museum in Peterborough, Ontario, home of some 600 canoes, the world's largest boat collection.

ACCESSION NO. 1981.111

The open Peterborough canoe, showing the light frames and one of the longitudinal battens that cover the plank seams in Peterborough construction. (Photo: Maynard Bray, Mystic Seaport 1981.111A)

The strip-planked Peterborough canoe. (Photo: Maynard Bray, Mystic Seaport 1984.146A)

OPEN CANOE
BY THE PETERBOROUGH
CANOE COMPANY
MODEL 42, SERIAL #42 2004
14' 9" x 2' 6"   ca. 1910-16

The costliest Peterborough canoes were the beveled strip-planked models, a method patented by John Stephenson in 1883 as "Stephenson's Longitudinal Rib Boat," and sold to James Z. Rogers of the Ontario Canoe Company. After the factory fire in 1892, the method continued, although it was considered inferior (heavier) to the patent open-rib canoe, which had a single-skin rib-less hull of interlocking single planks running across the boat. The Model 42 sold for $45 in 1892, a price that rose five dollars by 1914. The same model in a wide-board, batten-seam boat would have sold for $13 less. These boats were popular in the European market, being shipped in nests containing an 18' canoe at the bottom, and a 14' canoe at the top—assembly by dealer required. The 16' Model 44 was the choice of sophisticated canoeists in the United States. Under the onslaught of fiberglass, the company finally folded in 1961, after switching to cedar strip outboards as its primary product in the 1930s.

STATUS: Excellent refinished condition.

DONOR: Henry N. Silverman

FURTHER READING:

Cameron, G.D.W. "Birth of the "Peterborough Canoe: Four Builders Start a Revolution." *Wooden Canoe* 9, Winter, 1982.

Moores, Ted. *Canoecraft: An Illustrated Guide to Fine Woodstrip Construction*, 2nd ed. Willowdale, Ontario: Firefly Books, 2000. Has plans for numerous canoes like these, both copies of old and new designs.

Stephenson, Gerald F. "John Stephenson and the Famous 'Peterborough' Canoes." Occasional paper #8 published by the Peterborough Historical Society, November, 1987, reprinted in *Wooden Canoe* 51, 1992.

ACCESSION NO. 1984.146

This Peterborough Canoe Co. catalog from 1922 suggests the broad appeal of canoeing. (G.W. Blunt White Library, Mystic Seaport)

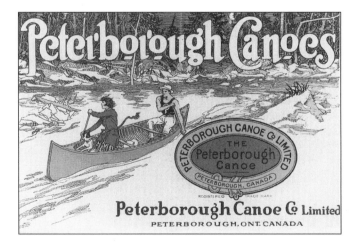

OPEN CANOE ATTRIBUTED TO ENGLISH

15' 6" x 2' 6"

All of the Peterborough, Ontario, canoe builders produced ship-lapped strip-planked cedar canoes like this one, as well as wide-plank, batten-seam boats. This canoe does not have the usual manufacturer's nameplate held in place by the screws in the side that hold a thwart support cleat in place. But her extreme deadrise and perfectly vertical stems are characteristic of William English's boats, which were among the raciest of the Peterborough designs. This would have been one of English's Model 6s, costing $92 in 1918. Starting in 1861, English was one of the first Peterborough-area builders. On his death, some of his models were continued by the Peterborough Canoe Company, particularly his fast 16' x 30" Model 20. This boat was bought from the "City Island Yacht Club"–a center of decked sailing canoe activity in the 1930s–and reconditioned by the buyer's grandson Reid Wulff. It has the long double-bladed paddle, the backrest, and the canvas-covered canoe seat popular amongst early A.C.A. paddlers, and is decorated by a totem or personal emblem of an earlier owner.

STATUS: Good condition, original with minor repairs.

DONOR: Mrs. Margaret Wulff in memory of Reid Wulff

ACCESSION NO. 1979.190

The strip-planked Peterborough canoe attributed to William English. (Photo: Maynard Bray, Mystic Seaport 1979.190A)

OPEN CANOE BY CANADIAN CANOE COMPANY MODEL 16

15' 11" x 2' 7"   ca. 1910

At the first American Canoe Association gathering, in 1880, Canadian canoe builders met the Americans, who favored decked sailing-cruising canoes. The Canadians won the paddling races. But they also learned that there was a market for sails, and soon they added leeboards and lateen sails to their offerings. These became popular as a cruising canoe rig after 1900.

This boat is in the Canadian standard rib-and-batten style. It was in the most popular 16' x 30" size and used a long double-bladed paddle for solo outings. After being refinished and used at a Mystic Seaport-sponsored Small Craft Workshop, her owner turned this canoe–still equipped with factory lateen sail and leeboards–over to the Museum for its collection. She carries the nameplate of her builder, the Canadian

The Canadian Canoe Co. canoe, rigged for cruising with her original long-bladed double paddle, spars, and leeboards.
(Photo: Maynard Bray, Mystic Seaport 1975-5-257)

Canoe Co. of Peterborough, Ontario (1892-1921). Because she'll paddle as well as she'll sail, one could enjoy quite unrestricted use of her in sheltered waters.

STATUS: Nearly original, fully equipped, refinished, very good condition.

DONOR: William B. Coolidge

FURTHER READING:

Gardner, John. *Building Classic Small Craft*. Camden, Maine: International Marine Publishing Co., 1984, 1997. Includes write-up and plans.

ACCESSION NO. 1975.47

OPEN CANOE BY
ST. LAWRENCE RIVER SKIFF,
CANOE AND STEAM LAUNCH
COMPANY

15' 5" x 2' 9"   ca. 1890

Despite heavy advertising and promotional work by the St. Lawrence River Skiff, Canoe and Steam Launch Co., boasting of boats sent all over the country, only a handful of the company's boats exist. This is one of the few surviving canoes. It combines the batten-seam construction of the Canadian canoe builders with the small side decks and low coaming of the St. Lawrence River skiff. Canoes and other craft were added to the A. Bain & Company line shortly after a New York investment group bought the company in 1887 and changed its name to the St. Lawrence River Skiff, Canoe and Steam Launch Company the following year. What had begun as a shop had become a factory with each part built by a specialist. What began as a single product line diversified to take advantage of a rapidly expanding recreational boating market.

STATUS: Fair; repaired and canvassed at some point.
DONOR: Denny Alsop
FURTHER READING:
(See St. Lawrence River skiff, *Annie*, 1980.76)

Keats, John. *The Skiff and the River*. Nantucket, Massachusetts: The Herrick Collection, 1988.

St. Lawrence River Skiff, Canoe and Steam Launch Company. *Illustrated Catalog for 1893*. Reprint, Clayton, New York: Thousand Islands Shipyard Museum, 1983.

The Rudder, March, April, 1891.

ACCESSION NO. 1981.163

A cross between a Peterborough-style Canadian canoe and a St. Lawrence River skiff, this is one of only a few products of the St. Lawrence River Skiff, Canoe and Steam Launch Co. to survive. The canvas covering was added at some later date. (Photo: Maynard Bray, Mystic Seaport 1981.163A)

FLATWATER RACING CANOE
BY H.B. ARNOLD & COMPANY

19' 11" x 2' 9"   ca. 1900

Between 1880 and the 1920s, Boston's Charles River in the Lakes District around Newton, Waltham, and Weston was a canoeist's paradise. Several thousand canoes made this area their home, especially after the Norumbega Amusement Park was built in the Auburndale section of Newton in 1897.

The Arnold "Club 4" 20' racing canoe in 1978. (Photo: Maynard Bray, Mystic Seaport 1978.220A)

Bostonians could take the trolley car out to flee downtown on a hot summer's day. At the river, they could rent a canoe at one of several liveries or paddle their own canoe from a club. Norumbega Park alone had a 600-canoe boathouse, including space for 300 rental canoes.

Club racing was a popular sport, and Arnold and other U.S. and Canadian companies built these 20' "Club 4s" for paddling with single or double blades. This one features brass battens covering the seams for ultralight construction. It was purchased by the Swastika Canoe Club of Cranston, Rhode Island. In 1965, the Waterford Canoe Club bought her and, after reconditioning, paddled the boat to a first place in the American Canoe Association's New England Championships, first in the National Junior Division, and third in the Senior, all with about four practices in the boat. This was an excellent showing for a design more than 40 years old. Over the next decade, club members paddled her to more national championships.

STATUS: Original, good condition.
DONOR: Ralph G. Clark
FURTHER READING:

Audette, Susan T., with David E. Baker. *The Old Town Company: Our First Hundred Years.* Gardiner, Maine: Tilbury House, 1998. Includes a chapter on the Boston "canoe craze."

Joy, Arthur F. "Canoeing on the Charles… gone are the days!" *Wooden Canoe* 59, 1993.

ACCESSION NO: 1978.220

The Swastika Canoe Club, ca. 1900. Swastika is a Sanscrit term for good or well-being. Before it was appropriated by the Nazis, the term and the associated bent-armed cross was often used by paddlers and canoe clubs, as the cross was also a symbol found among Native Americans with the same meaning as the Sanscrit. Along the Seekonk River on the east side of Providence, Rhode Island, the Swastika Canoe Club's size shows what could be achieved by a group working together to allow people of modest means access to the water. (Photo: Courtesy of Mr. & Mrs. Roger I. Wilkinson, Mystic Seaport 1984.151.204)

Racing a similar "Club 4" canoe, George Ames, Fred Mahern, Charles Hougton, and George E. Merritt of the Dedham Boat Club show the style that won them the New England Amateur Oarsman's four-man canoe race on the Fourth of July, 1910. (Photo: Courtesy of William Ames, Mystic Seaport 1995.51.2)

Skitch

OPEN PADDLING AND SAILING CANOE BY WILLITS

17' 2" x 2' 11"   1936-37

Besides the Peterborough style of all-wood canoes, another all-wood method was invented by the Willits Brothers of Tacoma, Washington. In the years between 1914 and 1962, they built up to 50 canoes a year using a technique that featured two layers of planking, with a layer of glue-soaked muslin in between. The inner layer ran athwartships, giving a perfectly smooth surface inside the boat. The brothers standardized their production with just one model, to "give the customers a better canoe for less money than would otherwise be possible." Their methods allowed for pre-production of planks and parts, and they also could furnish a customer a complete sailing rig and even outriggers and oars. The costs of this durable wooden boat in 1920 was $84, or actually less than an equivalent wood-canvas canoe. By the time that production ceased, the price had risen to $280; a sailing rig and paddles doubled the price.

Karl A. Staley of Ohio bought *Skitch* in 1937 and built a lateen-style sailing rig according to the then-current American Canoe Association designs. The boat often went to the A.C.A.'s annual encampment on Sugar Island in the Thousand Islands to race, and was finally taken to Florida when Mr. Staley retired. When *Skitch* became hard for him to lift, he mounted a skateboard wheel on the bow, which allowed him to turn the canoe over and roll it to the water's edge.

STATUS: Good condition, with owner-built outfit and modifications.

DONOR: Mrs. Karl A. Staley in memory of Karl A. Staley

FURTHER READING:

Chapman, Patrick F. "'You Take no Risk in Ordering from Us' The Willits Brothers and Their Careers." *Wooden Canoe* 104, 2001.

Fay, W. Roger. "The Mossgrove Willits." *Wooden Canoe* 104, 2001.

Hughes, Holly. "The Willits Brothers Canoes." *WoodenBoat* 55, Nov/Dec, 1983.

ACCESSION NO. 1986.19

Skitch in 1986. Notice that, with two layers of planking laid at right angles, the canoe has no frames. Owner Karl Staley mounted the skateboard wheel on the bow so he could roll his canoe to the water. (Photo: Maynard Bray, Mystic Seaport 1986.19A)

Sebal about 1958. (Photo: Louis Martel, Mystic Seaport 1950.2848)

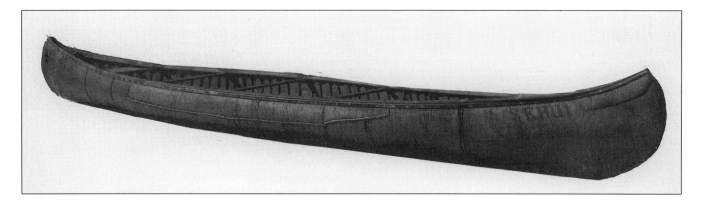

Sebal

OPEN CANOE OF BIRCH BARK

16′ 10″ x 3′ 0″   ca. 1890

Called in Passamaquoddy *aquiden*, in Penobscot *ul*, all that is certain is that this canoe came from Maine, where the two Native American groups were neighbors. In shape and detailing *Sebal* is Penobscot. Her caned seats and painted name show she was built in the late 1800s. Given the vibrant canoe-building business in the Penobscot Valley after the Civil War, she was probably built for a sporting camp.

Bark canoes are built by laying out the bark "envelope" with the gunwale assembly inside. The bark is bent up, with stakes to hold it in place. Then the gunwale is raised and lashed into place, with rocks holding down the bottom. The ends are shaped and sewn. Once this is done, sheathing is put inside the boat and ribs are forced in to hold the sheathing planks in place. An ax, a special carving knife called a crooked knife, and an awl are the only tools needed.

STATUS: Original except that stem has been externally strengthened.

DONOR: E. G. Rogers

FURTHER READING:

Adney, Edwin Tappan, and Howard I. Chapelle. *The Bark and Skin Boats of North America*. Washington, D.C.: U.S. Government PrintinhOffice, 1964.

Gidmark, David. "Building a Birchbark Canoe." *WoodenBoat* 135, Mar/Apr, 1997.

——. *Building a Birchbark Canoe: The Algonquin Wâbanäki Tcîmân*. Mechanicsburg, Pennsylvania: Stackpole Books, 1995.

——. *Birchbark Canoe, Living Among the Algonquin*. Willowdale, Ontario: Firefly Books, 1997.

Hofeman, William. "Birch Bark Canoe Builder." *Minnesota History*, Winter, 1972. Good information on the construction of birchbark canoes.

McPhee, John. *The Survival of the Bark Canoe*. New York: Farrar, Straus and Giroux, 1975. First published as a two-part article in the *New Yorker*, this is the story of a young builder of traditional birchbark canoes.

ACCESSION NO. 1950.2848

OPEN WOOD-CANVAS CANOE
BY OLD TOWN
CANOE COMPANY
HW MODEL, GRADE AA,
HULL #64582

16' 0" x 2' 9"   1921

The first canoe builder in Old Town, Maine, was Guy Carleton, a builder of lumbering boats and bark canoes, who added wood-canvas canoes to his line in the 1880s. E.M. White moved his business to Old Town in 1896. But it was the Gray family that made Old Town famous worldwide as a canoe-building center. In 1898, Old Town hardware store owner George Gray hired Alfred E. Wickett (trained by E.M. White), to set up a shop at his store. In 1900 they opened a new factory called the Indian Old Town Canoe Company. In 1902 the Gray's hired J.R. Robertson from his Auburndale shop; he returned there the following year, but from him Old Town probably learned of the potential markets for their canoes in Boston and other distant locations. In 1906 the company began to advertise in national weekly magazines. By 1908, you could buy an Old Town in France, Finland, Germany, Italy, Argentina, or on the West Coast. By 1912, when the company built a new factory, 4,000 canoes a year were being built by 60 people.

By the 1920s, the Old Town Canoe Company had clearly established its ascendancy over its rivals from the State of Maine. Many companies, active when Old Town began in 1899, were out of business, or would not survive the competition of aluminum and fiberglass to come. Old Town was building at a steady rate of 4,000 boats per year in their five-story factory built in 1912 and 1914 (still in use), a production rate that they kept up until the depths of the Great Depression in 1934. The HW (heavy water) model was the top-of-the-line boat in 1901 (then costing $35) and continued in production until 1954.

This canoe was completed in January of 1921, getting her rails and keel at the end of April, and being painted red and shipped in May to a "Wilder" at H.D. Luce Company. This may have been the donor's father, named Walker, as the record is hard to read. He paid $83.00 for the boat, as a present for his daughter—which was a bit more than $2,000 in today's dollars. Although the records don't show it, the canoe seems to have been equipped with sponsons for increased buoyancy, which were removed in 1940 according to Old Town's instructions. Removing them made it easier for the donor's husband to fit the canoe for leeboards and sailing in 1948. The canoe was used summers on Lake Ontario, surfing and sailing. It was taken to Florida in 1976.

STATUS: Excellent, refinished by donor.

DONOR: Virginia Walker Buell (Mrs. Charles K. Buell, Jr.)

FURTHER READING:

Audette, Susan T., with David E. Baker. *The Old Town Company: Our First Hundred Years*. Gardiner, Maine; Tilbury House, 1998.

Stelmok, Jerry, and Rollin Thurlow. *The Wood & Canvas Canoe*. Gardiner, Maine: The Harpswell Press, 1987.

The Old Town Canoe Company maintains building records for their boats, which allow building dates, model and initial purchaser to be traced based on serial number. These have been transferred to CD-ROM by the Wooden Canoe Heritage Association, and members answer research questions electronically. In addition, all of the catalogs of the Old Town Canoe Company are available on CD-ROM.

ACCESSION NO. 1985.83

The 16' wood-canvas Old Town canoe in 1985. (Photo: Maynard Bray, Mystic Seaport 1985.83A)

Adelaide with her sailing rig. (Photo: Courtesy of Karin and Lisa Whittemore, Mystic Seaport 1998-3-149)

Adelaide

OPEN WOOD-CANVAS CANOE BY OLD TOWN CANOE COMPANY FIFTY-POUND MODEL, GRADE CS, HULL #113038-11 WITH "BOY SCOUT" SAILING RIG

11' 0" x 3' 5"   1933

Old Town began making a 15' "Light Canoe" in 1905. "It is all right with proper care, but will not stand rough usage, banging about." It was reintroduced in 1910 as the Fifty Pound Model, ideal for one person with a heavy load, or two with a light load. The 11' version was produced in 1926-27 and 1930-65. This little model is relatively rare: less than 1 percent of the Fifty Pound boats were this small, and Old Town's production of Fifty Pound Canoes was only about 4 percent of their wood-canvas production.

When Harris Whittemore bought *Adelaide* from Abercrombie and Fitch in 1934, for $48.00, he named her for his grandmother. His selection was the lightest and smallest boat in the Old Town line. With it, he bought the "Boy Scout" 40-square-foot sailing rig, which added $31.50 to the package. Portaging was not the issue here, other than getting her between cottage and Lake Qassapaug in Middlebury, Connecticut. A small boat fitted the needs of his daughters, or was a good excuse for a solo sail.

STATUS: Excellent.

DONOR: Gift of Karin Whittemore and Lisa Whittemore. In Memory of Harris T. Whittemore III

FURTHER READING:

Audette, Susan T., with David E. Baker. *The Old Town Company: Our First Hundred Years*. Gardiner, Maine: Tilbury House, 1998.

ACCESSION NO. 1998.23

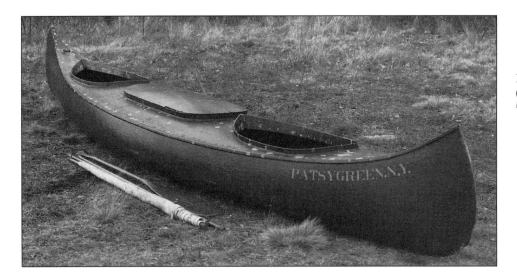

Patsy Green in 1980.
(Photo: Maynard Bray,
Mystic Seaport 1980.93A*)*

Patsy Green

DECKED WOOD-CANVAS CANOE BY J.R. ROBERTSON

16′ 3″ x 2′ 11″   ca. 1906

"Nowhere is too far" is the motto of the Cruising Club of America, drafted by founding member Henry A. Wise Wood. He had the experience to back it. It began in canoeing. With twelve years of sea paddling experience, in 1907 and 1908 he and his wife paddled and sailed *Patsy Green* from New York City to Prince Edward Island. The first year they cruised *Patsy Green* to Gloucester, traveling in the open Atlantic outside of Cape Cod. Leaving in mid-July of 1908 and averaging 30 to 35 miles a day, they arrived in St. John, New Brunswick, August 9, 1908, and then made the run up the Bay of Fundy in three days. After a short train portage they crossed to Charlottetown, Prince Edward Island.

J.R. Robertson of Auburndale, Massachusetts, custom-built *Patsy Green*, adding decks to one of his stock canoes. *Patsy Green* has two cockpits and a central watertight storage compartment. "We are often wet ourselves but our supplies are dry always. Our canoe has two sails which we use whenever practicable, but we put a great deal of dependency on our paddles. The canoe cannot be upset except under extraordinary conditions," commented Mr. Wood to the society page reporter of the *New York Herald*. Since the canoe had no permanent mast for a burgee, the Wood's New York Yacht Club colors were painted on the bow.

STATUS: Unrestored, original condition.

DONOR: Mrs. Horace Brock

FURTHER READING:

Audette, Susan T., with David E. Baker. *The Old Town Company: Our First Hundred Years*. Gardiner, Maine: Tilbury House, 1998.

New York Herald, September 13, 1908.

Robertson, J.R. *Catalogue of Boats and Canoes Designed and Built by J.R. Robertson, Auburndale, Massachusetts*. Auburndale, Massachusetts: J.R. Robertson, ca. 1881-1895.

Stelmok, Jerry, and Rollin Thurlow. *The Wood & Canvas Canoe*. Gardiner, Maine: The Harpswell Press, 1987.

ACCESSION NO. 1980.93

Mr. and Mrs. Henry A. Wise Wood made several open-ocean passages in Patsy Green *during their expedition from New York to Prince Edward Island, 1907-08. In its September 13, 1908, issue, the* New York Herald *described and illustrated their journey. (Photo:* Mystic Seaport*)*

Without its canvas cover, this canoe attributed to the wood-canvas canoe-builder B.N. Morris looks more like a wooden Peterborough-style canoe. (Photo: Maynard Bray, Mystic Seaport 1983.8A)

OPEN WOOD-CANVAS CANOE ATTRIBUTED TO B.N. MORRIS

15' 11" x 2' 6"   ca. 1887

This unusual open canoe descended in the family of pioneering wood-canvas canoe builder B.N. Morris of Veazie, Maine. In shape it resembles the Peterborough style, but it seems to have been covered with fabric, as there is a small scrap of it under a stem, and there are no battens, caulking, laps, or bevels to keep water out. But she does not have the flat frames of the classic wood-canvas canoe and is much more lightly built. The stamp "Patented Jan 18–and Aug. 9, 1887, Series No.–" indicates that this may have been an experimental model. Patent research is still ongoing, but the date is about right, for that is when most sources agree that Morris began his canoe-building enterprise. In 1893 he sold a 46-pound Light Paddling Canoe–which seems much like this boat–for $55 in the First Grade.

STATUS: Poor; cover missing, parts missing from topside.

DONOR: Don Keeney

FURTHER READING:
Stelmok, Jerry, and Rollin Thurlow. *The Wood & Canvas Canoe*. Gardiner, Maine: The Harpswell Press, 1987.

ACCESSION NO. 1983.8

Ne-O-Ga

OPEN WOOD-CANVAS CANOE BY B.N. MORRIS CANOE COMPANY TYPE A 64, MODEL 1, SERIAL #9023

17' 0" x 2' 10"   1912

When C. Edgar Blake bought *Ne-O-Ga* in 1912, he was buying a highly popular wood-canvas canoe style. Her high ends, while not especially functional, gave her a romantic "Indian" look. The gold-leaf stripe, the decorative name, and the fancy mahogany gunwale added $8.90 to the $40.00 price. Just 35 days after the order was taken, the boat was shipped to Twin Lakes, Connecticut, where she was used for 10 years. An adjunct to a summer cottage, *Ne-O-Ga* could be found tripping to the swimming float, doing a little casual racing, and taking leisurely lake paddles. She then went to the Farmington River, where she was used for another four years before being put in storage, where she remained for 58 years.

Starting on the second floor of his house in 1882, Bert Morris pioneered canoe sales through catalogs and national media exposure. "One Quality Only, the Best.... The Canoe that Nationalized Canoeing," was his slogan. Perhaps Blake chose the Morris company because it aimed at the high end of the recreational market and boasted of higher-quality production than the more common Old Town canoes. By 1910, Morris had 35 people working in his factory; when it burned in 1920, 75 people lost their jobs, and all company records were lost. Morris canoes are characterized by higher, more sweeping ends than most canoes of the period, and by the use of cedar stems that splay out where they join the keel.

STATUS: Excellent, original unrefinished condition.

DONOR: Richard S. Blake

FURTHER READING:

Morris Canoes, 1908. reprint, Madison, Wisconsin: Wooden Canoe Heritage Association, 1982.

Stelmok, Jerry, and Rollin Thurlow. *The Wood & Canvas Canoe*. Gardiner, Maine: The Harpswell Press, 1987.

Wooden Canoe 21 Winter, 1985, and 22, Spring, 1985 have a discussion of the history of Morris and information about Morris features.

ACCESSION NO. 1984.47.1

Ne-O-Ga in 1984. (Photo: Maynard Bray, Mystic Seaport 1984.47.1A)

This 1917 B.N. Morris catalog suggests the romantic possibilities of canoeing with paddler and passenger facing one another. (G.W. Blunt White Library, Mystic Seaport)

The rounded, tapered sponsons attached on either side for stability and flotation are a prominent feature of this Kennebec Canoe Co. 16' canoe. (Photo: Maynard Bray, Mystic Seaport 1991.183A*)*

OPEN WOOD-CANVAS SPONSON CANOE BY KENNEBEC

16' 0" x 2' 9"   ca. 1925

Like George Gray, the founder of Old Town, George F. Terry, the founder of the Kennebec Canoe Company, was an entrepreneur and a businessman, not a canoe builder. Around 1908, he saw a business opportunity and hired the skills needed to build boats. By 1911 his payroll had grown to $70,000 annually and his firm was on its way. After the Morris Company burned in 1920, he hired Walter Grant, its superintendent, who supervised the building of this canoe around 1925.

Seventeen-year-old Morrill Hall and his eighteen-year-old brother lived on a farm on the North River in Pembroke, Massachusetts, in the 1920s. They saved their money from "raising chickens and selling eggs" until they had the hundred or so dollars that they recall were needed to buy their new Kennebec canoe in the mid-1920s. They opted for a sponson model, which made the canoe "not only unsinkable, but it will not tip over.... for salt water or on large lakes where rough water is encountered." From the mid-1950s to 1970 the canoe was used on Cape Cod's Pleasant Bay, near Orleans, Massachusetts. She is in original condition, with the damage to the seat commonly seen on older wood-canvas boats.

This canoe has sponsons integrated into the structure of the canoe, not added afterwards the way Old Town did on 1985.83. In 1914, a 16' sponson canoe cost between $46 and $58. Kennebec advertised the sponson canoe as especially well suited for children, for fly fishing, or for use on large lakes and the ocean, all of which were part of this canoe's career. The Kennebec Company was hit hard by the Great Depression, finding in 1930 that it cost them $1.09 for every dollar of sales. In 1939, the Terry family sold the company, which stayed in business another two years, having produced some 20,000 boats by its close.

STATUS: Good structural condition, forward seat smashed, two canvas repairs by donor.

DONOR: Morrill K. Hall

FURTHER READING:

Kennebec Canoe Co. *Kennebec Canoes Boats and Accessories*, 1914; reprint, 1983 Madison, Wisconsin: Wooden Canoe Heritage Society, 1983.

Millis, Willard E., Jr. "History of the Kennebec Canoe Company." *Wooden Canoe* 19, Summer, 1984.

ACCESSION NO. 1991.183

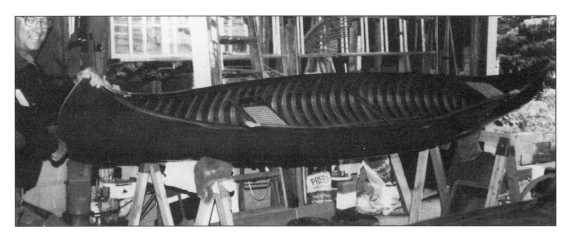

Fred Karshick shows off the refinished Sarah Ellen *before donating her to Mystic Seaport. (Photo: Courtesy of Kate and Fred Karshick,* Mystic Seaport 2000.40)

Sarah Ellen

OPEN WOOD-CANVAS CANOE BY RUSHTON INDIAN GIRL MODEL

16′ 0″ x 2′ 9″   1913

J. Henry Rushton introduced this model in 1901, attempting to maintain his leadership in canoe-building. His new Indian Girl could be built as an all-cedar canoe or as a canvas-covered wooden canoe. To get his production organized, Rushton hired a Bangor, Maine, builder who began to work in 1902. Rushton's all-wood Canadian models were twice as expensive as was the all-wood model of this boat. These wood-canvas canoes were popular and kept the shop in business for 10 years after Rushton died in 1906.

As a Clarkson College sophomore, Osborne Merrill bought his new Indian Girl for $41 from Van's, the Potsdam general store, May 1, 1913, putting down $10. Merrill planned to use his new boat on the St. Lawrence–the "Big River"– where he worked as a host on the tour boat *St. Lawrence*. On the rough windy afternoon of August 18, he took off to paddle a New York friend the 15 miles around Grindstone Island. Returning to Clayton, the canoe capsized about 40 feet from the dock. The friend waded ashore; Osborne never surfaced. Despite being pulled from the water in minutes, he never revived, a young heart-attack victim.

After his funeral, his mother, Sarah Ellen, arranged to have the canoe stored in a barn at their Heuvelton New York, farm, from whence his brother Aubrey "Doc" Merrill retrieved the boat in 1985. He gave the canoe to his daughter and son-in-law, who restored it in a WoodenBoat clinic at Buffalo in 1992.

In September 1913, Mr. Van Ness, proprietor of Van's, had to write Osborne's father apologetically for the balance of $31 due on the canoe, a sad postscript.

STATUS: Excellent, recanvassed and refinished by donor in 1992-93.

DONOR: Kate & Fred Karshick

FURTHER READING:

Bond, Hallie. *Boats and Boating in the Adirondacks*. Blue Mountain Lake, New York: The Adirondack Museum; Syracuse, New York: Syracuse University Press, 1995.

Crowley, William. *Rushton's Rowboats and Canoes, The 1903 Catalog in Perspective*. Blue Mountain Lake, New York: The Adirondack Museum; Camden Maine: International Marine Publishing Co., 1983.

Rushton Indian Girl Canoes, 1910; reprint, Madison, Wisconsin: Wooden Canoe Heritage Association, 1983.

ACCESSION NO. 2000.40

During a canoeing expedition in 1913, Osborne Merrill (chin on hands, right) looks out from under his Indian Girl canoe. (Photo: Courtesy of Kate and Fred Karshick, Mystic Seaport 2000.40.2)

OPEN WOOD-CANVAS CANOE ATTRIBUTED TO H.B. ARNOLD

16' 0" x 2' 7"   ca. 1920

Although makers like Old Town, Kennebec, and Robertson all built canoes in this "Torpedo" style, Waltham's Arnold Canoe Company's models had the most exaggerated recurved stems like this boat's stems. This one has long decks fore and aft and a single wide seat or thwart for a solo paddler. Generally the paddler faced a passenger; often a lady. This model encouraged such "girling," as it was called between the world wars. The Arnold Company sold many of these models to the Norumbega Ballroom for its 300-canoe livery on the Charles River.

STATUS: Original, relic.
DONOR: George B. Kelley and Richard White

FURTHER READING:

Audette, Susan T., with David E. Baker. *The Old Town Company: Our First Hundred Years*. Gardiner, Maine: Tilbury House, 1998. Includes a chapter on the Boston "canoe craze."

Joy, Arthur F. "Canoeing on The Charles... gone are the days!" *Wooden Canoe* 59, 1993.

ACCESSION NO. 1978.221

There is a similar style canoe in the Maine Maritime Museum Collection attributed to Old Town.

Despite its relic condition, this canoe is distinctive for its recurved "torpedo" ends, a style distinctive of the Arnold Canoe Co. (Photo: Maynard Bray, Mystic Seaport 1978.221A)

OPEN WOOD-CANVAS CANOE

18' 0" x 3' 0"

Canoes whose makers did not give them a plate or decal are known in canoe collecting circles as UCLOs, "unidentified canoe-like objects." This is one of them, owned and used by the family of yacht designer and builder Frederick Lawley. She differs from most canoes by having lowered caned seats and two rowing positions.

STATUS: Good original condition.
DONOR: Constance LaRue
ACCESSION NO. 1981.104.234

This "unidentified canoe-like object" came from the family of yacht designer and builder Frederick Lawley. (Photo: Maynard Bray, Mystic Seaport 1981.104.234A)

Unidentified members of the Lawley family fish from a canoe that may be the one in the Museum's collection, ca. 1930. (Photo: Courtesy of Constance LaRue, Mystic Seaport 1982.8.12)

FOLDING BOAT BY OSGOOD

15' 0" x 3' 0"   ca. 1890

Around 1890, N.A. Osgood of Battle Creek, Michigan, invented a folding boat with a shape that resembled an open canoe. Depending on the model, the boat could be paddled or rowed. Its portability was its virtue, but it was also quite light in weight as indicated by the following quote from an advertisement in an 1891 issue of *The Rudder* for a 12' model. "Weight, for trout fishing, and paddling, 25 lbs. With stretcher, sideboards, gunwale and paddle, 32 lbs. With stretcher, sideboards, gunwale, stools and oars, 40 lbs. With bottom board, sideboards, gunwale, stools and oars, 50 lbs."

With a waterproof canvas skin stretched over bent frames, the boat could fold up like an accordion; interlocking bottom panels were inserted when it was set up for use. These folding boats were advertised as being "The best! The safest! The lightest! The steadiest! The staunchest and most durable! Impossible to tip over

Osgood's folding boat, with storage box, in 1975. (Photo: Jack Deupree, Mystic Seaport 1975-12-46)

by rocking! Easy to row! Safest and best hunting and fishing boat made."

STATUS: Original, excellent condition.

DONOR: Given in the name of Kenneth Osgood Huff by Mrs. Richard Siller

ACCESSION NO. 1975.455

OPEN COLLAPSIBLE CANOE BY LINK MANUFACTURING COMPANY

15' 0" X 3' 0"   ca. 1947

In 1945, Edwin Link, inventor of the "Link" stationary flight trainer, introduced a new type of boat, a folding canoe. "Check it like luggage, stow it in the closet, or leave it in the trunk of your car," went the advertising slogan, aimed at the apartment dweller.

Link's design resembled, in principle, the Osgood folding boat (1975.455) with a rigid shell covered with canvas. Only now the inventor took advantage of the World War II resin-based technologies to use a phenolic resin impregnated fabric, called Mikarta, to form the hull, made of 10 pieces clipped together.

At his factory in Gananoque, Ontario, Link added rowboats, outboards, and skiffs to his line of sectional boats in 1946. By 1948 he had built some 4,000. But ultimately they

were not a success, and on the first of November 1949, the factory held a closeout sale.

STATUS: Excellent, original.

DONOR: Martin Cohen

FURTHER READING:

Bond, Hallie E. *Boats and Boating in the Adirondacks*. Blue Mountain Lake, New York: The Adirondack Museum; Syracuse, New York: Syracuse University Press, 1995.

ACCESSION NO. 1986.91

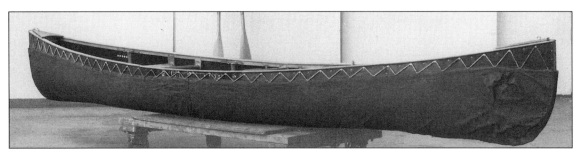

The Link canoe in 1986. (Photo: Deborah Patterson, Mystic Seaport 1986.91A)

OPEN RACING CANOE
BY MAX ANDERSEN

17' 0" x 2' 5"   ca. 1951

During World War II, a new woodworking technique was developed called hot molding. Thin veneers were bent into complex shapes, with glue in between the layers. These then went into an autoclave and were baked under pressure. Out came rigid, light plywood structures for everything from aircraft to radomes. After the war, builders of light boats embraced this new technology. Sweden's Max Andersen was one of the most successful. His racing canoes and kayaks were first seen in the 1948 Olympics, and he began advertising in the U.S. in 1951. Hot molding had size limits, and it has been superseded by cold molding using composites and epoxy glued-wood.

American paddler Frank B. Havens bought this C-1 (single-person canoe) and paddled it to victory in the 1952 Helsinki Olympic games in the 10,000-meter race.

Today this would have meant instant fame, but then his victory and the 1948 10,000-meter victory of Steve Lysak and Steve Macknowski were barely mentioned in the sporting press. Not until 1988 did Americans again paddle to Olympic Gold.

STATUS: Excellent, original condition.

DONOR: Mr. and Mrs. Roger I. Wilkinson

ACCESSION NO. 1984.151.11

The hot-molded Andersen racing canoe in 1984. (Photo: Maynard Bray, Mystic Seaport 1984.151.11A*)*

361

The Grumman canoe in 1995. (Photo: Judy Beisler, Mystic Seaport 1995.95)

OPEN CANOE BY GRUMMAN
MODEL G 15
HULL #7036-GP-5-15

15' 0" x 2' 0"   1973

Portaging an aging, heavy Old Town in the Adirondacks in 1944 convinced William J. Hoffman, Grumman Aircraft's chief tool engineer, that there had to be a way to use his aluminum aircraft-building skill to make a lighter canoe. At work, Hoffman built an aluminum 13' prototype that weighed 38 pounds—just half the weight of the Old Town he used as a model. Further experiments resulted in a new design and after the end of World War II, Leroy Grumman gave Hoffman space to build canoes. By the end of 1945, they had received 95 orders; by the end of 1946, 10,000. Six years later, Grumman canoe building moved to a new plant in Marathon, New York.

Lighter, cheaper, and tougher aluminum canoes almost put Old Town out of business. A standard 15' Grumman, like this one, became synonymous with "canoe" in most paddlers' minds, until the advent of higher tech (and more expensive) fiberglass canoes and newer ones of single sheet and powdered thermoplastic materials. In August 1996, OMC Inc., Grumman canoe's then-owner, announced the Marathon plant would close; no more "Grummans" would be built. The following month, employees bought the canoe-building business and began building "Marathons." Recently Grumman, now no longer building aircraft, has let them use the Grumman name again.

STATUS: Excellent, little used. With outboard bracket.

DONOR: Milton Menl

FURTHER READING:

Bond, Hallie E. *Boats and Boating in the Adirondacks*. Blue Mountain Lake, New York: The Adirondack Museum; Syracuse: Syracuse University Press, 1995.

"Grumman Closes Doors." *Paddler*, December, 1996.

ACCESSION NO. 1995.95

Chapter Two
SAILING CANOES

The Everson Lassie Model canoe, with sliding seat added. (Photo: Maynard Bray, Mystic Seaport 1986.59A)

DECKED SAILING CANOE BY EVERSON LASSIE MODEL

15' 0" x 2' 6"   ca. 1885

When W.L. Alden, a founder of the New York Canoe Club in 1871, wanted one of the new cruising canoes popularized by MacGregor (see 1958.1286), he turned to the best New York City Whitehall builder, James Everson. Alden gave Everson the "Nautilus" design sent by W. Baden-Powell, a MacGregor disciple. Alden needed to "take forcible possession of Everson," a conservative boatbuilder, but it was to Everson's lasting benefit, as he became one of the best-known builders of sailing and paddling canoes for the recreational market, where he actively advertised until 1892.

This canoe is one of Everson's Lassie models, designed and built in 1885. She is lightly framed, relying on full bulkheads and natural crook deck knees to hold her shape. The canoe features twin centerboards, one fairly far forward and one under the afterdeck, allowing six clear feet in the cockpit for sleeping when cruising, with a tent rigged over the boat. W.P. Stephens recommended this system to prospective cruising-canoe builders instead of the patented Radix folding centerboards introduced in 1885. But patent boards saved building time, and they became the centerboard of choice for manufacturers of canoes and row-sail boats like Rushton.

Sixteen-year-old Henry J. Condit received this canoe in 1888 in celebration of his recovery from typhoid fever. He sailed it at the family's summer home at Huletts Landing, Lake George, New York. His son, W. Chapin, added a sliding seat around 1920 and sailed the canoe until World War II.

Only three other Everson boats seem to have survived: a canoe in the collection of The Mariners' Museum built to lines by A. Cary Smith; another, in private hands, that belonged to canoe-sailor C. Boyer Vaux; and a Whitehall in the collection of the Adirondack Museum.

STATUS: Fair original condition, planks well checked, with most of original parts and rig.
DONOR: William C. Condit, Jr.
FURTHER READING:
Bond, Hallie E. *Boats and Boating in the Adirondacks*. Blue Mountain Lake, New York: The Adirondack Museum; Syracuse, New York: Syracuse University Press, 1995.

Stephens, William P. *Canoe and Boat Building for Amateurs*. New York: Forest and Stream, 1889. See plate 18 and 19 on page 16.

Timberman, O.J., ed. *New York Canoe Club Yearbooks*, 1871-1921.

Vaux, C. Boyer. "History of American Canoeing." *Outing*, June-August, 1887.

ACCESSION NO. 1986.59

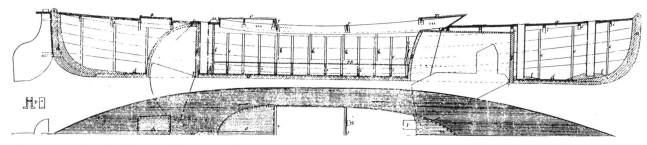

Construction details of Everson's Lassie model, from W.P. Stephens, Canoe and Boat Building for Amateurs.

Kestrel

DECKED SAILING CANOE

15' 0" x 2' 8"   ca. 1885

Canoe development for the two decades after the first Rob Roy was introduced in 1865 is well told in Maurice Wilt's "Canoeing Under Sail," published as a chapter in Edwin Schoettle's *Sailing Craft* and from which the following lines are directly taken.

"These early decked canoes, Rob Roys, were not much as sailing craft. They were too low in the water, had too little bearings, and were altogether too wet for anything but pretty fairly smooth water. Also they were steered by paddle alone, a very ineffective method.

"About 1868, several Englishmen, among them Messrs. W. Baden-Powell, Walter Stewart, and E. B. Tredwen, became interested in the possibility of developing better sailing qualities in the decked canoes. Baden-Powell's Nautilus No. 2 was the first model designed mainly for sailing. She had good beam, considerable sheer, a well crowned deck, and carried two sails, the larger, a standing lug, being forward. The paddle was still the means of steering. The rudder was introduced soon afterward, with lines and attached to a yoke, or to pedals in the fore part of the cockpit, the actual steering being done with the feet. The sailing was done with the crew sitting or lying on the floor-boards. The lines of Nautilus No.

4 were brought to America by a member of the New York Canoe Club, and in 1870 the first canoes of this sailing type were built by James Everson of Williamsburg, N. Y.

"Very soon after the sailing canoe was introduced into the United States, its type began to diverge from that of the English canoes. The English designs became deeper and somewhat wider, with fuller bodies and deep ballasted keels or heavy centerboards. As they were almost always sailed with the crew in a reclining position, the decks at the location of the crew's shoulders were often fitted with hinged flaps, so that the sailor could lean further to windward, when reaching or on the wind.

"Some of these features were found

Kestrel *with sails set, in 1971. (Photo: Claire L. White,* Mystic Seaport 1971-3-18*)*

in the early American sailing canoes, as long as the American canoe sailors remained below deck in the English fashion. It was not very long, however, until the American sailors were sitting on the windward deck, at first during reaching and windward work only, but finally at all times. Almost immediately the necessity for the big-bodied heavy canoes, with heavy centerboards and inside ballast disappeared. The crew was his own ballast, carried in the most advantageous position, well out on the windward side. The canoe could be built lighter with finer lines, and it was easier to handle both afloat and ashore, because of its lessened weight, and much safer in case of a capsize."

Deck flaps and foot-yoke steering indicate that *Kestrel* was normally sailed from inside the cockpit. Yet in size and general shape she is much like *Vesper*, the boat that proved the superiority of sailing from the windward deck to the English challengers while winning the New York Canoe Club's first International Challenge Cup in 1886.

Kestrel was built for the donor's father, Rev. Francis Goodwin. Family legend has W.P. Stephens as designer; building details indicate she may have been a custom Rushton commission. She is unballasted and is fitted with the Radix folding fan centerboard of 1885, which allows her to sail close-hauled. With her deck-mounted tiller, it would have been possible at times to have sailed her while sitting on the deck. After 1886, canoes were almost always sailed from this position, and the need for deck flaps vanished.

STATUS: Restored 1971, original, excellent condition.

DONOR: Charles A. Goodwin

FURTHER READING:

Baden-Powell, Warrington. *Canoe Traveling*. London: Smith, Elder & Co., 1871.

Bishop, Nathaniel H. *The Voyage of the Paper Canoe*. Boston: Lee and Shepard, 1878.

Bond, Hallie E. *Boats and Boating in the Adirondacks*. Blue Mountain Lake, New York: The Adirondack Museum; Syracuse, New York: Syracuse University Press, 1995.

Gardner, John. "Sailing Canoes." *The Log of Mystic Seaport*, Summer, 1971.

———. "Sailing Canoes Once Held Brief Place in the Sun." *National Fisherman*, June, 1977.

Hoffman, Ronald C. "The History of the American Canoe Association 1880-1960." Dissertation, Springfield College, 1967.

Kemp, Dixon. *A Manual of Yacht and Boat Sailing*. 6th ed. London: Horace Cox, 1886.

Manley, Atwood. *Rushton and His Times in American Canoeing*. Syracuse: Syracuse University Press for Adirondack Museum, 1968. Includes a good description of the development of *Vesper* and of the 1886 meet at Grindstone Island.

Schoettle, Edwin J., ed. *Sailing Craft*. New York: MacMillan Co., 1928.

Stephens, W. P. *Canoe and Boat Building*. New York: Forest and Stream Publishing Co., 1885. This book together with its pack of 50 separate plans went through several editions. Mystic Seaport has reprinted the set of plans, which include the original *Vesper* canoe.

ACCESSION NO. 1947.1508

Kestrel's cockpit, with the starboard deck flap open. (Photo: Claire L. White, Mystic Seaport 1971-3-23)

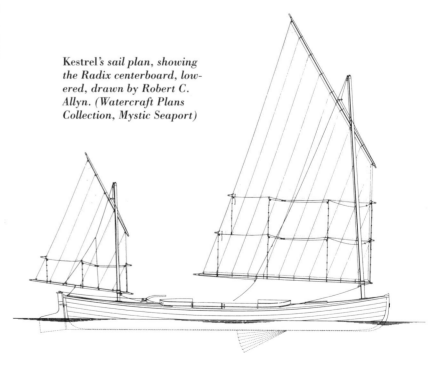

Kestrel's sail plan, showing the Radix centerboard, lowered, drawn by Robert C. Allyn. (Watercraft Plans Collection, Mystic Seaport)

Bill Kramer refinishes Argonaut's varnish work in 1971. The narrow overlapping blades of the Radix centerboard are clearly visible in this view. (Photo: Lester D. Olin, Mystic Seaport 1971-3-170)

Argonaut

VESPER-TYPE SAILING CANOE

16' 10" x 2' 7"   ca. 1910

Rushton's Vesper canoes sold well after the original *Vesper*, designed and sailed by Robert H. Gibson and built by J. Henry Rushton, won the International Challenge Cup at the Grindstone Island meet of 1886. J. Henry wasn't at all bashful about puffing up his boats and made much of *Vesper's* success, paying little heed that a competitor's boat, Fletcher Joyner's *Pecowsic*, was favored by some as the faster boat at the same event. In spite of being born from a racing environment and of being altered a bit from the original *Vesper*, Rushton's model was considered the ultimate in cruising canoes with which one could explore America's vanishing wilderness. It was classed as a "paddleable" sailing canoe and had refinements such as easily reefed batwing sails, a swing-up rudder, a small sliding seat, a smooth skin (made possible by flush-lapping the planking in guideboat fashion) and the wonderful Radix centerboard. This last item was in the form of a telescoping fan, each leaf of which was of hollow sheet brass. So conceived, the whole affair was housed inside a small box whose top came about flush with the floorboards and left the cockpit free for comfortable sleeping. It was operated by a folding rod with a handle on its upper end, which worked through a stuffing tube in the top of the centerboard box.

The Rushton shop continued building its standard Vesper canoes, of which *Argonaut* is one, until shortly before its closing in the winter of 1916-17, although other models had long before surpassed it in popularity.

STATUS: Restored 1971, original, excellent condition.
DONOR: William R. Wilson, M. D.
FURTHER READING:
(Same as for *Kestrel*, 1947.1508)
ACCESSION NO. 1969.207

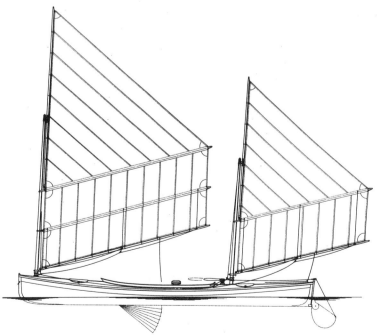

Argonaut's sail plan, drawn by Robert C. Allyn. (Watercraft Plans Collection, Mystic Seaport)

The Rushton Nomad canoe in 1983. (Photo: Maynard Bray, Mystic Seaport 1983.17B*)*

SAILING CANOE BY RUSHTON
NOMAD MODEL

16' 4" x 2' 8"   1910

To equip his hundred-foot motor yacht *Indian* with boats for his sons, Joseph Van Vleck spent $175 each for a brace of Nomad sailing canoes from J. H. Rushton, Inc. Rushton had died four years earlier, but the company still produced the sailing version of the Ugo paddling canoe introduced in 1887. An adaptation was an inexpensive way of keeping sailing canoes in the Rushton line at a time when canoeists' tastes had turned toward paddling. For hoisting aboard *Indian,* Van Vleck's pair had eyebolts into which davit lines hooked. These were removed in a later reconditioning. After use at the Forest Lake Club in the Poconos, one of these canoes was donated to the Antique Boat Museum, and this one was used on Cape Cod until 1979–a testament to the durability of Rushton's workmanship. Other Rushton Nomads are at the Adirondack Museum. With their smooth lap planking and handsome stripped decks, they represent the pinnacle of cruising sailing canoe construction.

STATUS: Excellent condition, all equipment and modern sails.
DONOR: Howard Van Vleck
FURTHER READING:
Manley, Atwood. *Rushton and His Times in American Canoeing.* Syracuse, New York: Syracuse University Press for the Adirondack Museum, 1968.
ACCESSION NO. 1983.17

Bee

DECKED SAILING CANOE BY BUTLER & STEVENS

16' 0" x 2' 6"   ca. 1890

The emphasis on racing under sail at the great American Canoe Association meet of 1886 spurred Paul Butler, who had joined only a year earlier, to develop so many advanced features for these boats that he later became known as the "father of the modern sailing canoe." In eulogizing Butler, as quoted in Edwin Schoettle's *Sailing Craft*, his friend H. Dudley Murphy said: "Few in this generation realize to what extent the sport of decked canoe sailing is indebted to Paul Butler. In the early days the canoe had no bulkheads, nor self draining cockpit; it was unmanageable after an upset, could carry only some fifty or sixty square feet of sail, with the sailor sitting on deck, and was steered by means of rudder chains and a short fore and aft tiller. Butler, weighing only one hundred and ten pounds, invented the cross sliding deck seat, added bulkheads, self-draining cockpit, and the Norwegian tiller (an athwartship tiller with a rod to the rudder head) and invented the most wonderful hollow spars ever made. He invented the clutch cleats for the sheet lines, reefing gears, and many appliances used with the enormous sails carried before sail-area was limited. From a craft little better or more seaworthy than our present open cruising canoe, he developed by his inventive genius the fastest sailing craft for its displacement the world has ever seen, a seaworthy, unsinkable boat capable of a speed of fifteen miles an hour. He designed his own boats, and started W.F. Stevens, a shell builder, to building canoes that after 35 years are still in fine condition and among our fastest. Every man who has sailed on a sliding seat in a good breeze of wind and experienced the thrill of the speed owes a debt of gratitude for the invention and development of the finest of all water sports to the memory of Paul Butler."

Bee was one of Paul Butler's boats and reflects many of the above-mentioned inventions, including featherlight hollow masts laid up of spirally wrapped 1/16" veneers, five layers for the main, three for the mizzen. Sailed by Murphy, *Bee* was the 1902 national champion and was kept at Butler's home club, the Winchester Boat Club outside of Boston, until 1970. She was built by W.F. Stevens, who did all of Butler's canoe-building; *Wasp*, now at the Adirondack Museum, is another of his Butler commissions.

STATUS: Fiberglass-covered hull, mostly original, fair condition.

DONOR: William L. Saltonstall

FURTHER READING: (Same as for *Kestrel*, 1947.1508)

Murphy, H.D. "Sailing Canoes." *American Canoe Association Yearbook, 1930.* Murphy was a prominent Boston artist who started sailing canoes in 1889.

Tyson, Irwin W. "The Modern Sailing Canoe." *Yachting*, July, 1949.

ACCESSION NO. 1970.639

Bee, set up to sail. (Photo: Maynard Bray, Mystic Seaport 1975-5-28)

Leprechaun

DECKED SAILING CANOE BY STEVENS AND GILBERT MERMAID MODEL

16' 0" x 2' 7"   1923

When the first *Mermaid* came out in 1913 to defend the New York Canoe Club's International Challenge Cup (the same trophy *Vesper* captured at the 1886 A.C.A. meet) she had the sliding seat, self-bailing cockpit, cam cleats, and Norwegian tiller developed earlier by Paul Butler. She carried the restricted sail area then imposed by Association rules. Indeed she was an out-and-out 16 x 30 (length in feet and beam in inches) racer, probably W.F. Stevens's most famous one, and he not only built her, but designed her as well. The combination of Leo Friede, *Mermaid*'s owner and skipper, and Stevens was practically unbeatable. Sailing the first *Mermaid* again the following year, Friede won the International Challenge Cup from the Canadians as well as the A.C.A. National Sailing Trophy for that year.

He continued to win with that boat until she was destroyed by fire in 1923. Stevens was dead by then so Fred Gilbert, a boatbuilder from Brockville, Ontario, was given the contract to duplicate *Mermaid* and build several others like her. *Mermaid II* proved just as fast, and Friede continued as undisputed champion, having won more important sailing canoe races by 1927 than anyone, ever. The 16 x 30 Mermaid-type canoe was brought up short, however, in 1933 when Uffa Fox and Roger deQuincy challenged the New York Canoe Club for its coveted International Challenge Cup. Using their wider, heavier, longer, sloop-rigged canoes of Fox's design, they beat Friede in his *Mermaid* and Walter Busch in *Loon*, another 16 x 30. The two English boats, *East Anglian* and *Valiant*, cleaned up in American waters that year, also winning the A.C.A. National Sailing Trophy, the National Paddling and Sailing Combined Championship, and the Paul Butler Trophy.

This canoe was one of a pair owned by the Friede family, both *Mermaid*s.

However, recent investigation shows that this is the one usually sailed by Leo Friede's son Kenneth, which he called *Leprechaun*. It was one of the canoes that attempted to defend the cup. The one that Friede sailed against Fox (now in a private collection) had the now-faint name *Mermaid II* painted on her, and photos of *Mermaid II* don't show the paddle carrying strap that this boat has.

As a result of Fox's victory, a joint British-American rule developed, borrowing the 17' size and the 100 square feet of sail from the British and the sliding seat from the Americans. In 1948, other canoe-sailing nations adopted the rule, and the boat was called the International Canoe. A development rule, allowing changes in hull design, governed the class until 1971, when a one-design hull was introduced.

STATUS: Refinished 1972, original, excellent condition.
DONOR: Leo Friede
FURTHER READING: (Same as for *Kestrel*, 1947.1508, and *Bee*, 1970.639)

Leprechaun in 1975. (Photo: Maynard Bray, Mystic Seaport 1975-5-165)

Fenger, Frederic A. *Alone in the Caribbean*. Belmont: Wellington Books, 1958. A firsthand account of adventures in *Yakaboo*, a 17-foot rudderless canoe designed and built by Stevens.

Fox, Uffa. *Sailing, Seamanship and Yacht Construction*. New York: Charles Scribner's Sons, 1934. A firsthand account of the international canoe races of 1933.

Schoettle, Edwin J., ed. *Sailing Craft*. New York: MacMillan Co., 1928. The chapter by Maurice Wilt, "Canoeing Under Sail," shows plans and photographs of *Mermaid* and contains a comprehensive history of the sport by one who participated in it.

Stephens, W.P. "The International Canoe Matches." *Yachting*, October, 1933.

ACCESSION NO. 1959.1373

Leo Friede aboard the first Mermaid, *during competition in 1913. (Photo: Courtesy of Mr. And Mrs. Roger I. Wilkinson, Mystic Seaport 1984.151)*

SAILING CANOE BY BURGESS
18' 5 " x 2' 6"   ca. 1920

W. Starling Burgess was fascinated by things that went fast. Around 1900 the fastest small sailing watercraft were decked sailing canoes with their tall rigs and tremendous power made possible by the sliding seat. So in 1906 Burgess joined the American Canoe Association and built a canoe called *Twilight*. He hired designer/builder W.F. Stevens to work in his Marblehead, Massachusetts, boatyard (Burgess & Packard) and produced a number of

boats. In the early 1920s, he introduced his protegés L. Francis Herreshoff and Norman Skene to the pleasures of paddling and sailing in canoes. The builder's plate indicates that this boat dates from the 1919-22 period, when Burgess was living in Provincetown. The canoe seems to have been converted for paddling, as the mast-partner holes have been covered and the deck and sternpost may have been replaced. Certainly neither has any sign of sailing hardware or rudder fittings. A cockpit coaming and metal hardware to hold a pair of backrests also look to be

additions. Her long and narrow proportions show the state of sailing canoe thinking before Uffa Fox's British canoeing invasion in 1933.

STATUS: Excellent, unrestored, no equipment.

DONOR: Museum purchase

FURTHER READING:

Howland, Lewellyn III. "The Burgess Legacy," parts 3 and 4, *WoodenBoat* 73 and 74, Dec, 1986, Jan/Feb, 1987.

ACCESSION NO. 1983.9

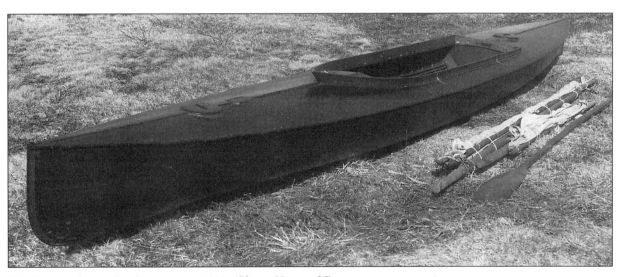

The Burgess-designed sailing canoe in 1983. (Photo: Maynard Bray, Mystic Seaport 1983.9A)

Blackbird

CLASS A OPEN
SAILING CANOE BY
OLD TOWN CANOE CO.
OTCA MODEL, GRADE AA
HULL #93669

20' 0" x 3' 3"   1927

In 1931, Brooklyn, New York, canoe sailors formed the Associated Canoe Clubs of Sheepshead Bay to unite the canoe clubs that grew up there in the 1920s and to write a set of rules for sailing wood-canvas canoes that would be accepted by the American Canoe Association. Among the half-dozen clubs on a beach called Oriental Point was the Mic Mac Canoe Club, run by Dewey W. Kantro who also sold canoes and parts. In 1927, he ordered *Blackbird*, a lengthened version of the stock model Otca, customized further with bilge keels and heavier rails than normal, and set up with mast steps and thwarts to carry a ketch rig and leeboards. He got the boat in May, and Ritchie Romaine and Lou Einsman bought her. In 1935 she was listed as #1 on the A.C.C.S.B. list. Class A canoes had a maximum 20' length, could carry up to 140 square feet of sail either as sloops or ketches, and were crewed with a minimum of three. At about $300 ready to sail, they were half the price of all-wood, decked, single-handed sailing canoes. These big, powerful canoes made notable trips, including crossing the Chesapeake, crossing New York Bay to New Jersey beaches, and sailing around Long Island. The ketch rig's low center of effort made these boats especially good in heavy weather, and they developed a reputation for sailing when no one else went out. Smooth water in Sheepshead Bay during a northwester gave them an advantage. After about a decade of active sailing, the Sheepshead Bay clubs were pretty much all destroyed with the building of the Belt Parkway in 1938.

Blackbird in 1975. (Photo: Maynard Bray, Mystic Seaport 1975-10-89)

STATUS: Original, good condition.
DONOR: Arnold Rupp
URTHER READING:
The Dope, the newsletter of the A.C.C.B.S., is in the G.W. Blunt White Library at Mystic Seaport.

Dugan, Francis A. "The Canvas Covered Racing Canoe." *Yachting*, May, 1934.
Tyson, O.S. *Sailing Canoes: A Brief History*. Worcester, Massachusetts: American Canoe Association, 1935.

ACCESSION NO. 1957.842

Charging across Brooklyn's Sheepshead Bay, the crew of Debonair shows how hard these Class A canoes were sailed. Similar in size and rig to Blackbird, Debonair won the A-Class championship, 1932-33. (Photo: Courtesy of Mr. And Mrs. Roger I. Wilkinson, Mystic Seaport 1984.151)

Doris

DECKED SAILING CANOE
BY FROHLING
& PETERBOROUGH

17' 1" x 3' 3" ca. 1930

"Imagine if you can, a 17' boat that will sail at 16 knots–and one that you can watch from a distance of five feet while you sail her," wrote Irwin Tyson in the July 1949 issue of *Yachting*. "Imagine yourself taking a full capsize, getting your boat up again and under full way in just 30 seconds without a drop of water in her bilge. And, if you are interested in design, imagine a boat of 450 pounds displacement putting a 900-pound stress on her weather shroud–a boat whose center of gravity may sometimes be a good two feet outboard of her weather rail."

Doris was designed by Hilding Frohling of Lubec, Maine, and built by the Peterborough Canoe Co. of Ontario. Frohling preferred larger canoes, the same size as Uffa Fox's *East Anglian*. H. Dudley Murphy sold the canoe to the donor in 1930 for $250. He sailed her in Hamburg Cove off the Connecticut River with her original cat-ketch rig. *The Rudder* of May, 1918, shows plans for another 17' canoe by Frohling. In 1946, Irwin Tyson borrowed *Doris* to be part of the American effort to recover the New York Cup. He rerigged her as a sloop the following year and made the three-boat team that challenged the British in vain in 1948. When his father became ill, Tyson pulled *Doris* off the ocean liner before the departure for England and returned the boat to Parsons, who complained that she was never as easy to sail as she had been before the alterations.

STATUS: Modified, excellent condition.

DONOR: John S. Parsons

FURTHER READING: (Same as for *Kestrel*, 1947.1508, Bee 1970.639, *Leprechaun*, 1959.1373, and *Blackbird*, 1957.842)

ACCESSION NO. 1974.996

Doris *on the water in 1974.*
(Photo: Kenneth E. Mahler,
Mystic Seaport 1974-10-152*)*

Foam, *ex-A.W.W.A., in 1983. (Photo: Judy Beisler,* Mystic Seaport 1983.7A*)*

Foam, (ex-*A.W.W.A.*)

DECKED SAILING CANOE BY FOX & PERSSON

17' 1" x 3' 4"   1938

In 1936, the American Gordon K. Douglass challenged the Royal Canoe Club in an attempt to recapture the International Challenge Cup. His canoe, *Nymph II*, was an enlarged version of Leo Friede's *Mermaid* model (1959.-1373), similar to *Doris* (1974.996), with a sharp, symmetrical hull that would capsize if not in motion. To meet the challenge, Uffa Fox designed and built *Wake*, a relatively beamy canoe with flat, planing after sections and a sharp bow. The challenger was beaten easily, and in a gesture of goodwill Fox gave Douglass a set of *Wake*'s plans. Douglass subsequently built a number of these, calling his first one *Foxy Nymph* in Fox's honor. Seth Persson of Old Saybrook, Connecticut, built this boat to the *Wake* plans for Al Thomas in 1938. Al sailed *A.W.W.A.* for many years out of the Horseshoe Harbor Yacht Club near Larchmont, New York, later selling her to Roger Wilkinson, a past A.C.A. commodore and experienced sailor of open canoes like *Blackbird* (1957.842). *Foam*, as she was renamed, shows the highest development of light double-planked canoe construction with her 1/4" x 3/8" oak frames on 3" centers, and two-layer 1/4" hull. She retains the crosshead tiller control system invented by Paul Butler, with many specialized fittings including a bronze combination tiller head and mainsheet cam cleat. This design was superseded in the U.S. by Lou Whitman's *Manana II* model, represented by *Teal II* (1974.1059).

STATUS: Fair; complete and original, except for a fiberglass covered hull.

DONOR: Mr. and Mrs. Roger I. Wilkinson

FURTHER READING:
American Canoe Association, Measurement Records.

Fox, Uffa, *Sail and Power*, New York, Scribners, 1936.

Douglass, Gordon K. *Sixty Years Behind the Mast: The Fox on the Water.* Parsons, West Virginia: McClain Printing Co., 1986.

ACCESSION NO. 1983.7

Foam *under sail in 1949. (Courtesy of Mr. and Mrs. Roger I. Wilkinson,* Mystic Seaport 1984.151*)*

Uffa Fox, sailing his decked sailing canoe East Anglian *before the 1933 New York Canoe Club Challenge Cup races in which he defeated Leo Friede and* Mermaid. *With canoes like* East Anglian *and* Wake, *Fox was among the most influential sailing-canoe designers and racers of the 1900s. (Photo:* ©Mystic Seaport, Rosenfeld Collection 65588F*)*

Teal II *in 1975. (Photo: Maynard Bray,* Mystic Seaport 1975-10-90*)*

Teal II

DECKED SAILING CANOE BY WHITMAN, ANDERSEN & FISHMAN

17' 0" x 3' 4"   1953

Teal II was designed by Louis Whitman and is built to the same plans as his *Manana II* with which Whitman won back the International Challenge Cup in 1952. She was built of molded plywood by Max Andersen of Vasteras, Sweden, who manufactured these Whitman hulls on special order. *Teal II* was completed and rigged by her donor in this country, after which he raced her near his home on Great South Bay, Long Island, and occasionally took part in the A.C.A. races at Sugar Island. With a modern rig and rebuilt to today's standards, the *Manana II* model remains competitive.

STATUS: Original, excellent condition.

DONOR: David S. Fishman

FURTHER READING: (*Same as for Kestrel*, 1947.1508, *Bee*, 1970.639, *Leprechaun*, 1959.1373, and *Blackbird*, 1957.842)

Wascheck, George. "The International Decked Sailing Canoe." *American Canoeist*, July, 1962. This brief history of the sport gives a good description of the Whitman canoe and its accessories. Also contains the lines of the Whitman canoe and instructions on how to sail one of these craft.

ACCESSION NO. 1974.1059

Jesse Fishman balancing Teal *in 1949. (Photo: Courtesy of Mr. and Mrs. Roger I. Wilkinson,* Mystic Seaport 1984.151*)*

National Champion Louis Whitman sailing his Manana II *on a breezy day. An athletic plumber from City Island, New York, Whitman was inspired by Uffa Fox and built himself a decked sailing canoe in 1939. As the best American canoe sailor of the postwar decade, Whitman won the New York Canoe Club International Challenge Cup in 1952 and defended it in 1955. (Photo: Courtesy of Mr. and Mrs. Roger I. Wilkinson,* Mystic Seaport 1984.151*)*

Phoenix *in 1992. (Photo: Judy Beisler, Mystic Seaport 1992.36.1A)*

Phoenix

DECKED SAILING CANOE
BY WHITMAN
CLASS #109

17' 1" x 3' 8"   1968

For the 1969 Canoe Sailing World Championships, Louis Whitman (a young 61) designed, built, and sailed this canoe, his "old man's boat." He used cold-molded construction over longitudinal battens, with toothpicks to hold the veneers in place, to build the hull. The hull later served as a plug for a fiberglass mold from which some 20 boats were built. The boat featured a hollow wood, rotating mast, the American-style cross-head tiller introduced by Paul Butler, and a maximum-beam V-shaped hull that combined final stability with relatively low wetted surface. *Phoenix* represents the last U.S. international design in this evolving class. In 1970, a 1969 English design by Peter Nethercott, whose roots went back to the Uffa Fox canoes of the 1930s, was selected for international competition. But U.S. designers still experiment with different shapes for national competition and have been responsible for introducing innovations like carbon-fiber masts into both the class and the wider sailing market. Modern boats have carbon fiber/kevlar hulls and highly tunable rigs. Experimentation is going on with asymmetric spinnakers, which may be the next chapter in the long history of sailing canoes.

STATUS: Excellent condition with all equipment.
DONOR: Ruth Whitman
FURTHER READING: (Same as for *Teal II*, 1974.1059)
Beaver, Bill. "IC Hullform Development." *International Canoes Letter*, May, 1996.

Miller, Paul H., and David L. Dillon. "The International Canoe: A Technical Review." *Marine Technology*, October, 1994.

Pettingill, Dana, "In Memoriam, Louis Whitman." *International CanoesLetter*, July, 1991.

ACCESSION NO. 1992.36.1

Showing how it's done, Louis Whitman sails at Miami in 1963. (Photo: Courtesy of Mr. and Mrs. Roger I. Wilkinson, Mystic Seaport 1984.151)

ICEBOATS

*H. Prescott Shreeve
at the helm of the X-
Class iceboat* Polaris
*on Lake Hopatcong,
New Jersey, ca. 1940.
Derived from Dutch
ice yachting, iceboat-
ing was established in
the New York area
and became increas-
ingly popular after
the Civil War.
(Photo: Courtesy of
H. Prescott Shreeve,*
Mystic Seaport 1997.27.599)

ICEBOATS

The early Dutch settlers of the Hudson River Valley brought with them a long tradition of using iceboats for work and pleasure in the Netherlands. As New York's transportation systems improved in the 1800s, their descendants used iceboats primarily for pleasure and, especially, racing. To achieve a faster boat, they developed a "hull" of spars and wire bracing with the crew on a tiny tray located in the stern over the steering runner. The boats were often propelled by a gaff-rigged main and jib set on a mast located forward, close to the runner plank. On the open reaches of the Hudson River, the larger boats often attained phenomenal speeds for the time, sometimes keeping up with the New York Central Railroad express steam trains that ran along the Hudson's east bank. One of the largest Hudson iceboats, *Icicle*, built around 1870 by Jacob Buckhout of Poughkeepsie, New York, was almost 70′ overall and carried more than a thousand square feet of sail.

The opening of the Hudson River to year-round navigation in 1902 encouraged the shift of iceboat sailing to the lakes of northern New Jersey, Michigan, Wisconsin, and Minnesota in the early 1900s. As in "soft-water" sailing, one-design classes were developed, with an emphasis on shorter boats with less sail area, and on technological innovation. Developed in the 1930s, the still very successful Skeeter Class was Marconi-cat-rigged with a sail area of only 75 square feet set on an aft-raking mast. The steering runner was located forward and, over time, the hull was lengthened and took on a distinctly aerodynamic shape, and a springboard to dampen vibration of the steering runner was added. As a result of a design competition sponsored by the *Detroit News*, a smaller, more economical one-design class, the single-seater DN60, was introduced in 1937, based in part on the design features of the Skeeter. By 1960, there were over 200 skeeters and 700 DNs. Other successful one-design iceboat classes are the Renegade (1947), Yankee (1948), and Arrow (1960). The Arrow Class was among the first to adopt a fiberglass hull.

Another iceboat tradition developed along the south shore of Long Island, where the frozen salt water of Great South Bay offered far less reliable ice. There, winter sailors developed the "scooter," somewhat like a sneakbox with a pair of runners on the bottom. Scooters danced across ice and open water, steered only by weight and the trim of the jib. Like the class iceboats of the freshwater lakes, scooters continue to sail the hard waters of winter.

Polaris
X-CLASS ICEBOAT
26'   ca. 1940

Herbert Prescott Shreeve, an engineer for the New Jersey Bell Telephone Company, designed and built *Polaris* to conform to the Class X Eastern Ice Yacht Association rules, which required a sail area of no more than 250 square feet. A stern-steerer with low-aspect Marconi sails, varnished wood, pin-striping, and massive steel runners, *Polaris* is out of the old pre-World War II iceboating era. This world has largely been supplanted by lightweight bow steerers often built with exotic materials, although a few of the old boats are still sailed.

STATUS: Good condition.

DONOR: H. Prescott Shreeve

FURTHER READING FOR 1997.27.1 AND 1997.27.2:

Andresen, Jack. *Sailing on Ice.* South Brunswick, New Jersey and New York: A.S. Barnes and Company, 1944.

Gardiner, Frederic M. *Wings on the Ice, A Comprehensive View of the Sport of Ice Boating.* New York: Yachting Publishing Corporation, 1938.

Levy, Natalie. *Ice Boating.* New York: David McKay Co., 1978.

Smith, S. Calhoun. *Ice Boating, A Complete Guide to Ice Boat Development, Design, Construction and Sailing.* Princeton, New Jersey: D. Van Nostrand Company, 1962.

Stone, Herbert L., ed. *Ice Boating.* New York: Outing Publishing Co., 1913.

ACCESSION NO. 1997.27.1

Polaris on Greenwood Lake, New Jersey, ca. 1950. (Photo: Bob Brousseau, courtesy of H. Prescott Shreeve, Mystic Seaport 1997.27.579)

Polaris in storage at Mystic Seaport. (Photo: Claire White-Peterson, Mystic Seaport 1997.27.1)

Whistling Wind *in storage at Mystic Seaport. (Photo:* Mystic Seaport 1997.27.2*)*

H. Prescott Shreeve sailing his new Arrow-Class iceboat Whistling Wind *on New Jersey's Lake Hopatcong in March 1963. (Photo:* Mystic Seaport 1997.27.720*)*

Whistling Wind
ARROW CLASS ICEBOAT
17' 4" x 12' 0"

Herbert Prescott Shreeve assembled *Whistling Wind*, Arrow Class iceboat hull #15, from a kit during the winter of 1962-63 and sailed it out of the Lake Hopatcong Ice Yacht Club in New Jersey. Howard Boston designed the Arrow Class in 1959 to be a strict one-design class. Its fiberglass fuselage and extruded aluminum spars meant it could not be scratch-built from plans, but it could be bought in finished and kit form from the Arrow Boat Company of Mount Clemens, Michigan. The class became widely accepted and eventually included 500 boats. A bow-steerer, the boat carries 80 square feet of sail.

STATUS: Good.
DONOR: H. Prescott Shreeve
FURTHER READING:
(Same as 1997.27.1)
ACCESSION NO. 1997.27.2

With a good breeze, H. Prescott Shreeve "hikes" Whistling Wind *at Shrewsbury, New Jersey in 1971. (Photo:* Mystic Seaport 1997.27.377*)*

GREAT SOUTH BAY ICE SCOOTER

16' 10" x 6' 0"

At home on both "hard" and "soft" water, scooters were developed for sailing on the saltwater ice of Great South Bay on the back side of Long Island. They were steered by shifting one's weight and by hauling or slacking the jib sheet (the main sheet remains cleated most of the time). The name came from "scooting" over holes in the ice after hitting them at high speed, slacking the sheets to keep from capsizing, and letting the momentum carry the craft to the firm ice on the other side. A "pike pole" was standard equipment, taking the place of oars or a paddle on the bay's shallow waters. The skipper of a scooter sits forward to tend the sheet of the balanced jib, while his crew is aft awaiting orders to trim or slack the main sheet. The sport of scooting was first organized in 1904 and was at one time very active.

STATUS: Some equipment missing, mostly original, fair condition.

DONOR: W. Dorsey Smith

FURTHER READING:

Dodge, Henry Irving. "A Day's Scooting on Great South Bay." *Yachting*, March, 1910.

Ice scooter 1963.249. (Photo: Louis Martel, Mystic Seaport 1963.249B)

——. "Dimensions and Specifications for Building a Scooter." *Yachting*, January, 1919.

——. "The Scooter." *Yachting*, December, 1918.

Harless, William H. "The Great South Bay Scooter." *Long Island Forum*, June, 1970.

Seidman, David. "The Great South Bay Scooters." *WoodenBoat* 92, Jan/Feb, 1990.

Underhill, Andrew M., and Hervey Garrett Smith. "What! No Rudder?" *Yachting*, Jan/Feb, 1963.

ACCESSION NO. 1963.249

Ice scooter 1963.249 at Bellport, Long Island, about 1954. Bay Shore restaurateur Gil Clark owned this scooter for most of her long life. (Photo: Courtesy of John F. Young)

Great South Bay ice scooter 1979.27 at Mystic Seaport. (Photo: Maynard Bray, Mystic Seaport 1979.27A*)*

GREAT SOUTH BAY ICE SCOOTER

14′ 8″ x 4′ 8″   1904

Racing a Great South Bay ice scooter was a bit like racing a sandbagger sloop. The expert skippers would place their "live ballast" to hold the boat at a slight angle of heel so that the inner of the two runners held the ice. Not all the live ballast made it home. The ride was rough, there was little to hold on to, and it was easy to fall off when traveling at more than a mile a minute.

Powered by a low-aspect jib and gaff-mainsail rig, most of the early scooters were equipped with two angle-iron runners on each side. The runners were shaped with a gentle fore-and-aft rocker so that when the crew shifted their weight forward, and the jib was eased, the scooter tended to round up into the wind.

N.V. Watkins of Bellport, New York, built this boat in 1904. It was his boat number 9 or 6, depending on how the number is read. When equipped to race, it carried close to 160 square feet of sail.

STATUS: Worn but good condition. Cockpit opening partially decked in forward.

DONORS: Dr. Raymond Siatkowski and JoAnn Greenwood

FURTHER READING: (Same as 1963.249)

ACCESSION NO. 1979.27

Similar to 1979.27, the ice scooter Eagle skims along in this photograph from The Rudder, *January, 1909. The skipper sits forward, steering by tending the jib. (Photo: Mary Anne Stets,* Mystic Seaport 1978-4-52*)*

Index of Watercraft Names

Index of Subjects and Proper Names

INDEX

INDEX

Index of Donors

INDEX

Chronological Index of Accession Numbers

INDEX